D1223285

THE ESSENCE OF HAYEK

THE ESSENCE OF
H·A·Y·E·K

EDITED BY
CHIAKI NISHIYAMA
KURT R. LEUBE
FOREWORD BY W. GLENN CAMPBELL

HOOVER INSTITUTION PRESS
STANFORD UNIVERSITY, STANFORD, CALIFORNIA

The Hoover Institution on War, Revolution and Peace, founded at Stanford University in 1919 by the late President Herbert Hoover, is an interdisciplinary research center for advanced study on domestic and international affairs in the twentieth century. The views expressed in its publications are entirely those of the authors and do not necessarily reflect the views of the staff, officers, or Board of Overseers of the Hoover Institution.

Grateful acknowledgment is made to the University of Chicago Press and to Routledge & Kegan Paul (London) for permission to reprint copyrighted selections used in this book.

Frontispiece and jacket photograph courtesy of Bank Hofmann AG

Hoover Press Publication 301

First printing, 1984
Manufactured in the United States of America
88 87 86 85 84 9 8 7 6 5 4 3 2

Library of Congress Cataloging in Publication Data
Hayek, Friedrich A. von (Friedrich August), 1899–
The essence of Hayek.

Includes bibliographical references and index.
1. Economics—Addresses, essays, lectures.
I. Nishiyama, Chiaki, 1924– . II. Leube, Kurt R.
III. Title.
HB171.H428 1984 330 84-6706
ISBN 0-8179-8011-3
ISBN 0-8179-8012-1 (pbk.)

Design by P. Kelley Baker

DEDICATED IN GRATITUDE TO
PROFESSOR FRIEDRICH A. VON HAYEK,
OUR TEACHER AND INTELLECTUAL LEADER,
ON THE OCCASION OF HIS 85TH BIRTHDAY

Contents

PART THREE: HAYEK'S CONTRIBUTIONS TO THE HISTORY OF IDEAS

PART FOUR: THEORETICAL BASIS OF THE HAYEKIAN SYSTEM

PART FIVE: HAYEK'S POLITICAL ECONOMY: A PHILOSOPHICAL-REALISTIC CONCEPT

Foreword

This volume is being published to honor the eighty-fifth birthday of one of the most distinguished intellectuals of our century. Friedrich Hayek's path-breaking contributions to economic theory during the 1930s earned him the Nobel Prize in 1974. But his achievements extend far beyond those early writings on the trade cycle and capital theory. We salute him for a lifetime of wide-ranging intellectual creativity, as well as for his personal courage, integrity, and independence.

All of these qualities were displayed conspicuously forty years ago, when Professor Hayek wrote *The Road to Serfdom.* At a time when socialism was dominant in Western, and especially European, intellectual circles, he identified the role that the socialists in Germany had played in paving the way for Adolf Hitler's National Socialism. And he warned, incisively and eloquently, that democratic socialism could not guarantee the preservation of individual liberty or limited government, because men entrusted with power would be tempted to exceed the constitutional restraints placed upon their exercise of authority.

In effect, Professor Hayek warned the West about the perils of *1984* several years before George Orwell did, but he paid a high price for his prescience. If he had been afraid of controversy, if he had lacked courage or integrity, he would have kept silent. Instead, he spoke out, provoking attacks upon himself and his ideas by the defenders of socialism and central planning. But his message was too provocative and persuasive to be ignored. Although some reviewers reacted by maligning him and misrepresenting his ideas, many readers turned directly to his book and were convinced by his dispassionate analysis. Today, *The Road to Serfdom* is recognized as a classic of twentieth-century thought, one of the books that fundamentally changed the way a whole field of thought is perceived.

In an age when scholars increasingly restrict their area of expertise, Professor Hayek has not constricted his fields of inquiry. True, he is primarily an economist, but only in the same sense that Leonardo Da Vinci was primarily an artist and Isaac Newton a scientist. Like them, his interests have spanned many fields, and he has left his indelible mark on all of them. He is, for example, a leading innovator in the disciplines of intellectual history, economic history, political philosophy, scientific methodology, and jurisprudence, as well as in psychology, the field of his earliest interest.

It has been said that winning a Nobel Prize is the highest honor and the greatest curse that can be bestowed upon an individual. The recipients are besieged with invitations to lecture, to be interviewed, and to serve on the boards of foundations, universities, and commissions. Fortunately, Professor Hayek has managed to take on these commitments without sacrificing his scholarly pursuits. But if he had not been able to do so, it would have been entirely understandable. When the Nobel Prize was awarded to him, he was, after all, 75 years old, a time in life when a man is entitled to rest on his laurels. Amazingly, though, during the past decade Professor Hayek has been more productive and creative than ever. If advancing age has forced him to curtail his lifelong passion for mountain-climbing, it has not otherwise diminished his energies, his acuity, or his devotion to preserving liberty as a legacy to future generations.

The Essence of Hayek ably captures the diversity, subtlety, and complexity of F. A. Hayek's system of thought. We are grateful to Professors Chiaki Nishiyama and Kurt R. Leube for taking time from their own research and writings to select the essays and excerpts that best convey Hayek's distinctive viewpoint. Of course, this selection is no substitute for reading the full corpus of Professor Hayek's writings, but it is an excellent starting point, one which soon will be supplemented by publication of Hayek's next major book, *The Fatal Conceit*.

Professor Hayek has been an honorary fellow of the Hoover Institution since June 1977. He has visited us frequently, has lectured often under our auspices, and given generously of his time to scholars, young and old alike, who value his assessments of their ideas. My colleagues join me in offering him birthday greetings, as well as in expressing the hope that his long and close association with us will continue for many more years.

W. GLENN CAMPBELL

Director, Hoover Institution

Acknowledgments

The idea for publishing this book to celebrate F. A. Hayek's eighty-fifth birthday stems from a discussion between the editors in September 1983.

It will always be difficult to select the essence out of such an extensive oeuvre as Hayek's. To the editors' satisfaction, their final choice received Professor Hayek's full and spontaneous approval. We wish to thank him for his cooperation.

Without the assistance of the Hoover Institution and its director, W. Glenn Campbell, deputy director John H. Moore, associate directors Dennis L. Bark and Thomas H. Henriksen, and senior research fellow Robert Hessen, this book would never have been produced. We are especially thankful for their generous support and patience.

Our thanks are given to the fine Hoover Institution Press staff, especially to Patricia Baker, Marshall Blanchard, Phyllis M. Cairns, Diane McCubbin, and to John R. Ziemer, who prepared the index. Their cooperation in publishing this book in such a short span of time is highly appreciated.

We also want to thank Andy Eisenberg and Shinichi Sano for their diligent help in reading the proofs.

FRIEDRICH AUGUST VON HAYEK: A BIOGRAPHICAL INTRODUCTION

• *Kurt R. Leube* •

I

Friedrich August von Hayek was born on May 8, 1899, in Vienna into a family that could lay claim to a great academic tradition. His paternal grandfather taught zoology at the University of Vienna, and Franz von Juraschek, his maternal grandfather and a colleague and climbing partner of the famous economist Eugen von Böhm-Bawerk of the Austrian School, was professor of public law at the University of Innsbruck and later became first president of the K.u.K. Statistische Zentralkommission (National Statistical Office of Imperial Austria) in Vienna. His father was a physician and taught plant geography as a *Privatdozent* at the University of Vienna. Additionally, the professional careers of his two brothers, as well as his children's, reflect the scholarly tradition of the Hayek family. One of his younger brothers became professor of anatomy at the University of Vienna, the other, professor of chemistry at the University of Innsbruck. Hayek's daughter, Christine, is a biologist at the British Museum in London; his son, Laurence, who also resides in England, is a medical doctor specializing in pathology.

In March 1917, Hayek entered the K.u.K. army as an artillery officer; in November 1918 he returned to Vienna after serving on the Piave front in Italy. In October 1918, while still in service, Hayek was allowed to obtain his gymnasium degree, which enabled him to enroll at the University of Vienna shortly after World War I. Late in November of the same year, he began to study law, preferring to attend the lectures of Friedrich von Wieser and Othmar Spann, and courses on psychology and philosophy. Wieser was the other leading economist of the second generation of the Austrian School of Economics; Spann was a relatively obscure figure in the fields of economics and sociology. During this time Hayek took a great deal of interest in the writings of Ernst Mach, the famous physicist and philosopher of science, which had a lasting influence on Hayek's philosophical and psychological thinking. After obtaining a Dr. Juris. degree in November 1921, Hayek decided to continue studying political science and in March 1923 received a doctorate in political science (*Doctor rerum politicarum*).

During the cold winter of 1919 – 20, when the University of Vienna had to be closed for lack of heating material, Hayek spent a few intellectually stimulating months in Zurich, where he came across Moritz Schlick's influential *General Theory of Knowledge*.

In those days, long since gone, when Vienna had a lively intellectual climate, Hayek, still a student in 1921, had helped to found a small circle of young social scientists who met regularly and informally to present papers and discuss problems of mutual interest. More than half of the participants later became world-famous, such as the economists Gottfried von Haberler, Fritz Machlup, and Oscar Morgenstern; the sociologist Alfred Schütz; the political philosopher Eric Voegelin; the historian Friedrich Engel-Janosi; the art historians Otto Benesch and Johannes Wilde; the musicologist Emanuel Winternitz; the philosopher Felix Kaufmann; the psycho-analyst Robert Waelder; and the mathematician Karl Menger. A few years later, most of the participants also joined the famous Mises-Seminar, which Mises had established in his office at the Vienna Chamber of Commerce. This *Privatseminar*, conducted by Mises, was more or less the nucleus of the fourth generation of the Austrian School of Economics, the most important representative of which is Hayek.

In October 1921, Hayek took a job in the Österreichische Abrechnungsamt (a government office for settling prewar debts), one of whose directors was Ludwig von Mises. This was the beginning of a most fruitful intellectual relationship. In March 1923, Hayek undertook at his own risk a visit to New York in order to become a research assistant to Professor Jeremiah W. Jenks of New York University, a leading authority on trusts and a professor of government.

While in New York, Hayek attended the lectures at Columbia University of Wesley C. Mitchell on the history of economic thought and the last seminar of John B. Clark, where he read a paper on the value of money.

Greatly stimulated and with an intense interest in the newly developed techniques and the new forms of monetary policy with which the Federal Reserve System was experimenting, Hayek returned to Vienna in May 1924. He then published some articles in this field[1] and began the research in monetary theory that paved the way to his later work.

In the summer of 1926, Hayek married Hella Fritsch in Vienna.

II

Stimulated by the advanced techniques for analyzing time series and forecasting industrial fluctuations that had just been developed in the United States, Hayek, together with Ludwig von Mises, founded the Austrian Institute for Business Cycle Research in 1927. Under Hayek's directorship until 1931, this institute soon became a European center for trade cycle research. As a result of some penetrating work on monetary theory, in February 1929 in one of the institute's periodicals, Hayek published a comment that anticipated ideas that he was later to develop more fully on the monetary aspects of the investment cycle. In this note, Hayek became the first to predict the coming crisis in the United States.

In 1929, Hayek presented his *Habilitation* lecture, "Geldtheorie und Konjunkturtheorie," which under this title was later published as his first book.[2] His test lecture, "The Paradox of Savings," led to an invitation from Professor Lionel Robbins to the London School of Economics, where in 1931 Hayek delivered four lectures entitled "Prices and Production."[3] That same year, Hayek was offered a professorship at the London School of Economics and became the first foreign professor at this then unique stronghold of theoretical economic research.

From those early days at the London School of Economics, a deep and stimulating friendship with Lord Robbins originated. Hayek was to spend the next eighteen years in England and to become the only intellectual opponent of John Maynard Keynes. Their points of disagreement were often to turn into heated debates.

III

"When the definitive history of economic analysis during the nineteen thirties comes to be written, a leading character in the drama (it was quite a drama) will be Professor Hayek . . . there was a time when the new theories of Hayek were the principal rival of the new theories of Keynes. Which was right, Keynes or Hayek?"[4]

During the course of these heated controversies, Hayek was asked to review Keynes's recently published *Treatise on Money,* and Keynes to evaluate Hayek's *Prices and Production.* Hayek's powerful review was published in two parts;[5] Keynes replied to the first part only, mainly criticizing *Prices and Production.* (Soon afterward Keynes changed his basic ideas.) Hayek reacted with a brilliant rejoinder[6] and also published a reply to Pierro Sraffa's review of his *Prices and Production.*[7] This major intellectual controversy, in a way comparable only to the *Methodenstreit* between the Historical School and the Austrian School, involved all eminent economists. In addition to his extensive reviews, replies, and reactions, Hayek in the years 1931 – 1937 published some ten essays on capital theory, investment theory, and the theory of savings, all of them crucial to his later work.[8]

The most striking characteristic of the "Austrian" trade cycle and monetary theory, as represented by Hayek, is the idea that any shortage of capital immediately causes a crisis. Classical economic theory never elucidated what causes such a shortage. Hayek's theory is that overinvestment leads to a capital shortage, which unavoidably leads to a decline in investment and hence to the loss of a part of the real capital, produced because of the overly high investment rate. The central thesis of Hayek's trade cycle theory, in sharp contrast to that of Keynes, maintains that the monetary factors are the original ones and that the cycle arises from real alterations in the structure of production.

When, in 1935, Gottfried von Haberler drew Hayek's attention to Karl Popper's *The Logic of Scientific Discovery,* Hayek discovered thoughts similar to those he had worked out in the introduction to his *Collectivist Economic Planning.* But Hayek found Popper's hypothetico-deductive approach to scientific explanation much more satisfactory than his own interpretation. This was the beginning of a mutually stimulating influence and a long-lasting friendship.

In 1936, Hayek invited Popper to the London School of Economics to read his *Poverty of Historicism* in the seminar Hayek held together with Lionel Robbins, Ernst Gombrich, G. L. S. Shackle, and others.

Even as Hayek's interest in technical economics finally culminated in the publication of *The Pure Theory of Capital* (1942), which the late Fritz Machlup, one of Hayek's world-famous contemporaries and his old friend, rated as "the first full treatise on capital since Böhm-Bawerk's *Positive Theory*," Hayek devoted himself more and more to the socio-philosophical problems of economics. In a lecture entitled "Economics and Knowledge," published in 1937,[9] Hayek first introduced his basic idea of the "division of knowledge." Here he criticized Mises's *a priorism* and argued very convincingly that only the pure logic of choice was an *a priori* discipline, whereas the market process itself was an empirical one. This essay, originally presented as a presidential address to the London Economic Club, clearly shows Hayek's turn toward the more philosophical concerns of the economic sciences.

The London School of Economics, then in Cambridge because of the bombing of London, granted Hayek a D.Sc. (econ.) in 1941.

IV

When the second edition of Ludwig von Mises's *Gemeinwirtschaft* (Socialism) initiated the big debate on socialism in the 1930s, with Mises and Hayek on one side and Oskar Lange and Henry Douglas Dickinson on the other, Hayek contributed three path-breaking and still extremely relevant essays. These thoughts, later assembled in *Individualism and Economic Order,*[10] demolished the theories of the so-called market socialism. His intensive engagement with the various insoluble problems of socialism, the terror of fascism, and the outbreak of World War II made Hayek write a book that, when first published in 1944, was a revelation for those who desperately wanted freedom. This best-seller of the immediate postwar years, significantly dedicated "to the Socialists of all parties," became a ray of hope, especially in Europe. An excellent condensation appeared in the *Reader's Digest* and made Hayek world-famous overnight. This popular book, still in print and of great relevance, as are all of his works, celebrated its fortieth anniversary in 1984.

The Road to Serfdom,[11] which even Joseph A. Schumpeter called a book written by "one of the most eminent economists of our time,"[12] has been translated into some sixteen different languages, including recently Polish and Russian. This stimulating book was Hayek's warning against not only the dangerous totalitarianism then rampant under the mantle of socialism and fascism but also against the risks of welfare statism and welfare dictatorship. In the philosophical parts of this courageous book, Hayek does not hesitate to demonstrate the links between socialisms of all stripes and fascism. Hayek shows that no variety of socialism, no matter what its name or however modified by adjectives, carries with it any adequate provisions for the preservation of political and economic freedom. The popular view of the convergence of economic systems, quite widespread in the German-speaking world and invoked on more than one occasion, is rooted in an economic error, as Hayek impressively illustrates. He also concludes that efforts to establish a so-called Third Way, often suggested in recent times, are a totally unsatisfactory experiment and an attempt to link principles of economic orders that in reality exclude one another.

In this period, Hayek became increasingly interested in methodological questions concerning the social sciences in general, and he particularly concentrated his efforts on refuting the ideas of a dangerous train of thought — scientism.

To this very important field, he contributed three outstanding essays, which were first published in *Economica* for 1941 and 1942 – 1944 respectively. These essays in intellectual history are crucial for understanding Hayek's work as a whole and are collected in his book *The Counter-Revolution of Science.*[13] The essays trace the roots of scientism to the Ecole Polytechnique and the early socialists influenced by Saint-Simon. These hubris-filled thoughts lead in a direct line to contemporary late Marxism. Here, we find the origin of the idea of scientism, which claims to be able to "foresee the future progress of the human race, accelerate and direct it. But to establish laws which will enable us to predict the future, history must cease to be a history of individuals and must become a history of the masses."[14] This statement of Hayek's makes the illogic of a mechanistic interpretation of historical evolution and the collectivistic view of history obvious. It is like the man in the well-known German fable who tries to pull himself out of a bog by his own hair. Hayek shows that the pretense of knowledge is an error fatal to individual freedom.

In the second part of *Studies on the Abuse of Reason,* Hayek systematically treats a comprehensive problem that, at first glance, seems to be a somewhat remote subject. To the contrary, however, it is the source of all the methodological confusions of the social sciences.

Hayek accuses scientism of being "a very prejudiced approach which, before it has considered its subject, claims to know what is the most appropriate way of investigating it."[15]

In the third part of this book, written later from notes collected at the same time as those for the other parts, Hayek points out with striking clarity that whereas the ideas of Hume and Voltaire, of Adam Smith and Kant, produced the liberalism of the nineteenth century, those of Hegel and Comte, Feuerbach and Marx, produced the totalitarianism of the twentieth century. (Note: throughout this essay, the word "liberalism" is used in the classical sense.)

V

With the publication of his very influential essay "The Use of Knowledge in Society,"[16] Hayek refined an argument previously treated in his "Economics and Knowledge." He once joked that he had made "one discovery and two inventions" and believes this work, in which the leading role of the "division of knowledge" is clearly developed, to be his most important discovery. According to Hayek, what counts in this connection is not scientific knowledge but the unorganized knowledge of the particular circumstances of time and place. The central problem of economics is how the spontaneous interaction of a number of people, each possessing only certain bits of knowledge, creates circumstances that could be brought about only by somebody who possessed the combined knowledge of all these individuals. In our society, in which the knowledge of the relevant facts is dispersed among many people, the price system is the only mechanism that communicates information. The price mechanism is a system of signals that puts us in the situation of adapting to circumstances and experiences of which we know nothing. Our whole modern order and well-being rest on the possibility of adapting to processes that we do not know.

Hayek's "Individualism: True and False,"[17] the twelfth Finlay Lecture at the University College, Dublin, is a masterpiece in the history of ideas. Here, he relentlessly exposes the whole confused state of thought regarding the terms of philosophical individualism.

Still in London, Hayek in 1947 organized a conference for like-minded liberal scientists, journalists, and politicians in a hotel on Mont Pelerin near Vevey, Switzerland. From this first important meeting of Hayek's contemporaries, called together to exchange ideas about the nature of a free society and about the ways and means of strengthening its intellectual support, derived the exclusive Mont Pelerin Society. Hayek served for over twelve years as president and, when he resigned from this office in 1960, was elected honorary president; he is still the society's intellectual mentor. This scholarly association now has about 400 members, drawn from nearly all the states of the free world.

During his almost twenty years in England, Hayek spent some time in Gibraltar doing field research in order to prepare his "Report on the Changes in the Cost of Living in Gibraltar, 1939 – 1944, and on Wages and Salaries."

VI

Due to the outstanding success of his best-known book, *The Road to Serfdom,* Hayek was invited to the United States to address countless audiences in many locales.

In December 1949, he resigned from the London School of Economics, spent the spring quarter at the University of Arkansas, Fayetteville, and in October 1950 accepted a professorship in social and moral sciences at the University of Chicago. That same year, he married his second wife, Helene Bitterlich, in Vienna.

At the University of Chicago, he associated with such figures as Frank Knight, Milton Friedman, and Aaron Director; somewhat later George Stigler joined this outstanding group of liberal scholars.

In this intellectually stimulating climate — many prominent scholars from different fields attended his seminar as regular members or as visitors — Hayek published a great number of important works. I shall concentrate here on surveying the most important ones only.

In his inaugural lecture, "Comte and Hegel,"[18] Hayek returned to the subject of scientism. He published the substance of this lecture as the third part of his *Counter-Revolution of Science: Studies on the Abuse of Reason.*

The Sensory Order (1952) once again shows Hayek's continuing interest in psychology. This book contains some of his most original and important ideas and thoughts[19] and, as such, deserves much more attention than it has received to date. It is a discourse in pure psychology, the preliminary thoughts and notes dating back to the early 1920s, when Hayek spent a few months in Zurich and was still uncertain whether to become a psychologist or an economist. This ambitious book was highly acclaimed by some eminent experts and has recently become the central topic of scholarly conferences.

With the penetrating essay "History and Politics,"[20] written as the introduction to *Capitalism and the Historians,* which Hayek edited, he initiated a long-overdue critical approach to economic history and the treatment of capitalism.

His deep concern with social, political, and legal philosophy led to the work that is regarded as his magnum opus. Hayek finished the typescript of his monumental *The Constitution of Liberty*[21] on his sixtieth birthday. In this milestone in the literature of social philosophy, he developed the ethical, anthropological, legal, and economic bases of a liberal economic and social order.

While for most modern social philosophers the chief aim of politics consists in setting up an ideal social order through utopian reforms, Hayek sees its main task as that of finding rules to enable men with different values and convictions to live together. These rules should be so constructed as to permit each individual to fulfill his aims. In this famous book, Hayek further develops his unique idea of spontaneous order, through which things are brought about that no individual can comprehend. In this massive contribution to the persistent question of the limits of state action, Hayek composed one of the great books of our times.

VII

After twelve years of exceptionally successful lecturing at the University of Chicago, Hayek accepted a call to a professorship of political economy at the University of Freiburg (Germany) in the spring of 1962. He assumed the chair of his old friend Walter Eucken, who had established the famous Ordo-School there shortly after World War II. This typically German-liberal school provided some of the theoretical base for the so-called German Economic Miracle.

In Hayek's first Freiburg period, which lasted seven years, besides translations, he published two books, five brochures, and some thirty articles. Only the most important among these will briefly be described.

With his essay entitled "Competition as a Discovery Procedure,"[22] Hayek contributed some major new insights of lasting significance to the somewhat deadlocked area of the theory of competition. Although the successor of Walter Eucken, who might be considered the head of the Freiburger School, Hayek never changed his characteristically Austrian point of view. To the contrary, he built the basis for the revival of the Austrian School, now so visible, especially in the Anglo-American academic world.

During this time, Hayek repeatedly returned to technical economics and refined, so to speak, as a by-product of his social-philosophical work, some of his arguments on pure economic theory.[23]

In 1964, Rikkyo University in Tokyo awarded him an honorary doctorate. There he delivered his influential lecture "Kinds of Rationalism," which reveals his preoccupation with themes that he would much later publish in the three-volume *Law, Legislation, and Liberty*.

Hayek included his inaugural lecture at Freiburg, "The Economy, Science, and Politics," in his famous *Studies in Philosophy, Politics, and Economics,*[24] which he dedicated to his old friend Sir Karl Popper. This volume contains an important selection of his work dating from the early 1950s to the mid-1960s.

Hayek's lecture on Bernard Mandeville,[25] delivered to the British Academy in 1966, again reveals him as a master in the history of ideas.

During his years in Freiburg, he was invited by the Austrian government to discuss the possibility of taking over the presidency of the Austrian National Bank, which he refused in order to complete his monumental *Law, Legislation, and Liberty.* It seems to be typical of Hayek's uncompromising devotion to scholarship that he leaves a country the moment he is offered a public position. This was the case in the late 1920s in Austria, after almost twenty years in England, after twelve years in the United States, and after seven years in Freiburg.

Some of the preliminary studies to his *Law, Legislation, and Liberty* were collected in a German book entitled *Freiburger Studien: Gesammelte Aufsätze* (1969).

Hayek contributed two very important articles to the *International Encyclopedia of the Social Sciences,* one on the Austrian School and one on Carl Menger. Both of these became noted for their detailed treatment of these subjects.

VIII

After becoming professor emeritus at the University of Freiburg in 1969, Hayek accepted a visiting professorship at the recently reestablished University of Salzburg and returned to his native Austria after spending almost forty years abroad. But a number of factors made this temporary move to Salzburg somewhat disappointing. One of them was the fact that at this university economics was taught as a subsidiary to law, and therefore the faculty's and the students' level did not meet his academic expectations. Also the Anglo-American scholarly tradition seemed more distant than in Freiburg.

In spite of his rather poor health and his intellectual isolation, he published a number of significant works. Again, I shall confine myself to mentioning the most interesting ones only.

In his famous essay "The Errors of Constructivism,"[26] delivered as an inaugural lecture at the University of Salzburg, Hayek developed the idea of constructivism and introduced this term into sociophilosophical discussion, in order to depict the errors of "social engineering" and "welfare statism." This preliminary study points toward Hayek's later fully developed theory of evolution.

Due to the undeniable fact that the liberal aim of a free society runs the risk of collapsing because of a misconstruction and misunderstanding of the democratic ideal, Hayek made a striking proposal for reform and reconstruction of democratic institutions. In the fourth Wincott Memorial Lecture,[27] Hayek for the first time criticized democratic institutions for enforcing mainly egalitarian targets and proposed a quite unorthodox model constitution in order to limit the powers of government. This important idea, which lately has become the subject of a very lively political discussion, is one of Hayek's intellectual inventions. He has since elaborated on this subject.[28]

In 1973, he published the first of the three volumes of *Law, Legislation, and Liberty*.[29] In this first volume, subtitled *Rules and Order,* Hayek refined his argument that a spontaneous order and an organization are distinct and that their distinctiveness is closely related to the two different kinds of rules that prevail in them. Special attention should be drawn to his treatment of "principles and expediencies"[30] in politics in this major work on political philosophy.

In May 1974, on the occasion of his seventy-fifth birthday, Hayek was awarded an honorary doctorate by the University of Salzburg.

The totally unexpected award of the Nobel Prize in Economics in the late fall of 1974 forced Hayek to write his courageous Nobel lecture, "The Pretence of Knowledge,"[31] which was composed in a very short span of time. In this essay, written during a visit to Japan, Hayek again successfully refuted Keynesian economics, basing himself on his concept of the division of knowledge. Ironically enough, he had to share the Nobel Prize with a complete adversary, Gunnar Myrdal, one of the founders of the Swedish welfare state. Nevertheless, this award to some extent initiated the long-overdue counteroffensive against Keynesianism and strengthened the revival of the Austrian School of Economics.

His second important invention originated in Salzburg, where he prepared an address entitled "International Money," for the Geneva Gold and Monetary Conference. Hayek's unusual proposal, which he later developed in detail in his *Denationalization of Money*,[32] aroused a fierce discussion in the field of monetary theory and, of course, contributed to the debate over interventionism. He seems to have been developing this idea since its first mention in *The Constitution of Liberty* (p. 520, *n*2). Hayek argues that inflation can be avoided only if the monopolistic power of issuing money is taken away from government and state authorities and the task given to private industry in order to promote competition in currencies.

Three years after publication of the first volume of *Law, Legislation, and Liberty,* Hayek published the second volume, subtitled *The Mirage of Social Justice.*[33] In this fundamental analysis, he explains why the misleading term "social justice" has meaning in a strict organization only and not in the spontaneous order of a free society. The dangerous and narcotic term "social or distributive justice" is meaningless in, and totally incompatible with, any free or "open" society.

Hayek regained his old form in the summer of 1974, just prior to his vacation, which he and his wife always spend in a tiny village high in the Tyrolian Alps.

IX

Somewhat disappointed with Salzburg, as mentioned above, Hayek decided to leave his native Austria for Freiburg in early 1977, reluctantly leaving behind his unique library of some 7,000 volumes, which he had sold for financial reasons to the University of Salzburg when he assumed the visiting professorship.

Back in Freiburg, he published a third volume of collected essays as his *New Studies in Philosophy, Politics, Economics, and the History of Ideas.*[34]

Three years after the publication of the second volume of his *Law, Legislation, and Liberty,* he concluded this trilogy with the final volume, *The Political Order of a Free People.*[35] Hayek here refined his proposal for reform and reconstruction of democracy. The predominant tendency of liberal democratic institutions, in which the same representative body sets up "rules of just conduct" and directs government, necessarily creates a gradual transformation of the spontaneous order of a free society, which in the long run unavoidably leads to a totalitarian system dominated by "coalitions of organized interests."

Since moving back to Freiburg, Hayek has published numerous other works, out of which I can mention only two of the more outstanding examples. In 1977, he presented an enlarged German translation of *Denationalization of Money — The Argument Refined: An Analysis of the Theory and Practice of Concurrent Currencies.*

In May 1978, Hayek gave the Hobhouse Lecture at the London School of Economics. Entitled "The Three Sources of Human Value," this lecture treated "the destruction of indispensable values by scientific error." It was published as the epilogue to the third volume of *Law, Legislation, and Liberty.*

In the late 1970s, Hayek became attracted to the idea of a public confrontation with socialist thinkers and wanted to organize a conference in Paris that would bring together some of his liberal colleagues with contemporary left-wing intellectuals. In order to structure this "Paris challenge," he laid down some twelve points of discussion, which since have "exploded" into a monumental work now being composed.

In this forthcoming work, significantly entitled *The Fatal Conceit,* Hayek not only further develops his theory of cultural evolution, but also offers some striking new insights into group selection and moral tradition.[36] He argues that cultural evolution is not a result of human reason consciously building institutions, but a process in which culture and reason develop concurrently. Since we owe the order of our society to a tradition of rules and morals that we understand only imperfectly, both cultural and economic progress must be based on tradition.

The book is bound to become an extraordinary critique of rationalism, socialism, and constructivism as a whole.

When not lecturing throughout the world, Hayek devotes himself entirely to the completion of this great work, which will contain some of the most significant developments in his intellectual thought.

X

Hayek's work arose and still develops from a comprehensive approach to various intellectual disciplines that condition and influence one another. We owe to Hayek's tireless labors not only important contributions to pure economic theory and profound studies in the philosophy of science, the history of ideas, and political philosophy, but also the most penetrating insights into social philosophy and psychology.

His work in pure economic theory was pioneering and is still very influential in the further development of theories of the trade cycle, monetary factors, and capital. Within the history of ideas, his careful studies of Mandeville, John Stuart Mill, Menger, Ricardo, Wieser, and the Austrian School are intellectual masterpieces.

His achievements in the philosophy of science are widely acknowledged. Hayek's unique books — *The Constitution of Liberty; Law, Legislation, and Liberty; Individualism and Economic Order;* both of his *Studies . . .* ; and *The Road to Serfdom* — have become classics of the literature of liberty. The better part of his work has been translated into the major languages of the world. It seems to be almost impossible to count all his memberships in distinguished societies and academies, his honarary doctorates, his honors, awards, and orders. (An almost complete bibliography of Hayek's published work has been prepared by John Cody of the Institute for Humane Studies, Menlo Park, California; see *Literature of Liberty,* Menlo Park, 4, no. 4 [1982]).

Notes

1. Cf. "Das Stabilisierungsproblem in Goldwährungsländern," *Zeitschrift für Volkswirtschaft und Sozialpolitik,* Vienna, n.s. 4 (1924); "Die Währungspolitik der Vereinigten Staaten seit der Überwindung der Krise von 1920," in ibid., n.s. 5 (1925); "Das amerikanische Bankwesen seit der Reform von 1914," *Der österreichische Volkswirt,* Vienna, no. 17 (1926); and "Die Bedeutung der Konjunkturforschung für das Wirtschaftsleben," in ibid., no. 5 (1926).

2. *Geldtheorie und Konjunkturtheorie* (Vienna and Leipzig, 1929); 2nd ed. (Munich, 1976); English trans.: *Monetary Theory and the Trade Cycle* (London, 1933; New York, 1933 and 1966).

3. See Chapter 2 of this volume.

4. Sir John Hicks, "The Hayek Story," in *Critical Essays in Monetary Theory* (Oxford, 1967), p. 203.

5. "Reflections on the Pure Theory of Money of Mr. J. M. Keynes," Part 1, *Economica* 11, no. 33 (August 1931): 270 – 95; Part 2, *Economica* 12 (February 1932): 22 – 44.

6. "The Pure Theory of Money: A Rejoinder to Mr. Keynes," *Economica* 11, no. 34 (November 1931): 398 – 413. (Keynes's reply appears on pp. 387 – 97.)

7. "Money and Capital: A Reply to Mr. Sraffa," *Economic Journal* 42 (June 1932): 237 – 49.

8. See *Profits, Interest and Investment* (London, 1939; Clifton, N.J., 1969 and 1975); *Monetary Nationalism and International Stability* (Geneva, 1937; London, 1937; New York, 1964, 1971, and 1974); "Über Neutrales Geld," *Zeitschrift für Nationalökonomie,* Vienna, 4 (1933); and "On the Relationship Between Investment and Output," *Economic Journal* 44 (1934).

9. "Economics and Knowledge," *Economica,* n.s. 4 (1937); reprinted in *Individualism and Economic Order*; see also Chapter 11 of this volume.

10. For bibliographical details, see Chapters 4, 7, and 11 of this volume.

11. *The Road to Serfdom* (London, 1944, 1945, 1960; Chicago, 1944, 1945, 1969; German trans.: Zurich, 1945 and 1952; 6th ed., Munich, 1976).

12. *Journal of Political Economy* 54 (1946): 269.

13. *The Counter-Revolution of Science: Studies on the Abuse of Reason* (Glencoe, Ill., 1952 and 1964; Indianapolis, 1979; German trans.: 1959; 2nd enl. ed., Munich, 1979).

14. Ibid., p. 192.

15. Ibid., p. 24.

16. See Chapter 11 of this volume.

17. See Chapter 7 of this volume.

18. See note 13 for details.

19. For bibliographical details, see Chapter 12 of this volume.

20. For bibliographical details, see Chapter 8 of this volume.

21. For bibliographical details, see Chapters 15 and 18 of this volume.

22. See Chapter 13 of this volume.

23. See "Alte Wahrheiten und neue Irrtümer," in *Freiburger Studien* (Tübingen, 1969); and "Three Elucidations of the 'Ricardo Effect,' " *Journal of Political Economy* 77 (March – April 1969).

24. See Chapter 8 of this volume.

25. See Chapter 9 of this volume.

26. See Chapter 9 of this volume.

27. *Economic Freedom and Representative Government,* Institute for Economic Affairs, Occasional Papers 39 (London, 1973).

28. See Chapters 19 and 21 of this volume.

29. For bibliographical details, see Chapter 16 of this volume.

30. See Chapter 16 of this volume.

31. See Chapter 14 of this volume.

32. *Denationalization of Money: An Analysis of the Theory and Practice of Concurrent Currencies,* Hobart Paper Special 70 (London, 1978).
33. For bibliographical details, see Chapter 5 of this volume.
34. For bibliographical details, see Chapter 9 of this volume.
35. For bibliographical details, see Chapter 21 of this volume.
36. Cf. Chapter 17 of this volume.

Suggestions for Further Reading

I. Hayekian Economics

In addition to the writings reprinted in this book, the following books, works and articles also contain essential writings by Hayek on economics:

Understanding How Markets Function and Why They Exist

"Economics and Knowledge" (in *Individualism and Economic Order*).
"Engineers and Planners" (in *Counter-Revolution of Science*).
"The Telecommunications System of the Market" (in *1980's Unemployment and the Unions*).
"Socialist Calculation" (chapters 7 – 9 in *Individualism and Economic Order*).
"The New Confusion About Planning" (in *New Studies*).
"The Market Order or Catallaxy" (in *Law, Legislation, and Liberty,* vol. 2).
"Government Policy and the Market" (in *Law, Legislation, and Liberty,* vol. 3).

Harmful Effects of Government Manipulation of Money and Credit

"The Campaign Against Keynesian Inflation" (in *New Studies*).
"Can We Still Avoid Inflation?" (in *A Tiger by the Tail*).
Denationalisation of Money.

II. Hayek's Refutation of Socialism

In addition to the writings reprinted in this section, the following books, works, and articles also contain essential writings by Hayek on socialism:

Theoretical, Historical, and Normative Analysis of Socialist Ideas

"The Source of the Scientistic Hubris: L'Ecole Polytechnique" (in *Counter-Revolution of Science*).

"Comte and Hegel" (in *Counter-Revolution of Science*).

"Socialist Roots of Naziism" (in *The Road to Serfdom*).

"The Intellectuals and Socialism" (in *Studies in Philosophy, Politics, and Economics*).

The Road to Serfdom (whose dedication reads, "To the Socialists of All Parties.")

See also the works listed below under Section III in the category, "Liberalism Versus Socialism."

Each of the works listed below under Section III in the category, "The History and Importance of the Idea of Spontaneous Order" should be viewed as constituting anthropological refutations of socialism, i.e., as showing how socialist norms are predicated on a set of naive and archaic misunderstandings of how complex institutions such as language, law, money, and markets have come to exist.

Each of the works listed below under Section I in the category "Understanding How Markets Function and Why They Exist" should be viewed as constituting economic refutations of socialism, i.e., as showing how socialist ideas are, in particular, predicated on a set of naive and archaic failures to comprehend the communications functions of markets and market prices. These works further show how any attempt to implement socialist economic theories necessarily produces waste and economic chaos.

Each of the works listed at the beginning of Section V should be viewed as constituting additional refutations of socialism, demonstrating that socialist ideals are undesirable either in theory or in practice, and that even the attempt to implement these undesirable and unrealizable ideals is destructive of an advanced (nontribal) civilization such as Western civilization.

Socialism Under a Different Name Still Doesn't Work

"The Atavism of Social Justice" (in *New Studies*).

"Engineers and Planners" (in *Counter-Revolution of Science*).

"The Confusion of Language in Political Thought" (in *New Studies*).

"The New Confusion About Planning" (in *New Studies*).

III. Hayek's Contributions to the History of Ideas

In addition to the writings reprinted in this section, the following books, works, and articles also contain essential writings by Hayek on the history of ideas:

Liberalism Versus Socialism

"Liberalism" (in *New Studies*).
"The Origins of the Rule of Law" (in *The Constitution of Liberty*).
"The Abandoned Road" (in *The Road to Serfdom*).
The Counter-Revolution of Science (chapters 11 – 17).
"The Socialist Roots of Naziism" (in *The Road to Serfdom*).
"The Transmission of the Ideals of Economic Freedom" (in *Studies*).

The History and Importance of the Idea of Spontaneous Order

"Kinds of Rationalism" (in *Studies in Philosophy, Politics, and Economics*).
"The Products of Human Action But Not of Human Design" (in *Studies*).
"Reason and Evolution" (in *Law, Legislation, and Liberty,* vol. 1).
"Cosmos and Taxis" (in *Law, Legislation, and Liberty,* vol. 1).
"The Confusion of Language in Political Thought" (in *New Studies*).
"The Containment of Power and the Dethronement of Politics" (in *Law, Legislation and Liberty*, vol. 3).
"Our Moral Heritage" (in *Knowledge, Evolution, and Society*).
The Fatal Conceit (forthcoming).
The Constitution of Liberty (whose dedication reads, "To the unknown civilization that is growing in America").

IV. Theoretical Basis of the Hayekian System

In addition to the writings reprinted in this section, the following books, works, and articles also contain essential writings by Hayek on the foundations of psychology, epistemology, economics, anthropology (especially of Western Civilization), and methodology in the social sciences:

Psychology and Epistemology

The Sensory Order.
"Rules, Perception, and Intelligibility" (in *Studies*).
"Notes on the Evolution of Systems of Rules of Conduct" (in *Studies*).
"Kinds of Rationalism" (in *Studies*).
"Our Moral Heritage" (in *Knowledge, Evolution, and Society*).
"The Primacy of the Abstract" (in *New Studies*).

Anthropology

"The Products of Human Action But Not of Human Design" (in *Studies*).
"Notes on the Evolution of Systems of Rules of Conduct" (in *Studies*).

"The Atavism of Social Justice" (in *New Studies*).
"Reason and Evolution" (in *Law, Legislation, and Liberty*, vol. 1).
"The Three Sources of Human Values" (in *Law, Legislation, and Liberty*, vol. 3).
Knowledge, Evolution, and Society.
The Fatal Conceit (forthcoming).

Economics

Individualism and Economic Order (chapters 1 – 9).
Counter-Revolution of Science (chapters 1 – 10).
"Degrees of Explanation" (in *Studies*).
"The Theory of Complex Phenomena" (in *Studies*).

Critique and Reformulation of Foundations of Social Science

Studies in Philosophy, Politics, and Economics (especially, "The Theory of Complex Phenomena," "Rules, Perception and Intelligibility," "Kinds of Rationalism," and "Degrees of Explanation").
The Sensory Order (chapters 1 – 8).
The Counter-Revolution of Science ("Scientism and the Study of Society").
"Economics and Knowledge" (in *Individualism and Economic Order*).
"The Facts of the Social Sciences" (in *Individualism and Economic Order*).
"A Digression on Articulated and Non-Articulated Rules" (in *The Confusion of Language in Political Thought*).
"Reason and Evolution" and "Cosmos and Taxis" (in *Law, Legislation, and Liberty*, vol. 1).
"The Three Sources of Human Values" (in *Law, Legislation, and Liberty*, vol. 3).
"The Primacy of the Abstract" (in *New Studies*).

V. Hayekian Political Economy: A Philosophical-realistic Concept

In addition to the writings reprinted in this section, the following books, works, and articles also contain essential writings by Hayek on law, morals, and politics:

Rules and Laws

Law, Legislation, and Liberty, vol. 1, *Rules and Order*.
"Rules, Perception, and Intelligibility" (in *Studies*).
"Notes on the Evolution of Systems of Rules of Conduct" (in *Studies*).
"A Digression on Articulated and Non-Articulated Rules" (in *The Confusion of Language in Political Thought*).

Morals

"Notes on the Evolution of Systems of Rules of Conduct" (in *Studies*).
"The Three Sources of Human Values" (in *Law, Legislation, and Liberty*, vol. 3).
"Our Moral Heritage" (in *Knowledge, Ignorance, and Society*).
The Fatal Conceit (forthcoming).

Politics, Political Theory, and the History of Political Ideals

Law, Legislation, and Liberty, vol. 1, *Rules and Order*.
vol. 2, *The Mirage of Social Justice*.
vol. 3, *The Political Order of a Free People*.
The Road to Serfdom.
The Counter-Revolution of Science (chapters 11 – 17).
The Constitution of Liberty.
"Liberalism" (in *New Studies*).
"The Confusion of Language in Political Thought" (in *New Studies*).

Socialism Versus Liberalism Versus Conservatism

See the works listed at the beginning of Section II.
See also the works listed under Section III.

INTRODUCTION

• *Chiaki Nishiyama* •

In the hope that they might present the essence of Friedrich von Hayek's thought, the 21 papers that follow were selected from the staggering number that Hayek has written in the past sixty years. As he would put it, however, any choice is very much a value judgment. His own selection, or that of another editor, would undoubtedly differ. The criterion for our choice was to present as total a picture of what we like to call the Hayekian "order" of ideas as possible. We could not, of course, include as many writings as we wished in this volume. One eminent example is the regrettable omission of any selection from his important *Pure Theory of Capital* (University of Chicago Press, 1941).

Our purpose will be fulfilled if readers use this book as a stepping-stone to further study of Hayek's works. Even this brief selection serves as a reminder of the number of intellectually stimulating ideas and novel practical suggestions contained in his writings. The corpus of Professor Hayek's works is very much like a rich mine, from which we can dig up various gems. Whether we succeed or not depends on our alertness. The problem we are studying may at first appear quite different from those he is discussing, yet will later prove to be fundamentally akin to them.

It is in a way contradictory to the purpose of this book to write an introduction. We decided not to publish the usual *Festschrift* because we felt that it was far more important for readers to study the writings of Professor Hayek directly than to read secondhand versions written by others. In order, however, to assist readers, an introductory note may not be totally useless. Many readers seem at first to be repelled by Hayek's unique use of otherwise familiar terminology and only later come to appreciate the meaning of his terms thoroughly. Moreover, mastery of the few bits and pieces of his writings presented here may lead to quite erroneous understanding and interpretation of his theories.

Consistency and coherence are very characteristic of his order of ideas. But this does not mean that his theories were deduced from a few ideas or that they did not evolve. On the contrary, the "evolution" of his thought is as striking as the evolution of social institutions he emphasizes. An introduction to his works may help readers overcome difficulties in grasping a true picture of Hayek's order of ideas and its genuine significance.

This introduction attempts to paraphrase his unique terminology, which results from his rather innovative reasoning process, and to elucidate the interrelationships among his different theories. The notable coherence of Hayek's theories has itself led many readers to make utterly unfounded assumptions in interpreting the diverse parts of his thought. In the case of the Hayekian order of ideas, self-consistency does not mean that everything in this order becomes self-evident as soon as some basic ideas of that order are grasped. Does, for example, Hayek approve of the concept of utility? If we regard utility as a cardinal number and mean by it a certain "absolute" quantity of satisfaction, then his answer would definitely be no. If, however, we regard it as an ordinal number and discuss relations among different utilities (the relative values of different goods and services) as expressed by the marginal rates of substitutions among them, which in return are reflected in their relative prices, he would certainly approve. Yet he clearly refuses either to regard a total national product as a meaningful sum of those utilities or to make intertemporal comparisons of the utilities of those same goods and services.

"Complexity" is the other characteristic of the Hayekian order of ideas. Yet readers should not assume that this complexity implies difficulty in understanding his theories. On the contrary, once readers master Hayekian terminology and his innovative way of thinking, they find it surprisingly easy to appreciate his arguments, none of which is self-evident at first glance. The so-called great discoveries and widely accepted "truths" are almost without exception rather easy to understand. So it is with the Hayekian order of ideas.

The Hayekian Revolution

The word *revolution* is not quite appropriate to Hayek's intellectual world. Many people may even assume that the term is utterly alien to his thought. He has, after all, insisted upon the indispensable importance of traditional morals, in clear contrast to the positivistic jurisprudence that dominates our age. For example, he has stated:

> Morals are not something we can choose at pleasure. At least the general outline of those we have inherited are an irreplaceable means for keeping alive the number of human beings they have called into being [see Chapter 17].

Nevertheless he has described the academic contributions of Carl Menger as a (marginal utility) revolution (see Chapter 10). In that sense, we can perhaps use "revolution" to emphasize the epoch-making significance of Hayek's works.

Moreover, many readers, in order to understand the real implications of his writings, may need to abandon their usual terminology and accustomed way of thinking and to change their "paradigm" or "switch their *Gestalt*."[1] Hayek himself used the words *paradigmata* and *paradigm* and expressed his fondness for the term *Gestalt* when he discussed "the order of the apparatus of classification" in *The Sensory Order*, the last chapter of which is reproduced here as Chapter 12.

According to him, "Mandeville for the first time developed all the classical *paradigmata* of the spontaneous growth of orderly social structures: of law and morals, of language, the market, and of money, and also of the growth of technological knowledge" (see Chapter 9; italics added). Contrary to the impressions people often receive from Hayek's theories, he declares that "cultural evolution is founded wholly on *group selection*" (see Chapter 17; italics added). He goes on to state:

> In some fields, such as language and law, the fact that these institutions could develop only through *group selection* is obvious: language could clearly be of no use to its sole possessor, and the benefits derived from it will normally accrue to all those who can communicate through it. All the *paradigms* of culturally evolved institutions, morals, exchange, and money refer to such practices whose benefits transcend the individuals who practice them in the particular instances [see Chapter 17; italics added].

It appears here that Hayek makes an unnecessarily strong statement. The sole possessor of any language will certainly find it useful for the development of his own thinking. But the real point is that "sole possession" in the strict sense of the term is impossible.

In the case of Bernard Mandeville, Hayek meant by *paradigmata* the hard core of the evolutionary theory of social institutions — the core that scholars have developed and will change and reformulate in accordance with their falsification efforts on the one hand and with their endeavors to develop hypotheses on the other. In the case of "group selection," he meant by *paradigm* the hard core of the results, both intended and unintended, of various individuals' activities, the control of the entire body of which was beyond the ability of any individual as well as of any particular group of individuals. For convenience' sake, let us differentiate the two by calling the former the "individual paradigm" and the latter the "group paradigm." What is most remarkable here is that in both cases Hayek is asserting the fundamental "changeability" of both of these paradigms. He also insists that even the framework of what he calls the "order of the apparatus of classification," which is the basis as well as the precondition not only for our cognition and perception, experience, and knowledge but also for our intuition, drive, emotion, and so forth, would change over the course of the development of either individual or group history (see Chapter 12). For Hayek, fundamentally nothing is fixed or perpetual. Everything is changeable. From time to time, steady structures of the rules of conduct, which show "homeostatic control," may arise,[2] but they will become unstable as unanticipated circumstances are encountered, and consequently the rules themselves will become self-contradictory.

Professor Hayek has often been accused of being a dogmatist. Readers must, however, be aware of his fundamental admission of the changeability of everything, including his own theories. He maintains that the rules of individual conduct may "mutate"; the results of such mutations, when transmitted to other individuals, will progressively change the overall order of actions itself.[3] And he also states that "the whole of our civilization and all human values" will "continue to change."[4] Hayek criticized past philosophico-scientific endeavors for having been "monocausal or nomothetic approaches" and for having reduced the world to "relatively simple or mechanical phenomena" (see Chapter 17).

Insofar as this assertion of the fundamental changeability of everything is concerned, Hayek appears more Platonic than Plato himself. There are, without doubt, more dissimilarities than similarities between Hayek and Plato. Because of his prominently logical consistency, however, many people may well categorize him more as an Aristotelian. But according to A. E. Taylor's lucid explanation of the basic difference between Plato and Aristotle,

> It is not necessary to the argument that the world should have had a beginning "in time," in the sense that there was a time when the world was not there. All that Timaeus commits himself to by saying that the world is *gennētón* (what must grow) is that "passage" is a fundamental character of it. Aristotle, on the other hand, maintains the "eternity of the world" not in the sense that "becoming" is not derivative . . . but in the different sense that the regular astronomical movements have no beginning and will have no end, and go on with absolute uniformity.[5]

In Plato's system of thought, "passage" and "becoming" were the fundamental characteristics of the "world." But then the "world" for Plato was "Nature"[6] and did not include the ideas, on whose absolutely general validity Plato insisted. In flat opposition to this, Hayek insists on the changeability, or even the mutability, of the basic framework of the apparatus for our cognition — that is, the framework that in Hayek's terminology is the fundamental set of classifications, but which in ordinary terminology would be called the hard-core group of ideas or, in short, ideas themselves. And this insistence implies also the variability of Nature, whose existence we can surmise thanks to such a framework. Many of those who have consciously or unconsciously been indoctrinated by the excessive positivism of the modern era are dissatisfied with Hayek's repeated criticism of the kind of scientific theories that make specific predictions and demand indiscreet social experiments based on those theories.

They cannot appreciate the wisdom of the Socratic or Platonic assertion of the need to realize our fundamental ignorance in our attempts to understand existence. Precisely because of their failure to understand the cardinal importance of this assertion, they cannot realize that in their scientific endeavors they are actually creating a rigid, mechanical, and oversimplified world out of both human and natural phenomena (the most significant characteristics of which are their "becomings" and "growth," whose results we can never exhaustively predict). Therefore, rather naturally they are unable to realize the profound sagacity of Hayek's repeated assertions that

> if man is not to do more harm than good in his efforts to improve the social order, he will have to learn that in this, as in all other fields where essential complexity of an organized kind prevails, he cannot acquire the full knowledge which would make mastery of the events possible. He will therefore have to use what knowledge he can achieve, not to shape the results as the craftsman shapes his handiwork, but rather to *cultivate a growth* by providing the appropriate environment, in the manner in which the gardener does this for his plants [see Chapter 14; italics added].

The issue here is whether or not we regard it as of the greatest importance to let every individual develop his or her potential to the utmost degree. Or to put it differently, whether we are so eager to experiment with our own theories of governmental intervention that we do not care if we end up putting individuals into straitjackets, or if the failures of our experiments give rise to vicious cycles of further expansions of such interventions. Readers who approach Hayek in the rationalistic, mechanistic, and deterministic tradition of Aristotle may not comprehend the significance of the Hayekian appeal for the cultivation of growth in socio-human affairs.

Even though Hayek emphasizes the changeability of even the most basic framework of the "apparatus of classification" or of our cognition, he does not mean by this either that such a change will take place in a revolutionary way or that the *Gestalt*-switch will occur abruptly. A long-established theory may yet suddenly be falsified by new facts. A rule of individual conduct may unexpectedly be contradicted by new experiences. But both the hard cores of theories and the overall rule of actions will gradually evolve as the cumulative results of interactions among their parts (some of which are still surviving, and some of which have failed). The very slowness or gradualness of such a change of the hard core of theories or of the overall order of actions is typical of evolution in the world of Hayek. Yet readers of his works may well find it useful to change their accustomed paradigm and their habitual terminology in order to appreciate the real significance of Hayek's abstruse arguments.

Subjective or Objective

Norman P. Barry, in *Hayek's Social and Economic Philosophy* (London: Macmillan, 1979), often displays keen insight into the subtle reasonings of Professor Hayek. Such a book on Hayek after so many years of malicious attacks is welcome. Barry clearly made a sincere effort to explain Hayek's works to the public. It is, therefore, all the more a pity that by being restricted to his own "paradigm," Barry ended up presenting Hayek's thought in utterly erroneous ways when he expressed his own views on the topics discussed by Hayek. Moreover, Barry appears to have created a monster out of Hayek. According to him, Hayek is not only "dogmatic" (see, e.g., pp. 70 – 71 and 121) but also "omniscient," "complete," and "self-sufficient." Barry claims that all the intellectual inquiries of Hayek "add up to a *complete*, integrated system of ideas" (p. 2) and that "Hayek has stressed, on a number of occasions, the necessity of understanding the *whole range* of academic disciplines for a proper appreciation of the forces that determine social phenomena" (p. 76; italics added).

Such an excessive eulogy amounts to the negation of one of Hayek's central theses. He denies the possibility of anyone's becoming "complete" in his or her thought or of acquiring the "whole" range of knowledge. This is precisely the reason why he adamantly opposes any kind of planned economy and has consistently been distrustful of the various forms of governmental intervention. And that is exactly why he asserts "methodological individualism." Barry is quite aware of this point. Should, however, we lose sight, as Barry did, of the Hayekian thesis of the inescapable and constitutional limitation of anyone's knowledge in the course of our examination of Hayekian thought, we might well be led to a similarly unfounded interpretation of Hayek's ideas.

According to Barry, for the Austrian economists, including Hayek, "cost is an entirely subjective phenomenon: it is not the observable money expenditure required to produce a commodity but the value of foregone output from *an alternative use* of the same resources" (p. 44; italics added). If the issue is inflation or a change in prices, or if the analysis of cost is to be made in real terms, then, indeed, cost is not the "observable quantity of money expenditure," which is the nominal amount of such an outlay. Clearly, however, these are not what Barry has in mind. What he is trying to say is that the Austrian economists regard "observable monetary expenditure" as an *objectivistic* variable. If this were the case, Barry would be making an utterly nonsensical statement, which could be made only by those with no knowledge of economics or of Hayek's writings in the field of economics.

The "value of foregone output" is usually called "opportunity cost," and the emphasis on this cost is characteristic of, but not limited to, the Austrian economists. Moreover, the use of the term "opportunity cost" is not restricted to the value of foregone output, which otherwise may have been produced by a *single* alternative use of the same resources as Barry apparently suggests. Those resources may well have been used for a number of different purposes, which will come to be known thanks to the free market, and many of which will remain unknown if the government tampers with the market. That is one of the reasons why Hayek emphasizes over and over again the need for a spontaneous order in the market. In the actual computation, we do use the value of foregone product from the second best use of the same resources (the second best to the actual use).

But each individual who uses resources can say what is the best or the second best only among those unknown opportunities that come to be disclosed to that individual by the market. And, more important, it is the free market and not any individual that can find out what are really the best and the second best, thanks to competitive as well as cooperative interactions among individuals. Furthermore, prices do reflect opportunity costs, which in turn are determined by the interactions among relative utilities such as those expressed by the marginal rates of substitutions (or transformations) on the one hand and cost conditions (expressed by the "displacement functions" that determine the rates at which some goods and services can be produced in place of the others) on the other.[7] In a monetary economy, those prices and costs are expressed only in "observable monetary terms." Or as Professor Hayek has put it, the "actual numerical values" of the rates of exchanges among different goods and services will "be different, according as one commodity or another is chosen as the standard of comparison or 'numeraire.'"[8]

Barry claims that Hayek "believes in the superiority of hunch and intuition over rational argument" (p. 14). I simply cannot understand why Barry, who creates an omniscient man out of Hayek and complains of the high degree of abstractness of Hayek's theories as well as of their theoretical complexity, makes such an unbelievable statement. If there could be any rational explanation for such an irrational claim, it might be that Barry was overly impressed by Hayek's assertion of "introspective method" (see, e.g., Chapter 12). According to Barry, Hayek maintains that "the major characteristic of knowledge in the social sciences is that it is *subjective*, that is, there are no observable facts of the social sciences, there are only the attitudes, beliefs and opinions of the actors in a social process and knowledge of this kind is acquired introspectively" (p. 16).

Barry also claims that in Hayekian economics, or "praxeology," that there are "no objective social facts which can be observed and measured," but only the knowledge of the "properties of our own minds," which we can acquire through "introspection" and thanks to which "we can understand the behavior of others"; and "therefore the theorems of [Hayekian] economics cannot be tested empirically" (pp. 20 – 21). I would very much like to learn from Barry which economic theory of Hayek was developed by the so-called introspective method. His "monetary" business cycle theory was certainly not. In *The Pure Theory of Capital* (pp. 420 – 23), Hayek stressed not only the importance of separating "relative costs" (in essence, relations among physical factors) and "relative utilities" (which are fundamentally subjective in their nature) more clearly than Alfred Marshall was willing to, but also the importance of retaining both concepts.

Barry himself has made a very penetrating explication of Hayekian reasoning. That is, in the world of Hayek all that we know about the "external world" is an "order of events *subjectively* known" (italics added). Yet Barry explains that the general statements that we make about the "external world" in terms of such an order will be sustainable because, as Hayek states, "what appears alike or different to us usually appears alike or different to other men" (p. 12). As explained above, Hayek maintains that social institutions have developed only through group selection. Do we not usually call what is cognitively common to us "concrete"?

Whatever objectivists, positivists, or behaviorists may claim, do they not base the reliabilities of their claims explicitly or implicitly on the very fact of the knowledge common among us? It is one thing to insist that we must always endeavor to falsify our hypotheses by contrasting them with "facts." It is entirely another, however, to claim that "facts" are invariably, or permanently, "facts." "Facts" are "facts" only in the context of the paradigm that allows the development of those hypotheses that are to be examined. This means that when the paradigm changes, facts may no longer be facts. That is why, as Professor Hayek puts it, " 'facts which everybody knows' have long been proved not to have been facts at all" (see Chapter 8).

A common misconception of Hayek's arguments is that he holds that since through "introspection," we can understand the behavior of others, we have no objective social facts that can be observed and measured. Suppose through introspection we develop a theory that we hope can explain the behavior of others. How can we ever hope then that our theory will succeed, unless our theory is tested by others, who also introspectively examine their minds, and by social phenomena such as the evolution of social institutions discussed by Hayek above?

Hayek, of course, asserts that our knowledge of those social institutions is the result of the order of the apparatus of classification that each of us has developed within ourselves. But he is not claiming the self-evident irrefutability of such knowledge. On the contrary, he humbly presented his theory of the sensory order as a plausible hypothesis for professional psychologists. And he insists on the supremacy of morals over reason (see Chapter 9) because they result from the experiences of many generations (see Chapter 9) in which the rational actions of individuals certainly played important roles, but in which *interactions* among the rational and nonrational, altruistic and self-regarding, intentional and unintentional, activities of those individuals played far more dominant roles.

Social science, in the genuine sense of the term, studies nothing other than those interactions. The social sciences, which claim either that they can study society directly or that they can establish reliable theories by studying individuals alone, are simply shams. What may really be worth regarding as "subjectivistic" in the Hayekian order of ideas is his assertion that we cannot explain even in principle why any person decides and acts in a particular way at any particular time and therefore must accept those decisions and actions as givens in our study of social phenomena. All the rest of his theories are "objective" in so far as they are based, however remotely or partly, on experience.

A Remarkable Synthesis of A Priori and A Posteriori: The Revival of Philosophy

A mind imbued with positivism and shallow in its understanding of socio-human phenomena cannot appreciate the really revolutionary significance of the Hayekian order of ideas. The most fundamental characteristics of those phenomena are complexity and mutual interrelatedness. Yet positivism has made them "dead" phenomena by stripping off their vital complexities and, at the same time, by disjoining their pregnant interrelatedness. No theory can grasp those complexities and mutual interrelations (which are the results of intricate interactions among relevant factors) as they are. Fundamental oversimplification is inevitable in scientific analysis. But it is one thing to say this, and another to negate that essential complexity and primary interrelatedness.

Yet under the influence of positivism, philosophy has long abdicated its sovereign role of integrating different aspects of socio-human phenomena, opting instead for breaking them up into disconnected parts. In spite of repeated calls for interdisciplinary studies, the social sciences have been able to establish only monocausal interrelationships among the phenomena analyzed by the different disciplines and not the resultant general interlinkages that emerge out of multiple causes. The fundamental feature of society is polycentricity. It is basically always individuals, or rather their various activities, that — however controlled and regimented they may be by government or other coercive power — generate socio-human phenomena. Yet those phenomena are characterized by an amazing degree of coherence and order.

It is the basic task of the social sciences to provide explanations for these. And it is precisely here that the Hayekian order of ideas comes in. Barry correctly and emphatically states that *The Sensory Order* constitutes the core of Hayekian methodology (see, e.g., p. 12). Hayek himself prefers to regard his theory of the sensory order as a work in the field of psychology. However, statements similar to those in *The Sensory Order* appear, for example in *The Counter-Revolution of Science* (Glencoe, Ill.: Free Press, 1952) and do constitute his methodological arguments. He once told me that he had conceived the idea of the sensory order at a very young age and had thought through this idea for many years before publishing.

Even when we realize the methodological significance of *The Sensory Order*, we often overlook an assertion of cardinal importance in that book. Hayek maintains there that human perception and cognition are, without exception, directly and indirectly, immediately and remotely, based on experience alone. Moreover, he insists that his theory of the sensory order should be tested by experience. Some of Hayek's admirers occasionally complain that he rarely discusses liberty or freedom as "moral values" or for their own sake.

Although he does say, for example, that "I doubt if we could even fully understand what someone says if we had no values whatever in common with him" (see Chapter 6), thus admitting the *objective* communicability of values among different individuals, such complaints are rather justified precisely because Hayek has consistently made an effort to argue "scientifically." This means in the world of Hayek to do two things simultaneously — to be logically consistent and to base theories on experience.

In the Hayekian theory of the sensory order, our theoretical knowledge, our daily perceptions, and, in fact, even our instinctive drives, emotions, and so forth result, without exception, from our classifications of "external" stimuli. Some of these external stimuli may well ordinarily be described as "internal" because they take place within ourselves. But they are external to the Hayekian order of the apparatus of classification. However external those stimuli may be, they are inseparable ingredients of this order because without them cognition, perceptions, drives, and so forth do not take place.

Some critics' obsession with Hayekian "subjectivism" is therefore all the more curious. They repeatedly insist that Hayek's theories are "mental constructs." This misrepresentation of the Hayekian order of ideas is typical of a mind impregnated with positivism. All theories are mental constructs. Differences of opinion about this occur only when we discuss, for example, how those mental constructs come to be produced, from what sort of origins they arise, in what way they acquire reliability.

Metaphysics was unique to an intellectual world in which people held an unwavering belief that without exception knowledge was ultimately deduced either from a set of *a priori* truths or from *the a priori* truth. Let us call this type of people "apriorists." When Immanuel Kant cried out that he had awaken from the slumber of metaphysical (or *a priori*) dogmatism, metaphysics was replaced by philosophy, in which the methodological primacy of such ideas as categories was still retained. But as logical positivism gained influence, even philosophy came to be abandoned. If there is anything left in the field called philosophy, it is a theory of syntax, semantics, ordinary language, or some such, or at best a theory of scientific discovery. The end result of all this has been the view that a theory owes it acceptability only to facts, objective conditions, quantifiable phenomena, observable behavior, and so forth, if not to some sort of intuitive knowledge; unless, of course, they are tautologies. Let us call the people who share this view "aposteriorists."

Professor Hayek is both an apriorist and an aposteriorist. He has attained a remarkable synthesis of *a priori* and *a posteriori* and thus revived philosophy. Herein lies the most unique significance of his contribution, which is indeed worthy of the name "Hayekian revolution." According to his theory of the sensory order (see Chapter 12), we can learn about the "external" (in the sense of the term mentioned before) world thanks to some presuppositions, which are *a priori* true. Those presuppositions themselves are, however, products of past experience. In this regard, Hayek is an apriorist. But this does not imply that those presuppositions constitute the "pure" or "primary" core of sensations (or, for that matter, hunch or intuition, as some critics seem to suggest).

Instead they simply represent generic reproductions of the relationships among various elements of our environment, which, without exception, each of us has *experienced* before. As far as this aspect of his theory of the sensory order is concerned, Hayek is an aposteriorist. Indeed, he goes so far as to maintain that "experience is not a function of mind or consciousness, but mind and consciousness are rather products of experience" (see Chapter 12). Therefore, there are no "irreducible mental atoms or elements." It is thus totally irrelevant to accuse him of subjectivism. Since all presensory or *a priori* suppositions are based on *experiences*, they cannot be invariable but will change as each of us encounters conflicting experiences that disappoint *expectations* resulting from existing sets of presuppositions. To this extent, our knowledge always contains *a posteriori* elements.

In other words, part of our knowledge is *a priori* true in the sense that it cannot be controlled by new experience but is rather the necessary precondition for making such experience possible. Insofar as, however, this *a priori* true part of knowledge is founded on past experience, it can be culturally intertransmitted among us. And its reliability can be examined by each one of us, though *a posteriori*, by contrasting it with our own orders of the apparatus of classifications or, to put it more plainly, with our own experience. This implies that the higher level of the Hayekian apparatus of classification, the reliability of which is greater than the lower one simply because it is grounded upon the experiences not only of each individual but also of the group those individuals constitute, may well be able to form a body of ideas (or generic reproductions of various relations in the "external world" in the Hayekian sense of the term).

This body can perhaps be common both to different individuals and to the different disciplines, which respectively examine more particular reproductions of external relations. In other words, thanks to Hayek's renewed recognition of the *a priori* true part of our knowledge, philosophy can now be revived as a discipline, which may be shared by different individuals on the one hand and may be able to integrate different disciplines into an orderly body on the other. And this is precisely what Hayek has been doing all these years. His philosophy combines different disciplines into a mutually interrelated body and provides us once again with a coherent picture of our lives. Under Hayek, the fragmentation of the "universe" is over.

This, of course, does not mean that Hayekian philosophy claims either general validity or completeness. On the contrary, our knowledge may well *a posteriori* have to be changed because of new experiences. That is why in the world of Hayek science is an endless pursuit of more general and more reliable theories, or, as he puts it, science consists "in a constant search for new classes" (see Chapter 12). And the history of mankind is the continuous expansion, through many turns and twists, of what he calls the "order of human interaction" (see, e.g., Chapter 17). The uniqueness of Hayekian philosophy is that it does not require either completeness or total comprehensiveness. It is always incomplete and never closed. It keeps growing and evolving.

Viewed as a logico-theoretical network, the Hayekian body of ideas keeps expanding both by knitting new nets and reknitting old ones and by connecting internal nets that had previously not been linked together. It is rather misleading to describe the entire body of Hayekian ideas as a "system" or, for that matter, a "complete system." He is not a system builder. That is why he opposes the rationalists and, as will be seen later, argues for "methodological individualism." And that is why I prefer to call this total body of ideas the Hayekian "order" of ideas. Whether the order is that of his own theories or that of human interaction or human action, "evolution" toward unknown frontiers is its pre-eminent characteristic.

Hayek has come to embrace an astounding number of different disciplines. But this is only the result of, not the necessary precondition to, his philosophy. He began, as it were, to make a voyage toward an unknown land. But what he calls the *a priori* true part of knowledge has provided him with a good ship. And just like a compass, new experience has given him a direction. Hayekian philosophy is not merely discursive but also empirical since it is based on experiences of its own and of those different disciplines his philosophy integrates. Should we miss this theoretico-empirical nature of his order of ideas, we might well be led to utterly erroneous, and even contrary, interpretations of his various arguments.

Abstract or Concrete

According to Hayek, "law in the proper sense of the term is abstract." In Hayekian terminology, a law against murder is an abstract law because it is on a higher plane than a law forbidding the murder of one's fellow "free men" but not nonfree persons, noncitizens, or slaves. The latter law is more particular and "concrete" in content than the former. Yet the nonfree persons, noncitizens, or slaves would almost certainly regard the former as more concrete. I do not believe that Professor Hayek would oppose this choice.

By "abstract" Hayek is emphasizing the need for laws to acquire greater generality and wider applicability so that the character of "command" is lessened. If, however, we do not come to understand the substance of Hayekian reasoning but remain perplexed by Hayek's unique use of the term "abstract," we may be led to a ridiculous interpretation of his theories. For example, according to Barry, Hayek

> was not detecting an observable historical trend from which he was, inductively, making a kind of prophecy about the likely course of events, but rather moving within the traditional Austrian methodology. That is, the road to serfdom thesis was an inference and not an empirical observation. A totalitarian order could be mentally reconstructed by inferring what would happen if there were certain departures from the principles of spontaneous evolution [p. 184].

In other words, Hayek's theorizing, for example, in *The Road to Serfdom* is only a process of logical reasoning that tries to attain logical self-consistency and thus is devoid of falsifiability. Barry is possessed with the idea that the Hayekian order of ideas is a closed system, within which alone logical coherence is attained and which has no relationship with empirical factors. This may be the reason why Barry cannot realize either Hayek's devotion to selecting fundamental assumptions for his theories from well-tested experience or the great swing from socialism to liberalism (in the original sense of the term) in the past forty years, thanks very much to Hayek's unyielding assertions over those years.

Hayek has repeatedly emphasized the "abstract" character of what he thought worthy of the name law. Yet he has consistently opposed the assertion that laws were deliberately and discursively designed. And he has always insisted that laws develop by evolutionary processes out of the experience and the trial and error of many generations.

Hayek uses the term *abstractness* in two meanings. First, he maintains that all perceptions and cognitions are "abstract" even though they are, without exception, based on experience. Any positivistic perception, any behavioristic cognition, any pragmatic apprehension, is inescapably "abstract" in its basic character. What can legitimately be said to be "concrete" are the subject matters of our perceptions and cognitions, of which we can know only some general characteristics at best. According to Hayek, we can only assume that concrete things and phenomena may exist. But we can never absolutely be sure. All that we can say is that we may be justified in supposing the existence of the "concrete" world insofar as our abstract knowledge of that world succeeds in surviving falsification tests or being free from contradiction.

Hayek's assertion could also be reversed. Even our most abstract knowledge should be regarded as concrete in its basic nature precisely because in some way or another it is based on our experience or on what we usually call "concrete" — or exactly because of the thoroughness of Hayek's use of the terms *abstract* and *concrete*.

Hayek then proceeds to use "abstract" and "concrete" to differentiate (or classify) kinds of perceptions, knowledge, theories, laws, etc., or the degree of their abstractness or concreteness.

The results of these classifications can never be exact reproductions of either the stimuli or what caused the stimuli. In Hayekian terminology, the results are "abstract." They are merely general and systematically simplified aspects of the "external" world. But this implies different degrees of classifications, generalizations, and simplifications and varying degrees of abstractness or concreteness. Some classifications are rather rudimentary. Some are highly theoretical and general in their nature since they are made on the basis of "lower" and "more immediate" classifications. Hayek describes these as abstract and contrasts them with the results of more unrefined, particular, and preliminary classifications, which he calls "concrete."

Karl Popper insists that we maximize the empirical (and concrete) contents of our theories so that we can perhaps easily falsify them by facts. Should we even then fail to invalidate those theories, we can only accept them as working hypotheses until we find new facts that might disprove them. This does not mean, however, that the Popperian world is a mere bundle of bits and pieces of working hypotheses. On the contrary, some of them have been tested so many times over such a long period and came to be so logically well interrelated that they now constitute the hard core of whatever the entire body of those theories may be called. These hard-core theories have more general applicability than the rest and thus are usually regarded as more abstract than theories that can be applied to more particular cases and are ordinarily considered to be more concrete. Hayek is in complete agreement with Popper in this regard.

Hayek is not infallible. Parts of his explanation of competition (see Chapter 13), for example, are either too strong or deviations from his fundamental order of ideas. He states that "the validity of the theory" of competition "can never be tested empirically" (see Chapter 13). Yet he also maintains that "the history of civilization seems eminently to have confirmed" that "on the whole, societies which rely . . . on competition have achieved their aims more successfully than others" (see Chapter 13). Indeed, there is abundant evidence that competition not only brought economic prosperity but also, and more significantly, gave rise to innovative ideas, new inventions, and great discoveries and stimulated both art and science.

Nevertheless, this is rather a reversed way of arguing for competition and contrary to Professor Hayek's fundamental order of ideas. In the true spirit of his extraordinary theory of the evolution of society, the real case for competition must be that it is one of the evolutionary results produced by interactions among human beings. We have tried various forms of transaction and organization over many years and only then gradually came to realize the great merit of competition.

Yet our ancestors practiced it only on a limited scale and under special circumstances. And even today many human beings sway this way and that in deciding whether competition is really beneficial. This is because competition resembles a scientific theory, which can concern itself only with particular ("concrete") facts and unique cases and yet tries to attain a general ("abstract") applicability. The general theory of competition can be established only on the basis of as many instances of the failure to falsify its central theses as possible. It is almost certain, however, that the coming "information revolution" will provide the crucial experiment that fails to falsify them once and for all. For that, however, we must be ready with a theory of competition better than current one. Otherwise competition may well become a matter of what Hayek calls "group selection."

Hayek's "monetary" theory of business cycles made him world famous before he was thirty years old. But this is only a part of his economics. He later established a "real term" theory of the business cycle in which he analyzed the problems of not only the business cycle but also, and more fundamentally, "capital" in real terms. He regarded this pure theory of capital as more general and thus more "abstract" than his earlier one. In his terminology, his monetary business cycle theory is more particular and concrete than the latter. Hayek never claimed that all laws in the history of mankind have been abstract. On the contrary, the central thesis of his jurisprudence is that laws have gradually developed from quite particular and concrete laws ("commands") by gaining abstractness and a more general character, thus becoming more universally applicable.

He states, for example, "as rules which have originally been developed in small, purpose-connected groups ('organizations') are progressively extended to larger and larger groups and finally universalized to apply to the relations between any members of an Open Society who have no concrete purposes in common and merely submit to the same abstract rules, they will in this process have to shed all references to particular purposes" (see Chapter 20). Rationalistic positivists in the field of modern jurisprudence ignore this fundamental and important nature of law. They claim that whatever was legislated through "due process" and supported by the majority (which is often nothing more than a rabble of special interest groups that join together for convenience' sake) at any given time is law.

Methodological Individualism: A Dynamic Method of Analysis

Methodological individualism is not sociopolitical individualism. If it were, we would not trouble to call it "methodological" individualism. Yet readers of Hayek's works often overlook this self-evident point. For example, according to a certain critic, methodological individualism allegedly asserts that all statements about *collectives* are logically deducible from statements about *individuals*. This is wrong on two counts. First, Hayek's use of the expressions "collectives" and "wholes" in his writings were concessions he made in order to let those who were thoroughly indoctrinated by these expressions understand his arguments more easily. His own terms for them are "complexes," "patterns," or "orders." "Collective" signifies a mere (mechanical) collection of things or factors. Methodological individualism denies, above all, the assertion that social phenomena are merely collections of their constituent parts.

Second, Hayek also holds that the social sciences start from our knowledge of "individual attitudes," never of "individuals" as such. Many people think that there hardly exists any meaningful difference between individual attitudes and individuals as such. However, the same individual assumes quite different attitudes at different times. Or the same good (or service) may well have different utilities for the same person at different times. That is why Hayek is opposed to accepting without reservation any intertemporal comparison of utilities.

It may not be easy, however, to see, as Hayek maintains, why any optimum economic policy that presupposes a conception of maximizing national income in real terms must always imply "an illegitimate comparison of the utility to different persons" (see Chapter 20). There can, of course, be a total social product that is appropriate only to the kind of economy that serves a single (or a greatly regimented) hierarchy of ends. But the *free* market, in which the price mechanism is left alone to work itself out, means that in this market every person is allowed to act in accordance with his or her own standard of values. The relative prices that emerge out of such a free market do reflect the relative utilities of various goods and services to those different persons; that is, their relative utilities as valued in this way or that way by different individuals (during a certain limited span of time). It is difficult to understand how the illegitimacy, if there is any, involved in an interspacial comparison of relative utilities to different persons can be dissolved by saying that an optimal policy is to aim at increasing "the chance that, whatever [an individual's] share in total income may be, the real equivalent of this share will be as large as we know how to make it" (see Chapter 20).

Any humanly possible maximization of such a share can, of course, be expressed in real terms but is not attainable without relying on the function of the system of relative prices, which mirror relative utilities as they appear differently to different persons (at a given time). It goes without saying, however, that such an aggregate as total national product must not indiscreetly be accepted at its face value without maximum precaution. It definitely tends, as Hayek warns, to conceal the difference of the kinds of economic orders under which that total was produced and whether in the economy concerned the standard of values is decided by each individual or by somebody else. Besides it is not necessarily the case that the higher the growth rate of total national product, the better off individuals are. Nevertheless, I do not think it advisable to write off such a aggregate as total national product in real terms. This is because such a real-term aggregate is fundamentally measured in terms of relative prices and is neither a statistical average nor a mere statistical construct.

To return to the subject, methodological individualism is, fundamentally, an asertion that in the field of socio-human phenomena, every whole is a constituent of something larger. It used to be claimed in this field that there were decisive wholes, in various forms, that are larger and more intrinsic than their constituents. But the reverse is the truth. A "whole" is simply a certain part that is demarcated in some way or other out of a more essential and complex whole. Methodological individualism, then, maintains that it is not humanly possible to grasp *whole* as such; (which is a version of the thesis of Socrates, Scotus, Ockham, Huygens, Mandeville, Hume, and Hayek that the cognitive ability of the human being is constitutionally limited).

Furthermore, methodological individualism holds that in the field of social phenomena any whole is always the result of *interactions* among its constituent factors. Yet such a result does not always exist but *emerges* only as interactions among the constituent factors take place and vanish as the degree of interactions is reduced (or diminishes as a larger whole is reduced to smaller and smaller constituents). Moreover, constituent factors do not remain constant but change in character, behavior, value, and so on to reflect the effects of interactions among them. That is, they *vary* as they interact (directly and indirectly) with each other. Neither the *emergent* results of interactions among constituent factors nor the *variations* of those factors can ever be analyzed either in terms of a whole alone or of the constituent units. Methodological individualism fills the need for a dynamic type of analytical method of socio-human phenomena.

Bernard Mandeville's unprecedented and remarkable theory of the evolution of social institutions amounted to the earliest attempt to establish methodological individualism systematically. In his case, this methodology consisted of two principles: "the principle of self-liking and the principle of self-love."[9] But it was Carl Menger, the founder of the Austrian School of Economics, who began the methodological efforts to make explicit the "dynamic" nature of methodological individualism. He asserted, for example, that

> every theory, of whatever kind it may be and whatever degree of rigorousness of knowledge it may strive for, has the primary task of teaching us to understand the concrete phenomena of the real world as exemplifications of a certain regularity in the *emergent* sequence of phenomena. Every theory, accordingly, strives first and foremost to make us understand the complicated phenomena which are peculiar to its research field as the result of the coming together and acting upon each other of all factors responsible for its original formation. *This principle of emergence is inseparable from the concept of the theoretical sciences.*[10]

Moreover, Menger tried to explain by means of methodological individualism the evolution not only of such economic institutions as the market, money, and so on, but also such social institutions as language and law. But his analysis of the latter was only very limited and rather cursory.

It was Hayek who brought methodological individualism to maturity and, by making excellent use of it, has developed his theories in various fields. He is a very good student of Carl Menger. He not only inherited Menger's thought but also created a rather innovative and quite extensive order of ideas out of it. The fundamental problem he posed to himself in Mengerian fashion was

> How can the combination of fragments of knowledge existing in different minds bring about results which, if they were to be brought about deliberately, would require a knowledge on the part of the directing mind which no simple person can possess [see Chapter 11]?

He paraphrased the problem in the following manner:

> The character of the problem is . . . the same if we ask why such and such action regularly produces unemployment, or leads to the waste of resources, although *in neither case was this result intended* by those whose actions produce an order or desirable pattern, and the extent to which they fail to do so, raises problems to which social theory has to supply an answer. Questions of similar nature are raised by language or of any other social formation or institution.[11] [Italics added.]

Many social scientists, including even economists, are quite puzzled by Professor Hayek, when, for example, he maintains that

> by tracing the combined effects of individual actions, we discover that many of the institutions on which human achievements rest have arisen and are functioning *without a designing and directing mind;* that, as Adam Ferguson expressed it, "nations stumble upon establishments, which are indeed the result of human action but *not the result of human design*" [see Chapter 4].

Or, for instance, that

> the spontaneous collaboration of free men often creates things which are *greater than their individual minds can ever fully comprehend* [see Chapter 4; italics added].

It is common knowledge that economics liberally uses mathematical functions to analyze economic phenomena. It does this not simply because there are functional relations among different economic variables, but because out of the interactions among those variables, a certain pattern often does emerge. Furthermore, through the emergence of this pattern, the value of each variable comes, from time to time, to be determined, while the end result of all this also determines the value of the pattern itself. The use of functional analysis is no longer limited to economics but has spread to such disciplines as sociology, political science, and anthropology. This functional (or algebraic) technique that is the mathematico-statistical version of methodological individualism.[12] In this analytical method, it is neither the whole (of all equations) nor its constituent units (or its various variables) themselves but *interactions* among all these that produce the emergence of a certain general pattern.

Some variables may respectively represent expectations of different individuals, and others may reflect the various kinds of intentional activities of those persons. And some parameters, which are represented by diverse constants in equations, may mirror societally purposeful customs of the people. But the most significant feature of functional analysis is that it tries to obtain its solution from *interactions* among the variables and parameters concerned. Such an analysis is *impossible* without reducing phenomena to their most fundamental variables, or, in other words, their "individual" components. Precisely because of this epistemological impossibility, methodological individualism came to be asserted by Duns Scotus and William of Ockham and especially by Mandeville, David Hume, Adam Smith, and Ferguson at the dawn of the social sciences and was developed more fully and systematically by Menger and Hayek. It should be quite easy to see the error of regarding it as "methodological atomism" or a "Robinson Crusoe type" of methodological approach. Either of these views represents the unsustainable claim that we can derive general propositions, patterns, and so on for socioeconomic phenomena directly from the analyses of "atomistic" units alone or of a totally isolated individual like Robinson Crusoe.

Many critics think that Hayek is rather unorthodox and quite alien to modern social science. Hayek has indeed been shunned by the so-called intellectuals since publication of *The Road to Serfdom* (1944). But Hayek's influence on economics is more extensive than many are aware or even more than the awarding of the Nobel Prize may suggest. Barry appears to regard Hayek as an eccentric because Hayek asserts that "the major characteristic of knowledge in the social sciences is that it is *subjective*" in the sense that it is knowledge of the "attitudes, beliefs and opinions of the actors in a social process" (see Barry, p. 16, and Chapter 11 of this book). Economics, however, has increasingly tended to express variables in terms of the "expectations" of individuals, or of magnitudes, volumes, prices, quantities, etc., *as they are subjectively expected* by each individual, firm, or other agent. Economists finally began to catch up with Hayek in the 1970s and gradually became aware both of the central role of "information" (or "knowledge") in the economy[13] and of the cardinal importance of the Hayekian problem of "information cost" (the costs involved in the process through which knowledge comes to be known by an individual and transmitted to others).

The field called microfoundation of macroeconomics owes much of its birth to Hayekian economics; so does the so-called economics of information. Some critics suggest that Hayekian economics has been refuted by the works of the Virginia school of economics, more specifically of James Buchanan and Gordon Tullock. But the truth is quite the reverse. Their models beautifully fit into the Hayekian order of ideas. Although they have not done so, we can derive those models from Hayekian theory by adding what he calls an "auxiliary hypothesis." Some critics seem to be puzzled by Hayek's argument that while the Walrasian type of equilibrium theory is tautological, Hayekian "economics of the process toward a state of equilibrium" is an empirical science (see Chapter 11 of this book).

Walrasian theory never analyzed the process of the emergence of equilibrium, but left the solution of this problem to utterly fictional "gropings." Then it simply made a purely mathematical analysis of the equilibrium system of relative prices under the assumption that thanks to the system the market was completely "cleared," that is, total demand perfectly matched total supply. But the real task of economics is to explain how in fact such an equilibrium does or does not emerge (that is, how in reality disequilibrium emerges). And this is exactly what Hayek has argued for, for example, in Chapter 11 of this book. Noneconomists might be surprised at how far economics has moved toward the direction Hayek pointed out some fifty years ago.

Although econometrics is a mathematico-statistical version of methodological individualism, all of the conclusions of econometrics are not necessarily consistent with the latter.[14] This is because econometrics often uses for its parameters and variables the kind of magnitudes that, since they are only statistically constructed, often dissolve differences of cardinal importance among individual units by regimenting different persons into a certain hierarchy of ends (or values). Moreover, while unquantifiable variables are often far more important than quantifiable ones in the field of socio-human phenomena, econometrics tends to give the opposite impression to the people. That is why Professor Hayek stated in his Nobel lecture that "the superstition that only measurable magnitudes can be important has done positive harm in economic field" (see Chapter 14).

Finally, methodological individualism is not an assertion of "economic man" (or *homo oeconomicus*). For too long, liberal economics has been accused of relying on this concept. With the exception of those who attacked liberal economics, almost the only liberal economist to suggest the methodological need for this concept in economics was John Stuart Mill.[15] And even Mill rarely practiced this methodology. From the beginning methodological individualism has had nothing to do with egoism, selfishness, or anything of this sort, even in Mandeville, Hume, Ferguson, or Adam Smith (see Chapters 7 and 11). It has always been nothing more than an assertion of our need to realize the inescapable limitation of individual knowledge and to analyze socio-human phenomena in terms of interactions such as those mentioned above.

A Socrates Who Survived and Began to Prevail

Hayek is, as it were, a modern Socrates who not only survived the "people's court" but came to prevail. He was once condemned by the so-called intellectuals to intellectual death. Within the academic circle, he came to be regarded almost as an untouchable, if not a convenient whipping boy, whom academics could attack at whim whenever they thought they had discovered a "failure" of the market or of a free society. Thanks, however, to his academic integrity, tenacity, will power, and, especially, his foresight, he has not only endured this intellectually almost unbearable life but also developed his thought and deepened his order of ideas. I became a student of his in 1952 and was privileged to study directly (in fact, for an innumerable number of his tutorial hours) and indirectly (while I began to teach as a lecturer) under him for nearly eight years at the University of Chicago. He used to tell me then that he was writing for the next century.

Indeed, we were a tiny minority of social outcasts denounced as a bunch of "reactionaries." Who would have imagined at that time that we would see the day when we could proudly argue for freedom? Both *The Sensory Order* and *The Counter-Revolution of Science* were published in 1952. But the former was almost completely ignored, and the latter was bitterly criticized by the "secondhand dealers of ideas." And it was just at that time that he began to write *The Constitution of Liberty* (and a little later that Professor Milton Friedman started to write his *Capitalism and Freedom* [Chicago: University of Chicago Press, 1962]).

Luckily we did not have to wait until the next century before people came to appreciate Hayekian thought. First, people were impressed by the fact that events did not falsify his predictions as the kinds of theories he strongly opposed were put into practice. Second, when they began to look for remedies for the serious difficulties into which they had inevitably fallen, they discovered that Hayek had been presenting a body of guiding principles just for that purpose. And the astonishing breadth of the entire order of his theories, which were mutually interrelated and consistent with each other, has given people a coherent picture of their lives, which had become increasingly chaotic because of active, indiscriminate, and hasty experiment in government intervention and planning.

Thanks to the impressive depth of the Hayekian order of ideas, people came not only to understand the superficial reasons for the disorder of modern society but also to gain insight into the real nature of their problems. These problems should be analyzed from the various and yet interrelated points of view of, among other disciplines, philosophy, jurisprudence, economics, political science, psychology, and anthropology, and historical science. It may well not be an exaggeration to say that Professor Hayek is one of the greatest thinkers of the twentieth century because of the striking breadth, depth, and consistency of the entire body of his theories, and especially because of his very innovative ideas.

Some contemporary observers erroneously believe that the historical evidence of this century is that experiments in planning have not led in the direction of omnipotent government or a new despotism. Unlike earlier in the twentieth century, however, we can now assert that the failure of government intervention based on theory *X* leads not to the reduction of governmental activity but only to further interferences founded on other theories (or for that matter obsolete theories), thus expanding both the power and the size of government. We have accumulated a rather overwhelming body of evidence that this is indeed the case.

Why, for example, has the vigor of England gradually but clearly diminished over the past forty years? Does this really have nothing to do with its welfare statism? What about government deficits, which are growing faster than national products in so many countries? Do we not now have enough cases that perhaps not individually but collectively tell us clearly the grave dangers involved in experiments in governmental activism? Because of self-admiration, intellectuals tend to prefer "active" government and fail to recognize that by doing so they often end up handing their intellects over to the chosen few. They are frequently totally blind to the plainest veracities simply because they are so plain.

Those who are obsessed with the Popperian demand for making theories as falsifiable as possible tend to regard Hayekian "experiences" as nonempirical and Hayek's "abstract" theories as totally devoid of any empirical content. Such minds are inclined to accept the shallow theories of Keynesian economics as empirical. Predictions based on mathematically complex Keynesian models seemed for a while to be verified by events, but they inevitably came to be falsified by facts, exactly as Hayek had been predicting for a long time. (In the case of the United States, the apparent Keynesian successes of the Kennedy administration were actually due to the stabilization policies of the Eisenhower administration.) When implemented, Keynesian theories not only accelerated inflation but also rapidly aggravated unemployment and thus caused "stagflation." This was because the Keynesians dealt superficially only with aggregate variables and never heeded the great dangers involved in experimenting with their theories in government, especially the detrimental impact on the system of relative prices and thus on the structure of the economy.

Hayek, in his monetary business cycle theory (see Chapter 2 of this book) has been arguing for almost sixty years that an expansionist monetary policy will not only cause accelerating inflation but also distort the *system of relative prices*. That is, the expansion of credit will enable the *capital goods* production sector (or plants and equipment) to bid up both wages and the prices of materials so that it can take these away from the *consumption goods* production sector. Thanks to the consequent increase in plant or equipment investment (or in Hayekian terminology, the lengthening of the roundabout way of production or the heightening of the complexity of capital production), the productivity of workers will increase, raising their wages still further.

But by that time, the production of consumption goods may well have been relatively reduced because of the loss of a relatively favorable capability of acquiring both workers and materials, as well as because of the relative reduction of the rate of increase in investment in this sector. The end result of all this will be a rise in the prices of consumption goods. This will consequently enable the consumption goods production sector to bid up wages and prices and take them away from the capital goods production sector.

This will inevitably cause a reduction in the rate of increase in plant and equipment investment (or in Hayekian terminology, a shortening of the roundabout way of production), which in turn will create redundancy or idling of production capacity. This is because production facilities are specialized and some of those facilities unavoidably become unusable as the rate of heightening in the complexity of production is reduced.

The consequent diminishing of the rate of increase in investment in this sector will lower the productivity of working individuals and thus the rate of increase in their wages. Their purchasing power will increasingly be reduced as the prices of consumption goods rise. The situation into which we eventually fall is "stagflation," where both the rate of inflation and the rate of unemployment are rising. It might appear that such a situation is avoidable if more doses of inflation are injected into the economy.

But we must not overlook another aspect of the damaging impact of such an inflationary policy—the change in the prices of production goods relative to wages. Because of the inevitable and quickening reduction of wages in the process of accelerating inflation, each household encounters intensified difficulties in maintaining its accustomed standard of living on the income of one worker or from one job alone. Thus the supply of those who wish to work will increase.

Now let us look at what happens in the business sector. Insofar as an accelerating inflationary policy is maintained, business firms will have no difficulty in finding demand for the goods and services they sell. In order, however, to satisfy that demand, business firms may well be increasingly unwilling to invest in plant and equipment even for renewal of existing structures. The purchasing power of depreciations for existing plants and equipments becomes more and more unrealistic, while the prices of new investment goods rise at a faster and faster tempo. Therefore, in order to meet the demand for their goods and services created by inflation, business firms will hire more workers (including part-time workers) instead of investing in plant and equipment. This is not only because wages are now cheaper relative to the cost of investment goods, it is also because an end to an inflationary policy would cause a sudden reduction in demand. It is easier for businesses to fire workers, especially part-time workers, than to sell plant and equipment. In the process of accelerated inflation, therefore, many business firms once again become "labor intensive."

This situation will reduce the rate of increase of "labor productivity" still further. This implies that demand in real terms for both investment and consumption goods will eventually grow more slowly than the expansion of production facilities and later on even begin to decline more rapidly than the latter does. Such a situation will unavoidably increase the rate of unemployment once again relative to the now increased supply of those who wish to work. Yet prices rise faster than before. What emerges is "stagflation." This, in fact, has actually been brought about, precisely as predicted by Professor Hayek (e.g., in the United States under the Carter administration), by detrimental changes in the system of relative prices and the structure of the economy; these changes were created by the so-called demand control policy of Keynesian economics (or more specifically by the policies that were thought by Keynesian economists as worthy of a "locomotive economy").

Hayek, of course, neither quantified his predictions, as mentioned above, nor made them specific or particular. What Hayek presented was a coherent body of general principles, some of which can be seen in Chapter 2 of this book. Contrary to what many critics of Hayek assume, however, this is nothing unusual to theoretical science, not only in the social sciences but also in the natural sciences. It is the task of the applied sciences to build testable models out of general theories. All the variables mentioned above can be quantified and at the same time fit into a dynamic model derivable from the Hayekian theory of the business cycle. Great thinkers provide us with general ideas and universal theories. And by the aid of them, we often come to establish particular models so that we can understand better various phenomena within and without ourselves. The greatness of Hayek lies in his untiring pursuit of general principles. That is precisely why he could revive philosophy and revolutionize the ideas pertaining to socio-human phenomena.

At no time, however, has Hayek been lost in meditation. The task he set for himself has been to answer the question of what liberalism means "when applied to the concrete problems of our time."[16] He passionately appealed to those who believe in freedom:

> There has never been a time when liberal ideas were fully realized and when liberalism did not look forward to further improvement of institutions. Liberalism is not averse to evolution and change; and where spontaneous change has been smothered by government control, it wants a great deal of change of policy. So far as much of current governmental action is concerned, there is in the present world very little reason for the liberal to wish to preserve things as they are. It would seem to the liberal, indeed, that what is most urgently needed in most parts of the world is a thorough sweeping-away of the obstacles to free growth [see Chapter 15 of this book].

True to this spirit, he has examined the problems, among others, of welfare statism, labor unions, taxation and transfer payments, money, housing and town planning, agriculture and natural resources, education and research, the "neighborhood effects" that later came to be identified with both positive and negative "public goods."[17]

But all this has led him to question democracy as it now exists — the kind of democracy based solely on the principle of majority rule, which has gradually been transformed into a new kind of despotism. Omnipotent democracy, which has emerged in one country after another, and under which legislative power and administrative power are increasingly combined into one, is in one sense quite strong since the individual can hardly escape from its far-reaching coercive power. But in another sense, it is rather weak in that it easily succumbs to the pressure of special-interest groups. In order to establish "liberal democracy," Hayek has spent his time more and more on analyzing law, legislation, and liberty.[18] Through this analysis, he came to assert more strongly than ever our need for establishing clearly and securely a "liberal Utopia," or "a truly liberal radicalism which does not spare the susceptibilities of the mighty" (see Chapter 15).

He used to be fond of saying that "if politics is the art of the possible, political philosophy is the art of making politically possible the seemingly impossible."[19] It is in this spirit that readers are advised to approach, for instance, the chapter entitled "A Model Constitution." Hayek is quite aware that *utopia* is "a bad word today."[20] Nevertheless,

> It is not to be denied that to some extent the guiding model of the overall order will always be an *utopia,* something to which the existing situation will be only a distant approximation and which many people will regard as wholly impractical. Yet it is only by constantly holding up the guiding conception of an internally consistent model which could be realized by the consistent application of the same

> principles, that anything like an effective framework for a functioning spontaneous order will be achieved. Adam Smith thought that "to expect, indeed, that freedom of trade should ever be entirely restored in Great Britain is as absurd as to expect an oceania or *Utopia* should ever be established." Yet seventy years later, largely as a result of his work, it was achieved [italics added].[21]

And, indeed, thanks to Hayek's own writings, people have come to demand smaller government and the abolition of arbitrary taxation. Perhaps one of these days the powers of the two legislative houses will be demarcated according to the Hayekian scheme.

Hayek's recurrent references to Mandeville, Hume, Ferguson, or Smith were not made simply to reiterate what they wrote. He has, in fact, been trying to rewrite the history of thought. "Enlightenment" is the English equivalent of the German *Aufklärung* or the French *illumination*. Hayek holds that it is wrong to believe that there was no English Enlightenment. Insofar as either the *Aufklärung* or the *illumination* brought about an intellectual movement for civil rights or fundamental human rights, there was no need for an English counterpart. The Magna Carta was established in 1215. Furthermore, English citizens won additional civil rights in the two civil wars (1642 – 1646 and 1648 – 1652).

But if we look at the intellectual movement initiated by Mandeville and developed further by others in Scotland and England, we cannot but realize that this movement was different from, and in many ways even contrary to, the *Aufklärung* or the *illumination*. The most remarkable feature of that intellectual movement was that it combined liberty, science, and history, that all the arguments for moral values and empirical facts were harmoniously synthesized by philosophy and yet at the same time were vigorously developed by different disciplines. It was clearly a unique movement and worthy of the name English Enlightenment.

Modern science eschews any discussion of liberty or freedom as a value simply because it would be normative. Positivistic jurisprudence has abandoned the concept of natural law because it was allegedly based on presuppositions of *a priori* truth. History has come to be viewed by modern positivism as having hardly any bearing on the positivistic sciences, insofar as those sciences are concerned with predictions of future events. Under the English Enlightenment, however, historical reflections, for the first time in the history of the mankind, gave rise to the scientific accounts of, among other things, law, language, the market, money, and the division of labor.

The resulting jurisprudence made it clear that the foundations of law consisted of "natural law" in the sense that it should not readily be changed, precisely because it was the fruit of the experiences of many generations. In their analyses, Scottish and English scholars discovered how indispensable freedom was to the advancement of civilization. For example, Mandeville said, "How the shortsighted wisdom, of perhaps well-meaning people, may rob us of a felicity, that would follow spontaneously from the nature of every large society, if none were diverted or interrupt this stream." And he asserted that "arbitrary exertions of government power must be minimized."[22]

Professor Hayek has emphasized the enormous importance of this coherent body of ideas, in which philosophical arguments for freedom as a moral value, the scientific analysis of social institutions, and historical examinations of their origins are inseparably interconnected. But he has not simply reminded us of the great significance of the English Enlightenment. In the spirit of the Renaissance, he has been trying to develop it still further. This is the ultimate contribution of his work.

Notes

1. See Thomas S. Kuhn, *The Structure of Scientific Revolutions,* 2nd ed. enl. (Chicago: University of Chicago Press, 1962); and idem, "Logic of Discovery or Psychology of Research?" in I. Lakatos and A. Musgrave, eds., *Criticism and the Growth of Knowledge* (Cambridge, Eng.: Cambridge University Press, 1970), p. 3.

2. F. A. Hayek, "Notes on the Evolution of Systems of Rules of Conduct," in idem, *Studies in Philosophy, Politics and Economics* (Chicago: University of Chicago Press, 1967), p. 71.

3. Ibid.

4. Hayek, "The Theory of Complex Phenomena," in *Studies in Philosophy,* p. 38.

5. A. E. Taylor, *A Commentary on Plato's Timaeus* (Oxford: Clarendon Press, 1928), p. 667.

6. Ibid.

7. Hayek, *The Pure Theory of Capital* (Chicago: University of Chicago Press, 1941), chaps. 11 – 17, and especially appendix 1.

8. See ibid., p. 167.

9. Chiaki Nishiyama, "The Theory of Self-love: An Essay in the Meth-

odology of the Social Sciences, and Especially of Economics," mimeo. (Ph.D. diss., University of Chicago, 1960), pt. 2.

10. Carl Menger, *Untersuchungen über die Methode der Socialwissenschaften, und der politischen Oeconomie insbesondere* (Leipzig: Duncker & Humblot, 1883), p. 88

11. Hayek, "Economics," *Chamber's Encyclopedia* (New York: Oxford University Press, 1950), 4:773.

12. Hayek, "Theory of Complex Phenomena," p. 28. See also Chapter 14 of this book.

13. See Hayek, *The Constitution of Liberty* (Chicago: University of Chicago Press, 1960), pp. 46 – 47.

14. Hayek was one of the founders of the Econometric Society.

15. John Stuart Mill, *Essays on Some Unsettled Questions of Political Economy* (London: London School of Economics and Political Science, 1948 reprint), essay 5.

16. Hayek, *Constitution of Liberty,* p. 3.

17. Ibid.

18. See Hayek, *Law, Legislation and Liberty,* vol. 1, *Rules and Order;* vol. 2, *The Mirage of Social Justice* (Chicago: University of Chicago Press, 1973, 1976).

19. Hayek, *Constitution of Liberty,* p. 114. Later he wrote that he had been led "to concentrate more and more on what at first seemed merely an attractive but impracticable idea, until the utopia lost its strangeness and came to appear to me the only solution of the problem in which the founders of Liberal constitutionalism failed" (*Law, Legislation and Liberty,* 1:4).

20. Hayek, *Constitution of Liberty,* p. 65.

21. Hayek, *Law, Legislation and Liberty,* 1:64 – 65.

22. Bernard Mandeville, *The Fable of the Bees, or, Private Vices, Public Benefits,* with a commentary by F. B. Kaye (Oxford: Clarendon Press, 1924), 2:353, 1:299 – 300.

THE ESSENCE OF HAYEK

Editors' Note: These chapters, with the exception of Chapter 17, are taken from previously published books and articles by F. A. Hayek. Other than corrections of spelling errors and the renumbering of some footnotes, the originals have been faithfully reproduced.

HAYEKIAN ECONOMICS

♦

♦ *PART* ♦ *ONE* ♦

Inflation, the Misdirection of Labour, and Unemployment

· 1 ·

Inflation and Unemployment

After a unique 25-year period of great prosperity the economy of the Western world has arrived at a critical point. I expect that the experience of the period will enter history under the name of The Great Prosperity as the 1930s are known as The Great Depression. We have indeed succeeded, by eliminating all the automatic brakes which operated in the past, namely the gold standard and fixed rates of exchange, in maintaining the full and even over-employment which was created by an expansion of credit and in the end prolonged by open inflation, for a much longer time than I should have thought possible. But the inevitable end is now near, if it has not already arrived.

I find myself in an unpleasant situation. I had preached for forty years that the time to prevent the coming of a depression is the boom. During the boom nobody listened to me. Now people again

---

From Occasional Paper 45, Institute of Economic Affairs, July 1975. Permission to reprint courtesy of the Cato Institute.

A revised version of a lecture delivered on 8 February, 1975, to the 'Convegno Internazionale: Il Problema della Moneta Oggi', organised in commemoration of the 100th birthday of Luigi Einaudi by the Academia Nazionale dei Lincei at Rome, and to be published in the proceedings of that congress.

turn to me and ask how the consequences of a policy of which I had constantly warned can be avoided. I must witness the heads of the governments of all the Western industrial countries promising their people that they will stop the inflation *and* preserve full employment. But I know that they *cannot* do this. I even fear that such attempts, as President Ford has just announced, to postpone the inevitable crisis by a new inflationary push, may temporarily succeed and make the eventual breakdown even worse.

Three Choices in Policy

The disquieting but unalterable truth is that a false monetary and credit policy, pursued through almost the whole period since the last war, has placed the economic systems of all the Western industrial countries in a highly unstable position in which *anything* we can do will produce most unpleasant consequences. We have a choice between only three possibilities:

– to allow a rapidly accelerating open inflation to continue until it has brought about a complete disorganisation of all economic activity;

– to impose controls of wages and prices which will for a time conceal the effects of a continued inflation but would inevitably lead to a centrally-directed totalitarian economic system; and

– finally, to terminate resolutely the increase of the quantity of money which would soon, through the appearance of substantial unemployment, make manifest all the misdirections of labour which the inflation of the past years has caused and which the two other procedures would further increase.

Lessons of the Great Inflation

To understand why the whole Western world allowed itself to be led into this frightful dilemma, it is necessary to glance briefly back at two events soon after the First World War which have largely determined the views that have governed the policy of the post-war years. I want first to recall an experience which has unfortunately been largely forgotten. In Austria and Germany the Great Inflation had directed our attention to the connection between changes in the quantity of money and changes in the degree of employment. It especially showed us that the employment created by inflation diminished as soon as the inflation slowed down, and that the termination of the inflation always produced what came to be called a 'stabilisation crisis' with substantial unemployment. It was the insight into this connection which made me and some of my contemporaries from the outset reject and oppose the kind of full employment policy propagated by Lord Keynes and his followers.

I do not want to leave this recollection of the Great Inflation without adding that I have probably learnt at least as much if not more than I learnt from personally observing it by being taught to see — then largely by my teacher, the late Ludwig von Mises — the utter stupidity of the arguments then propounded, especially in Germany, to explain and justify the increases in the quantity of money. Most of these arguments I am now encountering again in countries, not least Britain and the USA, which then seemed economically better trained and whose economists rather looked down at the foolishness of the German economists. None of these apologists of the inflationary policy was able to propose or apply measures to terminate the inflation, which was finally ended by a man, Hjalmar Schacht, who firmly believed in a crude and primitive version of the quantity theory.

British Origin of Inflation as Cure for Unemployment

The policy of the recent decades, or the theory which underlies it, had its origin, however, in the specific experiences of Great Britain during the 1920s and 1930s. Great Britain had after what now seems the very modest inflation of the First World War, returned to the gold standard in 1925, in my opinion very sensibly and honestly, but unfortunately and unwisely at the former parity. This had in no way been required by classical doctrine: David Ricardo had in 1821 written to a friend[1] that 'I never should advise a government to restore a currency, which was depreciated 30 per cent, to par'. I ask myself often how different the economic history of the world might have been if, in the discussion of the years preceding 1925, even only one English economist had remembered and pointed out this long-published passage from Ricardo.

In the event, the unfortunate decision taken in 1925 made a prolonged process of deflation inevitable, which process might have been successful in maintaining the gold standard if it had been continued until a large part of the wages had been reduced. I believe this attempt was near success when in the world crisis of 1931 Britain abandoned it together with the gold standard, which was greatly discredited by this event.

Keynes' Political 'Cure' for Unemployment

Development of Keynesian Ideas

It was during the period of extensive unemployment in Great Britain preceding the world-wide economic crisis of 1929 – 31 that John Maynard Keynes developed his basic ideas. It is important to note that this development of his economic thought happened in a very exceptional and almost unique position of his country. It was a period when, as a result of the big appreciation of the international value of the pound sterling, the real wages of practically all British workers had been substantially increased compared with the rest of the world, and British exporters had in consequence become substantially unable successfully to compete with other countries. In order to give employment to the unemployed it would therefore have been necessary either to reduce practically *all* wages or to raise the sterling prices of most commodities.

In the development of Keynes' thought it is possible to distinguish three distinct phases. First, he began with the recognition that it was necessary to reduce real wages. Second, he arrived at the conclusion that this was *politically* impossible. Third, he convinced himself that it would be vain and even harmful. The Keynes of 1919 had still understood that:

> There is no subtler, no surer means of overturning the existing basis of society than to debauch the currency. The process engages all the hidden forces of economic law on the side of destruction, and does it in a manner which not one man in a million is able to diagnose.[2]

His political judgement made him the inflationist, or at least avid anti-deflationist, of the 1930s. I have, however, good reason to believe that he would have disapproved of what his followers did in the post-war period. If he had not died so soon, he would have become one of the leaders in the fight against inflation.

'The Fatal Idea'

It was in that unfortunate episode of English monetary history in which he became the intellectual leader that he gained acceptance for the fatal idea: that unemployment is predominantly due to an insufficiency of aggregate demand compared with the total of wages which would have to be paid if all workers were employed at current rates.

This formula of employment as a direct function of total demand proved so extraordinarily effective because it seemed to be confirmed in some degree by the results of quantitative empirical data. In contrast, the alternative explanations of unemployment which I regard as correct could make no such claims. The dangerous effects which the 'scientistic' prejudice has had in this diagnosis is the subject of my Nobel lecture at Stockholm (Part II). Briefly, we find the curious situation that the (Keynesian) theory, which is comparatively best confirmed by statistics because it happens to be the only one which can be tested quantitatively, is nevertheless false. Yet it is widely accepted only because the explanation earlier regarded as true, and which I still regard as true, cannot *by its very nature* be tested by statistics.

The True Theory of Unemployment

The true, though untestable, explanation of extensive unemployment ascribes it to a discrepancy between the distribution of labour (and the other factors of production) between industries (and localities) and the distribution of demand among their products. This discrepancy is caused by a distortion of the system of *relative* prices and wages. And it can be corrected only by a change in these relations, that is, by the establishment in each sector of the economy of those prices and wages at which supply will equal demand.

The cause of unemployment, in other words, is a deviation from the equilibrium prices and wages which would establish themselves with a free market and stable money. But we can never know beforehand at what structure of relative prices and wages such an equilibrium would establish itself. We are therefore unable to measure the deviation of current prices from the equilibrium prices which make it impossible to sell part of the labour supply. We are therefore also unable to demonstrate a statistical correlation between the distortion of relative prices and the volume of unemployment. Yet, although not measurable, causes may be very effective. The current superstition that only the measurable can be important has done much to mislead economists and the world in general.

Keynes' Temptations to the Politicians

Probably even more important than the fashionable prejudices concerning scientific method which made the Keynesian theory attractive to professional economists were the temptations it held out for politicians. It offered them not only a cheap and quick method of removing a chief source of real human suffering. It also promised them release from the most confining restrictions that had impeded them in their striving for popularity. Spending money and budget deficits were suddenly represented as virtues. It was even argued persuasively that increased government expenditure was wholly meritorious, since it led to the utilisation of hitherto unused resources and thus cost the community nothing but brought it a net gain.

These beliefs led in particular to the gradual removal of all effective barriers to an increase in the quantity of money by the monetary authorities. The Bretton Woods agreement had tried to place the burden of international adjustment exclusively on the surplus countries, that is, to require them to expand but not to require the deficit countries to contract. It thus laid the foundation for a world inflation. But this was at least done in the laudable endeavour to secure fixed rates of exchange. Yet when the criticism of the inflation-minded majority of economists succeeded in removing this last obstacle to national inflation, no effective brake remained, as the experience of Britain since the late 1960s illustrates.

Floating Exchanges, Full Employment, Stable Currency

It is, I believe, undeniable that the demand for flexible rates of exchange originated wholly from countries such as Britain some of whose economists wanted a wider margin for inflationary expansion (called 'full employment policy'). They have, unfortunately, later received support also from other economists who were not inspired by the desire for inflation but who seem to me to have overlooked the strongest argument in favour of fixed rates of exchange: that they constitute the practically irreplaceable curb we need to *compel* the politicians, and the monetary authorities responsible to them, to maintain a stable currency.

The maintenance of the value of money and the avoidance of inflation constantly demand from the politicians highly unpopular measures which they can justify to people adversely affected only by showing that government was compelled to take them. So long as the preservation of the external value of the national currency is regarded as an indisputable necessity, as it is with fixed exchange rates, politicians can resist the constant demands for cheaper credits, avoidance of a rise in interest rates, more expenditure on 'public works', and so on. With fixed exchanges a fall in the foreign value of the currency or an outflow of gold or foreign exchange reserves acted as a signal requiring prompt government action. With flexible exchange rates, the effect of an increase in the quantity of money on the internal price level is much too slow to be generally recognised or to be charged to those ultimately responsible for it. Moreover, the inflation of prices is usually preceded by a welcome increase in employment, and it may therefore even be welcomed because its harmful effects are not visible until later.

It is therefore easy to understand why, in the hope of restraining countries all too inclined towards inflation, others like Germany, even while noticeably suffering from imported inflation, hesitated in the post-war period to destroy altogether the system of fixed rates of exchange. For a time it seemed likely to restrain the temptation further to speed up inflation. But now that the system of fixed rates of exchange appears to have totally collapsed, and there is scarcely any hope that self-discipline might induce some countries to restrain themselves, little reason is left to adhere to a system that is no longer effective. In retrospect one may even ask whether, out of a mistaken hope, the German Bundesbank or the Swiss National Bank have not waited too long, and then raised the value of their currency too little. But in the long run I do not believe we shall regain a system of international stability without returning to a system of fixed exchange rates which imposes upon the national central banks the restraint essential if they are successfully to resist the pressure of the inflation-minded forces of their countries — usually including Ministers of Finance.

Inflation Ultimately Increases Unemployment

But why all this fear of inflation? Should we not try to learn to live with it, as some South American States seem to have done, particularly if, as some believe, this is necessary to secure full employment? If this were true and the harm done by inflation were only that which many people emphasise, we would have to consider this possibility seriously.

Why We Cannot Live with Inflation

The answer, however, is twofold. *First,* such inflation, in order to achieve the goal aimed at, would have constantly to *accelerate,* and accelerating inflation would sooner or later reach a degree which makes all effective order of a market economy impossible. *Second,* and most important, in the long run such inflation makes much *more* unemployment inevitable than that which it was originally designed to prevent.

The argument often advanced that inflation produces merely a *redistribution* of the social product, while unemployment *reduces* it and therefore represents a worse evil, is thus false, because *inflation becomes the cause of increased unemployment.*

Harmful Effects of Inflation

I certainly do not wish to under-estimate the other harmful effects of inflation. They are much worse than anyone can conceive who has not himself lived through a great inflation. I count my first eight months in a job during which my salary rose to 200 times the initial amount as such an experience. I am indeed convinced that such a mismanagement of the currency is tolerated by the people only because, while the inflation proceeds, nobody has the time or energy to organise a popular rebellion.

What I want to say is that even the effects which every citizen experiences are not the worse consequence of inflation, which is usually not understood because *it becomes visible only when the inflation is past.* This must particularly be said to economists, politicians or others who like to point to the South American countries which have had inflations lasting through several generations and seem to have learnt to live with them. In these predominantly agrarian countries the effects of inflation are chiefly limited to those mentioned. The most serious effects that inflation produces in the labour markets of industrial countries are of minor importance in South America.

The attempts made in some of these countries, in particular Brazil, to deal with the problems of inflation by some method of indexing can, at best, remedy some of the consequences but certainly not the chief causes or the most harmful effects. They could not prevent the worst damage which inflation causes, that misdirection of labour which I must now consider more fully.

The Misdirection of Labour

Inflation makes certain jobs *temporarily* attractive. They will disappear when it stops or even when it ceases to accelerate at a sufficient rate. This result follows because inflation

(a) changes the distribution of the money stream between the various sectors and stages of the process of production, and
(b) creates expectation of a further rise of prices.

The defenders of a monetary full employment policy often represent the position as if a *single* increase of total demand were sufficient to secure full employment for an indefinite but fairly long period. This argument overlooks both the inevitable effects of such a policy on the distribution of labour between industries and those on wage policy of the trade unions.

As soon as government assumes the responsibility to maintain full employment at whatever wages the trade unions succeed in obtaining, they no longer have any reason to take account of the unemployment their wage demands might have caused. In this situation every rise of wages which exceeds the increase in productivity will make necessary an increase in total demand if unemployment is not to ensue. The increase in the quantity of money made necessary by the upward movement of wages thus released becomes a *continuous* process requiring a constant influx of additional quantities of money. The additional money supply must lead to changes in the relative strength of demand for various kinds of goods and services. And these changes in relative demand must lead to further changes in relative prices and consequent changes in the direction of production and the allocation of the factors of production, including labour. I must leave aside here all the other reasons why the prices of different goods — and the quantities produced — will react differently to changes in the demand (such as elasticities — the speed with which supply can respond to demand).

The chief conclusion I want to demonstrate is that the longer the inflation lasts, the larger will be the number of the workers whose jobs depend on a *continuation* of the inflation, often even on a continuing *acceleration* of the rate of inflation — not because they would not have found employment without the inflation, but because they were drawn by the inflation into *temporarily* attractive jobs which after a slowing down or cessation of the inflation will again disappear.

The Consequences Are Unavoidable

We ought to have no illusion that we can escape the consequences of the mistakes we have made.[3] Any attempt to preserve the jobs made profitable by inflation would lead to a complete destruction of the market order. *We have once again in the post-war period missed the opportunity to forestall a depression while there was still time to do so.* We have indeed used our emancipation from institutional restraints — the gold standard and fixed exchange rates — to act more stupidly than ever before.

But if we cannot escape the re-appearance of substantial unemployment, this is not the effect of a failure of 'capitalism' or the market economy, but exclusively due to our own errors which past experience and available knowledge ought to have enabled us to avoid. It is unfortunately only too true that the disappointment of expectations they have created may lead to serious social unrest. But this does not mean that we can avoid it. The most serious danger now is certainly that attempts, so attractive for the politicians, to postpone the evil day and thereby make things in the long run even worse, may still succeed. I must confess I have been wishing for some time that the inescapable crisis may come soon. And I hope now that any attempts made promptly to restart the process of monetary expansion will not succeed, and that we shall now be forced to face the choice of a new policy.

Temporary, Not Mass, Unemployment

Let me, however, emphasise at once that, although I regard a period of some months, perhaps even more than a year, of considerable unemployment as unavoidable, this does not mean that we must expect another long period of mass unemployment comparable with the Great Depression of the 1930s, provided we do not commit very bad mistakes of policy. Such a development can be prevented by a sensible policy which does not repeat the errors responsible for the duration of the Great Depression.

But before I turn to what our future policy ought to be I want to reject emphatically a misrepresentation of my point of view. I certainly do not recommend unemployment as a *means* to combat inflation. But I have to advise in a situation in which *the choice open to us is solely between some unemployment in the near future and more unemployment at a later date*. What I fear above all is the *apres nous le deluge* attitude of the politicians who in their concern about the next elections are likely to choose more unemployment later. Unfortunately even some commentators, such as the writers of the *Economist*, argue in a similar manner and have called for 'reflation' when the increase in the quantity of money is still continuing.

What Can Be Done Now?

The First Step

The first necessity now is to stop the increase of the quantity of money — or at least to reduce it to the rate of the real growth of production — and this cannot happen soon enough. Moreover, *I can see no advantage in a gradual deceleration,* although for purely technical reasons it may prove all we can achieve.

It does not follow that we should not endeavour to stop a real deflation when it threatens to set in. Although I do not regard deflation as the original cause of a decline in business activity, a disappointment of expectations has unquestionably tended to induce a process of deflation — what more than 40 years ago I called a 'secondary deflation'[4] — the effect of which may be worse, and in the 1930s certainly was worse, than what the original cause of the reaction made necessary, and which has no steering function to perform.

I have to confess that 40 years ago I argued differently. I have since altered my opinion — not about the theoretical explanation of the events but about the practical possibility of removing the obstacles to the functioning of the system by allowing deflation to proceed for a while.

I then believed that a short process of deflation might break the rigidity of money wages (what economists have since come to call their 'rigidity downwards') or the resistance to the reduction of some particular money wages, and that in this way we could restore relative wages determined by the market. This seems to me still an indispensable condition if the market mechanism is to function satisfactorily. But I no longer believe it is in practice possible to achieve it in this manner. I probably should have seen then that the last chance was lost after the British government in 1931 abandoned the attempt to bring costs down by deflation just when it seemed near success.

Prevent Recession Degenerating into Depression

If I were today responsible for the monetary policy of a country I would certainly try to prevent a threatening deflation, that is, an absolute decrease of the stream of incomes, by all suitable means, and would announce that I intended to do so. This alone would probably be sufficient to prevent a degeneration of the recession into a long-lasting depression. The re-establishment of a properly functioning market would however still require a re-structuring of the whole system of relative prices and wages and a re-adjustment to the expectation of stable prices, which presupposes a much greater flexibility of wages than exists now. What chance we have to achieve such a determination of relative wage-rates by the market and how long it may take I dare not predict. But, although I recognise that a *general* reduction of money wages is politically unachievable, I am still convinced that the required adjustment of the structure of *relative* wages can be achieved without inflation only through the reduction of the money wages of some groups of workers, and therefore must be thus achieved.

From a longer point of view it is obvious that, once we have got over the immediate difficulties, we must not avail ourselves again of the seemingly cheap and easy method of achieving full employment by aiming at the maximum of employment which in the short run can be achieved by monetary pressure.

The Keynesian Dream

The Keynesian dream is gone even if its ghost will continue to plague politics for decades. It is to be wished, though this is clearly too much to hope for, that the term 'full employment' itself, which has become so closely associated with the inflationist policy, should be abandoned — or that we should at least remember that it was the aim of classical economists long before Keynes. John Stuart Mill reports in his autobiography[5] how 'full employment with high wages' appeared to him in his youth as the chief *desideratum* of economic policy.

The Primary Aim: Stable Money, Not Unstable 'Full' Employment

What we must now be clear about is that our aim must be, not the maximum of employment which can be achieved in the short run, but a 'high and stable [i.e. *continuing*] level of employment', as one of the wartime British White Papers on employment policy phrased it.[6] This however we can achieve only through the re-establishment of a properly functioning market which, by the free play of prices and wages, establishes for each sector the correspondence of supply and demand.

Though it must remain one of the chief tasks of monetary policy to prevent wide fluctuations in the quantity of money or the volume of the income stream, the effect on employment must not be the dominating consideration guiding it. *The primary aim must again become the stability of the value of money.* The currency authorities must again be effectively protected against the political pressure which today forces them so often to take measures that are politically advantageous in the short run but harmful to the community in the long run.

Disciplining the Monetary Authorities

I wish I could share the confidence of my friend Milton Friedman who thinks that one could deprive the monetary authorities, in order to prevent the abuse of their powers for political purposes, of all discretionary powers by prescribing the amount of money they may and should add to circulation in any one year. It seems to me that he regards this as practicable because he has become used for statistical purposes to draw a sharp distinction between what is to be regarded as money and what is not. This distinction does not exist in the real world. I believe that, to ensure the convertibility of all kinds of near-money into real money, which is necessary if we are to avoid severe liquidity crises or panics, the monetary authorities must be given some discretion. But I agree with Friedman that we will have to try and get back to a more or less automatic system for regulating the quantity of money in ordinary times. His principle is one that monetary authorities ought to aim at, not one to which they ought to be tied by law. The necessity of 'suspending' Sir Robert Peel's Bank Act of 1844 three times within 25 years after it was passed ought to have taught us this once and for all.

And although I am not as optimistic as the Editor of the London *Times,* Mr. William Rees-Mogg, who in a sensational article[7] (and now in a book)[8] has proposed the return to the gold standard, it does make me feel somewhat more optimistic when I see such a proposal coming from so influential a source. I would even agree that among the feasible monetary systems the international gold standard is the best, if I could believe that the most important countries could be trusted to obey the rules of the game necessary for its preservation. But this seems to me exceedingly unlikely, and no single country can have an effective gold standard: by its nature it is an international system and can function only as an international system.

It is, however, a big step in the direction of a return to reason when at the end of his book Mr. Rees-Mogg argues that

> We should be tearing up the full employment commitment of the 1944 White Paper, a great political and economic revolution.
>
> This would until very recently have seemed a high price to pay; now it is no great price at all. There is little or no prospect of maintaining full employment with the present inflation, in Britain or in the world. The full employment standard became a commitment to inflation, but the inflation has now accelerated past the point at which it is compatible with full employment.[9]

Equally encouraging is a statement of the British Chancellor of the Exchequer, Mr. Denis Healey, who is reported to have said:

> It is far better that more people should be in work, *even if that means accepting lower wages on average,* than that those lucky enough to keep their jobs should scoop the pool while millions are living on the dole.[10] (My italics.)

It would almost seem as if in Britain, the country in which the harmful doctrines originated, a reversal of opinion were now under way. Let us hope it will rapidly spread over the world.

Notes

1. David Ricardo to John Wheatley, 18 September, 1821, reprinted in *The Works of David Ricardo,* ed. Piero Sraffa, Cambridge University Press, Vol. IX, 1952, p. 73.

2. *The Economic Consequences of the Peace* (1919), reprinted in *The Collected Writings of John Maynard Keynes,* Macmillan for the Royal Economic Society, Vol. II, 1971, p. 149.

3. I should make it clear that, although I was addressing an audience in Italy, what I am saying certainly also applies to Britain and most other Western countries. There is little sign so far of this truth being understood in Britain. — F.A.H.

4. Defined and discussed in Part III, p. 44. I recall that the phrase was frequently used in the LSE Seminar from the 1930s.

5. *Autobiography and other Writings,* ed. J. Stillinger, Houghton Mifflin, Boston, 1969.

6. *Employment Policy,* Cmd. 6527, HMSO, May 1944, Foreword.

7. 'Crisis of Paper Currencies: Has the Time Come for Britain to Return to the Gold Standard?', *The Times,* 1 May, 1974.

8. *The Reigning Error. The Crisis of World Inflation,* Hamish Hamilton, London, 1974.

9. *Ibid.*, p. 112.

10. Speech at East Leeds Labour Club reported in *The Times,* 11 January, 1975.

The Conditions of Equilibrium Between the Production of Consumers' Goods and the Production of Producers' Goods

2

"The question of how far, and in what manner, an increase of currency tends to increase capital appears to us so very important, as fully to warrant our attempt to explain it. . . . It is not the quantity *of the circulating medium which produces the effects here described, but the* different distribution *of it . . . on every fresh issue of notes . . . a larger proportion falls into the hands of those who consume and produce, and a smaller proportion into the hands of those who only consume."*

T. R. Malthus

Edinburgh Review, vol. XVII (1811), p. 363 *et seq.*

(1) Before we can attempt to understand the influence of prices on the amount of goods produced, we must know the nature of the immediate causes of a variation of industrial output. Simple as this question may at first appear, contemporary theory offers at least three explanations.

(2) First of these, we may take the view that the main causes of variations of industrial output are to be found in changes of the willingness of individuals to expand effort. I mention this first, because it is probably the theory which has at present the greatest number of adherents in this country. That this point of view is so

widely accepted in England is probably due to the fact that a comparatively great number of economists here are still under the influence of "real cost" theories of value which make this type of explanation of any change in the total value of output the natural one. Mr. D. H. Robertson's stimulating book on *Banking Policy and the Price Level* provides, perhaps, the best example of reasoning based on this assumption. Yet I do not think that this assumption is at all justified by our common experience; it is a highly artificial assumption to which I would only be willing to resort when all other explanations had failed. But its correctness is a question of fact, and I shall make no attempt to refute it directly. I shall only try to show that there are other ways of accounting for changes in industrial output which seem less artificial.

(3) The second type of explanation is the one which "explains" variations of production simply by the changes of the amount of factors of production used. In my opinion this is no explanation at all. It depends essentially upon a specious appeal to facts. Starting from the existence of unused resources of all kinds, known to us in daily experience, it regards any increase of output simply as the consequence of bringing more unused factors into use, and any diminution of output as the consequence of more resources becoming idle. Now, that any such change in the amount of resources employed implies a corresponding change in output is, of course, beyond question. But it is not true that the existence of unused resources is a *necessary* condition for an increase of output, nor are we entitled to take such a situation as a starting point for theoretical analysis. If we want to explain fluctuations of production, we have to give a complete explanation. Of course this does not mean that we have to start for that purpose *ab ovo* with an explanation of the whole economic process. But it does mean that we have to start where general economic theory stops; that is to say at a condition of equilibrium when no unused resources exist. The existence of such unused resources is itself a fact which needs explanation. It is not explained by static analysis and, accordingly, we are not entitled to take it for granted. For this reason I cannot agree that Professor Wesley Mitchell is justified when he states that he considers it no part of his task "to determine how the fact of cyclical oscillations in economic activity can be reconciled with the general theory of equilibrium, or how that theory can be reconciled with facts".[1] On the contrary, it is my conviction that if we want to explain economic phenomena at all, we have no means available but to build on the foundations given by the concept of a tendency towards an equilib-

rium. For it is this concept alone which permits us to explain fundamental phenomena like the determination of prices or incomes, an understanding of which is essential to any explanation of fluctuation of production. If we are to proceed systematically, therefore, we must start with a situation which is already sufficiently explained by the general body of economic theory. And the only situation which satisfies this criterion is the situation in which all available resources are employed. The existence of unused resources must be one of the main objects of our explanation.[2]

(4) To start from the assumption of equilibrium has a further advantage. For in this way we are compelled to pay more attention to causes of changes in the industrial output whose importance might otherwise be underestimated. I refer to changes in the methods of using the existing resources. Changes in the direction given to the existing productive forces are not only the main cause of fluctuations of the output of individual industries; the output of industry as a whole may also be increased or decreased to an enormous extent by changes in the use made of existing resources. Here we have the third of the contemporary explanations of fluctuations which I referred to at the beginning of the lecture. What I have here in mind are *not* changes in the methods of production made possible by the progress of technical knowledge, but the increase of output made possible by a transition to more capitalistic methods of production, or, what is the same thing, by organising production so that, at any given moment, the available resources are employed for the satisfaction of the needs of a future more distant than before. It is to this effect of a transition to more or less "roundabout" methods of production that I wish particularly to direct your attention. For, in my opinion, it is only by an analysis of this phenomenon that in the end we can show how a situation can be created in which it is temporarily impossible to employ all available resources.

The processes involved in any such transition from a less to a more capitalistic form of production are of such a complicated nature that it is only possible to visualise them clearly if we start from highly simplified assumptions and work through gradually to a situation more like reality. For the purpose of these lectures, I shall divide this investigation into two parts. Today I shall confine myself to a consideration of the conditions under which an equilibrium between the production of producers' goods and the production of consumers' goods is established, and the relation of this equilibrium to the flow of money; I reserve for the next lecture a more detailed explanation of the working of the price mechanism during the period of transition, and of the relations between changes in the price system and the rate of interest.

(5) My first task is to define the precise meaning of certain terms. The term production I shall always use in its widest possible sense, that is to say, all processes necessary to bring goods into the hands of the consumer. When I mean land and labour, I shall speak of *original means of production*. When I use the phrase *factors of production* without further qualification this will cover capital also, that is to say this term will include all factors from which we derive *income* in the form of wages, rent, and interest. When I use the expression *producers' goods*, I shall be designating all goods existing at any moment which are not consumers' goods, that is to say, *all* goods which are directly or indirectly used in the production of consumers' goods, *including* therefore the original means of production, as well as instrumental goods and all kinds of unfinished goods. Producers' goods which are not original means of production, but which come between the original means of production and consumers' goods, I shall call *intermediate products*. None of these distinctions coincides with the customary distinction between durable and non-durable goods, which I do not need for my present purpose. I shall, however, have to use this distinction and to add a new one, which stands in some relation to it, in my next lecture.

(6) I have already pointed out that it is an essential feature of our modern, "capitalistic", system of production that at any moment a far larger proportion of the available original means of production is employed to provide consumers' goods for some more or less distant future than is used for the satisfaction of immediate needs. The raison d'être of this way of organising production is, of course, that by lengthening the production process we are able to obtain a greater quantity of consumers' goods out of a given quantity of original means of production. It is not necessary for my present purpose to enter at any length into an explanation of this increase of productivity by roundabout methods of production. It is enough to state that within practical limits we may increase the output of consumers' goods from a given quantity of original means of production indefinitely, provided we are willing to wait long enough for the product. The thing which is of main interest for us is that any such change from a method of production of any given duration to a method which takes more or less time implies quite definite changes in the organisation of production, or, as I shall call this particular aspect of organisation, to distinguish it from other more familiar aspects, changes in the *structure of production*.

In order to get a clear view of what is actually implied by these changes in the structure of production it is useful to employ a schematic representation.[3] For this purpose, I find it convenient to represent the successive applications of the original means of production which are needed to bring forth the output of consumers' goods accruing at any moment of time, by the hypotenuse of a right-angled triangle, such as the triangle in Figure 1. The value of these original means of production is expressed by the horizontal projection of the hypotenuse, while the vertical dimension, measured in arbitrary periods from the top to the bottom, expresses the progress of time, so that the inclination of the line representing the amount of original means of production used means that these original means of production are expended continuously during the whole process of production. The bottom of the triangle represents the value of the current output of consumers' goods. The area of the triangle thus shows the totality of the successive stages through which the several units of original means of production pass before they become ripe for consumption. It also shows the total amount of intermediate products which must exist at any moment of time in order to secure a continuous output of consumers' goods. For this reason we may conceive of this diagram not only as representing the successive stages of the production of the output of any given moment of time, but also as representing the processes of production going on simultaneously in a stationary society. To use a happy phrase of J. B. Clark's, it gives a picture of the "synchronised process of production".[4,5]

Now it should be clear without further explanation that the proportion between the amount of intermediate products (represented by the area of the triangle) which is necessary at any moment of time to secure a continuous output of a given quantity of consumers' goods, and the amount of that output,[6] must grow with the length of the roundabout process of production. As the average time interval between the application of the original means of production and the completion of the consumers' goods increases, production becomes more capitalistic, and vice versa. In the case we are contemplating in which the original means of production are applied at a constant rate throughout the whole process of production, this average time is exactly half as long as the time which elapses between the application of the first unit of original means of production and the completion of the process. Accordingly, the total amount of intermediate products may also be represented by a rectangle half as high as the triangle, as indicated by the dotted line in the

FIGURE I
OUTPUT OF CONSUMERS GOODS

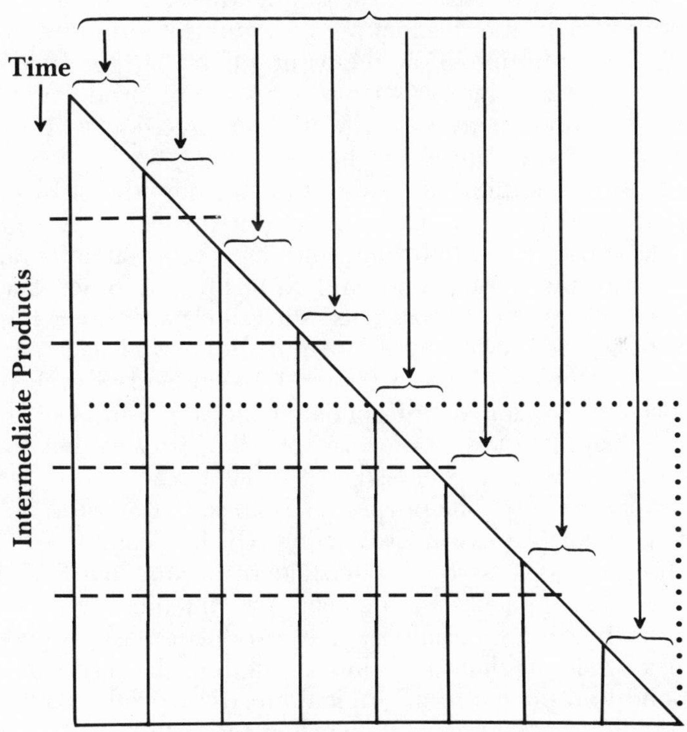

diagram. The areas of the two figures are necessarily equal, and it sometimes assists the eye to have a rectangle instead of a triangle when we have to judge the relative magnitude represented by the area of the figure. Furthermore, it should be noticed that, as the figure represents values and not physical production, the surplus return obtained by the roundabout methods of production is not represented in the diagram. In this lecture I have intentionally neglected interest. We shall have to take that into consideration next time. Until then we may assume that the intermediate products remain the property of the owners of the original means of production until they have matured into consumers' goods and are sold to consumers. Interest is then received by the owners of the original means of production together with wages and rent.

(7) A perfectly continuous process of this sort is somewhat unwieldy for theoretical purposes: moreover such an assumption is not perhaps sufficiently realistic. It would be open to us to deal with the difficulties by the aid of higher mathematics. But I, personally, prefer to make it amenable to a simpler method by dividing the continuous process into distinct periods, and by substituting for the concept of a continuous flow the assumption that goods move intermittently in equal intervals from one stage of production to the next. In this way, in my view, the loss of precision is more than compensated by the gain in lucidity.

Probably the simplest method of transforming the picture of the continuous process into a picture of what happens in a given period is to make cross sections through our first figure at intervals corresponding to the periods chosen, and to imagine observers being posted at each of these cross cuts who watch and note down the amount of goods flowing by. If we put these cross sections, as indicated by the broken lines in Figure 1, at the end of each period, and represent the amount of goods passing these lines of division in a period by a rectangle of corresponding size, we get the new illustration of the same process given in Figure 2.

It is convenient for the purposes of exposition to count only that part of the total process of production which is completed during one of these periods, as a separate stage of production. Each of the successive shaded blocks in the diagram will then represent the product of the corresponding stage of production as it is passed on to the next while the differences in the length of the successive blocks correspond to the amount of original means of production used in the succeeding stage. The white block at the bottom represents the output of consumers' goods during the period. In a stationary state, which is still the only state I am considering, this output of consumers' goods is necessarily equal to the total income from the factors of production used, and is exchanged for this income. The proportion of the white area to the shaded area, in this diagram 40:80 or 1:2, expresses the proportion between the output of consumers' goods and the output of intermediate products (or between the amount of consumption and the amount of new and renewed investment during any period of time).

So far, I have used this schematic illustration of the process of production only to represent the movements of goods. It is just as legitimate to use it as an illustration of the movement of money. While goods move downwards from the top to the bottom of our diagram, we have to conceive of money moving in the opposite di-

FIGURE 2
OUTPUT OF CONSUMERS' GOODS

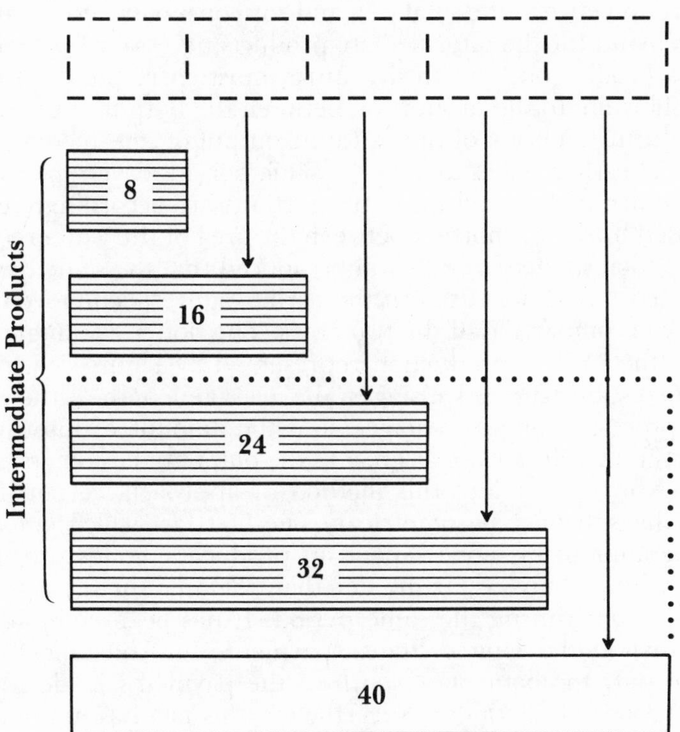

rection, being paid first for consumers' goods and thence moving upwards until, after a varying number of intermediary movements, it is paid out as income to the owners of the factors of production, who in turn use it to buy consumers' goods. But in order to trace the relation between actual money payments, or the proportional quantities of money used in the different stages of production, and the movements of goods, we need a definite assumption in regard to the division of the total process among different firms, which alone makes an exchange of goods against money necessary. For this does not by any means necessarily coincide with our division into separate stages of production of equal length. I shall begin with the simplest assumption, that these two divisions do coincide, that is to say that goods moving towards consumption do change hands against money in equal intervals which correspond to our unit production periods.

In such a case, the proportion of money spent for consumers' goods and money spent for intermediate products is equal to the proportion between the total demand for consumers' goods and the total demand for the intermediate products necessary for their continuous production; and this, in turn, must correspond, in a state of equilibrium, to the proportion between the output of consumers' goods during a period of time and the output of intermediate products of all earlier stages during the same period. Given the assumptions we are making, all these proportions are accordingly equally expressed by the proportion between the area of the white rectangle and the total shaded area. It will be noticed that the same device of the dotted line as was used in the earlier figure is employed to facilitate the comparison of the two areas. The dotted rectangle shows that, in the kind of production represented by Figure 2, which actually takes four successive stages, the average length of the roundabout process is only two stages, and the amount of intermediate products is therefore twice as great as the output of customers' goods.

(8) Now if we adopt this method of approach, certain fundamental facts at once become clear. The first fact which emerges is that the amount of money spent on producers' goods during any period of time may be far greater than the amount spent for consumers' goods during the same period. It has been computed, indeed, that in the United States, payments for consumers' goods amount only to about one-twelfth of the payments made for producers' goods of all kinds.[7] Nevertheless, this fact has not only very often been overlooked, it was even expressly denied by no less an authority than Adam Smith. According to Smith[8]: "The value of goods circulated between the different dealers never can exceed the value of those circulated between dealers and consumers; whatever is bought by the dealer being ultimately destined to be sold to the consumers." This proposition clearly rests upon a mistaken inference from the fact that the total expenditure made in production must be covered by the return from the sale of the ultimate products; but it remained unrefuted, and quite recently in our own day it has formed the foundation of some very erroneous doctrines.[9] The solution of the difficulty is, of course, that most goods are exchanged several times against money before they are sold to the consumer, and on the average exactly as many times as often as the

total amount spent for producers' goods is larger than the amount spent for consumers' goods.

Another point which is of great importance for what follows, and which, while often overlooked in current discussion,[10] is quite obvious if we look at our diagram, is the fact that what is generally called the capital equipment of society — the total of intermediate products in our diagram — is not a magnitude which, once it is brought into existence, will necessarily last for ever independently of human decisions. Quite the contrary: whether the structure of production remains the same depends entirely upon whether entrepreneurs find it profitable to re-invest the usual proportion of the return from the sale of the product of their respective stages of production in turning out intermediate goods of the same sort. Whether this is profitable, again, depends upon the prices obtained for the product of this particular stage of production on the one hand and on the prices paid for the original means of production and for the intermediate products taken from the preceding stage of production on the other. The continuance of the existing degree of capitalistic organisation depends, accordingly, on the prices paid and obtained for the product of each stage of production and these prices are, therefore, a very real and important factor in determining the direction of production.

The same fundamental fact may be described in a slightly different way. The money stream which the entrepreneur representing any stage of production receives at any given moment is always composed of net income which he may use for consumption without disturbing the existing method of production, and of parts which he must continuously re-invest. But it depends entirely upon him whether he re-distributes his total money receipts in the same proportions as before. And the main factor influencing his decisions will be the magnitude of the profits he hopes to derive from the production of his particular intermediate product.

(9) And now at last we are ready to commence to discuss the main problem of this lecture, the problem of how a transition from less to more capitalistic methods of production, or vice versa, is actually brought about, and what conditions must be fulfilled in order that a new equilibrium may be reached. The first question can be answered immediately: a transition to more (or less) capitalistic methods of production will take place if the total demand for producers' goods (expressed in money) increases (or decreases) relatively to the demand for consumers' goods. This may come about

in one of two ways: either as a result of changes in the volume of voluntary saving (or its opposite), or as a result of a change in the quantity of money which alters the funds at the disposal of the entrepreneurs for the purchase of producers' goods. Let us first consider the case of changes in voluntary saving, that is, simple shifts of demand between consumers' goods and producers' goods.[11]

As a starting point, we may take the situation depicted in Figure 2, and suppose that consumers save and invest an amount of money equivalent to one fourth of their income of one period. We may assume further that these savings are made continuously, exactly as they can be used for building up the new process of production. The proportion of the demand for consumers' goods to the demand for intermediate products will then ultimately be changed from 40:80 to 30:90, or 1:2 to 1:3. The additional amounts of money available for the purchase of intermediate products must now be so applied that the output of consumers' goods may be sold for the reduced sum of thirty now available for that purpose. It should now be sufficiently clear that this will only be the case if the average length of the roundabout processes of production and, therefore, in our instance, also the number of successive stages of production, is increased in the same proportion as the demand for intermediate products has increased relatively to the demand for consumers' goods, i.e., from an average of two to an average of three (or from an actual number of four to an actual number of six) stages of production. When the transition is completed, the structure of production will have changed from that shown in Figure 2 to the one shown in Figure 3. (It should be remembered that the relative magnitudes in the two figures are values expressed in money and not physical quantities, that the amount of original means of production used has remained the same, and that the amount of money in circulation and its velocity of circulation are also supposed to remain unchanged.)

If we compare the two diagrams, we see at once that the nature of the change consists in a stretching of the money stream flowing from the consumers' goods to the original means of production. It has, so to speak, become longer and narrower. Its breadth at the bottom stage, which measures the amount of money spent during a period of time on consumers' goods and, at the same time, the amount of money received as income in payment for the use of the factors of production, has permanently decreased from forty to thirty. This means that the price of a unit of the factors of production, the total amount of which (if we neglect the increase of capital) has re-

FIGURE 3
OUTPUT OF CONSUMERS' GOODS

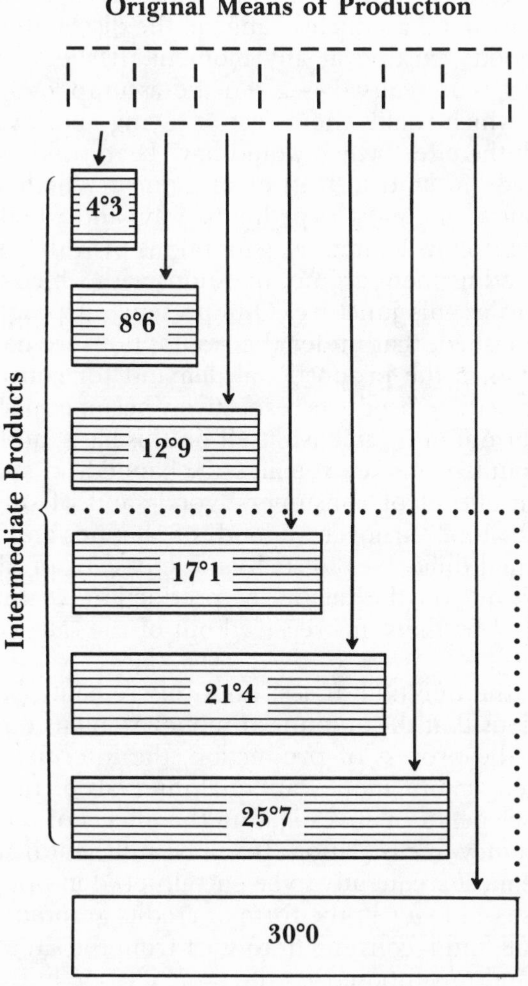

mained the same, will fall in the same proportion, and the price of a unit of consumers' goods, the output of which has increased as a consequence of the more capitalistic methods of production, will fall in still greater proportion. The amount of money spent in each of the later stages of production has also decreased, while the amount used in the earlier stages has increased, and the total spent on intermediate products has increased also because of the addition of a new stage of production.[12]

Now it should be clear that to this change in the distribution of the amounts of money spent in the different stages of production there will correspond a similar change in the distribution of the total amount of goods existing at any moment. It should also be clear that the effect thus realised — given the assumptions we are making — is one which fulfills the object of saving and investing, and is identical with the effect which would have been produced if the savings were made in kind instead of in money. Whether it has been brought about in the most expeditious way, and whether the price changes which follow from our assumptions provide a suitable stimulus to the readjustment are not questions with which we need concern ourselves at this juncture. Our present purpose is fulfilled if we have established, that under the assumptions we have made, the initial variation in the proportional demand for consumers' goods and for intermediate products respectively becomes permanent, that a new equilibrium may establish itself on this basis, and that the fact that the amount of money remains unchanged, in spite of the increase of the output of consumers' goods and of the still greater increase of the total turnover of goods of all kinds and stages, offers no fundamental difficulties to such an increase of production, since total expenditure on the factors of production, or total costs, will still be covered by the sums received out of the sales of consumers' goods.

But now the question arises: does this remain true if we drop the assumptions that the amount of money remains unchanged and that, during the process of production, the intermediate products are exchanged against money at equal intervals of time?

(10) Let us begin by investigating the effects of a change in the amount of money in circulation. It will be sufficient if we investigate only the case most frequently to be encountered in practice: the case of an increase of money in the form of credits granted to producers. Again we shall find it convenient to start from the situation depicted in Figure 2 and to suppose that the same change in the proportion between the demand for consumers' goods and the demand for intermediate products, which, in the earlier instance, was supposed to be produced by voluntary saving, is now caused by the granting of additional credits to producers. For this purpose, the producers must receive an amount of forty in additional money. As will be seen from Figure 4, the changes in the structure of production which will be necessary in order to find employment for the additional means

which have become available will exactly correspond to the changes brought about by saving. The total services of the original means of production will now be expended in six instead of in four periods; the total value of intermediate goods produced in the different stages during a period will have grown to three times instead of twice as large as the value of consumers' goods produced during the same period; and the output of each stage of production, including the

FIGURE 4

OUTPUT OF CONSUMERS' GOODS

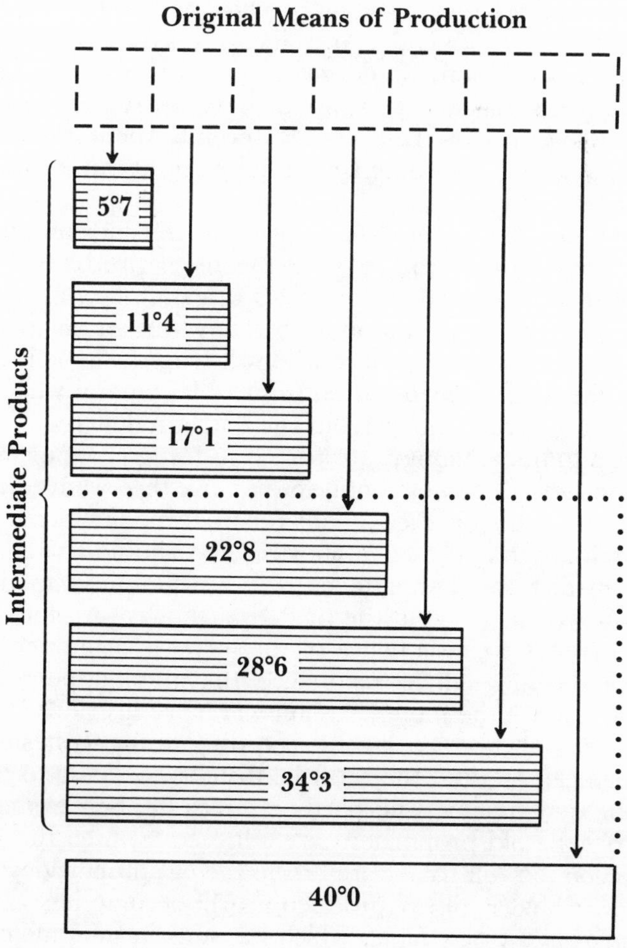

final one, measured in physical units will accordingly be exactly as great as in the case represented in Figure 3. The only difference at first apparent is that the money values of these goods have grown by one-third compared with the situation depicted in Figure 3.

There is, however, another and far more important difference which will become apparent only with the lapse of time. When a change in the structure of production was brought about by saving, we were justified in assuming that the changed distribution of demand between consumers' goods and producers' goods would remain permanent, since it was the effect of voluntary decisions on the part of individuals. Only because a number of individuals had decided to spend a smaller share of their total money receipts on consumption and a larger share on production was there any change in the structure of production. And since, after the change had been completed, these persons would get a greater proportion of the increased total real income, they would have no reason again to increase the *proportion* of their money receipts spent for consumption.[13] There would accordingly exist no inherent cause for a return to the old proportions.

In the same way, in the case we are now considering, the use of a larger proportion of the original means of production for the manufacture of intermediate products can only be brought about by a retrenchment of consumption. But now this sacrifice is not voluntary, and is not made by those who will reap the benefit from the new investments. It is made by consumers in general who, because of the increased competition from the entrepreneurs who have received the additional money, are forced to forego part of what they used to consume. It comes about not because they want to consume less, but because they get less goods for their money income. There can be no doubt that, if their money receipts should rise again, they would immediately attempt to expand consumption to the usual proportion. We shall see in the next lecture why, in time, their receipts will rise as a consequence of the increase of money in circulation. For the moment let us assume that this happens. But if it does, then at once the money stream will be re-distributed between consumptive and productive uses according to the wishes of the individual concerned, and the artificial distribution, due to the injection of the new money, will, partly at any rate, be reversed. If we assume that the old proportions are adhered to, then the structure of production too will have to return to the old proportion, as shown in Figure 5. That is to say production will become less capitalistic, and that part of the new capital which was sunk in equipment adapted only to the more capitalistic processes will be lost. We shall see in the next lecture that such a transition to less capitalistic methods of production necessarily takes the form of an economic crisis.

But it is not necessary that the proportion between the demand for consumers' goods and the demand for intermediate products should return exactly to its former dimensions as soon as the injection of new money ceases. In so far as the entrepreneurs have already succeeded, with the help of the additional money, in completing the new processes of longer duration,[14] they will, perhaps, receive increased money returns for their output which will put them in a position to continue the new processes, i.e., to expend permanently a larger share of their money receipts upon intermediate products without reducing their own consumption. It is only in consequence of the price changes caused by the increased demand for consumers' goods that, as we shall see, these processes too become unprofitable.

FIGURE 5
OUTPUT OF CONSUMERS' GOODS

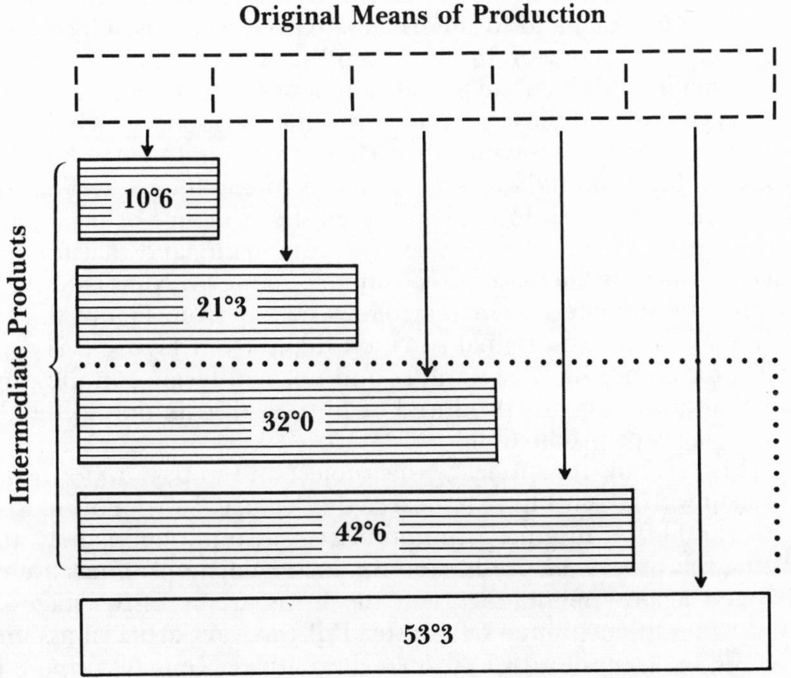

But for the producers who work on a process where the transition to longer roundabout processes is not yet completed when the amount of money ceases to increase the situation is different. They have spent the additional money which put them in a position to increase their demand for producers' goods and in consequence it has become consumers' income; they will, therefore, no longer be able to claim a larger share of the available producers' goods, and they will accordingly have to abandon the attempt to change over to more capitalistic methods of production.

(11) All this becomes easier to follow if we consider the simpler case in which an increase in demand for consumers' goods of this sort is brought about directly by additional money given to consumers. In recent years, in the United States, Messrs. Foster and Catchings have urged that, in order to make possible the sale of an increased amount of consumers' goods produced with the help of new savings, consumers must receive a proportionately larger money income. What would happen if their proposals were carried out? If we start with the situation which would establish itself as a consequence of new savings if the amount of money remained unchanged (as shown in Figure 3), and then assume that consumers receive an additional amount of money sufficient to compensate for the relative increase of the demand for intermediate products caused by the savings (i.e., an amount of 15) and spend it on consumers' goods, we get a situation in which the proportion between the demand for consumers' goods, and the demand for producers' goods, which, in consequence of the new savings, had changed from 40:80 to 30:90 or from 1:2 to 1:3 would again be reduced to 45:90 or 1:2. That this would mean a return to the less capitalistic structure of production which existed before the new savings were made, and that the only effect of such an increase of consumers' money incomes would be to frustrate the effect of saving follows clearly from Figure 6. (The difference from the original situation depicted in Figure 2 is again only a difference in money values and not a difference in the physical quantities of goods produced or in their distribution to the different stages of production.)

(12) It is now time to leave this subject and to pass on to the last problem with which I have to deal in this lecture. I wish now to drop the second of my original assumptions, the assumption, namely, that during the process of production the intermediate products are exchanged against money between the firms at successive stages of production in equal intervals. Instead of this very artificial assumption, we may consider two possible alternatives: we may suppose (a)

FIGURE 6

OUTPUT OF CONSUMERS' GOODS

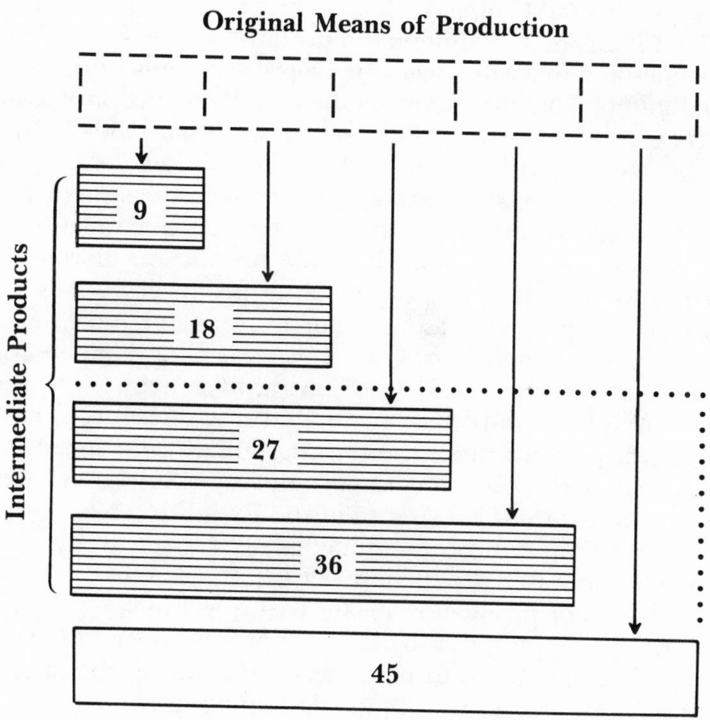

that in any line of production the whole process is completed by a single firm, so that no other money payments take place than the payments for consumers' goods and the payments for the use of the factors of production: or we may suppose (b) that exchanges of intermediate products take place, but at very irregular intervals, so that in some parts of the process the goods remain for several periods of time in the possession of one and the same firm, while in other parts of the process they are exchanged once or several times during each period.

(13) (a) Let us consider first the case in which the whole process of production in any line of production is completed by a single firm. Once again we may use Figure 1 to illustrate what happens. In this case the base of the triangle represents the total payments for consumers' goods and the hypotenuse (or, more correctly, its

horizontal projection) represents the amounts of money paid for the original means of production used. No other payments would be made and any amount of money received from the sale of consumers' goods could immediately be spent for original means of production. It is of fundamental importance to remember that we can assume only that any *single* line of production is in this way integrated into one big firm. It would be entirely inappropriate in this connection to suppose that the production of *all* goods is concentrated in one enterprise. For, if this were the case, of course the manager of this firm could, like the economic dictator of a communistic society, arbitrarily decide what part of the available means of production should be applied to the production of consumers' goods and what part to the production of producers' goods. There would exist for him no reason to borrow and, for individuals, no opportunity to invest savings. Only if *different* firms compete for the available means of production will saving and investing in the ordinary sense of the word take place, and it is therefore such a situation which we must make the starting point of our investigation.

Now, if any of these integrated industries decides to save and invest part of its profits in order to introduce more capitalistic methods of production, it must not immediately pay out the sums saved for original means of production. As the transition to more capitalistic methods of production means that it will be longer until the consumers' goods produced by the new process are ready, the firm will need the sums saved to pay wages, etc., during the interval of time between the sale of the last goods produced by the old process, and the getting ready of the first goods produced by the new process. So that, during the whole period of transition, it must pay out less to consumers than it receives in order to be able to bridge the gap at the end of this period, when it has nothing to sell but has to continue to pay wages and rent. Only when the new product comes on the market and there is no need for further saving will it again currently pay out all its receipts.

In this case, therefore, the demand for consumers' goods, as expressed in money, will be only temporarily reduced, while in the case where the process of production was divided between a number of independent stages of equal length, the reduction of the amount available for the purchase of consumers' goods was a permanent one. In the present case, the prices of the consumers' goods will, accordingly, fall only in inverse proportions as their quantity has increased, while the total paid as income for the use of the factors of production will remain the same. These conclusions are, however, only provisional as they do not take account of the relative position of the one firm considered to all other firms which will certainly be affected by a change of relative prices and interest rates which are necessarily connected with such a process. Unfortunately, these influences are too complicated to allow of treatment within the scope of these lectures, and I must ask you, therefore, to suspend judgment upon the ultimate effects of the price changes which will take place under these conditions.

But there is one point to which I must particularly direct your attention: the reason in this case why the unchanged amount of money used in production remains sufficient, in spite of the fact that a larger amount of intermediate products now exists, whereas in the former case, the use of an increased amount of intermediate products required the use of an increased quantity of money is this. In the former case the intermediate products passed from one stage of production to the next by an exchange against money. But in the present case this exchange is replaced by internal barter, which makes money unnecessary. Of course, our division of the continuous process of production into separate stages of equal length is entirely arbitrary: it would be just as natural to divide it into stages of different lengths and then speak of these stages as exhibiting so many more or less instances of internal barter. But the procedure which has been adopted serves to bring out a concept, which I shall need in a later lecture, the concept of the relative volume of the flow of goods during any period of time, as compared with the amount of goods exchanged against money in the same period. If we divide the path traversed by the elements of any good from the first expenditure of original means of production until it gets in the hands of the final consumer into unit periods, and then measure the quantities of goods which pass each of these lines of division during a period of time, we secure a comparatively simple measure of the flow of goods without having recourse to higher mathematics. Thus, we may say that, in the instance we have been considering, money has become more efficient in moving goods, in the sense that a given amount of exchanges against money has now become sufficient to make possible the movement of a greater volume[15] of goods than before.

(14) (b) Perhaps this somewhat difficult concept becomes more intelligible if I illustrate it by supposing that two of the independent firms which we have supposed to represent the successive stages of production in our diagrams 2 and 6 are combined into one firm. This is the second of the alternative possibilities I set out to consider. Once this has happened, the passage of the intermediate products

from the one to the next stage of production will take place without money payments being necessary, and the flow of goods from the moment they enter the earlier of the two stages until they leave the later will be effected by so much less money. A corresponding amount of money will thus be released and may be used for other purposes. The reverse effect will, of course, be witnessed if the two firms separate again. An increased amount of money payments will be required to effect the same movement of goods and the proportion of money payments to the flow of goods advancing towards consumption will have increased.

(15) Unfortunately, all names which might be used to designate this kind of monetary effectiveness have already been appropriated for designating different concepts of the velocity of money. Until somebody finds a fitting term, therefore, we shall have to speak somewhat clumsily of the proportion between the amount of goods exchanged against money and the total flow of goods or of the proportion of the total movements of goods which is effected by exchange against money.

Now this proportion must on no account be confused with the proportion of the volume of money payments to the physical volume of trade. The proportion I have in mind may remain the same while the volume of trade increases relatively to the total of money payments and the price level falls, if only the same proportion of the total flow of goods is exchanged against money, and it may change though the proportion of the total of money payments to the physical volume of trade remains the same. It is, therefore, not necessarily influenced either by changes in the amount of money or by changes in the physical volume of trade; it depends only upon whether, in certain phases of the process of production, goods do or do not change hands.

So far I have illustrated this concept only by instances from the sphere of production. It may be applied also to the sphere of consumption. Here, too, sometimes a larger and sometimes a smaller share of the total output of consumers' goods is exchanged for money before it is consumed. Accordingly, here, too, we may speak about the proportion which the total output of consumers' goods in a period of time bears to the output which is sold for money. And this proportion may be different in the different stages of production. But in its effect upon the structure of production, the efficiency of a given amount of money spent in any stage of production (including the last stage — consumption) is determined by the proportion in that stage; and any change in that proportion has the same effects as an alteration in the amount of money spent in this particular stage of production.

So much for the complications which arise when we drop the assumption that production is carried on in independent stages of equal length. It has been necessary to discuss them here at some length in order to clear the way for an investigation, into which I wish to enter in the last lecture, in connection with the arguments for and against an elastic money supply. But for the tasks which I shall have to face tomorrow, it will be expedient again to make use of the simplest assumption and to suppose that production is carried on in independent stages of equal length, as we did in our schematic representations, and that this proportion is not only the same in all stages of production, but also that it remains constant over time.

Notes

1. *Business Cycles, The Problem and its Setting*, New York, 1927, p. 462.

2. I have dealt more fully with the relation between pure economic theory and the explanation of business fluctuations in my book, *Monetary Theory and the Trade Cycle* (London, 1933), Chaps. I and II.

3. The following diagrams were originally the result of an attempt to replace the somewhat clumsy tables of figures, used for the same purpose in my Paradox of Saving (*Economica*, May, 1931), by a more easily grasped form of representation. Later I noticed that similar triangular figures had been used as representations of the capitalistic process of production not only by W. S. Jevons (*Theory of Political Economy*, 4th edit., 1911, pp. 230–7), but particularly also by K. Wicksell (*Lectures on Political Economy*, vol. I, p. 152 et seq.) and, following him, G. Åckerman (*Realkapital und Kapitalzins*, Part I. Stockholm, 1923). Dr. Marschak has recently made the very appropriate suggestion to designate these triangular figures as the "Jevonian Investment Figures".

4. The methodological bearing of the concept of a synchronised production is particularly well brought out by Hans Mayer in his article, "Produktion", in the *Handwörterbuch der Staatswissenschaften*, fourth edit., vol. VI, Jena, 1925, p. 1115 et seq.

5. So long as we confine ourselves to the real aspects of the capital structure the triangular figures may be taken to represent not only the stock of goods in process but also the stock of durable instruments existing at any moment of time. The different instalments of future services which such goods are expected to render will in that case have to be imagined to belong to different "stages" of production corresponding to the time interval which will elapse before these services mature. (For a more detailed

discussion of the problems arising out of the two different aspects, of actual duration of production and the durability of goods, in which time enters in the productive process, cf. my article "On the Relationship between Investment and Output", *Economic Journal*, June, 1934.) But as soon as it is tried to use the diagrammatic representations to show the successive transfers of the intermediate products from stage to stage in exchange for money it becomes evidently impossible to treat durable goods in the same way as goods in process since it is impossible to assume that the individual services embodied in any durable goods will regularly change hands as they approach a stage nearer to the moment when they will actually be consumed. For this reason it has been necessary, as has been pointed out in the preface, to abstract from the existence of durable goods so long as the assumption is made that the total stock of intermediate products as it gradually proceeds towards the end of the process of production is exchanged against money at regular intervals.

6. It would be more exact to compare the stock of intermediate products existing *at a moment* of time not with the output of consumers' goods *during a period* of time, but rather with the rate at which consumers' goods mature at the same moment of time. Since, however, this output at a moment of time would be infinitely small, that proportion could only be expressed as a differential quotient of a function which represents the flow of intermediate products at the point where this flow ends, i.e., where the intermediate products become consumers' goods. This relationship is essentially the same as that between the total quantity of water in a stream and the rate at which this water passes the mouth of this stream. (This *simile* seems to be more appropriate than the more familiar one which considers capital as a "stock" and only income as a "flow". Cf. on this point N. J. Polak, *Grundzüge der Finanzierung*, Berlin, 1926, p. 13.) It is convenient to treat the quantity of intermediate products at any point of this stream as a function of time $f(t)$ and accordingly the total quantity of intermediate products in the stream, as an integral of this function over a period r equal to the total length of the process of production. If we apply this to any process of production beginning at the moment x, the total quantity of intermediate products in the stream will be expressed by

$$\int_{x}^{x+r} f(t).\,dt$$

and the output of consumers' goods at a moment of time by $f(x+r)$. In the diagrams used in the text the function $f(t)$ is represented by the hypotenuse, its concrete value $f(x+r)$ by the horizontal side and the integral by the area of the triangle. There is of course no reason to assume that the function $f(t)$ will be linear, i.e., that the amount of original factors applied during successive stages of the process is constant, as is assumed in the diagrams. On these and some connected points see the article on "Investment and Output", quoted in the preceding footnote.

7. Cf. M. W. Holtrop, *De Omloopssnelheid van het Geld*, Amsterdam, 1928, p. 181.

8. *Wealth of Nations*, Book II, Chap. I, ed. Cannan, p. 305. It is interesting to note that this statement of Adam Smith is referred to by Thomas Tooke as a justification of the erroneous doctrines of the Banking School. (Cf. *An Inquiry into the Currency Principle*, London, 1844, p. 71.)

9. Cf. W. T. Foster and W. Catchings, *Profits*, Publications of the Pollak Foundation for Economic Research, No. 8, Boston and New York, 1925, and a number of other books by the same authors and published in the same series. For a detailed criticism of their doctrines, cf. my article, "The 'Paradox' of Saving", *Economica*, May, 1931.

10. J. S. Mill's emphasis on the "perpetual consumption and reproduction of capital", like most of his other penetrating, but often somewhat obscurely expressed observations on capital, has not had the deserved effect, although it directs attention to the essential quality of capital which distinguishes it from other factors of its production. More recently the misplaced emphasis which some authors, particularly Professors J. B. Clark, J. Schumpeter and F. H. Knight, have put on the tautological statement that so long as stationary conditions prevail capital is *ex definitione* permanent, has further contributed to obscure the problem.

11. I am deliberately discussing here the "strong case" where saving implies a reduction in the demand for *all* consumers' goods, although this is a highly unlikely case to occur in practice, since it is in this case that many people find it so difficult to understand how a general decrease in the demand for consumers' goods should lead to an increase of investment. Where, as will regularly be the case, the reduction in the demand for consumers' goods affect only a few kinds of such goods, these special difficulties would, of course, be absent.

12. To avoid misunderstandings I have now substituted the terms "earlier" and "later" stages used by Professor Taussig in this connection, for the expression "higher" and "lower" which are unequivocal only with reference to the diagrams but are liable to be confused with such expressions as "highly finished" products, particularly as A. Marshall has used the terms in this reverse sense (cf. *Industry and Trade*, p. 219).

13. It is important to bear in mind that, though the total money income would diminish, the total real income would increase.

14. It should, however, be remembered that a process cannot be regarded as completed in this sense, just because an entrepreneur at any one stage of production has succeeded in completing his section of it. A complete process, in the sense in which this concept is used in the text, comprises *all* the stages of any one line of production, whether they are part of one firm or divided between several. I have further elaborated this point in my article on "Capital and Industrial Fluctuations", *Econometrica*, April, 1934.

15. Even if this total of goods moving towards consumption during each period is not actually exchanged against money in each period, it is not an imaginary, but a real and important magnitude, since the value of this total is a magnitude which continually rests within our power to determine. It probably stands in close relation to what is commonly called free capital, and it is certainly the supply of this factor which — together with new saving — determines the rate of interest; the capital which remains invested in durable instruments affects the interest rate from the demand side only, i.e., by influencing opportunities for new investment.

The Keynes Centenary: The Austrian Critique

• 3 •

It will not be easy for future historians to account for the fact that, for a generation after the untimely death of Maynard Keynes, opinion was so completely under the sway of what was regarded as Keynesianism, in a way that no single man had ever before dominated economic policy and development. Nor will it be easy to explain why these ideas rather suddenly went out of fashion, leaving behind a somewhat bewildered community of economists who had forgotten much that had been fairly well understood before the "Keynesian Revolution." There can be no doubt that it was in Keynes's name and on the basis of his theoretical work that the modern world has experienced the longest period of general inflation, and has now again to pay for it by a widespread and severe depression. Yet it is more than doubtful whether Keynes himself would have approved of the policies pursued in his name.

It was Keynes who had told us in 1919 that

> there is no surer means of overturning the existing basis of society than to debauch the currency. The process engages all the hidden forces of economic law on the side of destruction, and does it in a manner which not one man in a million is able to diagnose.

From *The Economist,* June 11, 1983. Permission to reprint courtesy of *The Economist.*

It was Keynes who alleged that Lenin had concluded that "the best way to destroy the capitalist system was to debauch the currency."

During this crucial period I could watch much of this development and occasionally discuss the decisive issues with Keynes, whom I in many ways much admired and still regard as one of the most remarkable men I have known. He was certainly one of the most powerful thinkers and expositors of his generation. But, paradoxical as this may sound, he was neither a highly trained economist nor even centrally concerned with the development of economics as a science. In the last resort he did not even think much of economics as a science, tending to regard his superior capacity for providing theoretical justifications as a legitimate tool for persuading the public to pursue the policies which his intuition told him were required at the moment.

The question of Keynes's role in history is essentially one of how his teaching could succeed once more in opening the floodgates of inflation after it had become generally recognised that the temporary gain in employment achieved by credit expansion had necessarily to be paid for by even more severe unemployment at a later stage. This old truth is now being rediscovered. Bitter experience has again shown that the acceleration of inflation, which alone can preserve the kinds of jobs that have been created by inflation, cannot be indefinitely continued.

Keynes never recognised that progressive inflation was needed in order that any growth in monetary demand could lastingly increase the employment of labour. He was thoroughly aware of the danger of growing monetary demand degenerating into progressive inflation, and towards the end of his life greatly concerned that this might happen. It was not the living Keynes but the continuing influence of his theories that determined what did happen. I can report from first-hand knowledge that, on the last occasion I discussed these matters with him, he was seriously alarmed by the agitation for credit expansion by some of his closest associates. He went so far as to assure me that if his theories, which had been badly needed in the deflation of the 1930s, should ever produce dangerous effects he would rapidly change the public opinion in the right direction. A few weeks later he was dead and could not do it.

Yet it is undeniable that inflationary conclusions could in good faith be drawn from his teaching. This suggests that his theories must have suffered from a serious defect and raises the central question — whether the great influence that his views have had on professional opinion was due to a real advance of our understanding or to some definite error. Special circumstances made me from the very beginning regard his whole analysis as based on a crucial error.

I am afraid this obliges me to say frankly that I still have no doubt that Maynard Keynes was neither a full master of the body of economic theory then available, nor really cared to acquaint himself with any development which lay outside the Marshallian tradition which he had learnt during the second half of his undergraduate years at Cambridge. His main aim was always to influence current policy, and economic theory was for him simply a tool for this purpose. He trusted his intellectual powers readily to produce a better theory for this purpose, and tried to do so in several different forms.

In these theoretical efforts he was guided by one central idea — which in conversation he once described to me as an "axiom which only half-wits could question" — namely, that general employment was always positively correlated with the aggregate demand for consumer goods. This made him feel that there was more truth in that underconsumption theory preached by a long row of radicals and cranks for generations but by relatively few academic economists. It was his revival of this underconsumption approach which made his theories so attractive to the Left. John Stuart Mill's profound insight that demand for commodities is not demand for labour, which Leslie Stephen could in 1876 still describe as the doctrine whose "complete apprehension is, perhaps, the best test of an economist," remained for Keynes an incomprehensible absurdity.

The Role of Investment

In the Cambridge tradition that governed Keynes's brief study of economics, the Mill-Jevons theory of capital, later developed by Boehm-Bawerk and Wicksell, was not seriously considered. By about 1930 these ideas had been largely forgotten in the English-speaking world. Along with most of my professional colleagues, I might also have readily accepted Keynes's elaboration of the common-sense belief of a direct dependence of employment on aggregate demand. However, not only had I been brought up in the Boehm-Bawerk-Wicksell tradition but, just before Keynes's *Treatise on Money* appeared, I had also spent much time analysing a somewhat similar but much cruder American effort to develop a monetary theory of the causes of "underconsumption." For this purpose I had already developed a little further the Wicksell-Mises theory of monetary overstimulation of investment which, I felt, refuted the naive assumption of a direct dependence of investment on final demand from which Keynes had started.

In the course of the years I had several occasions to discuss these issues with Keynes. It became quite clear that our differences rested wholly on his refusal to question that assumption. On one occasion I succeeded in making him admit, with evident surprise, that in certain circumstances, preceding investment might cause an increase in the demand for capital. But when on a later occasion I had got him momentarily interested in the possibility that a fall in product prices might lead to investment in order to reduce units costs, he soon dismissed this brusquely as nonsense!

Since the determinants of employment other than final demand are the factors which Keynesian macroeconomics so fatally neglects, an assessment of its historical role must attempt to bring this aspect of economics briefly back to mind. It is helpful to conceive of the continuous flow of production as a great river that may, independently of the suction from its mouth, swell or shrink in its different parts as its countless tributaries further upstream add more or less to its volume. Fluctuations in investments and replacement will cause the stream to increase or reduce the volume in its upper reaches with consequent change in employment, as occurs in the course of industrial fluctuations. There is no necessary correspondence between the volume (or even the direction of the change) of the sale of the final products during a period and that of employment during that period.

The volume of investment is far from moving proportionally to final demand. Not only the rate of interest but also the relative prices of the different factors of production and particularly of the different kinds of labour will affect it, apart from technological change. Investment will depend on the volume of the different parts of the stream whether at any one moment total employment of factors of production will be greater or smaller than the effective demand for final products. The immediate determinants directing the tributaries to the main stream will not be final demand but the structure of relative prices of the different factors of production: the different kinds of labour, semi-finished products, raw materials and, of course, rates of interest.

When, as directed by these relative prices, the whole stream changes its shape, employment is bound to change at its different stages at very different rates: sometimes the whole stream will, as it were, happily stretch itself, providing additional jobs, while sometimes it will shrink. This may cause strong fluctuations in the volume of employment, particularly in the "heavy" industries and in building, without any changes of consumer demand in the same direction. It is a well-known historical fact that in a slump the revival of final demand is generally an effect rather than a cause of the revival in the upper reaches of the stream of production — activities generated by savings seeking investment and by the necessity of making up for postponed renewals and replacements.

The important point is that those independent swellings and shrinkings of the different reaches of the stream of production are caused by the changes in the relative prices of different factors: some being drawn by higher prices to earlier stages of the process or vice versa. This constant reallocation of resources is wholly concealed by the analysis Keynes chose to adopt and which has since come to be known as "macroeconomics": an analysis in terms of the relations between various aggregates or averages, such as aggregate demand or supply, average prices, etc. This approach obscures the character of the mechanism by which the demand for the different kinds of activities is determined.

The Myth of Measurement

The hope of becoming more "empirical" by becoming more macroeconomic is bound to be disappointed, because these statistical magnitudes — which are alone ascertainable by "measurement" — do not also make them significant as the cause of actions of individuals who do not know them. Economic phenomena are not mass phenomena of the kind to which statistical theory is applicable. They belong to that intermediate sphere that lies between the simple phenomena of which people can ascertain all the relevant data, and the true mass phenomena where one must rely on probabilities.

It cannot seriously be denied that monetary causes exert important effects on the order of the world of real goods, or that these effects were largely neglected by Keynes. Yet the purely monetary approach he had adopted created considerable difficulties for criticism by an opponent who felt that Keynes had missed the crucial issues. I ought to explain why I failed to return to the charge after I had devoted much time to a careful analysis of his writings — a failure for which I have reproached myself ever since. It was not merely (as I have occasionally claimed) the inevitable disappointment of a young man when told by the famous author that his objections did not matter since Keynes no longer believed in his own arguments. Nor was it really that I became aware that an effective refutation of Keynes's conclusions would have to deal with the whole "macroeconomic" approach. It was rather that his disregard of what seemed to me the crucial problems made me recognise that a proper critique would have to deal more with what Keynes had not gone into than with what he had discussed, and that in consequence an elaboration of the still inadequately developed theory of capital was a prerequisite for a thorough disposal of Keynes's argument.

So I started on this task intending it to lead to a discussion of the determinants of investment in a monetary system. But the preliminary "pure" part of this work proved to be much more difficult, and took me very much longer, than I had expected. When war broke out, making it doubtful that publication of such a voluminous work would be possible, I put out as a separate book what had been meant as a first step of an analysis of the Keynesian weaknesses, which itself was indefinitely postponed.

The main cause of this postponement was that I soon found myself supporting Keynes in his struggle against wartime inflation, and at that time wished nothing less than to weaken his authority. Although I regard Keynes's theories as chiefly responsible for the inflation of the past quarter of a century, I am convinced that this was a development which he did not intend and which he would have endeavoured with all his strength to prevent. I am not sure he could have succeeded because he had never seen clearly that only accelerating inflation could lastingly secure a high level of employment.

Deviating Disciples

Towards the end of his life Keynes was certainly not happy about the direction of the efforts of his closest associates. I can well believe his saying that, just as Marx was never a Marxist, so he was never a Keynesian. We have it also, on the authority of Professor Joan Robinson, that "there were moments when we had trouble in getting Maynard to see what the point of his revolution really was, but when he came to sum it up after the book was published he got it into focus." It was, in fact, the group of younger Keynesian doctrinaires whose ideas guided the inflationary "full-employment" policy for the next 30 years, not only of Britain but most of the rest of the world.

I am fully aware that, in effect, I am claiming that perhaps the most impressive intellectual figure I have ever encountered and whose general intellectual superiority I have readily acknowledged, was wholly wrong in the scientific work for which he is chiefly known. But I must add that I am convinced that he owed his extraordinary influence in this field, to which he gave only a small part of his energy, to an almost unique combination of other gifts. Irrespective of whether he was right or wrong, those gifts made him one of the outstanding figures of his age. He will in future appear as representative of his time as some of the famous renaissance figures now appear to us. I am not contending that his influence in other fields was necessarily more beneficial. Indeed I am convinced that, through his denial of conventional morals and his haughty "in the long run we are all dead" approach, his influence was disastrous.

Yet it was his great gifts which made it so difficult to escape his influence and to resist being drawn into his way of thinking. He not only possessed an incredible variety of intellectual interests but was perhaps even more drawn to the arts. He was also a great patriot, if that is the right word for a profound believer in the superiority of British civilisation. That his intellectual efforts were largely dominated by his aesthetic feelings was one of his strongest characteristics, and chief source of the personal fascination he exercised.

Alpha Plus

A little episode on the same last occasion when I met him at dinner at King's College may give an idea of the amazing richness of his mind. In the later years of the war he had been regularly sending me the *American Journal of the History of Ideas* to which he subscribed and which I found difficult to obtain. Two or three weeks before the dinner at King's he had sent me the latest issue; it happened that I had read in it the same morning an article on the circumstances of the posthumous publication of the second work of Copernicus. At coffee I sat opposite the College astronomer, who had not yet seen the article, so it provided a welcome topic of conversation.

Keynes, sitting a little further up the table and engaged in another conversation, was evidently at the same time following my account of the affair. He suddenly interrupted me in the rendering of a complicated detail with "You are wrong, Hayek." He then gave a much fuller and more accurate account of the circumstances, although it must have been two or three weeks since he had seen what I had read a few hours before.

I have confined myself here to the distinctive contributions Keynes made to economic theory. But his great influence far exceeded and also antedated the hopes this technical work held out of lastingly full employment. He had gained the ear of the "advanced" thinkers much earlier and greatly contributed to a trend very much in conflict with his own classical liberal beginnings. The time when he had become the idol of the leftist intellectuals was in fact when in 1933 he had shocked many of his earlier admirers by an essay on "National Self-Sufficiency" in the *New Statesman* and *Nation* (reprinted with equal enthusiasm by the *Yale Review*, the communist *Science and Society*, and the national-socialist *Schmollers Jahrbuch*). In the essay he proclaimed that "the decadent international but individualistic capitalism, in the hands of which we found ourselves after the war, is not a success. It is not intelligent, it is not beautiful, it is not just, it is not virtuous — and it does not deliver the goods. In short, we dislike it and are beginning to despise it." Later, still in the same mood, in his preface to the German translation of *The General Theory,* he frankly recommended his policy proposals as being more easily adapted to the conditions of a totalitarian state than those in which production is guided by free competition.

No wonder his disciples were shocked when, long after his death, it became known that less than a decade later he had, in a private letter, said of my book, *The Road to Serfdom,* that "morally and philosophically [he found himself] in agreement with virtually the whole of it; and not only in agreement, but in deeply moved agreement." He qualified this approval by the curious belief that "dangerous acts can be done safely in a country which thinks rightly, which could be the way to hell if they were executed by those who feel wrongly."

Inspired geniuses possessing a great power of conviction are not necessarily a blessing for the society in which they spring up. John Maynard Keynes was undoubtedly one of the great men of his age, in some respects representative and in others revolutionary, but hardly the great scientist whose growing insight moves along a single path. His *Collected Works,* "chiefly in the field of economics" and now approaching the thirtieth volume, are certainly a most revealing documentation of the intellectual movements of his time. But an economist may feel some doubt whether this distinction, for which Newton, Darwin, and the great British philosophers all still have to wait, is not rather a token of the idolatry he enjoyed among his personal admirers than proportionate to his contribution to the advance of scientific knowledge.

HAYEK'S REFUTATION OF SOCIALISM

♦ ♦

♦ *PART* ♦ *TWO* ♦

Two Pages of Fiction: The Impossibility of Socialist Calculation

· 4 ·

There is endless repetition of the claim that Professor Oskar Lange in 1936 refuted the contention advanced in 1921 by Ludwig von Mises that 'economic calculation is impossible in a socialist society'. The claim rests wholly on theoretical argument by Oskar Lange in little more than two pages, 59 to 61, in the most widely known reprint of his original essay, with Fred M. Taylor, *On the Economic Theory of Socialism* (ed. B.E. Lippincott, University of Minnesota Press, 1938). It will be timely to analyse this argument clause by clause. We shall here indent Lange's successive assertions with the crucial terms in italics, and examine their validity and bearing one by one. The theoretical argument commences as follows:

> Professor Mises' contention that a socialist economy cannot solve the problems of rational allocation of its sources is based on a confusion concerning the nature of prices. As Wicksteed has pointed out, the term 'price' has two meanings. It may mean either price in the ordinary sense, i.e. the exchange ratio of two commodities on a market, or it may have the generalized meaning of 'terms on which alternatives are offered'. Wicksteed says, '"Price", then, in the narrower sense of "the money for which a material thing, a

---

From *Economic Affairs*, April 1982. Permission to reprint courtesy of the Institute of Economic Affairs.

> service, or a privilege can be obtained", is simply a special case of "price" in the wider sense of "the terms on which alternatives are offered to us" '. [P.H. Wicksteed, *The Common Sense of Political Economy,* 2nd ed., London, 1933, p. 28]. It is only prices in the generalized sense which are indispensible to solving the problem of the allocation of resources.

Wicksteed's honest warning that for the purposes of analysis he would use the term 'price' in a wider sense in no way indicates that those quasi-prices can generally operate as substitutes for the money prices where they are not known. Within his range of knowledge the individual will certainly often have to balance alternatives between which he must choose, but the problem is precisely how he can do so where he does not know the particular concrete facts determining this necessity. That the 'alternatives which are offered to us' become known to us in most instances only as *money* prices is Mises' chief argument. To turn this against him is an inexcusable legerdemain of which a thinker not prejudiced by political preconceptions should be incapable.

Lange continues:

> The economic problem is a problem of choice between alternatives. To solve the problem three *data* are needed; (1) a preference scale which guides the acts of choice; (2) knowledge of the 'terms on which alternatives are offered'; and (3) knowledge of the amount of resources available. Those three *data* being *given,* the problem of choice is soluble.

The illiterate expression 'given data' constantly recurs in Lange. It appears to have an irresistable attraction to mathematical economists because it doubly assures them that they know what they do not know. It seems to bewitch them into making assertions about the real world for which they have no empirical justification whatever. On the confusion supported by this pleonasm the whole of Lange's 'refutation' of Mises' argument (and most of the theory of resource allocation descending from it) is based. Note the following:

> it is obvious that a socialist economy *may regard the data* under 1 and 3 as *given,* at least *in as great a degree* as they are given in a market economy.

One is bound to ask: known (which I presume is the meaning of 'given') to whom? These circumstances are in a market economy known to some thousands of different individuals, but this of course in no way implies that they can be known to the central planning authority of a socialist economy. Yet Lange continues:

> The *data* under 1 may be either *given* by the demand schedules of the individuals or be established by the judgement of the authorities administering the economic system. The question remains whether the *data* under 2 are accessible to the administrators of a socialist economy. Professor Mises denies this. However, a careful study of price *theory* and of the theory of production convinces us that the *data* under 1 and under 3 being given, the 'terms on which alternatives are offered' *are determined* ultimately by the *technical possibilities* of transformation of one commodity into another, i.e. by the production functions [the relationships between input and output — ED.].

It will be noticed that the assurance that these 'data' are being 'given' in no way explains *how* in day-to-day practice they become known to the socialist planning agency.

Before we go on to Lange's extraordinary answer to this question we ought first, perhaps, more carefully distinguish between the two senses in which the expression 'data' can be meaningfully employed. It can be used legitimately either for the assumption, necessarily made hypothetically by the theorist, that certain facts exist which are not known to him, or for the assumption that particular facts will be known to specified persons and will have certain effects on their actions. But it is an impermissible falsification of the sequence of cause and effect to claim that the 'data' presumed (though not known) by the theorist are also known to some agency without his showing the process by which they will become known to it. And when he claims that some further events are 'determined' by either kind of data, this does not show that these results are known to any particular person.

Now to Lange's most extraordinary 'solution' of this problem. He asserts that

> The administrators of the socialist economy will have exactly the same knowledge, or lack of knowledge, of the production functions as the capitalist entrepreneurs have.

This brazen assertion is crucial for Lange's refutation of Mises' argument, but he offers no evidence or justification for it, even in this limited form confined to production functions. Yet it has been expanded by Lange's pupils into the even more fantastic assertion that a central planning board 'would receive exactly the same information from a socialist economic system as did the entrepreneurs under the market systems'. (Thus Robert L. Heilbroner, *Between Capitalism and Socialism,* New York, 1980, p. 88.)

The Flaw in Socialist Planning

I am afraid this is a blatant untruth, an assertion so absurd that it is difficult to understand how an intelligent person could ever honestly make it. It asserts a sheer impossibility which only a miracle could realise. In the first instance: most of the information which the capitalist entrepreneurs have consists of prices determined on a competitive market. This knowledge would *not* be available to anyone in a socialist economy where prices are not provided by the market. So far as the particular case of the production function is concerned, the relevant production functions which guide the competitive market are, of course, not (as the theoretical models simplifyingly assume) relations between general, generic categories of commodities, but very *specific* relations showing how, in a particular plant under the specific local conditions, changes in the combinations of the particular goods and services employed will affect the size of the output.

The individual entrepreneur will not possess or require knowledge of general production functions, but he will currently learn from experience how at any given time variations in the qualities or the relative quantities of the different factors of production he uses will affect his output. The information relevant for and possessed by each entrepreneur will be very different from that possessed by others. To speak of the aggregate of such information dispersed among hundreds of different individuals as being available to the planning authority is pure fiction. What the planning authority would have to know would not be the mere totals but the distinct, peculiar conditions prevailing *in each enterprise* which affect the information about *values* transmitted through market prices but would be completely lost in any statistical information about *quantities* that might reach the authority from time to time.

Even if this purely technological information about the range of available physical possibilities could with reasonable promptness be communicated to the planning authority, it would by no means put it in command of all the information which capitalist entrepreneurs can and must use if they are to be successful. The production functions about which Lange is concerned indicate only the range of possibilities from which the individual producer has to choose. But the particular points on the curves by which the functions can be represented that they must choose to produce economically, depend on the relative scarcities of all the different factors of production. Entrepreneurs are informed about these scarcities solely by market prices. The planning authority would have no 'data' whatever. Lange appears to have been so confused between the knowledge possessed in day-to-day economic life by the individuals whose actions economics attempts to explain and the knowledge which the economist must pretend to possess in order to be able to do so, that he represents the latter as if it were something obviously perceivable to any observer of the economy. How the market brings about an adaptation to a multitude of circumstances which in their totality are not known to anyone is precisely the process which the science of economics has to explain. Yet Lange has the audacity to blame Mises for the very mistake he himself is committing.

> Professor Mises seems to have confused prices in the narrower sense, i.e. the exchange ratio of commodities on a market, with prices in the wider sense of 'terms on which alternatives are offered'. As, in consequence of public ownership of the means of production, there is in a socialist economy no market on which capital goods are actually exchanged, there are obviously no prices of capital goods in the sense of exchange ratios on a market. And hence Professor Mises argues, there is no *index* of alternatives available in the sphere of capital goods. But this confusion is based on a confusion of 'price' in the narrower sense with 'price' in the wider sense of an *index* of alternatives. It is only in the latter sense that 'prices' are indispensible for allocation of resources, and *on the basis of the technical possibilities of transformation of one commodity into another* they are also *given* in a socialist economy.

Now, if in this argument 'index' means, as it must for the conclusions to follow, a sign or indicator visible to anyone who cares to look for it, it is, of course, simply false. That 'price' can also measure 'terms on which alternatives are offered' does not mean that these terms are generally known or readily discoverable. The whole of Mises' argument is precisely that, though the theoretician will recognise that the increase of the output of some good will usually be possible only 'at the price' of the reduction of the output of some other goods, without market prices nobody will know how large that 'price' is. As we have seen, even if all the technical possibilities of transformation of one commodity to another could be known to the planning authorities (which, interpreted as particular local and temporal possibilities, is of course not the case), this would be far from sufficient to allow the planning authority rationally to decide which of these possibilities to use.

The muddle involved in this is the same as that which makes so many contemporary socialist writers allege that, even before Mises, Vilfredo Pareto and Enrico Barone had shown that the problem of socialist calculation was soluble. It is perfectly true that these two authors had shown which information a socialist planning authority would have to possess in order to perform its task. But to know which kind of information would be required to solve a problem does not imply that it can be solved if the information is dispersed among millions of people.

Dispersed Market Knowledge Cannot Be Mobilised Centrally

I feel I should perhaps make it clear that I have never conceded, as is often alleged, that Lange had provided the theoretical solution of the problem, and I did not thereafter withdraw to pointing out practical difficulties. What I *did* say (in *Individualism and Economic Order*, p. 187) was merely that from the factually false hypothesis that the central planning board could command all the necessary information, it could *logically* follow that the problem was in principle soluble. To deduce from this observation the 'admission' that the real problem can be solved in theory is a rather scandalous misrepresentation. Nobody can, of course, transfer to another all the knowledge he has, and certainly not the information he could discover only *if* market prices told him what was worth looking for.

Neither Pareto nor Barone ever claimed that he knew how this knowledge could ever be obtained. Indeed, Pareto, on the contrary, explicitly denied it. After describing in his celebrated *Manuel d'économie politique* (2nd ed. 1971, pp. 233 – 34) all the information that would have to be taken into account to determine a market equilibrium, he continued: 'this determination has by no means the purpose to arrive at a numerical calculation of prices. Let us make the most favourable assumption for such a calculation, let us assume that we have triumphed over all the difficulties of finding the data of the problem and that we know the *ophélimités* [utility] of all the different commodities for each individual, and all the conditions of production of all the commodities, etc. *This is already an absurd hypothesis to make.* Yet it is not sufficient to make the solution of the problem possible. We have seen that in the case of 100 persons and 700 commodities there will be 70,699 conditions. [Actually, a great number of circumstances we have so far neglected] will further increase the number: we shall therefore have to solve a system of 70,699 equations. This exceeds practically the power of algebraic analysis, and this is even more true if one contemplates the fabulous number of equations which one obtains for a population of forty millions and several thousand commodities. In this case the roles would be changed; it would not be mathematics which would assist political economy, but political economy which would assist mathematics. In other words, if one really could know all these equations, the only means to solve them which is available to human powers is *to observe the practical solution given by the market*' (my italics).

Even today the solution of 100,000 equations is still an unachieved ambition of the constructors of computers. And it is regrettable that the mathematical difficulties Pareto introduced to illustrate further what he had called the 'absurdity' of the assumption have gained most attention. For the real problem is the impossibility of concentrating all the information required in the hands of any single agency. Apparently it was J.A. Schumpeter who gave currency to the myth that Pareto and Barone had solved the problem. At any rate, it was Schumpeter who in particularly drastic form tacitly re-introduced this assumption in his celebrated *Capitalism, Socialism and Democracy* (1942, pp. 172 – 77), as one of the 'general logic of choice' where it is 'possible to derive, from the data and from the rules of rational behaviour, uniquely determined solutions'. This assumes that the planning authority knows all these 'data'.

A 'logic of choice' can say something only about the consequences to be drawn from a set of statements known to some one mind, and in this sense it can account for the behaviour of one individual. But, as I showed about 45 years ago (*Individualism and Economic Order,* pp. 35 – 45), the step from this logic of choice to an empirical science which tells us anything about what can happen in the real world requires additional knowledge about the process by which information is transmitted or communicated.

Like so many mathematical economists Schumpeter appears to have been seduced by the habitual assumption of 'given data' to believe that the relevant facts that for his construction the theorist must assume to exist are actually known to any one mind. This becomes evident in Schumpeter's most startling assertion that the possibility of 'economic rationality', being attained in a planned system, follows for the theorist 'from the elementary proposition that consumers in evaluating ("demanding") consumers' goods *ipso facto* also evaluate the means of production which enter into the production of those goods'. This is a meaningful statement only in the context of a system or equation in which not only all the technical possibilities of production but also their relative scarcities are assumed to be known. As an assertion about what happens in the real world it is sheer nonsense. Even if we had full information about what Pareto called 'the *ophélimités* of all the different commodities for each indivdual', or even the prices they would be prepared to pay for each of any possible collection of commodities, we could not derive from them alone the prices of the different factors or intermediate products.

Schumpeter's attempt to prove his assertion to the layman characteristically begins by assuming that 'means of production are present in given and, for the moment, unalterable quantities'. He does not explain to *whom* these quantities are 'given', that is, known, nor how much about their various attributes and potentialities anybody knows. Yet the central planning board will allocate 'productive resources — all of which are under its control — to these industrial managements according to certain rules'. The first of these is that 'they must produce as economically as possible'.

Schumpeter's Equivocations

But if there are no market prices how do they know what is more and what is less economical? Apparently from 'stated "prices"' — presumably fixed by the board. But from which sources does the board know which prices represent the relative scarcities of these resources? All we get in reply is one equivocation after another, but no real explanation. This is surely not worthy of a distinguished thinker. I should perhaps add that it is mostly based on the result of a German doctoral thesis done some years earlier under Schumpeter's supervision, though no more satisfactory on the crucial issues than Schumpeter's own statements (K. Tisch, *Wirtschaftsrechnung und Verteiling im zentralisch organisierten sozialistischen Gemeinwesen,* doctoral thesis, University of Bonn, Wuppertal-Elberfeld, 1932).

It was probably the influence of Schumpeter's teaching more than the direct influence of Oskar Lange that has given rise to the growth of an extensive literature of mathematical studies of 'resource allocation processes' (most recently summarised in K.J. Arrow and L. Hurwicz, *Studies in Resource Allocation Processes,* Cambridge University Press, 1977). As far as I can see they deal as irresponsibly with sets of fictitious 'data' which are in no way connected with what the acting individuals can learn as any of Lange's.

From Calculation to Accountability

In the later parts of Lange's exposition, and increasingly in the more recent literature, the claim that in a socialist order economic *calculation* is possible is replaced by the assertion that economic *accounting* is possible without market prices. If by this is meant that the managers of the socialist plants can be held responsible for not defrauding or misusing the resources entrusted to them, nobody will deny this. Any sort of recording in terms of physical quantities or any other magnitude will do this. But it has nothing to do with the original issue of rational allocation of resources. It does not answer any objection ever seriously raised against the capacity of a socialist order to fulfill the promises of its advocates. It is another symptom of the negligence and carelessness with which words have been used throughout this whole, long discussion. The mere idea that the planning authority could ever possess a complete inventory of the amounts and qualities of all the different materials and instruments of production of which the manager of a particular plant will know or be able to find out makes the whole proposal a somewhat comic fiction. Once this is recognised it becomes obvious that what prices ought to be can never be determined without relying on competitive markets. The suggestion that the planning authority could enable the managers of particular plants to make use of their specific knowledge by fixing uniform prices for certain classes of goods that will then have to remain in force until the planning authority learns whether at these prices inventories generally increase or decrease is just the crowning foolery of the whole farce.

A reconsideration of the discussion in which I took an active part more than 40 years ago has left me with a rather depressing view of the somewhat shameful state of what has become an established part of economic science, the subject of 'economic systems'. It appears to me that in this subject political attractiveness has been preserved by the flimsiest of arguments. The kindest thing one can say is that some well-meaning people have allowed themselves to be deceived by the vague and thoughtless language commonly used by specialists in the theory of these issues.

'SOCIAL' OR DISTRIBUTIVE JUSTICE

• 5 •

So great is the uncertainty of merit, both from its natural obscurity, and from the self-conceit of each individual, that no determinate rule of conduct could ever follow from it.

David Hume[1]

Welfare, however, has no principle, neither for him who receives it, nor for him who distributes it (one will place it here and another there); because it depends on the material content of the will, which is dependent upon particular facts and therefore incapable of a general rule.

Immanuel Kant[2]

THE CONCEPT OF 'SOCIAL JUSTICE'

While in the preceding chapter I had to defend the conception of justice as the indispensable foundation and limitation of all law, I must now turn against an abuse of the word which threatens to destroy the conception of law which made it the safeguard of individual freedom. It is perhaps not surprising that men should have applied to the joint effects of the actions of many people, even where these were never foreseen or intended, the conception of justice which they had developed with respect to the conduct of individuals towards each other. 'Social' justice (or sometimes 'economic' justice) came to be regarded as an attribute which the 'actions' of society, or the 'treatment' of individuals and groups by society, ought to possess. As primitive thinking usually does when first noticing some regular processes, the results of the spontaneous ordering of the market were interpreted as if some thinking being deliberately directed them, or as if the particular benefits or harm different persons derived from them were determined by deliberate acts of will, and could therefore be guided by moral rules. This conception of 'social' justice is thus a direct consequence of that anthropomorphism or personification by which naive thinking tries to account for all self-ordering processes. It is a sign of the immaturity of our minds that we have not yet outgrown these primitive concepts and still demand from an impersonal process which brings about a greater satisfaction of human desires than any deliberate human organization could achieve, that it conform to the moral precepts men have evolved for the guidance of their individual actions.[3]

The use of the term 'social justice' in this sense is of comparatively recent date, apparently not much older than a hundred years. The expression was occasionally used earlier to describe the organized efforts to enforce the rules of just individual conduct,[4] and it is to the present day sometimes employed in learned discussion to evaluate the effects of the existing institutions of society.[5] But the sense in which it is now generally used and constantly appealed to in public discussion, and in which it will be examined in this chapter, is essentially the same as that in which the expression 'distributive justice' had long been employed. It seems to have become generally current in this sense at the time when (and perhaps partly because) John Stuart Mill explicitly treated the two terms as equivalent in such statements as that

> society should treat all equally well who have deserved equally well of it, that is, who have deserved equally well absolutely. This is the highest abstract standard of social and distributive justice; towards which all institutions, and the efforts of all virtuous citizens should be made in the utmost degree to converge[6]

or that

> it is universally considered just that each person should obtain that (whether good or evil) which he deserves; and unjust that he should

> obtain a good, or be made to undergo an evil, which he does not deserve. This is perhaps the clearest and most emphatic form in which the idea of justice is conceived by the general mind. As it involves the idea of desert, the question arises of what constitutes desert.[7]

It is significant that the first of these two passages occurs in the description of one of five meanings of justice which Mill distinguishes, of which four refer to rules of just individual conduct while this one defines a factual state of affairs which may but need not have been brought about by deliberate human decision. Yet Mill appears to have been wholly unaware of the circumstance that in this meaning it refers to situations entirely different from those to which the four other meanings apply, or that this conception of 'social justice' leads straight to full-fledged socialism.

Such statements which explicitly connect 'social and distributive justice' with the 'treatment' by society of the individuals according to their 'deserts' bring out most clearly its difference from plain justice, and at the same time the cause of the vacuity of the concept: the demand for 'social justice' is addressed not to the individual but to society — yet society, in the strict sense in which it must be distinguished from the apparatus of government, is incapable of acting for a specific purpose, and the demand for 'social justice' therefore becomes a demand that the members of society should organize themselves in a manner which makes it possible to assign particular shares of the product of society to the different individuals or groups. The primary question then becomes whether there exists a moral duty to submit to a power which can co-ordinate the efforts of the members of society with the aim of achieving a particular pattern of distribution regarded as just.

If the existence of such a power is taken for granted, the question of how the available means for the satisfaction of needs ought to be shared out becomes indeed a question of justice — though not a question to which prevailing morals provide an answer. Even the assumption from which most of the modern theorists of 'social justice' start, namely that it would require equal shares for all in so far as special considerations do not demand a departure from this principle, would then appear to be justified.[8] But the prior question is whether it is moral that men be subjected to the powers of direction that would have to be exercised in order that the benefits derived by the individuals could be meaningfully described as just or unjust.

It has of course to be admitted that the manner in which the benefits and burdens are apportioned by the market mechanism would in many instances have to be regarded as very unjust *if* it were the result of a deliberate allocation to particular people. But this is not the case. Those shares are the outcome of a process the effect of which on particular people was neither intended nor foreseen by anyone when the institutions first appeared — institutions which were then permitted to continue because it was found that they improve for all or most the prospects of having their needs satisfied. To demand justice from such a process is clearly absurd, and to single out some people in such a society as entitled to a particular share evidently unjust.

The Conquest of Public Imagination by 'Social Justice'

The appeal to 'social justice' has nevertheless by now become the most widely used and most effective argument in political discussion. Almost every claim for government action on behalf of particular groups is advanced in its name, and if it can be made to appear that a certain measure is demanded by 'social justice', opposition to it will rapidly weaken. People may dispute whether or not the particular measure is required by 'social justice'. But that this is the standard which ought to guide political action, and that the expression has a definite meaning, is hardly ever questioned. In consequence, there are today probably no political movements or politicians who do not readily appeal to 'social justice' in support of the particular measures which they advocate.

It also can scarcely be denied that the demand for 'social justice' has already in a great measure transformed the social order and is continuing to transform it in a direction which those who called for it never foresaw. Though the phrase has undoubtedly helped occasionally to make the law more equal for all, whether the demand for justice in distribution has in any sense made society juster or reduced discontent must remain doubtful.

The expression of course described from the beginning the aspirations which were at the heart of socialism. Although classical socialism has usually been defined by its demand for the socialization of the means of production, this was for it chiefly a means thought to be essential in order to bring about a 'just' distribution of wealth; and since socialists have later discovered that this redistribution could in a great measure, and against less resistance, be brought about by taxation (and government services financed by it), and have in practice often shelved their earlier demands, the realization of 'social justice' has become their chief promise. It might indeed be said that the main difference between the order of society at which classical liberalism aimed and the sort of society into which it is now being transformed is that the former was governed by principles of just individual conduct while the new society is to satisfy the demands for 'social justice' — or, in other words, that the former demanded just action by the individuals while the latter more and more places the duty of justice on authorities with power to command people what to do.

The phrase could exercise this effect because it has gradually been taken over from the socialist not only by all the other political movements but also by most teachers and preachers of morality. It seems in particular to have been embraced by a large section of the clergy of all Christian denominations, who, while increasingly losing their faith in a supernatural revelation, appear to have sought a refuge and consolation in a new 'social' religion which substitutes a temporal for a celestial promise of justice, and who hope that they can thus continue their striving to do good. The Roman Catholic church especially has made the aim of 'social justice' part of its official doctrine;[9] but the ministers of most Christian denominations appear to vie with each other with such offers of more mundane aims — which also seem to provide the chief foundation for renewed ecumenical efforts.

The various modern authoritarian or dictatorial governments have of course no less proclaimed 'social justice' as their chief aim. We have it on the authority of Mr. Andrei Sakharov that millions of men in Russia are the victims of a terror that 'attempts to conceal itself behind the slogan of social justice'.

The commitment to 'social justice' has in fact become the chief outlet for moral emotion, the distinguishing attribute of the good man, and the recognized sign of the possession of a moral conscience. Though people may occasionally be perplexed to say which of the conflicting claims advanced in its name are valid, scarcely anyone doubts that the expression has a definite meaning, describes a high ideal, and points to grave defects of the existing social order which urgently call for correction. Even though until recently one would have vainly sought in the extensive literature for an intelligible definition of the term,[10] there still seems to exist little doubt, either among ordinary people or among the learned, that the expression has a definite and well understood sense.

But the near-universal acceptance of a belief does not prove that it is valid or even meaningful any more than the general belief in witches or ghosts proved the validity of these concepts. What we have to deal with in the case of 'social justice' is simply a quasi-religious superstition of the kind which we should respectfully leave in peace so long as it merely makes those happy who hold it, but which we must fight when it becomes the pretext of coercing other men. And the prevailing belief in 'social justice' is at present probably the gravest threat to most other values of a free civilization.

Whether Edward Gibbon was wrong or not, there can be no doubt that moral and religious beliefs can destroy a civilization and that, where such doctrines prevail, not only the most cherished beliefs but also the most revered moral leaders, sometimes saintly figures whose unselfishness is beyond question, may become grave dangers to the values which the same people regard as unshakeable. Against this threat we can protect ourselves only by subjecting even our dearest dreams of a better world to ruthless rational dissection.

It seems to be widely believed that 'social justice' is just a new moral value which we must add to those that were recognized in the past, and that it can be fitted within the existing framework of moral rules. What is not sufficiently recognized is that in order to give this phrase meaning a complete change of the whole character of the social order will have to be effected, and that some of the values which used to govern it will have to be sacrificed. It is such a transformation of society into one of a fundamentally different type which is currently occurring piecemeal and without awareness of the outcome to which it must lead. It was in the belief that something like 'social justice' could thereby be achieved, that people have placed in the hands of government powers which it can now not refuse to employ in order to satisfy the claims of the ever increasing number of special interests who have learnt to employ the open sesame of 'social justice'.

I believe that 'social justice' will ultimately be recognized as a will-o'-the-wisp which has lured men to abandon many of the values which in the past have inspired the development of civilization — an attempt to satisfy a craving inherited from the traditions of the small group but which is meaningless in the Great Society of free men. Unfortunately, this vague desire which has become one of the strongest bonds spurring people of good will to action, not only is bound to be disappointed. This would be sad enough. But, like most attempts to pursue an unattainable goal, the striving for it will also produce highly undesirable consequences, and in particular lead to the destruction of the indispensible environment in which the traditional moral values alone can flourish, namely personal freedom.

The Inapplicability of the Concept of Justice to the Results of a Spontaneous Process

It is now necessary clearly to distinguish between two wholly different problems which the demand for 'social justice' raises in a market order.

The first is whether within an economic order based on the market the concept of 'social justice' has any meaning or content whatever.

The second is whether it is possible to preserve a market order while imposing upon it (in the name of 'social justice' or any other pretext) some pattern of remuneration based on the assessment of the performance or the needs of different individuals or groups by an authority possessing the power to enforce it.

The answer to each of these questions is a clear no.

Yet it is the general belief in the validity of the concept of 'social justice' which drives all contemporary societies into greater and greater efforts of the second kind and which has a peculiar self-accelerating tendency: the more dependent the position of the individuals or groups is seen to become on the actions of government, the more they will insist that the governments aim at some recognizable scheme of distributive justice; and the more governments try to realize some preconceived pattern of desirable distribution, the more they must subject the position of the different individuals and groups to their control. So long as the belief in 'social justice' governs political action, this process must progressively approach nearer and nearer to a totalitarian system.

We shall at first concentrate on the problem of the meaning, or rather lack of meaning, of the term 'social justice', and only later consider the effects which the efforts to impose *any* preconceived pattern of distribution must have on the structure of the society subjected to them.

The contention that in a society of free men (as distinct from any compulsory organization) the concept of 'social justice' is strictly empty and meaningless will probably appear as quite unbelievable to most people. Are we not all constantly disquieted by watching how unjustly life treats different people and by seeing the deserving suffer and the unworthy prosper? And do we not all have a sense of fitness, and watch it with satisfaction, when we recognize a reward to be appropriate to effort or sacrifice?

The first insight which should shake this certainty is that we experience the same feelings also with respect to differences in human fates for which clearly no human agency is responsible and which it would therefore clearly be absurd to call injustice. Yet we do cry out against the injustice when a succession of calamities befalls one family while another steadily prospers, when a meritorious effort is frustrated by some unforeseeable accident, and particularly if of many people whose endeavours seem equally great, some succeed brilliantly while others utterly fail. It is certainly tragic to see the failure of the most meritorious efforts of parents to bring up their children, of young men to build a career, or of an explorer or scientist pursuing a brilliant idea. And we will protest against such a fate although we do not know anyone who is to blame for it, or any way in which such disappointments can be prevented.

It is no different with regard to the general feeling of injustice about the distribution of material goods in a society of free men. Though we are in this case less ready to admit it, our complaints about the outcome of the market as unjust do not really assert that somebody has been unjust; and there is no answer to the question of *who* has been unjust. Society has simply become the new deity to which we complain and clamour for redress if it does not fulfil the expectations it has created. There is no individual and no cooperating group of people against which the sufferer would have a just complaint, and there are no conceivable rules of just individual conduct which would at the same time secure a functioning order and prevent such disappointments.

The only blame implicit in those complaints is that we tolerate a system in which each is allowed to choose his occupation and therefore nobody can have the power and the duty to see that the results correspond to our wishes. For in such a system in which each is allowed to use his knowledge for his own purposes[11] the concept of 'social justice' is necessarily empty and meaningless, because in it nobody's will can determine the relative incomes of the different people, or prevent that they be partly dependent on accident. 'Social justice' can be given a meaning only in a directed or 'command' economy (such as an army) in which the individuals are ordered what to do; and any particular conception of 'social justice' could be realized only in such a centrally directed system. It presupposes that people are guided by specific directions and not by rules of just individual conduct. Indeed, no system of rules of just individual conduct, and therefore no free action of the individuals, could produce results satisfying any principle of distributive justice.

We are of course not wrong in perceiving that the effects of the processes of a free society on the fates of the different individuals are not distributed according to some recognizable principle of justice. Where we go wrong is in concluding from this that they are unjust and that somebody is to be blamed for this. In a free society in which the position of the different individuals and groups is not the result of anybody's design — or could, within such a society, be altered in accordance with a generally applicable principle — the differences in reward simply cannot meaningfully be described as just or unjust. There are, no doubt, many kinds of individual action which are aimed at affecting particular remunerations and which might be called just or unjust. But there are no principles of individual conduct which would produce a pattern of distribution which as such could be called just, and therefore also no possibility for the individual to know what he would have to do to secure a just remuneration of his fellows.

The Rationale of the Economic Game in Which Only the Conduct of the Players but Not the Result Can Be Just

We have seen earlier that justice is an attribute of human conduct which we have learnt to exact because a certain kind of conduct is required to secure the formation and maintenance of a beneficial order of actions. The attribute of justice may thus be predicated about the intended results of human action but not about circumstances which have not deliberately been brought about by men. Justice requires that in the 'treatment' of another person or persons, i.e. in the intentional actions affecting the well-being of other persons, certain uniform rules of conduct be observed. It clearly has no application to the manner in which the impersonal process of the market allocates command over goods and services to particular people: this can be neither just nor unjust, because the results are not intended or foreseen, and depend on a multitude of circumstances not known in their totality to anybody. The conduct of the individuals in that process may well be just or unjust; but since their wholly just actions will have consequences for others which were neither intended nor foreseen, these effects do not thereby become just or unjust.

The fact is simply that we consent to retain, and agree to enforce, uniform rules for a procedure which has greatly improved the chances of all to have their wants satisfied, but at the price of all individuals and groups incurring the risk of unmerited failure. With the acceptance of this procedure the recompense of different groups and individuals becomes exempt from deliberate control. It is the only procedure yet discovered in which information widely dispersed among millions of men can be effectively utilized for the benefit of all — and used by assuring to all an individual liberty desirable for itself on ethical grounds. It is a procedure which of course has never been 'designed' but which we have learnt gradually to improve after we had discovered how it increased the efficiency of men in the groups who had evolved it.

It is a procedure which, as Adam Smith (and apparently before him the ancient Stoics) understood,[12] in all important respects (except that normally it is not pursued solely as a diversion) is wholly analogous to a game, namely a game partly of skill and partly of chance. We shall later describe it as the game of catallaxy. It proceeds, like all games, according to rules guiding the actions of individual participants whose aims, skills, and knowledge are different, with the consequence that the outcome will be unpredictable and that there will regularly be winners and losers. And while, as in a game, we are right in insisting that it be fair and that nobody cheat, it would be nonsensical to demand that the results for the different players be just. They will of necessity be determined partly by skill and partly by luck. Some of the circumstances which make the services of a person more or less valuable to his fellows, or which may make it desirable that he change the direction of his efforts, are not of human design or foreseeable by men.

We shall in the next chapter have to return to the rationale of the discovery procedure which the game of competition in a market in effect constitutes. Here we must content ourselves with emphasizing that the results for the different individuals and groups of a procedure for utilizing more information than any one person or agency can possess, must themselves be unpredictable, and must often be different from the hopes and intentions which determined the direction and intensity of their striving; and that we can make effective use of that dispersed knowledge only if (as Adam Smith was also one of the first to see clearly)[13] we allow the principle of negative feedback to operate, which means that some must suffer unmerited disappointment.

We shall also see later that the importance for the functioning of the market order of particular prices or wages, and therefore of the incomes of the different groups and individuals, is not due chiefly to the effects of the prices on all of those who receive them, but to the effects of the prices on those for whom they act as signals to change the direction of their efforts. Their function is not so much to reward people for what they *have* done as to tell them what in their own as well as in general interest they *ought* to do. We shall then also see that, to hold out a sufficient incentive for those movements which are required to maintain a market order, it will often be necessary that the return of people's efforts do *not* correspond to recognizable merit, but should show that, in spite of the best efforts of which they were capable, and for reasons they could not have known, their efforts were either more or less successful than they had reason to expect. In a spontaneous order the question of whether or not someone has done the 'right' thing cannot always be a matter of merit, but must be determined independently of whether the persons concerned ought or could have known what was required.

The long and the short of it all is that men can be allowed to decide what work to do only if the remuneration they can expect to get for it corresponds to the value their services have to those of their fellows who receive them; and that *these values which their services will have to their fellows will often have no relations to their individual merits or needs.* Reward for merit earned and indication of what a person should do, both in his own and in his fellows' interest, are different things. It is not good intentions or needs but doing what in fact most benefits others, irrespective of motive, which will secure the best reward. Among those who try to climb Mount Everest or to reach the Moon, we also honour not those who made the greatest efforts, but those who got there first.

The general failure to see that in this connection we cannot meaningfully speak of the justice or injustice of the results is partly due to the misleading use of the term 'distribution' which inevitably suggests a personal distributing agent whose will or choice determines the relative position of the different persons or groups.[14] There is of course no such agent, and we use an impersonal process to determine the allocation of benefits precisely because through its operation we can bring about a structure of relative prices and remunerations that will determine a size and composition of the total output which assures that the real equivalent of each individual's share that accident or skill assigns to him will be as large as we know to make it.

It would serve little purpose to enquire here at greater length into the relative importance of skill and luck in actually determining relative incomes. This will clearly differ a great deal between different trades, localities and times, and in particular between highly competitive and less enterprising societies. I am on the whole inclined to believe that within any one trade or profession the correspondence between individual ability and industry is higher than is commonly admitted, but that the relative position of all the members of a particular trade or profession compared with others will more often be affected by circumstances beyond their control and knowledge. (This may also be one reason why what is called 'social' injustice is generally regarded as a graver fault of the existing order than the corresponding misfortunes of individuals.)[15] But the decisive point is not that the price mechanism does on the whole bring it about that rewards are proportioned to skill and effort, but that even where it is clear to us that luck plays a great part, and we have no idea why some are regularly luckier in guessing than others, it is still in the general interest to proceed on the presumption that the past success of some people in picking winners makes it probable that they will also do so in the future, and that it is therefore worthwhile to induce them to continue their attempts.

The Alleged Necessity of a Belief in the Justice of Rewards

It has been argued persuasively that people will tolerate major inequalities of the material positions only if they believe that the different individuals get on the whole what they deserve, that they did in fact support the market order only because (and so long as) they thought that the differences of remuneration corresponded roughly to differences of merit, and that in consequence the maintenance of a free society presupposes the belief that some sort of 'social justice' is being done.[16] The market order, however, does not in fact owe its origin to such beliefs, nor was originally justified in this manner. This order could develop, after its earlier beginnings had decayed during the middle ages and to some extent been destroyed by the restrictions imposed by authority, when a thousand years of vain efforts to discover substantively just prices or wages were abandoned and the late schoolmen recognized them to be empty formulae and taught instead that the prices determined by just conduct of the parties in the market, i.e. the competitive prices arrived at without fraud, monopoly and violence, was all that justice required.[17] It was from this tradition that John Locke and his contemporaries derived the classical liberal conception of justice for which, as has been rightly said, it was only 'the way in which competition was carried on, not its results',[18] that could be just or unjust.

It is unquestionably true that, particularly among those who were very successful in the market order, a belief in a much stronger moral justification of individual success developed, and that, long after the basic principles of such an order had been fully elaborated and approved by catholic moral philosophers, it had in the Anglo-Saxon world received strong support from Calvinist teaching. It certainly is important in the market order (or free enterprise society, misleadingly called 'capitalism') that the individuals believe that their well-being depends primarily on their own efforts and decisions. Indeed, few circumstances will do more to make a person energetic and efficient than the belief that it depends chiefly on him whether he will reach the goals he has set himself. For this reason this belief is often encouraged by education and governing opinion — it seems to me, generally much to the benefit of most of the members of the society in which it prevails, who will owe many important material and moral improvements to persons guided by it. But it leads no doubt also to an exaggerated confidence in the truth of this generalization which to those who regard themselves (and perhaps are) equally able but have failed must appear as a bitter irony and severe provocation.

It is probably a misfortune that, especially in the USA, popular writers like Samuel Smiles and Horatio Alger, and later the sociologist W. G. Sumner, have defended free enterprise on the ground that it regularly rewards the deserving, and it bodes ill for the future of the market order that this seems to have become the only defence of it which is understood by the general public. That it has largely become the basis of the self-esteem of the businessman often gives him an air of self-righteousness which does not make him more popular.

It is therefore a real dilemma to what extent we ought to encourage in the young the belief that when they really try they will succeed, or should rather emphasize that inevitably some unworthy will succeed and some worthy fail — whether we ought to allow the views of those groups to prevail with whom the over-confidence in the appropriate reward of the able and industrious is strong and who in consequence will do much that benefits the rest, and whether without such partly erroneous beliefs the large numbers will tolerate actual differences in rewards which will be based only partly on achievement and partly on mere chance.

There is No 'Value to Society'

The futile medieval search for the just price and just wage, finally abandoned when it was recognized that only that 'natural' price could be regarded as just which would be arrived at in a competitive market where it would be determined not by any human laws or decrees but would depend on so many circumstances that it could be known beforehand only by God,[19] was not the end of the search for that philosophers' stone. It was revived in modern times, not only by the general demand for 'social justice', but also by the long and equally abortive efforts to discover criteria of justice in connection with the procedures for reconciliation or arbitration in wage disputes. Nearly a century of endeavours by public spirited men and women in many parts of the world to discover principles by which just wage rates could be determined have, as more and more of them acknowledge, produced not a single rule which would do this.[20] It is somewhat surprising in view of this when we find an experienced arbitrator like Lady Wootton, after admitting that arbitrators are 'engaged in the impossible task of attempting to do justice in an ethical vacuum', because 'nobody knows in this context what justice is', drawing from it the conclusion that the criteria should be determined by legislation, and explicitly demand a political determination of all wages and incomes.[21] One can hardly carry any further the illusion that Parliament can determine what is just, and I don't suppose the writer would really wish to defend the atrocious principle implied that all rewards should be determined by political power.

Another source of the conception that the categories of just and unjust can be meaningfully applied to the remunerations determined by the market is the idea that the different services have a determined and ascertainable 'value to society', and that the actual remuneration frequently differs from the value. But though the conception of a 'value to society' is sometimes carelessly used even by economists, there is strictly no such thing and the expression implies the same sort of anthropomorphism or personification of society as the term 'social justice'. Services can have value only to particular people (or an organization), and any particular service will have very different values for different members of the same society. To regard them differently is to treat society not as a spontaneous order of free men but as an organization whose members are all made to serve a single hierarchy of ends. This would necessarily be a totalitarian system in which personal freedom would be absent.

Although it is tempting to speak of a 'value to society' instead of a man's value to his fellows, it is in fact highly misleading if we say, e.g., that a man who supplies matches to millions and thereby earns $200,000 a year is worth more 'to society' than a man who supplies great wisdom or exquisite pleasure to a few thousand and thereby earns $20,000 a year. Even the performance of a Beethoven sonata, a painting by Leonardo or a play by Shakespeare have no 'value to society' but a value only to those who know and appreciate them. And it has little meaning to assert that a boxer or a crooner is worth more to society than a violin virtuoso or a ballet dancer if the former renders services to millions and the latter to a much smaller group. The point is not that the true values are different, but that the values attached to the different services by different groups of people are incommensurable; all that these expressions mean is merely that one in fact receives a larger aggregate sum from a larger number of people than the other.[22]

Incomes earned in the market by different persons will normally not correspond to the relative values of their services to any one person. Although, in so far as any one of a given group of different commodities is consumed by any one person, he or she will buy so much of each that the relative values to them of the last units bought will correspond to their relative prices, many pairs of commodities will never be consumed by the same person: the relative price of articles consumed only by men and of articles consumed only by women will not correspond to the relative values of these articles to anybody.

The remunerations which the individuals and groups receive in the market are thus determined by what these services are worth to those who receive them (or, strictly speaking, to the last pressing demand for them which can still be satisfied by the available supply) and not by some fictitious 'value to society'.

Another source of the complaint about the alleged injustice of this principle of remuneration is that the remuneration thus determined will often be much higher than would be necessary to induce the recipient to render those services. This is perfectly true but necessary if all who render the same service are to receive the same remuneration, if the kind of service in question is to be increased so long as the price still exceeds costs, and if anyone who wishes to buy or sell it at the current price is to be able to do so. The consequence must be that all but the marginal sellers make a gain in excess of what was necessary to induce them to render the services in question — just as all but the marginal buyers will get what they buy for less than they were prepared to pay. The remuneration of the market will therefore hardly ever seem just in the sense in which somebody might endeavour justly to compensate others for the efforts and sacrifice incurred for his benefit.

The consideration of the different attitudes which different groups will take to the remuneration of different services incidentally also shows that the large numbers by no means grudge all the incomes higher than theirs, but generally only those earned by activities the functions of which they do not understand or which they even regard as harmful. I have never known ordinary people grudge the very high earnings of the boxer or torero, the football idol or the cinema star or the jazz king — they seem often even to revel vicariously in the display of extreme luxury and waste of such figures compared with which those of industrial magnates or financial tycoons pale. It is where most people do not comprehend the usefulness of an activity, and frequently because they erroneously regard it as harmful (the 'speculator' — often combined with the belief that only dishonest activities can bring so much money), and especially where the large earnings are used to accumulate a fortune (again out of the erroneous belief that it would be desirable that it should be spent rather than invested) that the outcry about the injustice of it arises. Yet the complex structure of the modern Great Society would clearly not work if the remunerations of all the different activities were determined by the opinion which the majority holds of their value — or indeed if they were dependent on any one person's understanding or knowledge of the importance of all the different activities required for the functioning of the system.

The main point is not that the masses have in most instances no idea of the values which a man's activities have to his fellows, and that it is necessarily their prejudices which would determine the use of the government's power. It is that nobody knows except in so far as the market tells him. It is true enough that our esteem of particular activities often differs from the value given to them by the market; and we express this feeling by an outcry about the injustice of it. But when we ask what ought to be the relative remunerations of a nurse and a butcher, of a coal miner and a judge at a high court, of the deep sea diver or the cleaner of sewers, of the organizer of a new industry and a jockey, of the inspector of taxes and the inventor of a life-saving drug, of the jet pilot or the professor of mathematics, the appeal to 'social justice' does not give us the slightest help in deciding — and if we use it it is no more than an insinuation that the others ought to agree with our view without giving any reason for it.

It might be objected that, although we cannot give the term 'social justice' a precise meaning, this need not be a fatal objection because the position may be similar to that which I have earlier contended exists with regard to justice proper: we might not know what is 'socially just' yet know quite well what is 'socially unjust'; and by persistently eliminating 'social injustice' whenever we encounter it, gradually approach 'social justice'. This, however, does not provide a way out of the basic difficulty. There can be no test by which we can discover what is 'socially unjust' because there is no subject by which such an injustice can be committed, and there are no rules of individual conduct the observance of which in the market order would secure to the individuals and groups the position which as such (as distinguished from the procedure by which it is determined) would appear just to us.[23] It does not belong to the category of error but to that of nonsense, like the term 'a moral stone'.

The Meaning of 'Social'

One might hope to get some help in the search for the meaning of 'social justice' by examining the meaning of the attribute 'social'; but the attempt to do so soon leads into a quagmire of confusion nearly as bad as that which surrounds 'social justice' itself.[24] Originally 'social' had of course a clear meaning (analogous to formations like 'national', 'tribal', or 'organizational'), namely that of pertaining to, or characteristic of the structure and operations of society. In this sense justice clearly is a social phenomenon and the addition of social' to the noun a pleonasm[25] such as if we spoke of 'social language' — though in occasional early uses it might have been intended to distinguish the generally prevailing views of justice from that held by particular persons or groups.

But 'social justice' as used today is not 'social' in the sense of 'social norms', i.e. something which has developed as a practice of individual action in the course of social evolution, not a product of society or of a social process, but a conception to be imposed upon society. It was the reference of 'social' to the whole of society, or to the interests of all its members, which led to its gradually acquiring a predominant meaning of moral approbation. When it came into general use during the third quarter of the last century it was meant to convey an appeal to the still ruling classes to concern themselves more with the welfare of the much more numerous poor whose interests had not received adequate consideration.[26] The 'social question' was posed as an appeal to the conscience of the upper classes to recognize their responsibility for the welfare of the neglected sections of society whose voices had till then carried little weight in the councils of government. 'Social policy' (or *Socialpolitik* in the language of the country then leading in the movement) became the order of the day, the chief concern of all progressive and good people, and 'social' came increasingly to displace such terms as 'ethical' or simply 'good'.

But from such an appeal to the conscience of the public to concern themselves with the unfortunate ones and recognize them as members of the same society, the conception gradually came to mean that 'society' ought to hold itself responsible for the particular material position of all its members, and for assuring that each received what was 'due' to him. It implied that the processes of society should be deliberately directed to particular results and, by personifying society, represented it as a subject endowed with a conscious mind, capable of being guided in its operation by moral principles.[27] 'Social' became more and more the description of the pre-eminent virtue, the attribute in which the good man excelled and the ideal by which communal action was to be guided.

But while this development indefinitely extended the field of application of the term 'social', it did not give it the required new meaning. It even so much deprived it of its original descriptive meaning that American sociologists have found it necessary to coin the new term 'societal' in its place. Indeed, it has produced a situation in which 'social' can be used to describe almost any action as publicly desirable and has at the same time the effect of depriving any terms with which it is combined of clear meaning. Not only 'social justice' but also 'social democracy', 'social market economy'[28] or the 'social state of law' (or rule of law — in German *sozialer Rechtsstaat*) are expressions which, though justice, democracy, the market economy or the *Rechtsstaat* have by themselves perfectly good meanings, the addition of the adjective 'social' makes them capable of meaning almost anything one likes. The word has indeed become one of the chief sources of confusion of political discourse and can probably no longer be reclaimed for a useful purpose.

There is apparently no end to the violence that will be done to language to further some ideal and the example of 'social justice' has recently given rise to the expression 'global justice'! Its negative, 'global injustice', was defined by an ecumenical gathering of American religious leaders as 'characterized by a dimension of sin in the economic, political, social, sexual, and class structures and systems of global society'![29] It would seem as if the conviction that one is arguing in a good cause produced more sloppy thinking and even intellectual dishonesty than perhaps any other cause.

'Social Justice' and Equality

The most common attempts to give meaning to the concept of 'social justice' resort to egalitarian considerations and argue that every departure from equality of material benefits enjoyed has to be justified by some recognizable common interest which these differences serve.[30] This is based on a specious analogy with the situation in which some human agency has to distribute rewards, in which case indeed justice would require that these rewards be determined in accordance with some recognizable rule of general applicability. But earnings in a market system, though people tend to regard them as rewards, do not serve such a function. Their rationale (if one may use this term for a role which was not designed but developed because it assisted human endeavour without people understanding how), is rather to indicate to people what they ought to do if the order is to be maintained on which they all rely. The prices which must be paid in a market economy for different kinds of labour and other factors of production if individual efforts are to match, although they will be affected by effort, diligence, skill, need, etc., cannot conform to any one of these magnitudes; and considerations of justice just do not make sense[31] with respect to the determination of a magnitude which does not depend on anyone's will or desire, but on circumstances which nobody knows in their totality.

The contention that all differences in earnings must be justified by some corresponding difference in deserts is one which would certainly not have been thought to be obvious in a community of farmers or merchants or artisans, that is, in a society in which success or failure were clearly seen to depend only in part on skill and industry, and in part on pure accident which might hit anyone — although even in such societies individuals were known to complain to God or fortune about the injustice of their fate. But, though people resent that their remuneration should in part depend on pure accident, that is in fact precisely what it must if the market order is to adjust itself promptly to the unavoidable and unforeseen changes in circumstances, and the individual is to be allowed to decide what to do. The now prevalent attitude could arise only in a society in which large numbers worked as members of organizations in which they were remunerated at stipulated rates for time worked. Such communities will not ascribe the different fortunes of its members to the operation of an impersonal mechanism which serves to guide the directions of efforts, but to some human power that ought to allocate shares according to merit.

The postulate of material equality would be a natural starting point only if it were a necessary circumstance that the shares of the different individuals or groups were in such a manner determined by deliberate human decision. In a society in which this were an unquestioned fact, justice would indeed demand that the allocation of the means for the satisfaction of human needs were effected according to some uniform principle such as merit or need (or some combination of these), and that, where the principle adopted did not justify a difference, the shares of the different individuals should be equal. The prevalent demand for material equality is probably often based on the belief that the existing inequalities are the effect of somebody's decision — a belief which would be wholly mistaken in a genuine market order and has still only very limited validity in the highly interventionist 'mixed' economy existing in most countries today. This now prevalent form of economic order has in fact attained its character largely as a result of governmental measures aiming at what was thought to be required by 'social justice'.

When the choice, however, is between a genuine market order, which does not and cannot achieve a distribution corresponding to any standard of material justice, and a system in which government uses its powers to put some such standard into effect, the question is not whether government ought to exercise, justly or unjustly, powers it must exercise in any case, but whether government should possess and exercise additional powers which can be used to determine the shares of the different members of society. The demand for 'social justice', in other words, does not merely require government to observe some principle of action according to uniform rules in those actions which it must perform in any case, but demands that it undertake additional activities, and thereby assume new responsibilities — tasks which are not necessary for maintaining law and order and providing for certain collective needs which the market could not satisfy.

The great problem is whether this new demand for equality does not conflict with the equality of the rules of conduct which government must enforce on all in a free society. There is, of course, a great difference between government treating all citizens according to the same rules in all the activities it undertakes for other purposes, and government doing what is required in order to place the different citizens in equal (or less unequal) material positions. Indeed, there may arise a sharp conflict between these two aims. Since people will differ in many attributes which government cannot alter, to secure for them the same material position would require that government treat them very differently. Indeed, to assure the same material position to people who differ greatly in strength, intelligence, skill, knowledge and perseverance as well as in their physical and social environment, government would clearly have to treat them very differently to compensate for those disadvantages and deficiencies it could not directly alter. Strict equality of those benefits which government could provide for all, on the other hand, would clearly lead to inequality of the material positions.

This, however, is not the only and not even the chief reason why a government aiming to secure for its citizens equal material positions (or any determined pattern of material welfare) would have to treat them very unequally. It would have to do so because under such a system it would have to undertake to tell people what to do. Once the rewards the individual can expect are no longer an appropriate indication of how to direct their efforts to where they are most needed, because these rewards correspond not to the value which their services have for their fellows, but to the moral merit or desert the persons are deemed to have earned, they lose the guiding function they have in the market order and would have to be replaced by the commands of the directing authority. A central planning office would, however, have to decide on the tasks to be allotted to the different groups or individuals wholly on grounds of expediency or efficiency and, in order to achieve its ends, would have to impose upon them very different duties and burdens. The individuals might be treated according to uniform rules so far as their rewards were concerned, but certainly not with respect to the different kinds of work they would have to be made to do. In assigning people to their different tasks, the central planning authority would have to be guided by considerations of efficiency and expediency and not by principles of justice or equality. No less than in the market order would the individuals in the common interest have to submit to great inequality—only these inequalities would be determined not by the interaction of individual skills in an impersonal process, but by the uncontradictable decision of authority.

As is becoming clear in ever increasing fields of welfare policy, an authority instructed to achieve particular results for the individuals must be given essentially arbitrary powers to make the individuals do what seems necessary to achieve the required result. Full equality for most cannot but mean the equal submission of the great masses under the command of some élite who manages their affairs. While an equality of rights under a limited government is possible and an essential condition of individual freedom, a claim for equality of material position can be met only by a government with totalitarian powers.[32]

We are of course not wrong when we perceive that the effects on the different individuals and groups of the economic processes of a free society are not distributed according to some recognizable principle of justice. Where we go wrong is in concluding from this that they are unjust and that somebody is responsible and to be blamed for this. In a free society in which the position of the different individuals and groups is not the result of anybody's design—or could within such a society not be altered in accordance with a principle of general applicability—the differences in rewards cannot meaningfully be described as just or unjust. There are, no doubt, many kinds of individual actions which are aimed at affecting particular remunerations and which might be regarded as unjust. But there are no principles of individual conduct which would produce a pattern of distribution which as such could be called just, and therefore also no possibility for the individual to know what he would have to do to secure a just remuneration of his fellows.

Our whole system of morals is a system of rules of individual conduct, and in a Great Society no conduct guided by such rules, or by decisions of the individuals guided by such rules, could produce for the individuals results which would appear to us as just in the sense in which we regard designed rewards as just or unjust: simply because in such a society nobody has the power or the knowledge which would enable him to ensure that those affected by his actions will get what he thinks right for them to get. Nor could anyone who is assured remuneration according to some principle which is accepted as constituting 'social justice' be allowed to decide what he is to do: remuneration indicating how urgent it was that a certain work should be done could not be just in this sense, because the need for work of a particular kind would often depend on unforeseeable accidents and certainly not on the good intentions or efforts of those able to perform it. And an authority that fixed remunerations with the intention of thereby reducing the kind and number of people thought necessary in each occupation could not make these remunerations 'just', i.e. proportionate to desert, or need, or the merits of any other claim of the persons concerned, but would have to offer what was necessary to attract or retain the number of people wanted in each kind of activity.

'Equality of Opportunity'

It is of course not to be denied that in the existing market order not only the results but also the initial chances of different individuals are often very different; they are affected by circumstances of their physical and social environment which are beyond their control but in many particular respects might be altered by some governmental action. The demand for equality of opportunity or equal starting conditions (*Startgerechtigkeit*) appeals to, and has been supported by, many who in general favour the free market order. So far as this refers to such facilities and opportunities as are of necessity affected by governmental decisions (such as appointments to public office and the like), the demand was indeed one of the central points of classical liberalism, usually expressed by the French phrase 'la carrière ouverte aux talents'. There is also much to be said in favour of the government providing on an equal basis the means for the schooling of minors who are not yet fully responsible citizens, even though there are grave doubts whether we ought to allow government to administer them.

But all this would still be very far from creating real equality of opportunity, even for persons possessing the same abilities. To achieve this government would have to control the whole physical and human environment of all persons, and have to endeavour to provide at least equivalent chances for each; and the more government succeeded in these endeavours, the stronger would become the legitimate demand that, on the same principle, any still remaining handicaps must be removed — or compensated for by putting extra burden on the still relatively favoured. This would have to go on until government literally controlled every circumstance which could affect any person's well-being. Attractive as the phrase of equality of opportunity at first sounds, once the idea is extended beyond the facilities which for other reasons have to be provided by government, it becomes a wholly illusory ideal, and any attempt concretely to realize it apt to produce a nightmare.

'Social Justice' and Freedom Under the Law

The idea that men ought to be rewarded in accordance with the assessed merits or deserts of their services 'to society' presupposes an authority which not only distributes these rewards but also assigns to the individuals the tasks for the performance of which they will be rewarded. In other words, if 'social justice' is to be brought about, the individuals must be required to obey not merely general rules but specific demands directed to them only. The type of social order in which the individuals are directed to serve a single system of ends is the organization and not the spontaneous order of the market, that is, not a system in which the individual is free because bound only by general rules of just conduct, but a system in which all are subject to specific directions by authority.

It appears sometimes to be imagined that a mere alteration of the rules of individual conduct could bring about the realization of 'social justice'. But there can be no set of such rules, no principles by which the individuals could so govern their conduct that in a Great Society the joint effect of their activities would be a distribution of benefits which could be described as materially just, or any other specific and intended allocation of advantages and disadvantages among particular people or groups. In order to achieve *any* particular pattern of distribution through the market process, each producer would have to know, not only whom his efforts will benefit (or harm), but also how well off all the other people (actually or potentially) affected by his activities will be as the result of the services they are receiving from other members of the society. As we have seen earlier, appropriate rules of conduct can determine only the formal character of the order of activities that will form itself, but not the specific advantages particular groups or individuals will derive from it.

This rather obvious fact still needs to be stressed since even eminent jurists have contended that the substitution of 'social' or distributive for individual or commutative justice need not destroy the freedom under the law of the individual. Thus the distinguished German legal philosopher Gustav Radbruch explicitly maintained that 'the socialist community would also be a *Rechtsstaat* [i.e., the Rule of Law would prevail there], although a *Rechtsstaat* governed not by commutative but by distributive justice.'[33] And of France it is reported that 'it has been suggested that some highly placed administrators should be given the permanent task of "pronouncing" on the distribution of national income, as judges pronounce on legal matters.'[34] Such beliefs, however, overlook the fact that no specific pattern of distribution can be achieved by making the individuals obey rules of conduct, but that the achievement of such particular pre-determined results requires deliberate co-ordination of all the different activities in accordance with the concrete circumstances of time and place. It precludes, in other words, that the several individuals act on the basis of their own knowledge and in the service of their own ends, which is the essence of freedom, but requires that they be made to act in the manner which according to the knowledge of the directing authority is required for the realization of the ends chosen by that authority.

The distributive justice at which socialism aims is thus irreconcilable with the rule of law, and with that freedom under the law which the rule of law is intended to secure. The rules of distributive justice cannot be rules for the conduct towards equals, but must be rules for the conduct of superiors towards their subordinates. Yet though some socialists have long ago themselves drawn the inevitable conclusion that 'the fundamental principles of formal law by which every case must be judged according to general rational principles . . . obtains only for the competitive phase of capitalism,'[35] and the communists, so long as they took socialism seriously, had even proclaimed that 'communism means not the victory of socialist law, but the victory of socialism over any law, since with the abolition of classes with antagonistic interests, law will disappear altogether',[36] when, more than thirty years ago, the present author made this the central point of a discussion of the political effects of socialist economic policies,[37] it evoked great indignation and violent protests. But the crucial point is implied even in Radbruch's own emphasis on the fact that the transition from commutative to distributive justice means a progressive displacement of private by public law,[38] since public law consists not of rules of conduct for private citizens but of rules of organization for public officials. It is, as Radbruch himself stresses, a law that subordinates the citizens to authority.[39] Only if one understands by law not the general rules of just conduct only but any command issued by authority (or any authorization of such commands by a legislature), can the measures aimed at distributive justice be represented as compatible with the rule of law. But this concept is thereby made to mean mere legality and ceases to offer the protection of individual freedom which it was originally intended to serve.

There is no reason why in a free society government should not assure to all protection against severe deprivation in the form of an assured minimum income, or a floor below which nobody need to descend. To enter into such an insurance against extreme misfortune may well be in the interest of all; or it may be felt to be a clear moral duty of all to assist, within the organized community, those who cannot help themselves. So long as such a uniform minimum income is provided outside the market to all those who, for any reason, are unable to earn in the market an adequate maintenance, this need not lead to a restriction of freedom, or conflict with the Rule of Law. The problems with which we are here concerned arise only when the remuneration for services rendered is determined by authority, and the impersonal mechanism of the market which guides the direction of individual efforts is thus suspended.

Perhaps the acutest sense of grievance about injustice inflicted on one, not by particular persons but by the 'system', is that about being deprived of opportunities for developing one's abilities which others enjoy. For this any difference of environment, social or physical, may be responsible, and at least some of them may be unavoidable. The most important of these is clearly inseparable from the institution of the family. This not only satisfies a strong psychological need but in general serves as an instrument for the transmission of important cultural values. There can be no doubt that those who are either wholly deprived of this benefit, or grew up in unfavourable conditions, are gravely handicapped; and few will question that it would be desirable that some public institution so far as possible should assist such unfortunate children when relatives and neighbours fail. Yet few will seriously believe (although Plato did) that we can fully make up for such a deficiency, and I trust even fewer that, because this benefit cannot be assured to all, it should, in the interest of equality, be taken from those who now enjoy it. Nor does it seem to me that even material equality could compensate for those differences in the capacity of enjoyment and of experiencing a lively interest in the cultural surroundings which a suitable upbringing confers.

There are of course many other irremediable inequalities which must seem as unreasonable as economic inequalities but which are less resented than the latter only because they do not appear to be man-made or the consequence of institutions which could be altered.

The Spatial Range of 'Social Justice'

There can be little doubt that the moral feelings which express themselves in the demand for 'social justice' derive from an attitude which in more primitive conditions the individual developed towards the fellow members of the small group to which he belonged. Towards the personally known member of one's own group it may well have been a recognized duty to assist him and to adjust one's actions to his needs. This is made possible by the knowledge of his person and his circumstances. The situation is wholly different in the Great or Open Society. Here the products and services of each benefit mostly persons he does not know. The greater productivity of such a society rests on a division of labour extending far beyond the range any one person can survey. This extension of the process of exchange beyond relatively small groups, and including large numbers of persons not known to each other, has been made possible by conceding to the stranger and even the foreigner the same protection of rules of just conduct which apply to the relations to the known members of one's own small group.

This application of the same rules of just conduct to the relations to all other men is rightly regarded as one of the great achievements of a liberal society. What is usually not understood is that this extension of the same rules to the relations to all other men (beyond the most intimate group such as the family and personal friends) requires an attenuation at least of some of the rules which are enforced in the relations to other members of the smaller group. If the legal duties towards strangers or foreigners are to be the same as those towards the neighbours or inhabitants of the same village or town, the latter duties will have to be reduced to such as can also be applied to the stranger. No doubt men will always wish to belong also to smaller groups and be willing voluntarily to assume greater obligations towards self-chosen friends or companions. But such moral obligations towards some can never become enforced duties in a system of freedom under the law, because in such a system the selection of those towards whom a man wishes to assume special moral obligations must be left to him and cannot be determined by law. A system of rules intended for an Open Society and, at least in principle, meant to be applicable to all others, must have a somewhat smaller content than one to be applied in a small group.

Especially a common agreement on what is the due status or material position of the different members is likely to develop only in the relatively small group in which the members will be familiar with the character and importance of each other's activities. In such small communities the opinion about appropriate status will also still be associated with a feeling about what one self owes to the other, and not be merely a demand that somebody provide the appropriate reward. Demands for the realization of 'social justice' are usually as a matter of course, though often only tacitly, addressed to national governments as the agencies which possess the necessary powers. But it is doubtful whether in any but the smallest countries standards can be applied nationally which are derived from the condition of the particular locality with which the individual is familiar, and fairly certain that few men would be willing to concede to foreigners the same right to a particular income that they tend to recognize in their fellow citizens.

It is true that in recent years concern about the suffering of large numbers in the poor countries has induced the electorates of the wealthier nations to approve substantial material aid to the former; but it can hardly be said that in this considerations of justice played a significant role. It is indeed doubtful whether any substantial help would have been rendered if competing power groups had not striven to draw as many as possible of the developing countries into their orbit. And it deserves notice that the modern technology which has made such assistance possible could develop only because some countries were able to build up great wealth while most of the world saw little change.

Yet the chief point is that, if we look beyond the limits of our national states, and certainly if we go beyond the limits of what we regard as our civilization, we no longer even deceive ourselves that we know what would be 'socially just', and that those very groups within the existing states which are loudest in their demands for 'social justice', such as the trade unions, are regularly the first to reject such claims raised on behalf of foreigners. Applied to the international sphere, the complete lack of a recognized standard of 'social justice', or of any known principles on which such a standard could be based, becomes at once obvious; while on a national scale most people still think that what on the level of the face-to-face society is to them a familiar idea must also have some validity for national politics or the use of the powers of government. In fact, it becomes on this level a humbug — the effectiveness of which with well-meaning people the agents of organized interests have learnt successfully to exploit.

There is in this respect a fundamental difference between what is possible in the small group and in the Great Society. In the small group the individual can know the effects of his actions on his several fellows, and the rules may effectively forbid him to harm them in any manner and even require him to assist them in specific ways. In the Great Society many of the effects of a person's actions on various fellows must be unknown to him. It can, therefore, not be the specific effects in the particular case, but only rules which define kinds of actions as prohibited or required, which must serve as guides to the individual. In particular, he will often not know who the individual people will be who will benefit by what he does, and therefore not know whether he is satisfying a great need or adding to abundance. He cannot aim at just results if he does not know who will be affected.

Indeed the transition from the small group to the Great or Open Society — and the treatment of every other person as a human being rather than as either a known friend or an enemy — requires a reduction of the range of duties we owe to all others.

If a person's legal duties are to be the same towards all, including the stranger and even the foreigner (and greater only where he has voluntarily entered into obligations, or is connected by physical ties as between parents and children), the legally enforceable duties to neighbour and friend must not be more than those towards the stranger. That is, all those duties which are based on personal acquaintance and familiarity with individual circumstances must cease to be enforceable. The extension of the obligation to obey certain rules of just conduct to wider circles and ultimately to all men must thus lead to an attenuation of the obligation towards fellow members of the same small group. Our inherited or perhaps in part even innate moral emotions are in part inapplicable to Open Society (which is an abstract society), and the kind of 'moral socialism' that is possible in the small group and often satisfies a deeply ingrained instinct may well be impossible in the Great Society. Some altruistic conduct aimed at the benefit of some known friend that in the small group might be highly desirable, need not be so in the Open Society, and may there even be harmful (as e.g., the requirement that members of the same trade refrain from competing with each other).[40]

It may at first seem paradoxical that the advance of morals should lead to a reduction of specific obligations towards others: yet whoever believes that the principle of equal treatment of all men, which is probably the only chance for peace, is more important than special help to visible suffering, must wish it. It admittedly means that we make our rational insight dominate over our inherited instincts. But the great moral adventure on which modern man has embarked when he launched into the Open Society is threatened when he is required to apply to all his fellowmen rules which are appropriate only to the fellow members of a tribal group.

Claims for Compensation for Distasteful Jobs

The reader will probably expect me now to examine in greater detail the particular claims usually justified by the appeal to 'social justice'. But this, as bitter experience has taught me, would be not only an endless but also a bootless task. After what has been said already, it should be obvious that there are no practicable standards of merit, deserts, or needs, on which in a market order the distribution of material benefits could be based, and still less any principle by which these different claims could be reconciled. I shall therefore confine myself to considering two arguments in which the appeal to 'social justice' is very commonly used. The first case is usually quoted in theoretical argument to illustrate the injustice of the distribution by the market process, though little is done about it in practice, while the second is probably the most frequent type of situation in which the appeal to social justice leads to government action.

The circumstance which is usually pointed out to demonstrate the injustice of the existing market order is that the most unpleasant jobs are commonly also the worst paid. In a just society, it is contended, those who have to dig coal underground or to clean chimneys or sewers, or who perform other unclean or menial tasks, should be remunerated more highly than those whose work is pleasurable.

It is of course true that it would be unjust if persons, although equally able as others to perform other tasks, were without special compensation assigned by a superior to such distasteful duties. If, e.g., in such an organization as an army, two men of equal capacity were made to perform different tasks, one of which was attractive and the other very unpleasant, justice would clearly require that the one who had regularly to perform the unpleasant duty should in some way be specially compensated for it.

The situation is entirely different, however, where people earn their living by selling their services to whoever pays best for them. Here the sacrifice brought by a particular person in rendering the service is wholly irrelevant and all that counts is the (marginal) value the services have to those to whom they are rendered. The reason for this is not only that the sacrifices different people bring in rendering the same kind of service will often be very different, or that it will not be possible to take account of the reason why some will be capable of rendering only less valuable services than others. But those whose aptitudes, and therefore also remunerations, will be small in the more attractive occupations will often find that they can earn more than they could otherwise by undertaking unpleasant tasks that are scorned by their more fortunate fellows. The very fact that the more unpleasant occupations will be avoided by those who can render services that are valued more highly by the buyers, will open to those whose skills are little valued opportunities to earn more than they otherwise could.

That those who have to offer to their fellows little that is valuable may have to incur more pain and effort to earn even a pittance than others who perhaps actually enjoy rendering services for which they are well paid, is a necessary concomitant of any system in which remuneration is based on the values the services have to the user and not on an assessment of merit earned. It must therefore prevail in any social order in which the individual is free to choose whatever occupation he can find and is not assigned to one by authority.

The only assumption on which it could be represented as just that the miner working underground, or the scavenger, or slaughterhouse workers, should be paid more highly than those engaged in more pleasant occupations, would thus be that this was necessary to induce a sufficient number of persons to perform these tasks, or that they are by some human agency deliberately assigned to these tasks. But while in a market order it may be a misfortune to have been born and bred in a village where for most the only chance of making a living is fishing (or for the women the cleaning of fish), it does not make sense to describe this as unjust. Who is supposed to have been unjust? — especially when it is considered that, if these local opportunities had not existed, the people in question would probably never have been born at all, as most of the population of such a village will probably owe its existence to the opportunities which enabled their ancestors to produce and rear children.

The Resentment of the Loss of Accustomed Positions

The appeal to 'social justice' which in practice has probably had the greatest influence is not one which has been much considered in literary discussion. The considerations of a supposed 'social injustice' which have led to the most far-reaching interference with the functioning of the market order are based on the idea that people are to be protected against an unmerited descent from the material position to which they have become accustomed. No other consideration of 'social justice' has probably exercised as widespread an influence as the 'strong and almost universal belief that it is unjust to disappoint legitimate expectations of wealth. When differences of opinion arise, it is always on the question of what expectations are legitimate'. It is believed, as the same author says, 'that it is legitimate even for the largest classes to expect that no very great and sudden changes will be made to their detriment'.[41]

The opinion that long established positions create a just expectation that they will continue serves often as a substitute for more substantial criteria of 'social justice'. Where expectations are disappointed, and in consequence the rewards of effort often disproportionate to the sacrifice incurred, this will be regarded as an injustice without any attempt to show that those affected had a claim in justice to the particular income which they expected. At least when a large group of people find their income reduced as a result of circumstances which they could not have altered or foreseen, this is commonly regarded as unjust.

The frequent recurrence of such undeserved strokes of misfortune affecting some group is, however, an inseparable part of the steering mechanism of the market: it is the manner in which the cybernetic principle of negative feedback operates to maintain the order of the market. It is only through such changes which indicate that some activities ought to be reduced, that the efforts of all can be continuously adjusted to a greater variety of facts than can be known to any one person or agency, and that that utilization of dispersed knowledge is achieved on which the well-being of the Great Society rests. We cannot rely on a system in which the individuals are induced to respond to events of which they do not and cannot know without changes of the values of the services of different groups occurring which are wholly unrelated to the merits of their members. It is a necessary part of that process of constant adaptation to changing circumstances on which the mere maintenance of the existing level of wealth depends that some people should have to discover by bitter experience that they have misdirected their efforts and are forced to look elsewhere for a remunerative occupation. And the same applies to the resentment of the corresponding undeserved gains that will accrue to others for whom things have turned out better than they had reason to expect.

The sense of injury which people feel when an accustomed income is reduced or altogether lost is largely the result of a belief that they have morally deserved that income and that, therefore, so long as they work as industriously and honestly as they did before, they are in justice entitled to the continuance of that income. But the idea that we have morally deserved what we have honestly earned in the past is largely an illusion. What is true is only that it would have been unjust if anybody had taken from us what we have in fact acquired while observing the rules of the game.

It is precisely because in the cosmos of the market we all constantly receive benefits which we have not deserved in any moral sense that we are under an obligation also to accept equally undeserved diminutions of our incomes. Our only moral title to what the market gives us we have earned by submitting to those rules which makes the formation of the market order possible. These rules imply that nobody is under an obligation to supply us with a particular income unless he has specifically contracted to do so. If we were all to be consistently deprived, as the socialists propose to do, of all 'unearned benefits' which the market confers upon us, we would have to be deprived of most of the benefits of civilization.

It is clearly meaningless to reply, as is often done, that, since we owe these benefits to 'society', 'society' should also be entitled to allocate these benefits to those who in its opinion deserve them. Society, once more, is not an acting person but an orderly structure of actions resulting from the observation of certain abstract rules by its members. We all owe the benefits we receive from the operation of this structure not to anyone's intention to confer them on us, but to the members of society generally obeying certain rules in the pursuit of their interests, rules which include the rule that nobody is to coerce others in order to secure for himself (or for third persons) a particular income. This imposes upon us the obligation to abide by the results of the market also when it turns against us.

The chance which any individual in our society has of earning an income approximating that which he has now is the consequence of most individuals obeying the rules which secure the formation of that order. And though this order provides for most good prospects for the successful employment of their skills, this success must remain dependent also on what from the point of view of the individual must appear as mere luck. The magnitude of the chances open to him are not of his making but the result of others submitting to the same rules of the game. To ask for protection against being displaced from a position one has long enjoyed, by others who are now favoured by new circumstances, means to deny to them the chances to which one's own present position is due.

Any protection of an accustomed position is thus necessarily a privilege which cannot be granted to all and which, if it had always been recognized, would have prevented those who now claim it from ever reaching the position for which they now demand protection. There can, in particular, be no right to share equally in a general increase of incomes if this increase (or perhaps even their maintenance at the existing level) is dependent on the continuous adjustment of the whole structure of activities to new and unforeseen circumstances that will alter and often reduce the contributions some groups can make to the needs of their fellows. There can thus be in justice no such claims as, e.g., those of the American farmer for 'parity', or of any other group to the preservation of their relative or absolute position.

The satisfaction of such claims by particular groups would thus not be just but eminently unjust, because it would involve the denial to some of the chances to which those who make this claim owe their position. For this reason it has always been conceded only to some powerfully organized groups who were in the position to enforce their demands. Much of what is today done in the name of 'social justice' is thus not only unjust but also highly unsocial in the true sense of the word: it amounts simply to the protection of entrenched interests. Though it has come to be regarded as a 'social problem' when sufficiently large numbers clamour for protection of their accustomed position, it becomes a serious problem chiefly because, camouflaged as a demand for 'social justice', it can engage the sympathy of the public. We shall see in volume 3 why, under the existing type of democratic institutions, it is in practice inevitable that legislatures with unlimited powers yield to such demands when made by sufficiently large groups. This does not alter the fact that to represent such measures as satisfying 'social justice' is little more than a pretext for making the interest of the particular groups prevail over the general interest of all. Though it is now usual to regard every claim of an organized group as a 'social problem', it would be more correct to say that, though the long run interests of the several individuals mostly agree with the general interest, the interests of the organized groups almost invariably are in conflict with it. Yet it is the latter which are commonly represented as 'social'.

Conclusions

The basic contention of this chapter, namely that in a society of free men whose members are allowed to use their own knowledge for their own purposes the term 'social justice' is wholly devoid of meaning or content, is one which by its very nature cannot be *proved*. A negative assertion never can. One may demonstrate for any number of particular instances that the appeal to 'social justice' in no way assists the choices we have to make. But the contention that in a society of free men the term has no meaning whatever can only be issued as a challenge which will make it necessary for others to reflect on the meaning of the words they use, and as an appeal not to use phrases the meaning of which they do not know.

So long as one assumes that a phrase so widely used must have some recognizable meaning one may endeavour to prove that attempts to enforce it in a society of free individuals must make that society unworkable. But such efforts become redundant once it is recognized that such a society lacks the fundamental precondition for the application of the concept of justice to the manner in which material benefits are shared among its members, namely that this is determined by a human will — or that the determination of rewards by human will could produce a viable market order. One does not have to prove that something is impracticable which cannot exist.

What I hope to have made clear is that the phrase 'social justice' is not, as most people probably feel, an innocent expression of good will towards the less fortunate, but that it has become a dishonest insinuation that one ought to agree to a demand of some special interest which can give no real reason for it. If political discussion is to become honest it is necessary that people should recognize that the term is intellectually disreputable, the mark of demagogy or cheap journalism which responsible thinkers ought to be ashamed to use because, once its vacuity is recognized, its use is dishonest. I may, as a result of long endeavours to trace the destructive effect which the invocation of 'social justice' has had on our moral sensitivity, and of again and again finding even eminent thinkers thoughtlessly using the phrase,[42] have become unduly allergic to it, but I have come to feel strongly that the greatest service I can still render to my fellow men would be that I could make the speakers and writers among them thoroughly ashamed ever again to employ the term 'social justice'.

That in the present state of the discussion the continued use of the term is not only dishonest and the source of constant political confusion, but destructive of moral feeling, is shown by the fact that again and again thinkers, including distinguished philosophers,[43] after rightly recognizing that the term justice in its now predominant meaning of distributive (or retributive) justice is meaningless, draw from this the conclusion that the concept of justice itself is empty, and who in consequence jettison one of the basic moral conceptions on which the working of a society of free men rests. But it is justice in this sense which courts of justice administer and which is the original meaning of justice and must govern men's conduct if peaceful coexistence of free men is to be possible. While the appeal to 'social justice' is indeed merely an invitation to give moral approval to demands that have no moral justification, and which are in conflict with that basic rule of a free society that only such rules as can be applied equally to all should be enforced, justice in the sense of rules of just conduct is indispensable for the intercourse of free men.

We are touching here upon a problem which with all its ramifications is much too big to try to be examined here systematically, but which must at least be mentioned briefly. It is that we can't have any morals we like or dream of. Morals, to be viable, must satisfy certain requirements, requirements which we may not be able to specify but may only be able to find out by trial and error. What is required is not merely consistency, or compatibility of the rules as well as the acts demanded by them. A system of morals also must produce a functioning order, capable of maintaining the apparatus of civilization which it presupposes.

We are not familiar with the concept of non-viable systems of morals and certainly cannot observe them anywhere in practice since societies which try them rapidly disappear. But they are being preached, often by widely revered saintly figures, and the societies in decay which we can observe are often societies which have been listening to the teaching of such moral reformers and still revere the destroyers of their society as good men. More often, however, the gospel of 'social justice' aims at much more sordid sentiments: the dislike of people who are better off than oneself, or simply envy, that 'most anti-social and evil of all passions' as John Stuart Mill called it,[44] that animosity towards great wealth which represents it as a 'scandal' that some should enjoy riches while others have basic needs unsatisfied, and camouflages under the name of justice what has nothing to do with justice. At least all those who wish to despoil the rich, not because they expect that some more deserving might enjoy that wealth, but because they regard the very existence of the rich as an outrage, not only cannot claim any moral justification for their demands, but indulge in a wholly irrational passion and in fact harm those to whose rapacious instincts they appeal.

There can be no moral claim to something that would not exist but for the decision of others to risk their resources on its creation. What those who attack great private wealth do not understand is that it is neither by physical effort nor by the mere act of saving and investing, but by directing resources to the most productive uses that wealth is chiefly created. And there can be no doubt that most of those who have built up great fortunes in the form of new industrial plants and the like have thereby benefited more people through creating opportunities for more rewarding employment than if they had given their superfluity away to the poor. The suggestion that in these cases those to whom in fact the workers are most indebted do wrong rather than greatly benefit them is an absurdity. Though there are undoubtedly also other and less meritorious ways of acquiring large fortunes (which we can hope to control by improving the rules of the game), the most effective and important is by directing investment to points where they most enhance the productivity of labour — a task in which governments notoriously fail, for reasons inherent in non-competitive bureaucratic organizations.

But it is not only by encouraging malevolent and harmful prejudices that the cult of 'social justice' tends to destroy genuine moral feelings. It also comes, particularly in its more egalitarian forms, into constant conflict with some of the basic moral principles on which any community of free men must rest. This becomes evident when we reflect that the demand that we should equally esteem all our fellow men is irreconcilable with the fact that our whole moral code rests on the approval or disapproval of the conduct of others; and that similarly the traditional postulate that each capable adult is primarily responsible for his own and his dependants' welfare, meaning that he must not through his own fault become a charge to his friends or fellows, is incompatible with the idea that 'society' or government owes each person an appropriate income.

Though all these moral principles have also been seriously weakened by some pseudo-scientific fashions of our time which tend to destroy all morals — and with them the basis of individual freedom — the ubiquitous dependence on other people's power, which the enforcement of any image of 'social justice' creates, inevitably destroys that freedom of personal decisions on which all morals must rest.[45] In fact, that systematic pursuit of the *ignis fatuus* of 'social justice' which we call socialism is based throughout on the atrocious idea that political power ought to determine the material position of the different individuals and groups — an idea defended by the false assertion that this must always be so and socialism merely wishes to transfer this power from the privileged to the most numerous class. It was the great merit of the market order as it has spread during the last two centuries that it deprived everyone of such power which can be used only in arbitrary fashion. It had indeed brought about the greatest reduction of arbitrary power ever achieved. This greatest triumph of personal freedom the seduction of 'social justice' threatens again to take from us. And it will not be long before the holders of the power to enforce 'social justice' will entrench themselves in their position by awarding the benefits of 'social justice' as the remuneration for the conferment of that power and in order to secure to themselves the support of a praetorian guard which will make it certain that their view of what is 'social justice' will prevail.

Before leaving the subject I want to point out once more that the recognition that in such combinations as 'social', 'economic', 'distributive' or 'retributive' justice the term 'justice' is wholly empty should not lead us to throw the baby out with the bath water. Not only as the basis of the legal rules of just conduct is the justice which the courts of justice administer exceedingly important; there unquestionably also exists a genuine problem of justice in connection with the deliberate design of political institutions, the problem to which Professor John Rawls has recently devoted an important book. The fact which I regret and regard as confusing is merely that in this connection he employs the term 'social justice'. But I have no basic quarrel with an author who, before he proceeds to that problem, acknowledges that the task of selecting specific systems or distributions of desired things as just must be 'abandoned as mistaken in principle, and it is, in any case, not capable of a definite answer. Rather, the principles of justice define the crucial constraints which institutions and joint activities must satisfy if persons engaging in them are to have no complaints against them. If these constraints are satisfied, the resulting distribution, whatever it is, may be accepted as just (or at least not unjust)'.[46] This is more or less what I have been trying to argue in this chapter.

Appendix: Justice and Individual Rights*

The transition from the negative conception of justice as defined by rules of individual conduct to a 'positive' conception which makes it a duty of 'society' to see that individuals have particular things, is often effected by stressing the *rights* of the individual. It seems that among the younger generation the welfare institutions into which they have been born have engendered a feeling that they have a claim in justice on 'society' for the provision of particular things which it is the duty of that society to provide. However strong this feeling may be, its existence does not prove that the claim has anything to do with justice, or that such claims can be satisfied in a free society.

There is a sense of the noun 'right' in which every rule of just individual conduct creates a corresponding right of individuals. So far as rules of conduct delimit individual domains, the individual will have a right to his domain, and in the defence of it will have the sympathy and the support of his fellows. And where men have formed organizations such as government for enforcing rules of conduct, the individual will have a claim in justice on government that his right be protected and infringements made good.

Such claims, however, can be claims in justice, or rights, only in so far as they are directed towards a person or organization (such as government) which can act, and which is bound in its actions by rules of just conduct. They will include claims on people who have voluntarily incurred obligations, or between people who are connected by special circumstances (such as the relations between parents and children). In such circumstances the rules of just conduct will confer on some persons rights and on others corresponding obligations. But rules as such, without the presence of the particular circumstances to which they refer, cannot confer on anyone a right to a particular sort of thing. A child has a right to be fed, clad, and housed because a corresponding duty is placed on the parents or guardians, or perhaps a particular authority. But there can be no such right in the abstract determined by a rule of just conduct with-

*This appendix has been published as an article in the 75th anniversary issue of the Norwegian journal *Farmand* (Oslo, 1966).

out the particular circumstances being stated which determine on whom the corresponding obligation rests. Nobody has a right to a particular state of affairs unless it is the duty of someone to secure it. We have no right that our houses do not burn down, nor a right that our products or services find a buyer, nor that any particular goods or services be provided for us. Justice does not impose on our fellows a general duty to provide for us; and a claim to such a provision can exist only to the extent that we are maintaining an organization for that purpose. It is meaningless to speak of a right to a condition which nobody has the duty, or perhaps even the power, to bring about. It is equally meaningless to speak of right in the sense of a claim on a spontaneous order, such as society, unless this is meant to imply that somebody has the duty of transforming that cosmos into an organization and thereby to assume the power of controlling its results.

Since we are all made to support the organization of government, we have by the principles determining that organization certain rights which are commonly called political rights. The existence of the compulsory organization of government and its rules of organization does create a claim in justice to shares in the services of government, and may even justify a claim for an equal share in determining what government shall do. But it does not provide a basis for a claim on what government does not, and perhaps could not, provide for all. We are not, in this sense, members of an organization called society, because the society which produces the means for the satisfaction of most of our needs is not an organization directed by a conscious will, and could not produce what it does if it were.

The time-honoured political and civil rights which have been embodied in formal Bills of Right constitute essentially a demand that so far as the power of government extends it ought to be used justly. As we shall see, they all amount to particular applications of, and might be effectively replaced by, the more comprehensive formula that no coercion must be used except in the enforcement of a generic rule applicable to an unknown number of future instances. It may well be desirable that these rights should become truly universal as a result of all governments submitting to them. But so long as the powers of the several governments are at all limited, these rights cannot produce a duty of the governments to bring about a particular state of affairs. What we can require is that so far as government acts it ought to act justly; but we cannot derive from them any positive powers government ought to have. They leave wholly open the question whether the organization for coercion which we call government can and ought in justice be used to determine the particular material position of the several individuals or groups.

To the negative rights which are merely a complement of the rules protecting individual domains and which have been institutionalized in the charters of organization of governments, and to the positive rights of the citizens to participate in the direction of this organization, there have recently been added new positive 'social and economic' human rights for which an equal or even higher dignity is claimed.[47] These are claims to particular benefits to which every human being as such is presumed to be entitled without any indication as to who is to be under the obligation to provide those benefits or by what process they are to be provided.[48] Such positive rights, however, demand as their counterpart a decision that somebody (a person or organization) should have the duty of providing what the others are to have. It is, of course, meaningless to describe them as claims on 'society' because 'society' cannot think, act, value, or 'treat' anybody in a particular way. If such claims are to be met, the spontaneous order which we call society must be replaced by a deliberately directed organization: the cosmos of the market would have to be replaced by a taxis whose members would have to do what they are instructed to do. They could not be allowed to use their knowledge for their own purposes but would have to carry out the plan which their rulers have designed to meet the needs to be satisfied. From this it follows that the old civil rights and the new social and economic rights cannot be achieved at the same time but are in fact incompatible; the new rights could not be enforced by law without at the same time destroying that liberal order at which the old civil rights aim.

The new trend was given its chief impetus through the proclamation by President Franklin Roosevelt of his 'Four Freedoms' which included 'freedom *from* want' and 'freedom *from* fear' together with the old 'freedom *of* speech' and 'freedom *of* worship'. But it found its definite embodiment only in the *Universal Declaration of Human Rights* adopted by the General Assembly of the United Nations in 1948. This document is admittedly an attempt to fuse the rights of the Western liberal tradition with the altogether different conception deriving from the Marxist Russian Revolution.[49] It adds to the list of the classical civil rights enumerated in its first twenty-one articles seven further guarantees intended to express the new 'social and economic rights'. In these additional clauses 'every one, as a member of society' is assured the satisfaction of positive claims to particular benefits without at the same time placing on anyone the duty or burden of providing them. The document also completely fails to define these rights in such a manner that a court could possibly determine what their contents are in a particular instance. What, for instance, can be the legal meaning of the statement that every one 'is entitled to the realization . . . of the economic, social, and cultural rights indispensible for his dignity and free development of his personality' (Art. 22)? Against whom is 'every one' to have a claim to 'just and favourable conditions of work' (Art. 23 (1)) and to 'just and favourable employment' (Art. 23 (3))? What are the consequences of the requirement that every one should have the right 'freely to participate in the cultural life of the community and to share in the scientific advances and its benefits' (Art. 27 (1))? 'Every one' is even said to be 'entitled to a social and international order in which the rights and freedoms set forth in this Declaration are fully realized' (Art. 28) — on the assumption apparently that not only is this possible but that there exists now a known method by which these claims can be satisfied for all men.

It is evident that all these 'rights' are based on the interpretation of society as a deliberately made organization by which everybody is employed. They could not be made universal within a system of rules of just conduct based on the conception of individual responsibility, and so require that the whole of society be converted into a single organization, that is, made totalitarian in the fullest sense of the word. We have seen that rules of just conduct which apply to everybody alike but subject nobody to the commands of a superior can never determine what particular things any person is to have. They can never take the form of 'everybody must have so and so'. In a free society what the individual will get must always depend in some measure on particular circumstances which nobody can foresee and nobody has the power to determine. Rules of just conduct can therefore never confer on any person as such (as distinct from the members of a particular organization) a claim to particular things; they can bring about only opportunities for the acquiring of such claims.

It apparently never occurred to the authors of the Declaration that not everybody is an employed member of an organization whose right 'to just and favourable remuneration, including reasonable limitations of working hours and periodic holidays with pay' (Art. 24) can be guaranteed. The conception of a 'universal right' which assures to the peasant, to the Eskimo, and presumably to the Abominable Snowman, 'periodic holidays with pay' shows the absurdity of the whole thing. Even the slightest amount of ordinary common sense ought to have told the authors of the document that what they decreed as universal rights were for the present and for any foreseeable future utterly impossible of achievement, and that solemnly to proclaim them as rights was to play an irresponsible game with the concept of 'right' which could result only in destroying the respect for it.

The whole document is indeed couched in that jargon of organization thinking which one has learnt to expect in the pronouncement of trade union officials or the International Labour Organization and which reflects an attitude business employees share with civil servants and the organization men of the big corporations, but which is altogether inconsistent with the principles on which the order of a Great Society rests. If the document were merely the production of an international group of social philosophers (as in origin it is), it would constitute only somewhat disturbing evidence of the degree to which organization thinking has permeated the thinking of these social philosophers and how much they have become total strangers to the basic ideals of a free society. But its acceptance by a body of presumably responsible statesmen, seriously concerned with the creation of a peaceful international order, gives cause for much greater apprehension.

Organization thinking, largely as a result of the sway of the rationalist constructivism of Plato and his followers, has long been the besetting vice of social philosophers; perhaps it should therefore not surprise us that academic philosophers in their sheltered lives as members of organizations should have lost all understanding of the forces which hold the Great Society together and, imagining themselves to be Platonic philosopher-kings, should propose a re-organization of society on totalitarian lines. If it should be true, as we are told, that the social and economic rights of the Universal Declaration of Human Rights would today be 'accepted by the vast majority of American and British moralists,'[50] this would merely indicate a sorry lack of critical acumen on the part of these thinkers.

The spectacle, however, of the General Assembly of the United Nations solemnly proclaiming that *every* individual (!), 'keeping this Declaration constantly in mind' (!), should strive to insure the universal observation of those human rights, would be merely comic if the illusions which this creates were not so profoundly tragic. To see the most comprehensive authority which man has yet created undermining the respect it ought to command by giving countenance to the naive prejudice that we can create any state of affairs which we think to be desirable by simply decreeing that it ought to exist, and indulging in the self-deception that we can benefit from the spontaneous order of society and at the same time mould it to our own will, is more than merely tragic.[51]

The fundamental fact which these illusions disregard is that the availability of all those benefits which we wish as many people as possible to have depends on these same people using for their production their own best knowledge. To establish enforceable rights to the benefits is not likely to produce them. If we wish everybody to be well off, we shall get closest to our goal, not by commanding by law that this should be achieved, or giving everybody a legal claim to what we think he ought to have, but by providing inducements for all to do as much as they can that will benefit others. To speak of rights where what are in question are merely aspirations which only a voluntary system can fulfil, not only misdirects attention from what are the effective determinants of the wealth which we wish for all, but also debases the word 'right', the strict meaning of which it is very important to preserve if we are to maintain a free society.

Notes

1. The first quotation is taken from David Hume, *An Enquiry Concerning the Principles of Morals,* sect. III, part II, *Works* IV, p. 187, and ought to be given here in its context: 'the most obvious thought would be, to assign the largest possessions to the most extensive virtue, and give every one the power of doing good proportioned to his inclination. . . . But were mankind to execute such a law; so great is the uncertainty of merit, both from its natural obscurity, and from the self-conceit of each individual, that no determinate rule of conduct would ever follow from it; and the total dissolution of society must be the immediate consequence.'

2. The second quotation is translated from Immanuel Kant (*Der Streit der Fakultäten* (1798), sect. 2, para. 6, note 2) and reads in the original: 'Wohlfahrt aber hat kein Prinzip, weder für den der sie empfängt, noch für den der sie austeilt (der eine setzt sie hierin, der andere darin); weil es dabei auf das *Materiale* des Willens ankommt, welches empirisch und so einer allgemeinen Regel unfähig ist.' An English translation of this essay in which the passage is rendered somewhat differently will be found in *Kant's Political Writings,* ed. H. Reiss, trs. H. B. Nisbett (Cambridge, 1970), p. 183, note.

3. Cf. P. H. Wicksteed, *The Common Sense of Political Economy* (London, 1910), p. 184: 'It is idle to assume that ethically desirable results will necessarily be produced by an ethically indifferent instrument.'

4. Cf. G. del Vecchio, *Justice* (Edinburgh, 1952), p. 37. In the eighteenth century the expression 'social justice' was occasionally used to describe the enforcement of rules of just conduct within a given society, so e.g. by Edward Gibbon, *Decline and Fall of the Roman Empire,* chapter 41 (World's Classics edn, vol. IV, p. 367).

5. E.g. by John Rawls, *A Theory of Justice* (Harvard, 1971).

6. John Stuart Mill, *Utilitarianism* (London, 1861), chapter 5, p. 92; in H. Plamenatz, ed., *The English Utilitarians* (Oxford, 1949), p. 225.

7. *Ibid.,* pp. 66 and 208 respectively. Cf. also J. S. Mill's review of F. W. Newman, *Lectures on Political Economy,* originally published in 1851 in the *Westminster Review* and republished in *Collected Works,* vol. V (Toronto and London, 1967), p. 444: 'the distinction between rich and poor, so slightly connected as it is with merit and demerit, or even with exertion and want of exertion, is obviously unjust.' Also *Principles of Political Economy,* book II, ch. 1, §, ed. W. J. Ashley (London, 1909), pp. 211ff.: 'The proportioning of remuneration to work done is really just only in so far as the more or less of the work is a matter of choice: when it depends on natural differences of strength and capacity, this principle of remuneration is itself an injustice, it gives to those who have.'

8. See e.g. A. M. Honoré, 'Social Justice' in *McGill Law Journal,* VIII, 1962 and revised version in R. S. Summers, ed., *Essays in Legal Philosophy* (Oxford, 1968), p. 62 of the reprint: 'The first [of the two propositions of which the principle of social justice consists] is the contention that *all men considered merely as men and apart from their conduct or choice have a claim to an equal share in all those things, here called advantages, which are generally desired and are in fact conducive to well-being.*' Also W. G. Runciman, *Relative Deprivation and Social Justice* (London, 1966), p. 261.

9. Cf. especially the encyclicals *Quadragesimo Anno* (1931) and *Divini Redemptoris* (1937) and Johannes Messner, 'Zum Begriff der sozialen Gerechtigkeit' in the volume *Die soziale Frage und der Katholizismus* (Paderborn, 1931) issued to commemorate the fortieth anniversary of the encyclical *Rerum Novarum.*

10. The term 'social justice' (or rather its Italian equivalent) seems to have been first used in its modern sense by Luigi Taparelli d'Azeglio, *Saggio teoretico di diritto naturale* (Palermo, 1840) and to have been made more generally known by Antonio Rosmini-Serbati, *La costitutione secondo la giustizia sociale* (Milan, 1848). For more recent discussions cf. N. W. Willoughby, *Social Justice* (New York, 1909); Stephen Leacock, *The Unsolved Riddle of Social Justice* (London and New York, 1920); John A. Ryan, *Distributive Justice* New York, 1916); L. T. Hobhouse, *The Elements of Social Justice* (London and New York, 1922); T. N. Carver, *Essays in Social Justice* (Harvard, 1922); W. Shields, *Social Justice, The History and Meaning of the Term* (Notre Dame, Ind., 1941); Benevuto Donati, 'Che cosa è giustizia sociale?', *Archivio giuridico,* vol. 134, 1947; C. de Pasquier, 'La notion de justice sociale', *Zeit-*

schrift für Schweizerisches Recht, 1952; P. Antoine, 'Qu-est-ce la justice sociale?', *Archives de Philosophie,* 24, 1961. For a more complete list of this literature see G. del Vecchio, op. cit., pp. 37 – 9.

In spite of the abundance of writings on the subject, when about ten years ago I wrote the first draft of this chapter, I found it still very difficult to find any serious discussion of what people meant when they were using this term. But almost immediately afterwards a number of serious studies of the subject appeared, particularly the two works quoted in note 6 above as well as R. W. Baldwin, *Social Justice* (Oxford and London, 1966), and R. Rescher, *Distributive Justice* (Indianapolis, 1966). Much the most acute treatment of the subject is to be found in a German work by the Swiss economist Emil Küng, *Wirtschaft und Gerechtigkeit* (Tübingen, 1967) and many sensible comments in H. B. Acton, *The Morals of the Market* (London, 1971), particularly p. 71: 'Poverty and misfortune are evils but not injustices'. Very important is also Bertrand de Jouvenel, *The Ethics of Redistribution* (Cambridge, 1951) as well as certain passages in his *Sovereignty* (London, 1957), two of which may here be quoted. P. 140: 'The justice now recommended is a quality not of a man and a man's actions, but of a certain configuration of things in social geometry, no matter by what means it is brought about. Justice is now something which exists independently of just men.' P. 164: 'No proposition is likelier to scandalise our contemporaries than this one: it is impossible to establish a just social order. Yet it flows logically from the very idea of justice, on which we have, not without difficulty, thrown light. To do justice is to apply, when making a share-out, the relevant serial order. But it is impossible for the human intelligence to establish a relevant serial order for all resources in all respects. Men have needs to satisfy, merits to reward, possibilities to actualize; even if we consider these three aspects only and assume that — what is not the case — there are precise *indicia* which we can apply to these aspects, we still could not weight correctly among themselves the three sets of *indicia* adopted.'

The at one time very famous and influential essay by Gustav Schmoller on 'Die Gerechtigkeit in der Volkswirtschaft' in that author's *Jahrbuch für Volkswirtschaft etc.,* vol. V, 1895 is intellectually most disappointing — a pretentious statement of the characteristic muddle of the do-gooder foreshadowing some unpleasant later developments. We know now what it means if the great decisions are to be left to the 'jeweilige Volksbewusstsein nach der Ordnung der Zwecke, die im Augenblick als die richtige erscheint'!

11. Cf. note 7 to chapter VII above.

12. Cf. Adam Smith, *The Theory of Moral Sentiments* (London, 1801), vol. II, part VII, sect. ii, ch. I, p. 198: 'Human life the Stoics appear to have considered as a game of great skill, in which, however, there was a mixture of chance or of what is vulgarly understood to be chance.' See also Adam Ferguson, *Principles of Moral and Political Science* (Edinburgh, 1792) vol. I, p. 7: 'The Stoics conceived of human life under the image of a Game, at which the entertainment and merit of the players consisted in playing at-

tentively and well whether the stake was great or small.' In a note Ferguson refers to the *Discourses of Epictetus* preserved by Arrian, book II, ch. 5.

13. Cf. G. Hardin, *Nature and Man's Fate* (New York, 1961), p. 55: 'In a free market, says Smith in effect, prices are regulated by negative feedback.' The much ridiculed 'miracle' that the pursuit of self-interest serves the general interest reduces to the self-evident proposition that an order in which the action of the elements is to be guided by effects of which they cannot know can be achieved only if they are induced to respond to signals reflecting the effects of those events. What was familiar to Adam Smith has belatedly been rediscovered by scientific fashion under the name of 'self-organizing systems'.

14. See L. von Mises, *Human Action* (Yale, 1949), p. 255 note: 'There is in the operation of the market economy nothing which could properly be called distribution. Goods are not first produced and then distributed, as would be the case in a socialist state.' Cf. also M. R. Rothbard, 'Towards a Reconstruction of Utility and Welfare Economics' in M. Sennholz (ed.), *On Freedom and Free Enterprise* (New York, 1965), p. 231.

15. Cf. W. G. Runciman, op. cit., p. 274: 'Claims for social justice are claims on behalf of a group, and the person relatively deprived within an individual category will, if he is the victim of an unjust inequality, be a victim only of individual injustice.'

16. See Irving Kristol, 'When Virtue Loses all Her Loveliness — Some Reflections on Capitalism and "The Free Society"', *The Public Interest,* no. 21 (1970), reprinted in the author's *On the Democratic Idea in America* (New York, 1972), as well as in Daniel Bell and Irving Kristol (eds.), *Capitalism Today* (New York, 1970).

17. Cf. J. Höffner, *Wirtschaftsethik und Monopole im 15. und 16. Jahrhundert* (Jena, 1941) und 'Der Wettbewerb in der Scholastik', *Ordo,* V, 1953; also Max Weber, *On Law in Economy and Society,* ed. Max Rheinstein (Harvard, 1954) pp. 295ff., but on the latter also H. M. Robertson, *Aspects on the Rise of Economic Individualism* (Cambridge, 1933) and B. Groethuysen, *Origines de l'esprit bourgeois en France* (Paris, 1927). For the most important expositions of the conception of a just price by the late sixteenth century Spanish Jesuits see particularly L. Molina, *De iustitia et de iure,* vol. 2, *De Contractibus* (Cologne, 1594), disp. 347, no. 3 and especially disp. 348, no. 3, where the just price is defined as that which will form 'quando absque fraude, monopoliis, atque aliis versutiies, communiter res aliqua vendi consuevit pretio in aliqua regione, aut loco, it habendum est pro mensura et regula judicandi pretium iustum rei illius in ea regione.' About man's inability to determine beforehand what a just price would be see also particularly Johannes de Salas, *Commentarii in Secundum Secundae D. Thomas de Contractibus* (Lyon, 1617), *Tr. de empt. et Vend.* IV, n. 6, p. 9: '. . . quas exacte comprehendere, et ponderare Dei est, not hominum'; and J. de Lugo, *Disputationes de Iustitia et Iure* (Lyon, 1643), vol. II, d. 26, s. 4, n. 40; 'pretium

iustum matematicum, licet soli Deo notum.' See also L. Molina, op. cit., disp. 365, no. 9: 'omnesque rei publicae partes ius habent conscendendi ad gradum superiorem, si cuiusque sors id tulerit, neque cuiquam certus quidam gradus debitur, qui descendere et conscendere possit.' It would seem that H. M. Robertson (op. cit., p. 164) hardly exaggerates when he writes 'It would not be difficult to claim that the religion which favoured the spirit of capitalism was Jesuitry, not Calvinism.'

18. John W. Chapman, 'Justice and Fairness', *Nomos VI, Justice* (New York, 1963), p. 153. This Lockean conception has been preserved even by John Rawls, at least in his earlier work, 'Constitutional Liberty and the Concept of Justice', *Nomos VI, Justice* (New York, 1963), p. 117, note: 'If one assumes that law and government effectively act to keep markets competitive, resources fully employed, property and wealth widely distributed over time, and maintains a reasonable social minimum, then, if there is equality of opportunity, the resulting distribution will be just or at least not unjust. It will have resulted from the working of a just system . . . a social minimum is simply a form of rational insurance and prudence.'

19. See passages quoted in note 15 above.

20. See M. Fogarty, *The Just Wage* (London, 1961).

21. Barbara Wootton, *The Social Foundation of Wage Policy* (London, 1962), pp. 120 and 162, and now also her *Incomes Policy, An Inquest and a Proposal* (London, 1974).

22. Surely Samuel Butler (*Hudibras*, II,I) was right when he wrote

> For what is worth in any thing
> But so much money as 'twill bring.

23. On the general problem of remuneration according to merit, apart from the passages by David Hume and Immanuel Kant placed at the head of this chapter, see chapter VI of my book *The Constitution of Liberty* (London and Chicago, 1960) and cf. also Maffeo Pantaleoni, 'L'atto economico' in *Erotemi di Economia* (2 vols., Padua, 1963), vol. I, p. 101.

24. On the history of the term 'social' see Karl Wasserrab, *Sozialwissenschaft und soziale Frage* (Leipzig, 1903); Leopold von Wiese, *Der Liberalismus in Vergangenheit und Zukunft* (Berlin, 1917), and *Sozial, Geistig, Kulturell* (Cologne, 1936); Waldemar Zimmermann, 'Das "Soziale" im geschichtlichen Sinn- und Begriffswandel' in *Studien zur Soziologie, Festgabe für L. von Wiese* (Mainz, 1948); L. H. A. Geck, *Über das Eindringen des Wortes 'sozial' in die deutsche Sprache* (Göttingen, 1963); and Ruth Crummenerl, 'Zur Wortgeschichte von "sozial" bis zur englischen Aufklärung', unpublished essay for the State examination in philology (Bonn, 1963). Cf. also my essay 'What is "Social"? What does it Mean?' in a corrected English version in my *Studies in Philosophy, Politics and Economics* (London and Chicago, 1967).

25. Cf. G. del Vecchio, op. cit., p. 37.

26. Very instructive on this is Leopold von Wiese, *Der Liberalismus in Vergangenheit und Zukunft* (Berlin, 1917) pp. 115ff.

27. Characteristic for many discussions of the issue by social philosophers is W. A. Frankena, 'The Concept of Social Justice', in *Social Justice,* ed. R. B. Brandt (New York, 1962), p. 4, whose argument rests on the assumption that 'society' *acts* which is a meaningless term if applied to a spontaneous order. Yet this anthropomorphic interpretation of society seems to be one to which utilitarians are particularly prone, although this is not often as naively admitted as by J. W. Chapman in the statement quoted before in note 21 to chapter VII.

28. I regret this usage though by means of it some of my friends in Germany (and more recently also in England) have apparently succeeded in making palatable to wider circles the sort of social order for which I am pleading.

29. Cf. the 'Statement of Conscience' received by the 'Aspen Consultation on Global Justice', an 'ecumenical gathering of American religious leaders' at Aspen, Colorado, 4 – 7 June 1974, which recognized that 'global injustice is characterised by a dimension of sin in the economic, political, social, racial, sexual and class structures and systems of global society.' *Aspen Institute Quarterly* (New York), no. 7, third quarter, 1974, p. 4.

30. See particularly A. M. Honoré, op cit. The absurdity of the contention that in a Great Society it needs moral justification if *A* has more than *B*, as if this were the result of some human artifice, becomes obvious when we consider not only the elaborate and complex apparatus of government which would be required to prevent this, but also that this apparatus would have to possess power to direct the efforts of all citizens and to claim the products of those efforts.

31. One of the few modern philosophers to see this clearly and speak out plainly was R. G. Collingwood. See his essay on 'Economics as a philosophical science,' *Ethics* 36, 1926, esp. p. 74: 'A just price, a just wage, a just rate of interest, is a contradiction in terms. The question of what a person ought to get in return for his goods and labour is a question absolutely devoid of meaning.'

32. If there is any one fact which all serious students of the claims for equality have recognized it is that material equality and liberty are irreconcilable. Cf. A. de Tocqueville, *Democracy in America,* book II, ch. I (New York, edn 1946, vol. II, p. 87): democratic communities 'call for equality in freedom, and if they cannot obtain that, they still call for equality in slavery'; William S. Sorley, *The Moral Life and the Moral Worth* (Cambridge, 1911), p. 110: 'Equality is gained only by constant interference with liberty'; or more recently Gerhard Leibholz, 'Die Bedrohung der Freiheit durch die Macht der Gesetzgeber', in *Freiheit der Persönlichkeit* (Stuttgart, 1958), p. 80: 'Freiheit erzeugt notwendig Ungleichheit und Gleichheit notwendig Un-

freiheit', are merely a few instances which I readily find in my notes. Yet people who claim to be enthusiastic supporters of liberty still clamour constantly for material equality.

33. Gustav Radbruch, *Rechtsphilosophie* (Stuttgart, 1956), p. 87: 'Auch das sozialistische Gemeinwesen wird also ein Rechtsstaat sein, ein Rechtsstaat freilich, der statt von der ausgleichenden von der austeilenden Gerechtigkeit beherrscht wird.'

34. See M. Duverger, *The Idea of Politics* (Indianapolis, 1966), p. 201.

35. Karl Mannheim, *Man and Society in an Age of Reconstruction* (London, 1940), p. 180.

36. P. J. Stuchka (President of the Soviet Supreme Court) in *Encyclopedia of State and Law* (in Russian, Moscow, 1927), quoted by V. Gsovski, *Soviet Civil Law* (Ann Arbor, Michigan, 1948), I, p. 70. The work of E. Paschukanis, the Soviet author who has most consistently developed the idea of the disappearance of law under socialism, has been described by Karl Korsch in *Archiv sozialistischer Literatur,* III, (Frankfurt, 1966) as the only consistent development of the teaching of Karl Marx.

37. *The Road to Serfdom* (London and Chicago, 1944), chapter IV. For discussions of the central thesis of that book by lawyers see W. Friedmann, *The Planned State and the Rule of Law* (Melbourne, 1948), reprinted in the same author's *Law and Social Change in Contemporary Britain* (London, 1951); Hans Kelsen, 'The Foundations of Democracy', *Ethics* 66, 1955; Roscoe Pound, 'The Rule of Law and the Modern Welfare State', *Vanderbilt Law Review,* 7, 1953; Harry W. Jones, 'The Rule of Law and the Modern Welfare State', *Columbia Law Review,* 58, 1958; A. L. Goodhart, 'The Rule of Law and Absolute Sovereignty', *University of Pennsylvania Law Review,* 106, 1958.

38. G. Radbruch, op. cit., p. 126.

39. Radbruch's conceptions of these matters are concisely summed up by Roscoe Pound (in his introduction to R. H. Graves, *Status in the Common Law,* London, 1953, p. XI): Radbruch

> starts with a distinction between commutative justice, a correcting justice which gives back to one what has been taken away from him or gives him a substantial substitute, and distributive justice, a distribution of the goods of existence not equally but according to a scheme of values. Thus there is a contrast between co-ordinating law, which secures interests by reparation and the like, treating all individuals as equal, and subordinating law, which prefers some or the interests of some according to its measure of value. Public law, he says, is a law of subordination, subordinating individual to public interests but not the interests of other individuals with those public interests.

40. Cf. Bertrand de Jouvenel, *Sovereignty* (Chicago, 1957), p. 136:

> The small society, as the milieu in which man is first found, retains for him an infinite attraction; he undoubtedly goes to it to renew his strength; but . . . any attempt to graft the same features on a large society is utopian and leads to tyranny. With that admitted, it is clear that as social relations become wider and more various, the common good conceived as reciprocal trustfulness cannot be sought in methods which the model of the small, closed society inspires; such a model is, in the contrary, entirely misleading.

41. Edwin Cannan, *The History of Local Rates in England,* 2nd edn (London, 1912), p. 162.

42. While one has become used to find the confused minds of social philosophers talking about 'social justice', it greatly pains me if I find a distinguished thinker like the historian Peter Geyl (*Encounters in History,* London, 1963, p. 358) thoughtlessly using the term. J. M. Keynes (*The Economic Consequences of Mr. Churchill,* London, 1925, *Collected Writings,* vol. IX, p. 223) also writes unhesitatingly that 'on grounds of social justice no case can be made for reducing the wages of the miners.'

43. Cf. e.g. Walter Kaufmann, *Without Guilt and Justice* (New York, 1973) who, after rightly rejecting the concepts of distributive and retributive justice, believes that this must lead him to reject the concept of justice altogether. But this is not surprising after even *The Times* (London) in a thoughtful leading article (1 March 1957) apropos the appearance of an English translation of Josef Pieper's *Justice* (London, 1957) had observed that 'roughly, it may be said that in so far as the notion of justice continues to influence political thinking, it has been reduced to the meaning of the phrase "distributive justice" and that the idea of commutative justice has almost entirely ceased to influence our calculations except in so far it is embodied in laws and customs — in the maxims for instance of the Common Law — which are preserved from sheer conservatism.' Some contemporary social philosophers indeed beg the whole issue by so *defining* 'justice' that it includes *only* distributive justice. See e.g. Brian M. Barry, 'Justice and the Common Good', *Analysis,* 19, 1961, p. 80: 'although Hume uses the expression "rules of justice" to cover such things as property rules, *"justice" is now analytically tied to "desert" and "need",* so that one could quite properly say that some of what Hume calls "rules of justice" were unjust' (italics added). Cf. ibid., p. 89.

44. J. S. Mill, *On Liberty,* ed. McCallum (Oxford, 1946), p. 70.

45. On the destruction of moral values by scientific error see my discussion in my inaugural lecture as Visiting Professor at the University of Salzburg, *Die Irrtümer des Konstruktivismus und die Grundlagen legitimer Kritik gesellschaftlicher Gebilde* (Munich, 1970, now reprinted for the Walter Eucken Institute at Freiburg i.Brg. by J. C. B. Mohr, Tübingen, 1975).

46. John Rawls, 'Constitutional Liberty and the Concept of Justice', *Nomos IV, Justice* (New York, 1963), p. 102, where the passage quoted is pre-

ceded by the statement that 'It is the system of institutions which has to be judged and judged from a general point of view.' I am not aware that Professor Rawls' later more widely read work *A Theory of Justice* (Harvard, 1971) contains a comparatively clear statement of the main point, which may explain why this work seems often, but as it appears to me wrongly, to have been interpreted as lending support to socialist demands, e.g. by Daniel Bell, 'On Meritocracy and Equality', *Public Interest,* Autumn 1972, p. 72, who describes Rawls' theory as 'the most comprehensive effort in modern philosophy to justify a socialistic ethic.'

47. For discussions of the problem cf. the papers assembled in the *Philosophical Review,* April 1955 and in D. D. Raphael (ed.), *Political Theory and the Rights of Man* (London, 1967).

48. See the *Universal Declaration of Human Rights* adopted by the General Assembly of the United Nations on 10 December 1948. It is reprinted, and the intellectual background of this document can be found, in the volume entitled *Human Rights, Comments and Interpretations,* a symposium edited by UNESCO (London and New York, 1945). It contains in the Appendix not only a 'Memorandum Circulated by UNESCO on the Theoretical Bases of the Rights of Men' (pp. 251 – 54), but also a 'Report of the UNESCO Committee on the Theoretical Bases of the Human Rights' (in other places described as the 'UNESCO Committee on the Principles of the Rights of Men'), in which it is explained that their efforts were directed towards reconciling the two different 'complementary' working concepts of human rights, of which one 'started, from the premises of inherent individual rights . . . while the other was based on Marxist principles', and at finding 'some common measure of the two tendencies'. 'This common formulation,' it is explained, 'must by some means reconcile the various divergent or opposing formulations now in existence'! (The British representatives on that committee were Professors H. J. Laski and E. H. Carr!).

49. Ibid., p. 22, Professor E. H. Carr, the chairman of the UNESCO Committee of experts, explains that 'If the new declaration of the rights of man is to include provisions for social services, for maintenance in childhood, in old age, in incapacity or in unemployment, it becomes clear that no society can guarantee the enjoyment of such rights unless it in turn has the right to call upon and direct the productive capacities of the individuals enjoying them'!

50. G. Vlastos, 'Justice', *Revue Internationale de la Philosophie,* 1957, p. 331.

51. On the whole document cf. Maurice Cranston, 'Human Rights, Real and Supposed' in the volume edited by D. D. Raphael quoted in note 47 above, where the author argues that 'a philosophically respectable concept of human rights has been muddied, obscured, and debilitated in recent years by an attempt to incorporate in it specific rights of a different logical category.' See also the same author's *Human Rights Today* (London, 1955).

Socialism and Science

·6·

I

Socialism is related to Science in various ways. Probably the least interesting relation today is that from which Marxism lays claim to the name of 'scientific socialism', and according to which by an inner necessity, and without men doing anything about it, capitalism develops into socialism. This may still impress some novices, but it is hardly any longer taken seriously by competent thinkers in either camp. Socialists certainly do not act as if they believed that the transition from capitalism to socialism will be brought about by an ineluctable law of social evolution. Few people now believe in the existence of any 'historical laws'.

Experience has certainly refuted the predictions Marx made concerning the particular developments of capitalism.

There is, secondly, the undeniable propensity of minds trained in the physical sciences, as well as of engineers, to prefer a deliberately created orderly arrangement to the results of spontaneous growth — an influential and common attitude, which frequently attracts intellectuals to socialist schemes. This is a widespread and im-

---

A lecture delivered on 19 October 1976 to the Canberra Branch of the Economic Society of Australia and New Zealand.

portant phenomenon which has had a profound effect on the development of political thought. However, I have already on several occasions discussed the significance of these attitudes, calling them 'scientism' and 'constructivism' respectively, so that it is unnecessary to revert to these questions.

II

What I want to examine today is rather the peculiar manner in which most socialists attempt to shield their doctrines against scientific criticism, by claiming that differences from opponents are of a nature which precludes scientific refutation. Indeed, they frequently succeed in conveying the impression that any use of science to criticise socialist proposals is ipso facto proof of political prejudice, because the differences are wholly based on different value judgments, which the rules of scientific procedure prohibit, so that it is even indecent to introduce them into scientific discussions.

Two experiences have long made me impatient with these contentions. One is that not only I, but I believe also the majority of my contemporary libertarian fellow-economists, were originally led to economics by the more or less strong socialist beliefs — or at least dissatisfaction with existing society — which we felt in our youth, and the study of economics turned us into radical anti-socialists. The other experience is that my concrete differences with socialist fellow-economists on particular issues of social policy turn inevitably, not on differences of value, but on differences as to the effects particular measures will have.

It is true that in such discussions we frequently end up with differences about the probable magnitude of certain effects of the alternative policies. With regard to this both parties must often honestly admit that they have no conclusive proof. Probably I also ought to admit that my conviction that ordinary common sense clearly supports my position is often matched by an equally strong conviction of my opponents that ordinary common sense supports theirs.

III

Yet, when we survey the history of the results of the application of scientific analysis to socialist proposals, it seems abundantly clear that not only has it been shown that the methods advocated by socialists can never achieve what they promise, but also that the different values they hope or claim to serve cannot by *any* possible procedure be all realised at the same time, because they are mutually contradictory.

I will begin by considering the second of these questions which, in the present state of the discussion, appears to be the more interesting one — chiefly because it makes it necessary to clear up certain prevailing confusions concerning the inadmissibility of value judgments in scientific discussions. These are often used to represent scientific arguments against socialism as illegitimate or scientifically suspect. Such an examination raises important and interesting questions as to the possibility of the scientific treatment of moral beliefs, which have been unduly neglected. Economists, whose daily bread is the analysis of those conflicts of value which all economic activity has constantly to solve, have fought shy of frankly and systematically facing the task. It is as if they feared to soil their scientific purity by going beyond questions of cause and effect and *critically* evaluating the desirability of certain popular measures. They usually maintain that they can merely 'postulate' values without examining their validity. (So long as measures for the benefit of some supposedly 'underprivileged' groups are tacitly assumed to be good, such limitations are, however, usually forgotten.)

It is indeed necessary in this connection to be very careful, and even pedantic, with regard to the expressions one chooses, because there exists a real danger of inadvertently slipping value judgments in an illegitimate manner into a scientific discussion, and also because those defending their socialist ideals are now mostly trained to use 'freedom from value judgments' as a sort of paradoxical defence mechanism for their creed, and are constantly on the lookout to catch their critics out in some incautious formulations. What play has not been made with occasional passages in the work of the greatest scientific critic of socialism, Ludwig von Mises, in which he described socialism as 'impossible'; Mises obviously meant that the proposed methods of socialism could not achieve what they were supposed to do! We can, of course, try any course of action, but what is questioned is whether any such course of action will produce the effects claimed to follow from it. This undoubtedly *is* a scientific question.

IV

So let me for a moment be pedantic and try to state precisely the kinds of value judgments which are admissible in a scientific discussion and the kinds that are not. Our starting point must be the logical truism that from premises containing *only* statements about cause and effect, we can derive no conclusions about what *ought* to be. No consequences whatever for action follow from such a statement, so long as we do not know (or agree) which consequences are desirable and which are undesirable. But once we include among our accepted premises *any* statement about the importance or harmfulness of different ends or consequences of action, all manner of different norms of action can be derived from it. Meaningful discussion about public affairs is clearly possible only with persons with whom we share at least some values. I doubt if we could even fully understand what someone says if we had no values whatever in common with him. This means, however, that in practically any discussion it will be in principle possible to show that some of the policies one person advocates are inconsistent or irreconcilable with some other beliefs he holds.

This brings me to a fundamental difference in the general attitudes to moral problems which seems to be characteristic of the now common political positions. The conservative is generally happy to cling to his belief in absolute values. While I envy him, I cannot share his beliefs. It is the fate of the economist continually to encounter true conflicts of value; indeed, to analyse the manner in which such conflicts can be resolved is his professional task. The conflicts I have in mind here are not so much the obvious conflicts between the values held by different persons, or the gaps between their individual systems of values, but the conflicts and gaps within the system of values of any one person. However much we dislike it, we are again and again forced to recognise that there are no truly absolute values whatever. Not even human life itself. This again and again we are prepared to sacrifice, and must sacrifice, for some other higher values, even if it be only one life to save a large number of other lives.

(I cannot here consider the interesting point that, though we may never feel entitled to sacrifice a particular known human life, we constantly take decisions which we know will cause the death of some unknown person.)

But the libertarians or true liberals — not those pink socialists who, as Josef Schumpeter said, 'as a supreme but unintended compliment . . . have thought it wise to appropriate this label' — therefore do not fall into the opposite extreme of believing, like the socialists, that they can hedonistically construct some other new system of morals which they like, because they think that it will most increase human happiness, but who in fact merely hark back to the primitive instincts inherited from the tribal society. Though the liberal must claim the right critically to examine every single value or moral rule of his society, he knows that he can and must do this while accepting as given for that purpose most of the other moral values of this society, and examine that about which he has doubts in terms of its compatibility with the rest of the dominant system of values.

Our moral task must indeed be a constant struggle to resolve moral conflict, or to fill gaps in our moral code — a responsibility we can discharge only if we learn to understand that order of peace and mutually adjusted efforts, which is the ultimate value that our moral conduct enhances. Our moral rules must be constantly tested against, and if necessary adjusted to, each other, in order to eliminate direct conflicts between the different rules, and also so as to make them serve the same functioning order of human actions.

V

Moral tasks are individual tasks, and moral advance by some groups results from their members adopting rules which are more conducive to the preservation and welfare of the group. Moral progress demands the possibility of individual experimentation; in particular, that within a limited framework of compulsory abstract rules the individual is free to use his own knowledge for his own purposes. The growth of what we call civilisation is due to this principle of a person's responsibility for his own actions and their consequences, and the freedom to pursue his own ends without having to obey the leader of the band to which he belongs. It is true that our moral beliefs are still somewhat schizophrenic, as I tried to show on an earlier occasion, divided between instincts inherited from the primitive band, and the rules of just conduct which have made the open society possible. The morality of individual responsibility of the able adult for the welfare of himself and his family is still the basis for most moral judgments of action. Thus it is the indispensable framework for the peaceful working of any complex society.

Call it science or not, no objective analysis of those basic beliefs on which our existing morals rest, and without the acceptance of which any communication on moral issues becomes impossible — namely, recognition of the responsibility of the individual and of the general grounds on which we esteem the actions of others—can leave any doubt that they are irreconcilable with the socialist demand for a forcible redistribution of incomes by authority. Such an assignment of a particular share according to the views of some authority as to the merits or needs of the different persons is immoral; not simply because I say so, but because it is in conflict with certain basic moral values which those who advocate it also share. The mere fact that commonly accepted ethics have no generally recognised solutions to the conflicts of values which undeniably arise in this sphere is, of course, of the greatest significance for the political problems which arise here, and for the moral evaluation of the use of coercion in enforcing any particular solution.

VI

That collectivist economic planning, which used earlier to be thought to require the nationalisation of the means of 'production, distribution and exchange', leads inevitably to totalitarian tyranny has come to be fairly generally recognised in the West since I analysed the process in some detail in *The Road to Serfdom* more than 40 years ago. I do not know if it was partly for this reason, or because socialists increasingly recognised the incurable economic inefficiency of central planning, about which I shall have to say a few words later, or whether they simply discovered that redistribution through taxation and aimed financial benefits was an easier and quicker method of achieving their aims; but, in any event, socialist parties in the West have almost all for the time being abandoned the most obviously dangerous demands for a centrally planned economy. Left wing doctrinaires in some countries, and the communist parties, still press for it, and may of course sooner or later gain power. But the supposedly moderate leaders, who at present guide most of the socialist parties of the free world, claim—or have it claimed by the media on their behalf—that as good democrats they can be trusted to prevent any such developments.

But can they? I do not mean to question their good faith. Nevertheless, I greatly doubt their capacity to combine their aim of a thorough governmental redistribution of wealth with the preservation, in the long run, of a modicum of personal freedom, even if they succeed in preserving the forms of democracy. It is true that the substitution of cold socialism has much slowed down the process which

I had predicted hot socialism would bring about. But can it lastingly avoid the same effects? There are strong reasons for doubting that cold socialism can avoid them.

Governments, to be successful, would at the same time have to preserve functioning markets, on which depends the possibility of competition so determining prices of all products and factors of production in such a way as to serve as reliable guides to production, *and* also somehow so to influence at least the prices of labour (obviously including those of the farmer and other 'self-employed') as to satisfy demands for just or equitable remuneration. To satisfy both of these requirements in full is impossible. Governments can aim at best at some kind of compromise, and refrain from many interventions in the market which would be necessary if they were even approximately to satisfy the most pressing demands. But governments bowing to the inevitabilities of the market, after commencing to manipulate the results of the market to favour some groups, would clearly be embarking on a political impossibility. Once claims for interference with the market in favour of particular groups have come to be frequently recognised, a democratic government cannot refuse to comply with similar demands of any groups on whose votes it depends. Though the process may be gradual, a government which begins to control prices to secure popular conceptions of justice is bound to be driven step by step towards the control of all prices; and, since this must destroy the functioning of the market, to a central direction of the economy. Even if governments try not to use such central planning as an instrument, if they persist in the endeavour to create a just distribution they will be driven to use central direction as the only instrument by which it is possible to determine the overall distribution of remunerations (without thereby making it just)—and thus be driven to establish an essentially totalitarian system.

VII

It took a long time to convince socialists that central planning is inefficient. Practical men were probably convinced not by argument but only by the warning example of the Russian system; contemporary theoreticians, however, retreated only slowly from the position laid down by the founders of Marxism and generally maintained by their leading theoreticians until 50 years ago. Somehow, however, they nevertheless managed, as they gave up successive positions and attempted new solutions of the problem, to convey the impression that they had victoriously beaten off the onslaughts of hostile critics.

The founders of socialism, including Marx and Engels, did not even understand that any central direction of the machinery of production owned by society required, if resources were to be effectively used, calculations in terms of value. As Friedrich Engels put it, the social plan of production 'will be settled very simply without the intervention of the famous value'. Even when discussion of the problem was seriously started, immediately after the First World War, it was caused by the social science expert among the Vienna school of logical positivists claiming that all calculations of the efficiency of social production could be carried out *in natura* — that is, without relying on any variable rates of conversion between the different physical units used. It was against this position that Ludwig von Mises and some of his contemporaries (including Max Weber) developed the first decisive critique of the socialist position.

The crucial point here — which, it must be admitted, even the leading classical economists down to John Stuart Mill did not understand — is the universal significance of changing rates of substitution between different commodities. This simple insight, which helped us at last to understand the role of differences and variability of the prices of different commodities, began slowly to develop with the recognition — I will not say the discovery, since of course every simple peasant knew the facts if not their theoretical significance — of decreasing returns from successive applications of labour and capital to land. It was next found to govern, under the name of decreasing marginal utility, the rates of marginal substitution between different consumers' goods. And it was finally discovered to be the universal relation prevailing between all useful resources, determining at once if they are economically the same or different, and if they are scarce or not. Only when it was understood that changing supplies of the different factors of production (or means of satisfaction) determines their variable marginal rate of substitution, was the indispensability of known rates of equivalence (or rates of marginal substitution) for any efficient calculation fully understood. Only when it was at last seen that through market prices this rate of equivalence in all their different uses, mostly known only to a few of the many persons who would like to use them, could be made equal to the rates at which any pair of commodities could be substituted in any of its countless uses, was the indispensable function of prices in a complex economy fully understood.

Variable 'marginal rates of substitution' for different commodities, to which I have previously referred, naturally mean their temporary rates of equivalence determined by the situation at the moment, and at which these things must be substitutable at the margin in all their possible uses — if we are to get their full capacity out of them.

It was both the understanding of the function of changing rates of equivalence between physically defined objects as the basis of calculation, and the communication function of prices which combined into a single signal all the information on these circumstances dispersed among large numbers of people, which at last made it fully clear to every person who could follow the argument that rational calculation in a complex economy is possible only in terms of values or prices, and that these values will be adequate guides only if they are the joint efforts, such as the values formed on the market, of all the knowledge of potential suppliers or consumers about their possible uses and availability.

The first reaction of the socialist theoreticians, once they could no longer refuse to admit this fact, was to suggest that their socialist planning boards should determine prices by the same system of simultaneous equations by which mathematical economists had attempted to explain market prices in equilibrium. They even tried to suggest that Wieser, Pareto and Barone had long ago pointed out the possibility of this. In fact, these three scholars had pointed out what a socialist planning board *would have to try to do* in order to equal the efficiency of the market — not, as the socialist theoreticians incorrectly suggested, how such an impossible result could be achieved. Pareto, in particular, had made clear that the system of simultaneous equations, development of which made him famous, was intended to show only the general pattern (as we would today express this), but could never be used to determine particular prices, because any central authority could never know all the circumstances of time and place which guide the actions of individuals, such actions being the information fed into the communication machine which we call the market.

So the first attempt by the socialists to answer the critique by Mises and others soon collapsed. The next step, by which particularly Oscar Lange, but also others, are supposed to have refuted Mises, consisted of various attempts to reduce more or less the role of central planning and to re-introduce some market features under the name of 'socialist competition'. I will not dwell here on how great an intellectual reversal this meant for all those who for so long had emphasised the great superiority of central direction over the so-called 'chaos of competition'. This self-contradictory approach raised new problems of an altogether new kind. However, it could in no way overcome two crucial difficulties. First, the socialist authority could not, as long as all the industrial equipment and other capital belonged to 'society' (that is, the government), let competition or the market decide how much capital each enterprise was to have, or what risks the manager would be allowed to run — both decisive points if a market is to operate properly. Second, if the government were otherwise to let the market operate freely, it could do nothing to secure that the remuneration the market gave to each participant would correspond to what the government regarded as socially just. Yet to achieve such a so-called 'just' remuneration was, after all, the whole intended purpose of the socialist revolution!

VIII

The answers to the three questions we have been discussing do not depend on particular value judgments, except the answer to the first question, in which certain values (such as personal liberty and responsibility) were taken for granted. It can be assumed that such values would be shared by all persons with whom one cared to discuss such problems. The fundamental problem was always whether socialism could achieve what it promised. This is a purely scientific problem, even if the answer may in part depend on points on which we cannot strictly demonstrate the correctness of our answer. Yet, the answers at which we have arrived on all three counts are purely negative. On the moral side, socialism cannot but destroy the basis of all morals, personal freedom and responsibility. On the political side, it leads sooner or later to totalitarian government. On the material side it will greatly impede the production of wealth, if it does not actually cause impoverishment. All these objections to socialism were raised a long time ago on purely intellectual grounds, which in the course of time have been elaborated and refined. There have been no serious attempts to refute these objections to socialism rationally. Indeed, the most surprising thing about the treatment of these problems by the majority of professional economists is how little they have made them the central point of their discussions. One would think that nothing could be of more concern for economists than the relative efficiency and conduciveness to general welfare of alternative orders of economic affairs. Instead they have fought shy of the topic, as if fearing to soil their hands by concerning themselves with 'political' topics. They have left the discussion to specialists in 'economic systems' who in their textbooks provide stale accounts of discussions of long ago, carefully avoiding taking sides. It is as if the circumstance that that issue had become the subject of political dispute were a cause for the silence of the scientists who knew they could definitely refute at least some of the arguments of one side. This kind of neutrality seems to me not discretion but cowardice. Surely it is high time for us to cry from the house-tops that the intellectual foundations of socialism have all collapsed.

I have to admit that, after vainly waiting for upwards of 40 years to find a respectably intellectual defence against objections raised to socialist proposals, I am becoming a little impatient. Since I have always acknowledged that the socialist camp includes many people of good will, I have tried to deal with their doctrines gently. But the time is overdue to proclaim loudly that intellectually the foundations of socialism are as hollow as can be, and that opposition to socialism is based, not on different values or on prejudice, but on unrefuted logical argument. This must be openly said, especially in view of the tactics so frequently employed by most advocates and defenders of socialism. Instead of reasoning logically to meet the substantial objections they have to answer, socialists impugn the motives and throw suspicion on the good faith of defenders of what they choose to call 'capitalism'. Such crude efforts to turn discussion from whether a belief is true to why it is being held seems to me itself an outgrowth of the weakness of the intellectual position of the socialists. Quite generally, the socialist counter-critique seems often to be more concerned to discredit the author than to refute his arguments. The favourite tactics of the counter-critiques is to warn the young against taking the author or his book seriously. This technique indeed has been developed to a certain mastership. What young man will bother with such a book as my *Constitution of Liberty* which, he is told by a 'progressive' British political science don, is one of those 'dinosaurs that still occasionally stalk on the scene, apparently impervious to natural selection'? The principle seems generally: if you can't refute the argument, defame the author. That the argument against them may be genuine, honest and perhaps true, these left-wing intellectuals do not seem prepared to consider even as a possibility, since it might mean that they themselves are entirely wrong.

Certainly, political differences are frequently based on differences of ultimate values, on which science has little or nothing to say. But the crucial differences which exist today at least between the socialist intellectuals, who, after all, invented socialism, and their opponents are not of this kind. They are intellectual differences which between people not irredeemably wed to a muddled dream can be sorted out and decided by logical reasoning. I have never belonged to any political party. Long ago I shocked many of my friends by explaining why I cannot be a conservative. Insight into the nature of the economic problems of society turned me into a radical anti-socialist, I can honestly say. Moreover, it convinced me that as an economist I can do more for my fellow-men by explaining the reasons for opposing socialism than in any other manner. Anti-socialism means here opposition to *all* direct government interference with the market, no matter in whose interest such interference may be exercised.

It is not correct to describe this as a laissez faire attitude — another of the smear-words so frequently substituted for argument — because a functioning market requires a framework of appropriate rules within which the market will operate smoothly. Strong reasons also exist for wishing government to render *outside the market* various services, which for one reason or another the market cannot supply. But the state certainly ought never to have the *monopoly* of any such service, especially not of postal services, broadcasting, or the issue of money.

Some signs are appearing of a return to sanity. But I do not really feel hopeful about prospects for the future. There is much talk about countries becoming 'ungovernable', but little realisation that attempts to govern too much are at the root of the trouble, and even less awareness of how deeply the evil has already become entrenched in prevailing institutions. For progress towards its aims, socialism needs government with unlimited powers, and has already got this. In such a system various groups must be given, not what a majority thinks they deserve, but what those groups themselves think they are entitled to. Granting these groups what they think they deserve therefore becomes the price that must be paid so that some groups may become a majority. Omnipotent democracy indeed leads of necessity to a kind of socialism, but to a socialism which nobody foresaw or probably wanted: a position in which the individual elected representative as well as the governing majority must work to redress every imagined grievance which it has power to redress, however little justified the claim may be. It is not the assessment of the merits of persons or groups by a majority, but the power of those persons or groups to extort special benefits from the government, which now determines the distribution of incomes.

The paradox is that the all-powerful government which socialism needs, must, if it is to be democratic, aim at remedying all such dissatisfaction, and to remove all dissatisfaction means that it must reward groups at their own estimates of their deserts. But no viable society can reward everyone at his own valuation. A society in which a few can use power to extort what they feel they are entitled to may be highly unpleasant for the others, but would at least be viable. A society in which everyone is organised as a member of some groups to force government to help him get what he wants is self-destructive. There is no way of preventing some from feeling that they have been treated unjustly — that is bound to be widespread in any social order — but arrangements which enable groups of disgruntled people to extort satisfaction of their claims — or the recognition of an 'entitlement', to use this new-fangled phrase — make any society unmanageable.

There is no limit to the wishes of the people which an unlimited democratic government is obliged to try to satisfy. We have indeed the considered opinion of a leading British Labour politician that he regards it as his task to remedy all dissatisfaction! It would be unfair, however, to blame the politicians too much for being unable to say 'no'. Under prevailing arrangements perhaps an established leader could afford occasionally to do so, but the ordinary representative cannot say 'no' to any large number of his constituents, however unjust their demands, and still hope to retain his seat.

In a society whose wealth rests on prompt adaptation to constantly changing circumstances, the individual can be left free to choose the directions of his efforts only if rewards fluctuate with the value of the services he can contribute to the society's common pool of resources. If his income is politically determined, he loses not merely the incentive but also the possibility of deciding what he ought to do in the general interest. And if he cannot know himself what he must do to make his services valuable to his fellows, he must be commanded to do what is required. To suffer disappointment, adversity and hardship is a discipline to which in any society most must submit, and it is a discipline by which it is desirable that all able persons ought to have to submit. What mitigates these hardships in a free society is that no arbitrary human will imposes them, but that their incidence is determined by an impersonal process and unforeseeable chance.

I believe that, after a little socialism, people generally recognise that it is preferable for one's well-being and relative status to depend on the outcome of the game of the market than on the will of a superior, to whom one is assigned by authority. Present trends, however, make it seem likely that, before such an insight spreads widely enough, existing political institutions will break down under stresses which they cannot bear. Unless people learn to accept that many of their grievances are unjustified, and give them no claims on others, and that in this world government cannot effectively assume responsibility for how well off particular groups of people are to be, it will be impossible to build a decent society. Indeed, the most idealistic among the socialists will be forced to destroy democracy to serve their idealistic socialist vision of the future. What present trends point to is the emergence of ever larger numbers, for whose welfare and status government has assumed a responsibility it cannot discharge, and whose revolt when they are not paid enough, or asked to do more work than they like, will have to be subdued with the knout and the machine-gun: this, too, by the very people who genuinely intended to grant all their wishes.

HAYEK'S CONTRIBUTIONS TO THE HISTORY OF IDEAS

♦ ♦ ♦

• *PART* • *THREE* •

INDIVIDUALISM: *TRUE AND FALSE*

· 7 ·

Du dix-huitième siècle et de la révolution, comme d'une source commune, étaient sortis deux fleuves: le premier conduisait les hommes aux institutions libres, tandis que le second les menait au pouvoir absolu.

Alexis de Tocqueville

I

To advocate any clear-cut principles of social order is today an almost certain way to incur the stigma of being an unpractical doctrinaire. It has come to be regarded as the sign of the judicious mind that in social matters one does not adhere to fixed principles but decides each question "on its merits"; that one is generally guided by expediency and is ready to compromise between opposed views. Principles, however, have a way of asserting themselves even if they are not explicitly recognized but are only implied in particular decisions, or if they are present only as vague ideas of what is or is not being done. Thus it has come about that under the sign of "nei-

---

The twelfth Finlay Lecture, delivered at University College, Dublin, on December 17, 1945. Published by Hodges, Figgis & Co., Ltd., Dublin, and B. H. Blackwell, Ltd., Oxford, 1946.

ther individualism nor socialism" we are in fact rapidly moving from a society of free individuals toward one of a completely collectivist character.

I propose not only to undertake to defend a general principle of social organization but shall also try to show that the aversion to general principles, and the preference for proceeding from particular instance to particular instance, is the product of the movement which with the "inevitability of gradualness" leads us back from a social order resting on the general recognition of certain principles to a system in which order is created by direct commands.

After the experience of the last thirty years, there is perhaps not much need to emphasize that without principles we drift. The pragmatic attitude which has been dominant during that period, far from increasing our command over developments, has in fact led us to a state of affairs which nobody wanted; and the only result of our disregard of principles seems to be that we are governed by a logic of events which we are vainly attempting to ignore. The question now is not whether we need principles to guide us but rather whether there still exists a body of principles capable of general application which we could follow if we wished. Where can we still find a set of precepts which will give us definite guidance in the solution of the problems of our time? Is there anywhere a consistent philosophy to be found which supplies us not merely with the moral aims but with an adequate method for their achievement?

That religion itself does not give us definite guidance in these matters is shown by the efforts of the church to elaborate a complete social philosophy and by the entirely opposite results at which many arrive who start from the same Christian foundations. Though the declining influence of religion is undoubtedly one major cause of our present lack of intellectual and moral orientation, its revival would not much lessen the need for a generally accepted principle of social order. We still should require a political philosophy which goes beyond the fundamental but general precepts which religion or morals provide.

The title which I have chosen for this chapter shows that to me there still seems to exist such a philosophy — a set of principles which, indeed, is implicit in most of Western or Christian political tradition but which can no longer be unambiguously described by any readily understood term. It is therefore necessary to restate these principles fully before we can decide whether they can still serve us as practical guides.

The difficulty which we encounter is not merely the familiar fact that the current political terms are notoriously ambiguous or even that the same term often means nearly the opposite to different groups. There is the much more serious fact that the same word frequently appears to unite people who in fact believe in contradictory and irreconcilable ideals. Terms like "liberalism" or "democracy," "capitalism" or "socialism," today no longer stand for coherent systems of ideas. They have come to describe aggregations of quite heterogeneous principles and facts which historical accident has associated with these words but which have little in common beyond having been advocated at different times by the same people or even merely under the same name.

No political term has suffered worse in this respect than "individualism." It not only has been distorted by its opponents into an unrecognizable caricature — and we should always remember that the political concepts which are today out of fashion are known to most of our contemporaries only through the picture drawn of them by their enemies — but has been used to describe several attitudes toward society which have as little in common among themselves as they have with those traditionally regarded as their opposites. Indeed, when in the preparation of this paper I examined some of the standard descriptions of "individualism," I almost began to regret that I had ever connected the ideals in which I believe with a term which has been so abused and so misunderstood. Yet, whatever else "individualism" may have come to mean in addition to these ideals, there are two good reasons for retaining the term for the view I mean to defend: this view has always been known by that term, whatever else it may also have meant at different times, and the term has the distinction that the word "socialism" was deliberately coined to express its opposition to individualism.[1] It is with the system which forms the alternative to socialism that I shall be concerned.

II

Before I explain what I mean by true individualism, it may be useful if I give some indication of the intellectual tradition to which it belongs. The true individualism which I shall try to defend began its modern development with John Locke, and particularly with Bernard Mandeville and David Hume, and achieved full stature for the first time in the work of Josiah Tucker, Adam Ferguson, and Adam Smith and in that of their great contemporary, Edmund Burke — the man whom Smith described as the only person he ever knew who thought on economic subjects exactly as he did without any previous communication having passed between them.[2] In the nineteenth century I find it represented most perfectly in the work of two of its greatest historians and political philosophers: Alexis de Tocqueville and Lord Acton. These two men seem to me to have more successfully developed what was best in the political philosophy of the Scottish philosophers, Burke, and the English Whigs than any other writers I know; while the classical economists of the nineteenth century, or at least the Benthamites or philosophical radicals among them, came increasingly under the influence of another kind of individualism of different origin.

This second and altogether different strand of thought, also known as individualism, is represented mainly by French and other Continental writers — a fact due, I believe, to the dominant role which Cartesian rationalism plays in its composition. The outstanding representatives of this tradition are the Encyclopedists, Rousseau, and the physiocrats; and, for reasons we shall presently consider, this rationalistic individualism always tends to develop into the opposite of individualism, namely, socialism or collectivism. It is because only the first kind of individualism is consistent that I claim for it the name of true individualism, while the second kind must probably be regarded as a source of modern socialism as important as the properly collectivist theories.[3]

I can give no better illustration of the prevailing confusion about the meaning of individualism than the fact that the man who to me seems to be one of the greatest representatives of true individualism, Edmund Burke, is commonly (and rightly) represented as the main opponent of the so-called "individualism" of Rousseau, whose theories he feared would rapidly dissolve the commonwealth "into the dust and powder of individuality,"[4] and that the term "individualism" itself was first introduced into the English language through the translation of one of the works of another of the great representatives of true individualism, de Tocqueville, who uses it in his *Democracy in America* to describe an attitude which he deplores and rejects.[5] Yet there can no doubt that both Burke and de Tocqueville stand in all essentials close to Adam Smith, to whom nobody will deny the title of individualist, and that the "individualism" to which they are opposed is something altogether different from that of Smith.

III

What, then, are the essential characteristics of true individualism? The first thing that should be said is that it is primarily a *theory* of society, an attempt to understand the forces which determine the social life of man, and only in the second instance a set of political maxims derived from this view of society. This fact should by itself be sufficient to refute the silliest of the common misunderstandings: the belief that individualism postulates (or bases its arguments on the assumption of) the existence of isolated or self-contained individuals, instead of starting from men whose whole nature and character is determined by their existence in society.[6] If that were true, it would indeed have nothing to contribute to our understanding of society. But its basic contention is quite a different one; it is that there is no other way toward an understanding of social phenomena but through our understanding of individual actions directed toward other people and guided by their expected behavior.[7] This argument is directed primarily against the properly collectivist theories of society which pretend to be able directly to comprehend social wholes like society, etc., as entities *sui generis* which exist independently of the individuals which compose them. The next step in the individualistic analysis of society, however, is directed against the rationalistic pseudo-individualism which also leads to practical collectivism. It is the contention that, by tracing the combined effects of individual actions, we discover that many of the institutions on which human achievements rest have arisen and are functioning without a designing and directing mind; that, as Adam Ferguson expressed it, "nations stumble upon establishments, which are indeed the result of human action but not the result of human design";[8] and that the spontaneous collaboration of free men often creates things which are greater than their individual minds can ever fully comprehend. This is the great theme of Josiah Tucker and Adam Smith, of Adam Ferguson and Edmund Burke, the great discovery of classical political economy which has become the basis of our understanding not only of economic life but of most truly social phenomena.

The difference between this view, which accounts for most of the order which we find in human affairs as the unforeseen result of individual actions, and the view which traces all discoverable order to deliberate design is the first great contrast between the true individualism of the British thinkers of the eighteenth century and the so-called "individualism" of the Cartesian school.[9] But it is merely one aspect of an even wider difference between a view which in general rates rather low the place which reason plays in human affairs, which contends that man has achieved what he has in spite of the fact that he is only partly guided by reason, and that his individual reason is very limited and imperfect, and a view which assumes that Reason, with a capital *R,* is always fully and equally available to all humans and that everything which man achieves is the direct result of, and therefore subject to, the control of individual reason. One might even say that the former is a product of an acute consciousness of the limitations of the individual mind which induces an attitude of humility toward the impersonal and anonymous social processes by which individuals help to create things greater than they know, while the latter is the product of an exaggerated belief in the powers of individual reason and of a consequent contempt for anything which has not been consciously designed by it or is not fully intelligible to it.

The antirationalistic approach, which regards man not as a highly rational and intelligent but as a very irrational and fallible being, whose individual errors are corrected only in the course of a social process, and which aims at making the best of a very imperfect material, is probably the most characteristic feature of English individualism. Its predominance in English thought seems to me due largely to the profound influence exercised by Bernard Mandeville, by whom the central idea was for the first time clearly formulated.[10]

I cannot better illustrate the contrast in which Cartesian or rationalistic "individualism" stands to this view than by quoting a famous passage from Part II of the *Discourse on Method.* Descartes argues that "there is seldom so much perfection in works composed of many separate parts, upon which different hands had been employed, as in those completed by a single master." He then goes on to suggest (after, significantly, quoting the instance of the engineer drawing up his plans) that "those nations which, starting from a semi-barbarous state and advancing to civilization by slow degrees, have had their laws successively determined, and, as it were, forced upon them simply by experience of the hurtfulness of particular crimes and disputes, would by this process come to be possessed of less perfect institutions than those which, from the commencement of their association as communities, have followed the appointment of some wise legislator." To drive this point home, Descartes adds that in his opinion "the past pre-eminence of Sparta was due not to the pre-eminence of each of its laws in particular . . . but to the circumstance that, originated by a single individual, they all tended to a single end."[11]

It would be interesting to trace further the development of this social contract individualism or the "design" theories of social institutions, from Descartes through Rousseau and the French Revolution down to what is still the characteristic attitude of the engineers to social problems.[12] Such a sketch would show how Cartesian rationalism has persistently proved a grave obstacle to an understanding of historical phenomena and that it is largely responsible for the belief in inevitable laws of historical development and the modern fatalism derived from this belief.[13]

All we are here concerned with, however, is that this view, though also known as "individualism," stands in complete contrast to true individualism on two decisive points. While it is perfectly true of this pseudo-individualism that "belief in spontaneous social products was logically impossible to any philosophers who regarded individual man as the starting point and supposed him to form societies by the union of his particular will with another in a formal contract,"[14] true individualism is the only theory which can claim to make the formation of spontaneous social products intelligible. And, while the design theories necessarily lead to the conclusion that social processes can be made to serve human ends only if they are subjected to the control of individual human reason, and thus lead directly to socialism, true individualism believes on the contrary that, if left free, men will often achieve more than individual human reason could design or foresee.

This contrast between the true, antirationalistic and the false, rationalistic individualism permeates all social thought. But because both theories have become known by the same name, and partly because the classical economists of the nineteenth century, and particularly John Stuart Mill and Herbert Spencer, were almost as much influenced by the French as by the English tradition, all sorts of conceptions and assumptions completely alien to true individualism have come to be regarded as essential parts of its doctrine.

Perhaps the best illustration of the current misconceptions of the individualism of Adam Smith and his group is the common belief that they have invented the bogey of the "economic man" and that their conclusions are vitiated by their assumption of a strictly rational behavior or generally by a false rationalistic psychology. They were, of course, very far from assuming anything of the kind. It would be nearer the truth to say that in their view man was by nature lazy and indolent, improvident and wasteful, and that it was only by the force of circumstances that he could be made to behave economically or carefully to adjust his means to his ends. But even this would be unjust to the very complex and realistic view which these men took of human nature. Since it has become fashionable to deride Smith and his contemporaries for their supposedly erroneous psychology, I may perhaps venture the opinion that for all practical purposes we can still learn more about the behavior of men from the *Wealth of Nations* than from most of the more pretentious modern treatises on "social psychology."

However that may be, the main point about which there can be little doubt is that Smith's chief concern was not so much with what man might occasionally achieve when he was at his best but that he should have as little opportunity as possible to do harm when he was at his worst. It would scarcely be too much to claim that the main merit of the individualism which he and his contemporaries advocated is that it is a system under which bad men can do least harm. It is a social system which does not depend for its functioning on our finding good men for running it, or on all men becoming better than they now are, but which makes use of men in all their given variety and complexity, sometimes good and sometimes bad, sometimes intelligent and more often stupid. Their aim was a system under which it should be possible to grant freedom to all, instead of restricting it, as their French contemporaries wished, to "the good and the wise."[15]

The chief concern of the great individualist writers was indeed to find a set of institutions by which man could be induced, by his own choice and from the motives which determined his ordinary conduct, to contribute as much as possible to the need of all others; and their discovery was that the system of private property did provide such inducements to a much greater extent than had yet been understood. They did not contend, however, that this system was incapable of further improvement and, still less, as another of the current distortions of their arguments will have it, that there existed a "natural harmony of interests" irrespective of the positive institutions. They were more than merely aware of the conflicts of individual interests and stressed the necessity of "well-constructed institutions" where the "rules and principles of contending interests and compromised advantages"[16] would reconcile conflicting interests without giving any one group power to make their views and interests always prevail over those of all others.

IV

There is one point in these basic psychological assumptions which it is necessary to consider somewhat more fully. As the belief that individualism approves and encourages human selfishness is one of the main reasons why so many people dislike it, and as the confusion which exists in this respect is caused by a real intellectual difficulty, we must carefully examine the meaning of the assumptions it makes. There can be no doubt, of course, that in the language of the great writers of the eighteenth century it was man's "self-love," or even his "selfish interests," which they represented as the "universal mover," and that by these terms they were referring primarily to a moral attitude, which they thought to be widely prevalent. These terms, however, did not mean egotism in the narrow sense of concern with only the immediate needs of one's proper person. The "self," for which alone people were supposed to care, did as a matter of course include their family and friends; and it would have made no difference to the argument if it had included anything for which people in fact did care.

Far more important than this moral attitude, which might be regarded as changeable, is an indisputable intellectual fact which nobody can hope to alter and which by itself is a sufficient basis for the conclusions which the individualist philosophers drew. This is the constitutional limitation of man's knowledge and interests, the fact that he *cannot* know more than a tiny part of the whole of society and that therefore all that can enter into his motives are the immediate effects which his actions will have in the sphere he knows. All the possible differences in men's moral attitudes amount to little, so far as their significance for social organization is concerned, compared with the fact that all man's mind can effectively comprehend are the facts of the narrow circle of which he is the center; that, whether he is completely selfish or the most perfect altruist, the human needs for which he *can* effectively care are an almost negligible fraction of the needs of all members of society. The real question, therefore, is not whether man is, or ought to be, guided by selfish motives but whether we can allow him to be guided in his actions by those immediate consequences which he can know and care for or whether he ought to be made to do what seems appropriate to somebody else who is supposed to possess a fuller comprehension of the significance of these actions to society as a whole.

To the accepted Christian tradition that man must be free to follow *his* conscience in moral matters if his actions are to be of any merit, the economists added the further argument that he should be free to make full use of *his* knowledge and skill, that he must be allowed to be guided by his concern for the particular things of which *he* knows and for which *he* cares, if he is to make as great a contribution to the common purposes of society as he is capable of making. Their main problem was how these limited concerns, which did in fact determine people's actions, could be made effective inducements to cause them voluntarily to contribute as much as possible to needs which lay outside the range of their vision. What the economists understood for the first time was that the market as it had grown up was an effective way of making man take part in a process more complex and extended than he could comprehend and that it was through the market that he was made to contribute "to ends which were no part of his purpose."

It was almost inevitable that the classical writers in explaining their contention should use language which was bound to be misunderstood and that they thus earned the reputation of having extolled selfishness. We rapidly discover the reason when we try to restate the correct argument in simple language. If we put it concisely by saying that people are and ought to be guided in their actions by *their* interests and desires, this will at once be misunderstood or distorted into the false contention that they are or ought to be exclusively guided by their personal needs or selfish interests, while what we mean is that they ought to be allowed to strive for whatever *they* think desirable.

Another misleading phrase, used to stress an important point, is the famous presumption that each man knows his interests best. In this form the contention is neither plausible nor necessary for the individualist's conclusions. The true basis of his argument is that nobody can know *who* knows best and that the only way by which we can find out is through a social process in which everybody is allowed to try and see what he can do. The fundamental assumption, here as elsewhere, is the unlimited variety of human gifts and skills and the consequent ignorance of any single individual of most of what is known to all the other members of society taken together. Or, to put this fundamental contention differently, human Reason, with a capital *R*, does not exist in the singular, as given or available to any particular person, as the rationalist approach seems to assume, but must be conceived as an interpersonal process in which anyone's contribution is tested and corrected by others. This argument does not assume that all men are equal in their natural endowments and capacities but only that no man is qualified to pass final judgment on the capacities which another possesses or is to be allowed to exercise.

Here I may perhaps mention that only because men are in fact unequal can we treat them equally. If all men were completely equal in their gifts and inclinations, we should have to treat them differently in order to achieve any sort of social organization. Fortunately, they are not equal; and it is only owing to this that the differentiation of functions need not be determined by the arbitrary decision of some organizing will but that, after creating formal equality of the rules applying in the same manner to all, we can leave each individual to find his own level.

There is all the difference in the world between treating people equally and attempting to make them equal. While the first is the condition of a free society, the second means, as de Tocqueville described it, "a new form of servitude."[17]

V

From the awareness of the limitations of individual knowledge and from the fact that no person or small group of persons can know all that is known to somebody, individualism also derives its main practical conclusion: its demand for a strict limitation of all coercive or exclusive power. Its opposition, however, is directed only against the use of *coercion* to bring about organization or association, and not against association as such. Far from being opposed to voluntary association, the case of the individualist rests, on the contrary, on the contention that much of what in the opinion of many can be brought about only by conscious direction, can be better achieved by the voluntary and spontaneous collaboration of individuals. The consistent individualist ought therefore to be an enthusiast for voluntary collaboration — wherever and whenever it does not degenerate into coercion of others or lead to the assumption of exclusive powers.

True individualism is, of course, not anarchism, which is but another product of the rationalistic pseudo-individualism to which it is opposed. It does not deny the necessity of coercive power but wishes to limit it — to limit it to those fields where it is indispensable to prevent coercion by others and in order to reduce the total of coercion to a minimum. While all the individualist philosophers are probably agreed on this general formula, it must be admitted that they are not always very informative on its application in specific cases. Neither the much abused and much misunderstood phrase of "laissez faire" nor the still older formula of "the protection of life, liberty, and property" are of much help. In fact, in so far as both tend to suggest that we can just leave things as they are, they may be worse than no answer; they certainly do not tell us what are and what are not desirable or necessary fields of government activity. Yet the decision whether individualist philosophy can serve us as a practical guide must ultimately depend on whether it will enable us to distinguish between the agenda and the nonagenda of government.

Some general rules of this kind which are of very wide applicability seem to me to follow directly from the basic tenets of individualism: If each man is to use *his* peculiar knowledge and skill with the aim of furthering the aims for which *he* cares, and if, in so doing, he is to make as large a contribution as possible to needs which are beyond his ken, it is clearly necessary, first, that he should have a clearly delimited area of responsibility and, second, that the relative importance to him of the different results he can achieve must correspond to the relative importance to others of the more remote and to him unknown effects of his action.

Let us first take the problem of the determination of a sphere of responsibility and leave the second problem for later. If man is to remain free to make full use of his knowledge or skill, the delimitation of spheres of responsibility must not take the form of an assignation to him of particular ends which he must try to achieve. This would be imposing a specific duty rather than delimiting a sphere of responsibility. Nor must it take the form of allocating to him specific resources selected by some authority, which would take the choice almost as much out of his hands as the imposition of specific tasks. If man is to exercise his own gifts, it must be as a result of his activities and planning that his sphere of responsibility is determined. The solution to this problem which men have gradually developed and which antedates government in the modern sense of the word is the acceptance of formal principles, "a standing rule to live by, common to every one of that society"[18] — of rules which, above all, enable man to distinguish between mine and thine, and from which he and his fellows can ascertain what is his and what is somebody else's sphere of responsibility.

The fundamental contrast between government by rules, whose main purpose is to inform the individual what is his sphere of responsibility within which he must shape his own life, and government by orders which impose specific duties has become so blurred in recent years that it is necessary to consider it a little further. It involves nothing less than the distinction between freedom under the law and the use of the legislative machinery, whether democratic or not, to abolish freedom. The essential point is not that there should be some kind of guiding principle behind the actions of the government but that government should be confined to making the individuals observe principles which *they* know and can take into account in *their* decisions. It means, further, that what the individual may or may not do, or what he can expect his fellows to do or not to do, must depend not on some remote and indirect consequences which his actions may have but on the immediate and readily recognizable circumstances which he can be supposed to know. He must have rules referring to typical situations, defined in terms of what can be known to the acting persons and without regard to the distant effects in the particular instance — rules which, if they are regularly observed, will in the majority of cases operate beneficially — even if they do not do so in the proverbial "hard cases which make bad law."

The most general principle on which an individualist system is based is that it uses the universal acceptance of general principles as the means to create order in social affairs. It is the opposite of such government by principles when, for example, a recent blueprint for a controlled economy suggests as "the fundamental principle of organisation . . . that in any particular instance the means that serves society best should be the one that prevails."[19] It is a serious confusion thus to speak of principle when all that is meant is that no principle but only expediency should rule; when everything depends on what authority decrees to be "the interests of society." Principles are a means to prevent clashes between conflicting aims and not a set of fixed ends. Our submission to general principles is necessary because we cannot be guided in our practical action by full knowledge and evaluation of all the consequences. So long as men are not omniscient, the only way in which freedom can be given to the individual is by such general rules to delimit the sphere in which the decision is his. There can be no freedom if the government is not limited to particular kinds of action but can use its powers in any ways which serve particular ends. As Lord Acton pointed out long ago: "Whenever a single definite object is made the supreme end of the State, be it the advantage of a class, the safety or the power of the country, the greatest happiness of the greatest number or the support of any speculative idea, the State becomes for the time inevitably absolute."[20]

VI

But, if our main conclusion is that an individualist order must rest on the enforcement of abstract principles rather than on the enforcement of specific orders, this still leaves open the question of the kind of general rules which we want. It confines the exercise of coercive powers in the main to one method, but it still allows almost unlimited scope to human ingenuity in the designing of the most effective set of rules; and, though the best solutions of the concrete problems will in most instances have to be discovered by experience, there is a good deal more that we can learn from the general principles of individualism with regard to the desirable nature and contents of these rules. There is, in the first instance, one important corollary of what has already been said, namely, that the rules, because they are to serve as signposts to the individuals in making their own plans, should be designed to remain valid for long periods. Liberal or individualist policy must be essentially long-run policy; the present fashion to concentrate on short-run effects, and to justify this by the argument that "in the long run we are all dead," leads inevitably to the reliance on orders adjusted to the particular circumstances of the moment in the place of rules couched in terms of typical situations.

We need, and get from the basic principles of individualism, however, much more definite aid than this for the construction of a suitable legal system. The endeavor to make man by the pursuit of his interests contribute as much as possible to the needs of other men leads not merely to the general principle of "private property"; it also assists us in determining what the contents of property rights ought to be with respect to different kinds of things. In order that the individual in his decisions should take account of all the physical effects caused by these decisions, it is necessary that the "sphere of responsibility" of which I have been speaking be made to comprise as fully as possible all the direct effects which his actions have on the satisfactions which other people derive from the things under his control. This is achieved on the whole by the simple conception of property as the exclusive right to use a particular thing where mobile effects, or what the lawyer calls "chattels," are concerned. But it raises much more difficult problems in connection with land, where the recognition of the principle of private property helps us very little until we know precisely what rights and obligations ownership includes. And when we turn to such problems of more recent origin as the control of the air or of electric power, or of inventions and of literary or artistic creations, nothing short of going back to *rationale* of property will help us to decide what should be in the particular instance the sphere of control or responsibility of the individual.

I cannot here go further into the fascinating subject of a suitable legal framework for an effective individualist system or enter into discussion of the many supplementary functions, such as assistance in the spreading of information and in the elimination of genuinely avoidable uncertainty,[21] by which the government might greatly increase the efficiency of individual action. I mention them merely in order to stress that there are further (and noncoercive!) functions of government beyond the mere enforcement of civil and criminal law which can be fully justified on individualist principles.

There is still, however, one point left, to which I have already referred, but which is so important that I must give it further attention. It is that any workable individualist order must be so framed not only that the relative remunerations the individual can expect from the different uses of his abilities and resources correspond to the relative utility of the result of his efforts to others but also that these remunerations correspond to the objective results of his efforts rather than to their subjective merits. An effectively competitive market satisfies both these conditions. But it is in connection with the second that our personal sense of justice so frequently revolts against the impersonal decisions of the market. Yet, if the individual is to be free to choose, it is inevitable that he should bear the risk attaching to that choice and that in consequence he be rewarded, not according to the goodness or badness of his intentions, but solely on the basis of the value of the results to others. We must face the fact that the preservation of individual freedom is incompatible with a full satisfaction of our views of distributive justice.

VII

While the theory of individualism has thus a definite contribution to make to the technique of constructing a suitable legal framework and of improving the institutions which have grown up spontaneously, its emphasis, of course, is on the fact that the part of our social order which can or ought to be made a conscious product of human reason is only a small part of all the forces of society. In other words, that the state, the embodiment of deliberately organized and consciously directed power, ought to be only a small part of the much richer organism which we call "society," and that the former ought to provide merely a framework within which free (and therefore not "consciously directed") collaboration of men has the maximum of scope.

This entails certain corollaries on which true individualism once more stands in sharp opposition to the false individualism of the rationalistic type. The first is that the deliberately organized state on the one side, and the individual on the other, far from being regarded as the only realities, while all the intermediate formations and associations are to be deliberately suppressed, as was the aim of the French Revolution, the noncompulsory conventions of social intercourse are considered as essential factors in preserving the orderly working of human society. The second is that the individual, in participating in the social processes, must be ready and willing to adjust himself to changes and to submit to conventions which are not the result of intelligent design, whose justification in the particular instance may not be recognizable, and which to him will often appear unintelligible and irrational.

I need not say much on the first point. That true individualism affirms the value of the family and all the common efforts of the small community and group, that it believes in local autonomy and voluntary associations, and that indeed its case rests largely on the contention that much for which the coercive action of the state is usually invoked can be done better by voluntary collaboration need not be stressed further. There can be no greater contrast to this than the false individualism which wants to dissolve all these smaller groups into atoms which have no cohesion other than the coercive rules imposed by the state, and which tries to make all social ties prescriptive, instead of using the state mainly as a protection of the individual against the arrogation of coercive powers by the smaller groups.

Quite as important for the functioning of an individualist society as these smaller groupings of men are the traditions and conventions which evolve in a free society and which, without being enforceable, establish flexible but normally observed rules that make the behavior of other people predictable in a high degree. The willingness to submit to such rules, not merely so long as one understands the reason for them but so long as one has no definite reasons to the contrary, is an essential condition for the gradual evolution and improvement of rules of social intercourse; and the readiness ordinarily to submit to the products of a social process which nobody has designed and the reasons for which nobody may understand is also an indispensable condition if it is to be possible to dispense with compulsion.[22] That the existence of common conventions and traditions among a group of people will enable them to work together smoothly and efficiently with much less formal organization and compulsion than a group without such common background, is, of course, a commonplace. But the reverse of this, while less familiar, is probably not less true: that coercion can probably only be kept to a minimum in a society where conventions and tradition have made the behavior of man to a large extent predictable.[23]

This brings me to my second point: the necessity, in any complex society in which the effects of anyone's action reach far beyond his possible range of vision, of the individual submitting to the anonymous and seemingly irrational forces of society — a submission which must include not only the acceptance of rules of behavior as valid without examining what depends in the particular instance on their being observed but also a readiness to adjust himself to changes which may profoundly affect his fortunes and opportunities and the causes of which may be altogether unintelligible to him. It is against these that modern man tends to revolt unless their necessity can be shown to rest upon "reason made clear and demonstrable to every individual." Yet it is just here that the understandable craving for intelligibility produces illusory demands which no system can satisfy. Man in a complex society can have no choice but between adjusting himself to what to him must seem the blind forces of the social process and obeying the orders of a superior. So long as he knows only the hard discipline of the market, he may well think the direction by some other intelligent human brain preferable; but, when he tries it, he soon discovers that the former still leaves him at least some choice, while the latter leaves him none, and that it is better to have a choice between several unpleasant alternatives than being coerced into one.

The unwillingness to tolerate or respect any social forces which are not recognizable as the product of intelligent design, which is so important a cause of the present desire for comprehensive economic planning, is indeed only one aspect of a more general movement. We meet the same tendency in the field of morals and conventions, in the desire to substitute an artificial for the existing languages, and in the whole modern attitude toward processes which govern the growth of knowledge. The belief that only a synthetic system of morals, an artificial language, or even an artificial society can be justified in an age of science, as well as the increasing unwillingness to bow before any moral rules whose utility is not rationally demonstrated, or to conform with conventions whose rationale is not known, are all manifestations of the same basic view which wants all social activity to be recognizably part of a single coherent plan. They are the results of that same rationalistic "individualism" which wants to see in everything the product of conscious individual reason. They are certainly not, however, a result of true individualism and may even make the working of a free and truly individualistic system difficult or impossible. Indeed, the great lesson which the individualistic philosophy teaches us on this score is that, while it may not be difficult to destroy the spontaneous formations which are the indispensable bases of a free civilization, it may be beyond our power deliberately to reconstruct such a civilization once these foundations are destroyed.

VIII

The point I am trying to make is well illustrated by the apparent paradox that the Germans, though commonly regarded as very docile, are also often described as being particularly individualistic. With some truth this so-called German individualism is frequently represented as one of the causes why the Germans have never succeeded in developing free political institutions. In the rationalistic sense of the term, in their insistence on the development of "original" personalities which in every respect are the product of the conscious choice of the individual, the German intellectual tradition indeed favors a kind of "individualism" little known elsewhere. I remember well how surprised and even shocked I was myself when as a young student, on my first contact with English and American contemporaries, I discovered how much they were disposed to conform in all externals to common usage rather than, as seemed natural to me, to be proud to be different and original in most respects. If you doubt the significance of such an individual experience, you will find it fully confirmed in most German discussions of, for example, the English public school system, such as you will find in Dibelius' well-known book on England.[24] Again and again you will find the same surprise about this tendency toward voluntary conformity and see it contrasted with the ambition of the young German to develop an "original personality," which in every respect expresses what he has come to regard as right and true. This cult of the distinct and different individuality has, of course, deep roots in the German intellectual tradition and, through the influence of some of its greatest exponents, especially Goethe and Wilhelm von Humboldt, has made itself felt far beyond Germany and is clearly seen in J. S. Mill's *Liberty*.

This sort of "individualism" not only has nothing to do with true individualism but may indeed prove a grave obstacle to the smooth working of an individualist system. It must remain an open question whether a free or individualistic society can be worked successfully if people are too "individualistic" in the false sense, if they are too unwilling voluntarily to conform to traditions and conventions, and if they refuse to recognize anything which is not consciously designed or which cannot be demonstrated as rational to every individual. It is at least understandable that the prevalence of this kind of "individualism" has often made people of good will despair of the possibility of achieving order in a free society and even made them ask for a dictatorial government with the power to impose on society the order which it will not produce itself.

In Germany, in particular, this preference for the deliberate organization and the corresponding contempt for the spontaneous and uncontrolled, was strongly supported by the tendency toward centralization which the struggle for national unity produced. In a country where what traditions it possessed were essentially local, the striving for unity implied a systematic opposition to almost everything which was a spontaneous growth and its consistent replacement by artificial creations. That, in what a recent historian has well described as a "desperate search for a tradition which they did not possess,"[25] the Germans should have ended by creating a totalitarian state which forced upon them what they felt they lacked should perhaps not have surprised us as much as it did.

IX

If it is true that the progressive tendency toward central control of all social processes is the inevitable result of an approach which insists that everything must be tidily planned and made to show a recognizable order, it is also true that this tendency tends to create conditions in which nothing but an all-powerful central government can preserve order and stability. The concentration of all decisions in the hands of authority itself produces a state of affairs in which what structure society still possesses is imposed upon it by government and in which the individuals have become interchangeable units with no other definite or durable relations to one another than those determined by the all-comprehensive organization. In the jargon of the modern sociologists this type of society has come to be known as "mass society" — a somewhat misleading name, because the characteristic attributes of this kind of society are not so much the result of mere numbers as they are of the lack of any spontaneous structure other than that impressed upon it by deliberate organization, an incapacity to evolve its own differentiations, and a consequent dependence on a power which deliberately molds and shapes it. It is connected with numbers only in so far as in large nations the process of centralization will much sooner reach a point where deliberate organization from the top smothers those spontaneous formations which are founded on contacts closer and more intimate than those that can exist in the large unit.

It is not surprising that in the nineteenth century, when these tendencies first became clearly visible, the opposition to centralization became one of the main concerns of the individualist philosophers. This opposition is particularly marked in the writings of the two great historians whose names I have before singled out as the leading representatives of true individualism in the nineteenth century, de Tocqueville and Lord Acton; and it finds expression in their strong sympathies for the small countries and for the federal organization of large units. There is even more reason now to think that the small countries may before long become the last oases that will preserve a free society. It may already be too late to stop the fatal course of progressive centralization in the bigger countries which are well on the way to produce those mass societies in which despotism in the end comes to appear as the only salvation. Whether even the small countries will escape will depend on whether they keep free from the poison of nationalism, which is both an inducement to, and a result of, that same striving for a society which is consciously organized from the top.

The attitude of individualism to nationalism, which intellectually is but a twin brother of socialism, would deserve special discussion. Here I can only point out that the fundamental difference between what in the nineteenth century was regarded as liberalism in the English-speaking world and what was so called on the Continent is closely connected with their descent from true individualism and the false rationalistic individualism, respectively. It was only liberalism in the English sense that was generally opposed to centralization, to nationalism and to socialism, while the liberalism prevalent on the Continent favored all three. I should add, however, that, in this as in so many other respects, John Stuart Mill, and the later English liberalism derived from him, belong at least as much to the Continental as to the English tradition; and I know no discussion more illuminating of these basic differences than Lord Acton's criticism of the concessions Mill had made to the nationalistic tendencies of Continental liberalism.[26]

X

There are two more points of difference between the two kinds of individualism which are also best illustrated by the stand taken by Lord Acton and de Tocqueville by their views on democracy and equality toward trends which became prominent in their time. True individualism not only believes in democracy but can claim that democratic ideals spring from the basic principles of individualism. Yet, while individualism affirms that all government should be democratic, it has no superstitious belief in the omnicompetence of majority decisions, and in particular it refuses to admit that "absolute power may, by the hypothesis of popular origin, be as legitimate as constitutional freedom."[27] It believes that under a democracy, no less than under any other form of government, "the sphere of enforced command ought to be restricted within fixed limits";[28] and it is particularly opposed to the most fateful and dangerous of all current misconceptions of democracy — the belief that we must accept as true and binding for future development the views of the majority. While democracy is founded on the convention that the majority view decides on common action, it does not mean that what is today the majority view ought to become the generally accepted view — even if that were necessary to achieve the aims of the majority. On the contrary, the whole justification of democracy rests on the fact that in course of time what is today the view of a small minority may become the majority view. I believe, indeed, that one of the most important questions on which political theory will have to discover an answer in the near future is that of finding a line of demarcation between the fields in which the majority views must be binding for all and the fields in which, on the contrary, the minority view ought to be allowed to prevail if it can produce results which better satisfy a demand of the public. I am, above all, convinced that, where the interests of a particular branch of trade are concerned, the majority view will always be the reactionary, stationary view and that the merit of competition is precisely that it gives the minority a chance to prevail. Where it can do so without any coercive powers, it ought always to have the right.

I cannot better sum up this attitude of true individualism toward democracy than by once more quoting Lord Acton: "The true democratic principle," he wrote, "that none shall have power over the people, is taken to mean that none shall be able to restrain or to elude its power. The true democratic principle, that the people shall not be made to do what it does not like, is taken to mean that it shall never be required to tolerate what it does not like. The true democratic principle, that every man's will shall be as unfettered as possible, is taken to mean that the free will of the collective people shall be fettered in nothing."[29]

When we turn to equality, however, it should be said at once that true individualism is not equalitarian in the modern sense of the word. It can see no reason for trying to make people equal as distinct from treating them equally. While individualism is profoundly opposed to all prescriptive privilege, to all protection, by law or force, of any rights not based on rules equally applicable to all persons, it also denies government the right to limit what the able or fortunate may achieve. It is equally opposed to any rigid limitation of the position individuals may achieve, whether this power is used to perpetuate inequality or to create equality. Its main principle is that no man or group of men should have power to decide what another man's status ought to be, and it regards this as a condition of freedom so essential that it must not be sacrificed to the gratification of our sense of justice or of our envy.

From the point of view of individualism there would not appear to exist even any justification for making all individuals start on the same level by preventing them from profiting by advantages which they have in no way earned, such as being born to parents who are more intelligent or more conscientious than the average. Here individualism is indeed less "individualistic" than socialism, because it recognizes the family as a legitimate unit as much as the individual; and the same is true with respect to other groups, such as linguistic or religious communities, which by their common efforts may succeed for long periods in preserving for their members material or moral standards different from those of the rest of the population. De Tocqueville and Lord Acton speak with one voice on this subject. "Democracy and socialism," de Tocqueville wrote, "have nothing in common but one word, equality. But notice the difference: while democracy seeks equality in liberty, socialism seeks equality in restraint and servitude."[30] And Acton joined him in believing that "the deepest cause which made the French revolution so disastrous to liberty was its theory of equality"[31] and that "the finest opportunity ever given to the world was thrown away, because the passion for equality made vain the hope for freedom."[32]

XI

It would be possible to continue for a long time discussing further differences separating the two traditions of thought which, while bearing the same name, are divided by fundamentally opposed principles. But I must not allow myself to be diverted too far from my task of tracing to its source the confusion which has resulted from this and of showing that there is one consistent tradition which, whether you agree with me or not that it is "true" individualism, is at any rate the only kind of individualism which I am prepared to defend and, indeed, I believe, the only kind which can be defended consistently. So let me return, in conclusion, to what I said in the beginning: that the fundamental attitude of true individualism is one of humility toward the processes by which mankind has achieved things which have not been designed or understood by any individual and are indeed greater than individual minds. The great question at this moment is whether man's mind will be allowed to continue to grow as part of this process or whether human reason is to place itself in chains of its own making.

What individualism teaches us is that society is greater than the individual only in so far as it is free. In so far as it is controlled or directed, it is limited to the powers of the individual minds which control or direct it. If the presumption of the modern mind, which will not respect anything that is not consciously controlled by individual reason, does not learn in time where to stop, we may, as Edmund Burke warned us, "be well assured that everything about us will dwindle by degrees, until at length our concerns are shrunk to the dimensions of our minds."

Notes

1. Both the term "individualism" and the term "socialism" are originally the creation of the Saint-Simonians, the founders of modern socialism. They first coined the term "individualism" to describe the competitive society to which they were opposed and then invented the word "socialism"

to describe the centrally planned society in which all activity was directed on the same principle that applied within a single factory. See on the origin of these terms the present author's article on "The Counter-Revolution of Science," *Economica,* VIII (new ser., 1941), 146.

2. R. Bisset, *Life of Edmund Burke* (2d ed., 1800), II, 429. Cf. also W. C. Dunn, "Adam Smith and Edmund Burke: Complimentary Contemporaries," *Southern Economic Journal* (University of North Carolina), Vol. VII, No. 3 (January, 1941).

3. Carl Menger, who was among the first in modern times consciously to revive the methodical individualism of Adam Smith and his school, was probably also the first to point out the connection between the design theory of social institutions and socialism. See his *Untersuchungen über die Methode der Sozialwissenschaften* (1883), esp. Book IV, chap. 2, toward the end of which (p. 208) he speaks of "a pragmatism which, against the intention of its representatives, leads inevitably to socialism."

It is significant that the physiocrats already were led from the rationalistic individualism from which they started, not only close to socialism (fully developed in their contemporary Morelly's *Le Code de la nature* [1755]), but to advocate the worst despotism. "L'État fait des hommes tout ce qu'il veut," wrote Bodeau.

4. Edmund Burke, *Reflections on the Revolution in France* (1790), in *Works* (World's Classics ed.), IV, 105: "Thus the commonwealth itself would, in a few generations, be disconnected into the dust and powder of individuality, and at length dispersed to all winds of heaven." That Burke (as A. M. Osborn points out in her book on *Rousseau and Burke* [Oxford, 1940], p. 23), after he had first attacked Rousseau for his extreme "individualism," later attacked him for his extreme collectivism was far from inconsistent but merely the result of the fact that in the case of Rousseau, as in that of all others, the rationalistic individualism which they preached inevitably led to collectivism.

5. Alexis de Tocqueville, *Democracy in America,* trans. Henry Reeve (London, 1864), Vol. II, Book II, chap. 2, where de Tocqueville defines individualism as "a mature and calm feeling, which disposes each member of the community to sever himself from the mass of his fellows, and to draw apart with his family and friends; so that, after he has thus formed a little circle of his own, he willingly leaves society at large to itself." The translator in a note to this passage apologizes for introducing the French term "individualism" into English and explains that he knows "no English word exactly equivalent to the expression." As Albert Schatz pointed out in the book mentioned below, de Tocqueville's use of the well-established French term in this peculiar sense is entirely arbitrary and leads to serious confusion with the established meaning.

6. In his excellent survey of the history of individualist theories the late Albert Schatz rightly concludes that "nous voyons tout d'abord avec évidence ce que l'individualisme n'est pas. C'est précisément ce qu'on croit

commununément qu'il est: un système d'isolèment dans l'existence et une apologie de l'égoisme" (*L'Individualisme économique et social* [Paris, 1907], p. 558). This book, to which I am much indebted, deserves to be much more widely known as a contribution not only to the subject indicated by its title but to the history of economic theory in general.

7. In this respect, as Karl Pribram has made clear, individualism is a necessary result of philosophical nominalism, while the collectivist theories have their roots in the "realist" or (as K. R. Popper now more appropriately calls it) "essentialist" tradition (Pribram, *Die Entstehung der individualistischen Sozialphilosophie* [Leipzig, 1912]). But this "nominalist" approach is characteristic only of true individualism, while the false individualism of Rousseau and the physiocrats, in accordance with the Cartesian origin, is strongly "realist" or "essentialist."

8. Adam Ferguson, *An Essay on the History of Civil Society* (1st ed., 1767), p. 187. Cf. also ibid.: "The forms of society are derived from an obscure and distant origin; they arise, long before the date of philosophy, from the instincts, not from the speculations of man. . . . We ascribe to a previous design, what came to be known only by experience, what no human wisdom could foresee, and what, without the concurring humour and disposition of his age, no authority could enable an individual to execute" (pp. 187 and 188).

It may be of interest to compare these passages with the similar statements in which Ferguson's contemporaries expressed the same basic idea of the eighteenth-century British economists:

Josiah Tucker, *Elements of Commerce* (1756), reprinted in *Josiah Tucker: A Selection from His Economic and Political Writings,* ed. R. L. Schuyler (New York, 1931), pp. 31 and 92: "The main point is neither to extinguish nor to enfeeble self-love, but to give it such a direction that it may promote the public interest by promoting its own. . . . The proper design of this chapter is to show that the universal mover in human nature, self-love, may receive such a direction in this case (as in all others) as to promote the public interest by those efforts it shall make towards pursuing its own."

Adam Smith, *Wealth of Nations* (1776), ed. Cannan, I, 421: "By directing that industry in such a manner as its produce may be of the greatest value, he intends only his own gain, and he is in this, as in many other cases, led by an invisible hand to promote an end which was no part of his intention. Nor is it always the worse for the society that it was no part of it. By pursuing his own interest he frequently promotes that of the society more effectually than when he really intends to promote it." Cf. also *The Theory of Moral Sentiments* (1759), Part IV (9th ed., 1801), chap. i, p. 386.

Edmund Burke, *Thoughts and Details on Scarcity* (1795), in *Works* (World's Classics ed.), VI, 9: "The benign and wise disposer of all things, who obliges men, whether they will or not, in pursuing their own selfish interests, to connect the general good with their own individual success."

After these statements have been held up for scorn and ridicule by the majority of writers for the last hundred years (C. E. Raven not long ago called the last-quoted statement by Burke a "sinister sentence" — see his *Christian Socialism* [1920], p. 34), it is interesting now to find one of the leading theorists of modern socialism adopting Adam Smith's conclusions. According to A. P. Lerner (*The Economics of Control* [New York, 1944], p. 67), the essential social utility of the price mechanism is that "if it is appropriately used it induces each member of society, while seeking his own benefit, to do that which is in the general social interest. Fundamentally this is the great discovery of Adam Smith and the Physiocrats."

9. Cf. Schatz, op. cit., pp. 41 – 42, 81, 378, 568 – 69, esp. the passage quoted by him (p. 41, n. 1) from an article by Albert Sorel ("Comment j'ai lu la 'Réforme sociale,' " in *Réforme sociale,* November 1, 1906, p. 614): "Quel que fut mon respect, assez commandé et indirect encore pour le *Discours de la méthode,* je savais déja que de ce fameux discours il était sorti autant de déraison sociale et d'aberrations métaphysiques, d'abstractions et d'utopies, que de données positives, que s'il menait à Comte il avait aussie mené à Rousseau." On the influence of Descartes on Rousseau see further P. Janet, *Histoire de la science politique* (3d ed., 1887), p. 423; F. Bouillier, *Histoire de la philosophie cartésienne* (3d ed., 1868), p. 643; and H. Michel, *L'Idée de l'état* (3d ed., 1898), p. 68.

10. The decisive importance of Mandeville in the history of economics, long overlooked or appreciated only by a few authors (particularly Edwin Cannan and Albert Schatz), is now beginning to be recognized, thanks mainly to the magnificent edition of the *Fable of the Bees* which we owe to the late F. B. Kaye. Although the fundamental ideas of Mandeville's work are already implied in the original poem of 1705, the decisive elaboration and especially his full account of the origin of the division of labor, of money, and of language occur only in Part II of the *Fable* which was published in 1728 (see Bernard Mandeville, *The Fable of the Bees,* ed. F. B. Kaye [Oxford, 1924], II, 142, 287 – 88, 349 – 50). There is space here to quote only the crucial passage from his account of the development of the division of labor where he observes that "we often ascribe to the excellency of man's genius, and the depth of his penetration, what is in reality owing to the length of time, and the experience of many generations, all of them very little differing from one another in natural parts and sagacity" (ibid., p. 142).

It has become usual to describe Giambattista Vico and his (usually wrongly quoted) formula, *homo non intelligendo fit omnia* (*Opere,* ed. G. Ferrari [2d ed.; Milan, 1854], V, 183), as the beginning of the antirationalistic theory of social phenomena, but it would appear that he has been both preceded and surpassed by Mandeville.

Perhaps it also deserves mention that not only Mandeville but also Adam Smith occupy honorable places in the development of the theory of language which in so many ways raises problems of a nature kindred to those of the other social sciences.

11. Réné Descartes, *A Discourse on Method* (Everyman's ed.), pp. 10 – 11.

12. On the characteristic approach of the engineer type of mind to economic phenomena compare the present author's study on "Scientism and the Study of Society," *Economica,* Vols. IX – XI (new ser., 1942 – 44), esp. XI, 34 ff.

13. Since this lecture was first published I have become acquainted with an instructive article by Jerome Rosenthal on "Attitudes of Some Modern Rationalists to History" (*Journal of the History of Ideas,* IV, No. 4 [October, 1943], 429 – 56), which shows in considerable detail the antihistorical attitude of Descartes and particularly his disciple Malebranche and gives interesting examples of the contempt expressed by Descartes in his *Recherche de la vérité par la lumière naturelle* for the study of history, languages, geography, and especially the classics.

14. James Bonar, *Philosophy and Political Economy* (1893), p. 85.

15. A. W. Benn, in his *History of English Rationalism in the Nineteenth Century* (1906), says rightly: "With Quesnay, following nature meant ascertaining by a study of the world about us and of its laws what conduct is most conducive to health and happiness; and the natural rights meant liberty to pursue the course so ascertained. Such liberty only belongs to the wise and good, and can only be granted to those whom the tutelary authority in the state is pleased to regard as such. With Adam Smith and his disciples, on the other hand, nature means the totality of impulses and instincts by which the individual members of society are animated; and their contention is that the best arrangements result from giving free play to those forces in the confidence that partial failure will be more than compensated by successes elsewhere, and that the pursuit of his own interest by each will work out in the greatest happiness of all" (I, 289).

On this whole question see Elie Halévy, *The Growth of Philosophic Radicalism* (1928), esp. pp. 266 – 70.

The contrast of the Scottish philosophers of the eighteenth century with their French contemporaries is also brought out in Gladys Bryson's recent study on *Man and Society: The Scottish Enquiry of the Eighteenth Century* (Princeton, 1945), p. 145. She emphasizes that the Scottish philosophers "all wanted to break away from Cartesian rationalism, with its emphasis on abstract intellectualism and innate ideas," and repeatedly stresses the "anti-individualistic" tendencies of David Hume (pp. 106, 155) — using "individualistic" in what we call here the false, rationalistic sense. But she occasionally falls back into the common mistake of regarding them as "representative and typical of the thought of the century" (p. 176). There is still, largely as a result of an acceptance of the German conception of "the Enlightenment," too much inclination to regard the views of all the eighteenth-century philosophers as similar, whereas in many respects the differences between the English and the French philosophers of the period are much more important than the similarities. The common habit of lumping Adam Smith and Quesnay together, caused by the former belief that Smith was greatly indebted to the physiocrats, should certainly cease, now that this belief has been disproved by W. R. Scott's recent discoveries (see his *Adam Smith as Student and Professor* [Glasgow, 1937], p. 124). It is also significant that both Hume and Smith are reported to have been stimulated to their work by their opposition to Montesquieu.

Some suggestive discussion of the differences between the British and the French social philosophers of the eighteenth century, somewhat distorted, however, by the author's hostility toward the "economic liberalism" of the former, will be found in Rudolf Goldscheid, *Grundlinien zu einer Kritik der Willenskraft* (Vienna, 1905), pp. 32 – 37.

16. Edmund Burke, *Thoughts and Details on Scarcity* (1795), in *Works* (World's Classics ed.), VI, 15.

17. This phrase is used over and over again by de Tocqueville to describe the effects of socialism, but see particularly *Oeuvres complètes,* IX (1886), 541, where he says: "Si, en définitive, j'avais à trouver une formule générale pour exprimer ce que m'apparait le socialisme dans son ensemble, je dirais que c'est une nouvelle formule de la servitude." Perhaps I may be allowed to add that it was this phrase of de Tocqueville's which suggested to me the title of a recent book of mine.

18. John Locke, *Two Treatises of Government* (1690), Book II, chap. 4, §22: "Freedom of men under government is to have a standing rule to live by, common to every one of that society and made by the legislative power erected in it."

19. Lerner, op. cit., p. 5.

20. Lord Acton, "Nationality" (1862), reprinted in *The History of Freedom and Other Essays* (1907), p. 288.

21. The actions a government can expediently take to reduce really *avoidable* uncertainty for the individuals are a subject which has given rise to so many confusions that I am afraid to let the brief allusion to it in the text stand without some further explanation. The point is that, while it is easy to protect a particular person or group against the loss which might be caused by an unforeseen change, by preventing people from taking notice of the change after it has occurred, this merely shifts the loss onto other shoulders but does not prevent it. If, e.g., capital invested in very expensive plant is protected against obsolescence by new inventions by prohibiting the introduction of such new inventions, this increases the security of the owners of the existing plant but deprives the public of the benefit of the new inventions. Or, in other words, it does not really reduce uncertainty for society as a whole if we make the behavior of the people more predictable by preventing them from adapting themselves to an unforeseen change in their knowledge of the world. The only genuine reduction of uncertainty consists in increasing its knowledge, but never in preventing people from making use of new knowledge.

22. The difference between the rationalistic and the true individualistic approach is well shown in the different views expressed by French observ-

ers on the apparent irrationality of English social institutions. While Henri de Saint-Simon, e.g., complains that "cent volumes *in folio,* de caractère plus fin, ne suffiraient pas pour rendre compte de toutes les inconséquences organiques qui existent en Angleterre" (*Oeuvres de Saint-Simon et d'Enfantin* [Paris, 1865 – 78], XXXVIII, 179), de Tocqueville retorts "que ces bizarreries des Anglais pussent avoir quelques rapports avec leurs libertés, c'est ce qui ne lui tombe point dans l'esprit" (*L'Ancien régime et la révolution* [7th ed.; Paris, 1866], p. 103).

23. Is it necessary to quote Edmund Burke once more to remind the reader how essential a condition for the possibility of a free society was to him the strength of moral rules? "Men are qualified for civil liberty," he wrote, "in exact proportion to their disposition to put moral chains upon their own appetites; in proportion as their love of justice is above their rapacity; in proportion as their own soundness and sobriety of understanding is above their vanity and presumption; in proportion as they are more disposed to listen to the councils of the wise and good, in preference to the flattery of knaves" (*A Letter to a Member of the National Assembly* [1791], in *Works* [World's Classics ed.], IV, 319).

24. W. Dibelius, *England* (1923), pp. 464 – 68 of 1934 English translation.

25. E. Vermeil, *Germany's Three Reichs* (London, 1944), p. 224.

26. Lord Acton, "Nationality" (1862), reprinted in *The History of Freedom,* pp. 270 – 300.

27. Lord Acton, "Sir Erskine May's Democracy in Europe" (1878), reprinted in *The History of Freedom,* p. 78.

28. Lord Acton, *Lectures on Modern History* (1906), p. 10.

29. Lord Acton, "Sir Erskine May's Democracy in Europe," reprinted in *The History of Freedom,* pp. 93 – 94.

30. Alexis de Tocqueville, *Oeuvres complètes,* IX, 546.

31. Lord Acton, "Sir Erskine May's Democracy in Europe," reprinted in *The History of Freedom,* p. 88.

32. Lord Acton, "The History of Freedom in Christianity" (1877), reprinted in *The History of Freedom,* p. 57.

History and Politics

8

Political opinion and views about historical events ever have been and always must be closely connected. Past experience is the foundation on which our beliefs about the desirability of different policies and institutions are mainly based, and our present political views inevitably affect and colour our interpretation of the past. Yet, if it is too pessimistic a view that man learns nothing from history, it may well be questioned whether he always learns the truth. While the events of the past are the source of the experience of the human race, their opinions are determined not by the objective facts but by the records and interpretations to which they have access. Few men will deny that our views about the goodness or badness of different institutions are largely determined by what we believe to have been their effects in the past. There is scarcely a political ideal or concept which does not involve opinions about a whole series of past events, and there are few historical memories which do not serve as a symbol of some political aim. Yet the historical beliefs which guide us in the present are not always in accord with the facts; sometimes they are even the effects rather than the cause of political beliefs.

Introduction to *Capitalism and the Historians.* Essays by T. S. Ashton, L. M. Hacker, W. H. Hutt, and B. de Jouvenel. London and Chicago, 1954.

Historical myths have perhaps played nearly as great a role in shaping opinion as historical facts. Yet we can hardly hope to profit from past experience unless the facts from which we draw our conclusions are correct.

The influence which the writers of history thus exercise on public opinion is probably more immediate and extensive than that of the political theorists who launch new ideas. It seems as though even such new ideas reach wider circles usually not in their abstract form but as the interpretations of particular events. The historian is in this respect at least one step nearer to direct power over public opinion than is the theorist. And long before the professional historian takes up his pen, current controversy about recent events will have created a definite picture, or perhaps several different pictures, of these events which will affect contemporary discussion as much as any division on the merits of new issues.

This profound influence which current views about history have on political opinion is today perhaps less understood than it was in the past. One reason for this probably is the pretension of many modern historians to be purely scientific and completely free from all political prejudice. There can be no question, of course, that this is an imperative duty of the scholar in so far as historical research, that is, the ascertainment of the facts, is concerned. There is indeed no legitimate reason why, in answering questions of fact, historians of different political opinions should not be able to agree. But at the very beginning, in deciding which questions are worth asking, individual value judgments are bound to come in. And it is more than doubtful whether a connected history of a period or of a set of events could be written without interpreting these in the light, not only of theories about the interconnection of social processes, but also of definite values — or at least whether such a history would be worth reading. Historiography, as distinguished from historical research, is not only at least as much an art as a science; the writer who attempts it without being aware that his task is one of interpretation in the light of definite values also will succeed merely in deceiving himself and will become the victim of his unconscious prejudices.

There is perhaps no better illustration of the manner in which for more than a century the whole political ethos of a nation, and for a shorter time of most of the Western world, was shaped by the writings of a group of historians than the influence exercised by the English 'Whig interpretation of history'. It is probably no exaggeration to say that, for every person who had firsthand acquaintance with the writings of the political philosophers who founded the liberal tradition, there were fifty or a hundred who had absorbed it from the writings of men like Hallam and Macaulay, or Grote and Lord Acton. It is significant that the modern English historian who more than any other has endeavoured to discredit this Whig tradition later came to write that 'those who, perhaps in the misguided austerity of youth, wish to drive out that Whig interpretation . . . are sweeping a room which humanly speaking cannot long remain empty. They are opening the doors for seven devils which, precisely because they are newcomers, are bound to be worse than this first'.[1] And, although he still suggests that 'Whig history' was 'wrong' history, he emphasizes that it 'was one of our assets' and that 'it had a wonderful effect on English politics'.[2]

Whether in any relevant sense 'Whig history' really was wrong history is a matter on which the last word has probably not yet been said but which we cannot discuss here. Its beneficial effect in creating the essentially liberal atmosphere of the nineteenth century is beyond doubt and was certainly not due to any misrepresentation of facts. It was mainly political history, and the chief facts on which it was based were known beyond question. It may not stand up in all respects to modern standards of historical research, but it certainly gave the generations brought up on it a true sense of the value of the political liberty which their ancestors had achieved for them, and it served them as a guide in preserving that achievement.

The Whig interpretation of history has gone out of fashion with the decline of liberalism. But it is more than doubtful whether, because history now claims to be more scientific, it has become a more reliable or trustworthy guide in those fields where it has exercised most influence on political views. Political history indeed has lost much of the power and fascination it had in the nineteenth century; and it is doubtful whether any historical work of our time has had a circulation or direct influence comparable with, say, T. B. Macaulay's *History of England*. Yet the extent to which our present political views are coloured by historical beliefs has certainly not diminished. As interest has shifted from the constitutional to the social and economic field, so the historical beliefs which act as driving forces are now mainly beliefs about economic history. It is probably justifiable to speak of a socialist interpretation of history which has governed political thinking for the last two or three generations and which consists mainly of a particular view of economic history. The remarkable thing about this view is that most of the assertions to which it has given the status of 'facts which everybody knows' have long been proved not to have been facts at all; yet they still continue, outside the circle of professional economic historians, to be almost universally accepted as the basis for the estimate of the existing economic order.

Most people, when being told that their political convictions have been affected by particular views on economic history, will answer that they never have been interested in it and never have read a book on the subject. This, however, does not mean that they do not, with the rest, regard as established facts many of the legends which at one time or another have been given currency by writers on economic history. Although in the indirect and circuitous process by which new political ideas reach the general public the historian holds a key position, even he operates chiefly through many further relays. It is only at several removes that the picture which he provides becomes general property; it is via the novel and the newspaper, the cinema and political speeches, and ultimately the school and common talk, that the ordinary person acquires his conceptions of history. But in the end even those who never read a book and probably have never heard the names of the historians whose views have influenced them come to see the past through their spectacles. Certain beliefs, for instance, about the evolution and effects of trade unions, the alleged progressive growth of monopoly, the deliberate destruction of commodity stock as the result of competition (an event which, in fact, whenever it happened, was always the result of monopoly and usually of government-organized monopoly), about the suppression of beneficial inventions, the causes and effects of 'imperialism', and the role of the armament industries or of 'capitalists' in general in causing war, have become part of the folklore of our time. Most people would be greatly surprised to learn that most of what they believe about these subjects are not safely established facts but myths, launched from political motives and then spread by people of good will into whose general beliefs they fitted. It would require several books like the present one to show how most of what is commonly believed on these questions, not merely by radicals but also by many conservatives, is not history but political legend. All we can do here with regard to these topics is to refer the reader to a few works from which he can inform himself about the present state of knowledge on the more important of them.[3]

There is, however, one supreme myth which more than any other has served to discredit the economic system to which we owe our present-day civilization and to the examination of which the present volume is devoted. It is the legend of the deterioration of the position of the working classes in consequence of the rise of 'capitalism' (or of the 'manufacturing' or 'industrial system'). Who has not heard of the 'horrors of early capitalism' and gained the impression that the advent of this system brought untold new suffering to large classes who before were tolerably content and comfortable? We might justly hold in disrepute a system to which the blame attached that even for a time it worsened the position of the poorest and most numerous class of the population. The widespread emotional aversion to 'capitalism' is closely connected with this belief that the undeniable growth of wealth which the competitive order has produced was purchased at the price of depressing the standard of life of the weakest elements of society.

That this was the case was at one time indeed widely taught by economic historians. A more careful examination of the facts has, however, led to a thorough refutation of this belief. Yet, a generation after the controversy has been decided, popular opinion still continues as though the older belief had been true. How this belief should ever have arisen and why it should continue to determine the general view long after it has been disproved are both problems which deserve serious examination.

This kind of opinion can be frequently found not only in the political literature hostile to capitalism but even in works which on the whole are sympathetic to the political tradition of the nineteenth century. It is well represented by the following passage from Ruggiero's justly esteemed *History of European Liberalism*:

> Thus it was precisely at the period of intensest industrial growth that the condition of the labourer changed for the worse. Hours of labour multiplied out of all measure; the employment of women and children in factories lowered wages: the keen competition between the workers themselves, no longer tied to their parishes but free to travel and congregate where they were most in demand, further cheapened the labour they placed on the market: numerous and frequent industrial crises, inevitable at a period of growth, when population and consumption are not yet stabilized, swelled from time to time the ranks of the unemployed, the reserves in the army of starvation.[4]

There was little excuse for such a statement even when it appeared a quarter-century ago. A year after it was first published, the most eminent student of modern economic history, Sir John Clapham, rightly complained:

> The legend that everything was getting worse for the working man, down to some unspecified date between the drafting of the People's

> Charter and the Great Exhibition, dies hard. The fact that, after the price fall of 1820 – 1, the purchasing power of wages in general — not, of course, of everyone's wages — was definitely greater than it had been just before the revolutionary and Napoleonic wars, fits so ill with the tradition that it is very seldom mentioned, the works of statisticians of wages and prices being constantly disregarded by social historians.[5]

In so far as general public opinion is concerned, the position is scarcely better today, although the facts have had to be conceded even by most of those who had been mainly responsible for spreading the contrary opinion. Few authors have done more to create the belief that the early nineteenth century had been a time in which the position of the working class had become particularly bad than Mr. and Mrs. J. L. Hammond; their books are frequently quoted to illustrate this. But towards the end of their lives they admitted candidly that

> statisticians tell us that when they have put in order such data as they can find, they are satisfied that earnings increased and that most men and women were less poor when this discontent was loud and active than they were when the eighteenth century was beginning to grow old in a silence like that of autumn. The evidence, of course, is scanty, and its interpretation not too simple, but this general view is probably more or less correct.[6]

This did little to change the general effect their writing had on public opinion. In one of the latest competent studies of the history of the Western political tradition, for instance, we can still read that, 'like all the great social experiments, however, the invention of the labour market was expensive. It involved, in the first instance, a swift and drastic decline in the material standard of living of the working classes'.[7]

I was going to continue here that this is still the view which is almost exclusively represented in the popular literature when the latest book by Bertrand Russell came to my hands in which, as if to confirm this, he blandly asserts:

> The industrial revolution caused unspeakable misery both in England and in America. I do not think any student of economic history can doubt that the average happiness in England in the early nineteenth century was lower than it had been a hundred years earlier; and this was due almost entirely to scientific technique.[8]

The intelligent layman can hardly be blamed if he believes that such a categorical statement from a writer of this rank must be true. If a Bertrand Russell believes this, we must not be surprised that the versions of economic history which today are spread in hundreds of thousands of volumes of pocket editions are mostly of the kind which spread this old myth. It is also still a rare exception when we meet a work of historical fiction which dispenses with the dramatic touch which the story of the sudden worsening of the position of large groups of workers provides.

The true fact of the slow and irregular progress of the working class which we now know to have taken place is of course rather unsensational and uninteresting to the layman. It is no more than he has learned to expect as the normal state of affairs; and it hardly occurs to him that this is by no means an inevitable progress, that it was preceded by centuries of virtual stagnation of the position of the poorest, and that we have come to expect continuous improvement only as a result of the experience of several generations with the system which he still thinks to be the cause of the misery of the poor.

Discussions of the effects of the rise of modern industry on the working classes refer almost always to the conditions in England in the first half of the nineteenth century; yet the great change to which they refer had commenced much earlier and by then had quite a long history and had spread far beyond England. The freedom of economic activity which in England had proved so favourable to the rapid growth of wealth was probably in the first instance an almost accidental by-product of the limitations which the revolution of the seventeenth century had placed on the powers of government; and only after its beneficial effects had come to be widely noticed did the economists later undertake to explain the connection and to argue for the removal of the remaining barriers to commercial freedom. In many ways it is misleading to speak of 'capitalism' as though this had been a new and altogether different system which suddenly came into being towards the end of the eighteenth century; we use this term here because it is the most familiar name, but only with great reluctance, since with its modern connotations it is itself largely a creation of that socialist interpretation of economic history with which we are concerned. The term is especially misleading when, as is often the case, it is connected with the idea of the rise of the propertyless proletariat which by some devious process have been deprived of their rightful ownership of the tools for their work.

The actual history of the connection between capitalism and the rise of the proletariat is almost the opposite of that which these theories of the expropriation of the masses suggest. The truth is that, for the greater part of history, for most men the possession of the tools for their work was an essential condition for survival or at least for being able to rear a family. The number of those who could maintain themselves by working for others, although they did not themselves possess the necessary equipment, was limited to a small proportion of the population. The amount of arable land and of tools handed down from one generation to the next limited the total number who could survive. To be left without them meant in most instances death by starvation or at least the impossibility of procreation. There was little incentive and little possibility for one generation to accumulate the additional tools which would have made possible the survival of a larger number to the next, so long as the advantage of employing additional hands was limited mainly to the instances where the division of the tasks increased the efficiency of the work of the owner of the tools. It was only when the larger gains from the employment of machinery provided both the means and the opportunity for their investment that what in the past had been a recurring surplus of population doomed to early death was in an increasing measure given the possibility of survival. Numbers which had been practically stationary for many centuries began to increase rapidly. The proletariat which capitalism can be said to have 'created' was thus not a proportion of the population which would have existed without it and which it had degraded to a lower level; it was an additional population which was enabled to grow up by the new opportunities for employment which capitalism provided. In so far as it is true that the growth of capital made the appearance of the proletariat possible, it was in the sense that it raised the productivity of labour so that much larger numbers of those who had not been equipped by their parents with the necessary tools were enabled to maintain themselves by their labour alone; but the capital had to be supplied first before those were enabled to survive who afterwards claimed as a right a share in its ownership. Although it was certainly not from charitable motives, it still was the first time in history that one group of people found it in their interest to use their earnings on a large scale to provide new instruments of production to be operated by those who without them could not have produced their own sustenance.

Of the effect of the rise of modern industry on the growth of population, statistics tell a vivid tale. That this in itself largely contradicts the common belief about the harmful effect of the rise of the factory system on the large masses is not the point with which we are at present concerned. Nor need we more than mention the fact that, so long as this increase of the numbers of those whose output reached a certain level brought forward a fully corresponding increase in population, the level of the poorest fringe could not be substantially improved, however much the average might rise. The point of immediate relevance is that this increase of population and particularly of the manufacturing population had proceeded in England at least for two or three generations before the period of which it is alleged that the position of the workers seriously deteriorated.

The period to which this refers is also the period when the problem of the position of the working class became for the first time one of general concern. And the opinions of some of the contemporaries are indeed the main sources of the present beliefs. Our first question must therefore be how it came about that such an impression contrary to the facts should have become widely held among the people then living.

One of the chief reasons was evidently an increasing awareness of facts which before had passed unnoticed. The very increase of wealth and well-being which had been achieved raised standards and aspirations. What for ages had seemed a natural and inevitable situation, or even as an improvement upon the past, came to be regarded as incongruous with the opportunities which the new age appeared to offer. Economic suffering both became more conspicuous and seemed less justified, because general wealth was increasing faster than ever before. But this, of course, does not prove that the people whose fate was beginning to cause indignation and alarm were worse off than their parents or grandparents had been. While there is every evidence that great misery existed, there is none that it was greater than or even as great as it had been before. The aggregations of large numbers of cheap houses of industrial workers were probably more ugly than the picturesque cottages in which some of the agricultural labourers or domestic workers had lived; and they were certainly more alarming to the landowner or to the city patrician than the poor dispersed over the country had been. But for those who had moved from country to town it meant an improvement; and even though the rapid growth of the industrial centres created sanitary problems with which people had yet slowly and painfully to learn to cope, statistics leave little doubt that even general health was on the whole benefited rather than harmed.[9]

More important, however, for the explanation of the change from an optimistic to a pessimistic view of the effects of industrialization than this awakening of social conscience was probably the fact that this change of opinion appears to have commenced, not in the manufacturing districts which had firsthand knowledge of what was happening, but in the political discussion of the English metropolis which was somewhat remote from, and had little part in, the new development. It is evident that the belief about the 'horrible' conditions prevailing among the manufacturing populations of the Midlands and the north of England was in the 1830's and 1840's widely held among the upper classes of London and the south. It was one of the main arguments with which the landowning class hit back at the manufacturers to counter the agitation of the latter against the Corn Laws and for free trade. And it was from these arguments of the conservative press that the radical intelligentsia of the time, with little firsthand knowledge of the industrial districts, derived their views which were to become the standard weapons of political propaganda.

This position, to which so much even of the present-day beliefs about the effects of the rise of industrialism on the working classes can be traced, is well illustrated by a letter written about 1843 by a London lady, Mrs. Cooke Taylor, after she had for the first time visited some industrial districts of Lancashire. Her account of the conditions she found is prefaced by some remarks about the general state of opinion in London:

> I need not remind you of the statements put forward in the newspapers, relative to the miserable conditions of the operatives, and the tyranny of their masters, for they made such an impression on me that it was with reluctance that I consented to go to Lancashire; indeed these misrepresentations are quite general, and people believe them without knowing why or wherefore. As an instance: just before starting I was at a large dinner party, at the west end of the town, and seated next a gentleman who is considered a very clever and intelligent man. In the course of the conversation I mentioned that I was going to Lancashire. He stared and asked, 'What on earth could take me there? That he would as soon think of going to St. Giles's; that it was a horrid place — factories all over; that the people, from starvation, oppression, and over-work, had almost lost the form of humanity; and that the mill-owners were a bloated, pampered race, feeding on the very vitals of the people'. I answered that this was a dreadful state of things; and asked 'In what part he had seen such misery?' He replied that 'he had never *seen* it, but had been *told* that it existed; and that for his part he never

> had been in the manufacturing districts, and that he never would'. This gentleman was one of the very numerous body of people who spread reports without ever taking the trouble of inquiring if they be true or false.[10]

Mrs. Cooke Taylor's detailed description of the satisfactory state of affairs which to her surprise she found ends with the remark:

> Now that I have seen the factory people at their work, in their cottages and in their schools, I am totally at a loss to account for the outcry that has been made against them. They are better clothed, better fed, and better conducted than many other classes of working people.[11]

But even if at the time itself the opinion which was later taken over by the historians was loudly voiced by one party, it remains to explain why the view of one party among the contemporaries, and that not of the radicals or liberals but of the Tories, should have become the almost uncontradicted view of the economic historians of the second half of the century. The reason for this seems to have been that the new interest in economic history was itself closely associated with the interest in socialism and that at first a large proportion of those who devoted themselves to the study of economic history were inclined towards socialism. It was not merely the great stimulus which Karl Marx's 'materialist interpretation of history' undoubtedly gave to the study of economic history; practically all the socialist schools held a philosophy of history intended to show the relative character of the different economic institutions and the necessity of different economic systems succeeding each other in time. They all tried to prove that the system which they attacked, the system of private property in the means of production, was a perversion of an earlier and more natural system of communal property; and, because the theoretical preconceptions which guided them postulated that the rise of capitalism must have been detrimental to the working classes, it is not surprising that they found what they were looking for.

But not only those by whom the study of economic history was consciously made a tool of political agitation — as is true in many instances from Marx and Engels to Werner Sombart and Sidney and Beatrice Webb — but also many of the scholars who sincerely believed that they were approaching the facts without prejudice produced results which were scarcely less biased. This was in part due to the fact that the 'historical approach' which they adopted had itself been proclaimed as a counterblast to the theoretical analysis of classical economics, because the latter's verdict on the popular remedies for current complaints had so frequently been unfavourable.[12] It is no accident that the largest and most influential group of students of economic history in the sixty years preceding the First World War, the German Historical School, prided themselves also on the name of the 'socialists of the chair' (*Kathedersozialisten*); or that their spiritual successors, the American 'institutionalists', were mostly socialists in their inclination. The whole atmosphere of these schools was such that it would have required an exceptional independence of mind for a young scholar not to succumb to the pressure of academic opinion. No reproach was more feared or more fatal to academic prospects than that of being an 'apologist' of the capitalist system; and, even if a scholar dared to contradict dominant opinion on a particular point, he would be careful to safeguard himself against such accusation by joining in the general condemnation of the capitalist system.[13] To treat the existing economic order as merely a 'historical phase' and to be able to predict from the 'laws of historical development' the emergence of a better future system became the hallmark of what was then regarded as the truly scientific spirit.

Much of the misrepresentation of the facts by the earlier economic historians was, in reality, directly traceable to a genuine endeavour to look at these facts without any theoretical preconceptions. The idea that one can trace the causal connections of any events without employing a theory, or that such a theory will emerge automatically from the accumulation of a sufficient amount of facts, is of course sheer illusion. The complexity of social events in particular is such that, without the tools of analysis which a systematic theory provides, one is almost bound to misinterpret them; and those who eschew the conscious use of an explicit and tested logical argument usually merely become the victims of the popular beliefs of their time. Common sense is a treacherous guide in this field, and what seem 'obvious' explanations frequently are no more than commonly accepted superstitions. It may seem obvious that the introduction of machinery will produce a general reduction of the demand for labour. But persistent effort to think the problem through shows that this belief is the result of a logical fallacy, of stressing one effect of the assumed change and leaving out others. Nor do the facts give any support to the belief. Yet anyone who thinks it to be true is very likely to find what seems to him confirming evidence. It is easy enough to find in the early nineteenth century instances of extreme poverty and to draw the conclusion that this must have been the effect of the introduction of machinery, without asking whether conditions had been any better or perhaps even worse before. Or one may believe that an increase of production must lead to the impossibility of selling all the product and, when one then finds a stagnation of sales, regard this as a confirmation of the expectations, although there are several more plausible explanations than general 'overproduction' or 'underconsumption'.

There can be no doubt that many of these misrepresentations were put forward in good faith; and there is no reason why we should not respect the motives of some of those who, to arouse public conscience, painted the misery of the poor in the blackest colours. We owe to agitation of this kind, which forced unwilling eyes to face unpleasant facts, some of the finest and most generous acts of public policy — from the abolition of slavery to the removal of taxes on imported food and the destruction of many entrenched privileges and abuses. And there is every reason to remember how miserable the majority of the people still were as recently as a hundred or a hundred and fifty years ago. But we must not, long after the event, allow a distortion of the facts, even if committed out of humanitarian zeal, to affect our view of what we owe to a system which for the first time in history made people feel that this misery might be avoidable. The very claims and ambitions of the working classes were and are the result of the enormous improvement of their position which capitalism brought about. There were, no doubt, many people whose privileged position, whose power to secure a comfortable income by preventing others from doing better what they were being paid for, was destroyed by the advance of freedom of enterprise. There may be various other grounds on which the development of modern industrialism might be deplored by some; certain aesthetic and moral values to which the privileged upper classes attached great importance were no doubt endangered by it. Some people might even question whether the rapid increase of population, or, in other words, the decrease in infant mortality, was a blessing. But if, and in so far as, one takes as one's test the effect on the standard of life of the large number of the toiling classes, there can be little doubt that this effect was to produce a general upward trend.

The recognition of this fact by the students had to wait for the rise of a generation of economic historians who no longer regarded themselves as the opponents of economics, intent upon proving that the economists had been wrong, but who were themselves trained economists who devoted themselves to the study of economic evolution. Yet the results which this modern economic history had largely established a generation ago have still gained little recognition outside professional circles. The process by which the results of research ultimately become general property has in this instance proved to be even slower than usual.[14] The new results in this case have not been of the kind which is avidly picked up by the intellectuals because it readily fits into their general prejudices but, on the contrary, are of a kind which is in conflict with their general beliefs. Yet, if we have been right in our estimate of the importance which erroneous views have had in shaping political opinion, it is high time that the truth should at last displace the legend which has so long governed popular belief. It was the conviction that this revision was long overdue which led to this topic being put on the programme of the meeting at which the first three of the following papers were originally presented and then to the decision that they should be made available to a wider public.

The recognition that the working class as a whole benefited from the rise of modern industry is of course entirely compatible with the fact that some individuals or groups in this as well as other classes may for a time have suffered from its results. The new order meant an increased rapidity of change, and the quick increase of wealth was largely the result of the increased speed of adaptation to change which made it possible. In those spheres where the mobility of a highly competitive market became effective, the increased range of opportunities more than compensated for the greater instability of particular jobs. But the spreading of the new order was gradual and uneven. There remained — and there remain to the present day — pockets which, while fully exposed to the vicissitudes of the markets for their products, are too isolated to benefit much from the opportunities which the market opened elsewhere. The various instances of the decline of old crafts which were displaced by a mechanical process have been widely publicized (the fate of the hand-loom weavers is the classical example always quoted). But even there it is more than doubtful whether the amount of suffering caused is comparable to that which a series of bad harvests in any region would have caused before capitalism had greatly increased the mobility of goods and of capital. The incidence on a small group among a prospering community is probably felt as more of an injustice and a challenge than was the general suffering of earlier times which was considered as unalterable fate.

The understanding of the true sources of the grievances, and still more the manner in which they might be remedied so far as possible, presupposes a better comprehension of the working of the market system than most of the earlier historians possessed. Much that has been blamed on the capitalist system is in fact due to remnants or revivals of precapitalistic features: to monopolistic elements which were either the direct result of ill-conceived state action or the consequence of a failure to understand that a smooth-working competitive order required an appropriate legal framework. We have already referred to some of the features and tendencies for which capitalism is usually blamed and which are in fact due to its basic mechanism not being allowed to work; and the question, in particular, why and to what extent monopoly has interfered with its beneficial operation is too big a problem for us to attempt to say more about it here.

This introduction is not intended to do more than to indicate the general setting in which the more specific discussion of the following papers must be seen. For its inevitable tendency to run in generalities I trust these special studies will make up by the very concrete treatment of their particular problems. They cover merely part of the wider issue, since they were intended to provide the factual basis for the discussion which they opened. Of the three related questions — What were the facts? How did the historians present them? and Why? — they deal primarily with the first and chiefly by implication with the second. Only the paper by M. de Jouvenel, which therefore possesses a somewhat different character, addresses itself mainly to the third question; and, in so doing, it raises problems which reach even beyond the complex of questions which have been sketched here.

Notes

1. Herbert Butterfield, *The Englishman and His History* (Cambridge: Cambridge University Press, 1944), p. 3.

2. Ibid., p. 7.

3. Cf. M. Dorothy George, 'The Combination Laws Reconsidered', *Economic History* (supplement to the *Economic Journal*), I (May 1927), 214 – 28; W. H. Hutt, *The Theory of Collective Bargaining* (London: P. S. King & Son, 1930) and *Economists and the Public* (London: J. Cape, 1936); L. C. Robbins, *The Economic Basis of Class Conflict* (London: Macmillan & Co., 1939) and *The Economic Causes of War* (London: J. Cape, 1939); Walter Sulzbach, *'Capitalistic Warmongers': A Modern Superstition* ('Public Policy Pamphlets', No. 35 (Chicago: University of Chicago Press, 1942)); G. J. Stigler, 'Competition in the United States', in *Five Lectures on Economic Problems* (London and New York: Longmans, Green & Co., 1949); G. Warren Nutter, *The Extent of*

Enterprise Monopoly in the United States, 1899 – 1939 (Chicago: University of Chicago Press, 1951); and, on most of these problems, the writings of Ludwig von Mises, especially his *Socialism* (London: J. Cape, 1936).

4. Guido de Ruggiero, *Storia del liberalismo europeo* (Bari, 1925), trans. R. G. Collingwood under the title *The History of European Liberalism* (London: Oxford University Press, 1927), p. 47, esp. p. 85. It is interesting that Ruggiero seems to derive his facts mainly from another supposedly liberal historian, Elie Halévy, although Halévy never expressed them so crudely.

5. J. H. Clapham, *An Economic History of Modern Britain* (Cambridge, 1926), I, 7.

6. J. L. and Barbara Hammond, *The Bleak Age* (1934) (rev. ed., London: Pelican Books, 1947), p. 15.

7. Frederick Watkins, *The Political Tradition of the West* (Cambridge, Mass.: Harvard University Press, 1948), p. 213.

8. Bertrand Russell, *The Impact of Science on Society* (New York: Columbia University Press, 1951), pp. 19 – 20.

9. Cf. M. C. Buer, *Health, Wealth and Population in the Early Days of the Industrial Revolution* (London: G. Routledge & Sons, 1926).

10. This letter is quoted in 'Reuben', *A Brief History of the Rise and Progress of the Anti-Corn-Law League* (London [1845]). Mrs. Cooke Taylor, who appears to have been the wife of the radical Dr. Cooke Taylor, had visited the factory of Henry Ashworth at Turton, near Bolton, then still a rural district and therefore probably more attractive than some of the urban industrial districts.

11. Ibid.

12. Merely as an illustration of the general attitude of that school a characteristic statement of one of its best-known representatives, Adolf Held, may be quoted. According to him, it was David Ricardo 'in whose hand orthodox economics became the docile servant of the exclusive interests of mobile capital', and his theory of rent 'was simply dictated by the hatred of the moneyed capitalist against the landowners' (*Zwei Bücher zur socialen Geschichte Englands*, Leipzig: Duncker & Humblot, 1881, p. 178).

13. A good account of the general political atmosphere prevailing among the German Historical School of economists will be found in Ludwig Pohle, *Die gegenwärtige Krise in der deutschen Volkswirtschaftslehre* (Leipzig, 1911).

14. On this, cf. my essay, 'The Intellectuals and Socialism', *University of Chicago Law Review*, Vol. XVI (1949), and reprinted as No. 12 in [*Capitalism and the Historians*].

DR. BERNARD MANDEVILLE

· 9 ·

I

It is to be feared that not only would most of Bernard Mandeville's contemporaries turn in their graves if they could know that he is today presented as a master mind to this august body, but that even now there may have been some raising of eyebrows about the appropriateness of such a choice. The author who achieved such a *succès de scandale* almost 250 years ago is still not quite reputable. Though there can be no doubt that his works[1] had an enormous circulation and that they set many people thinking on important problems, it is less easy to explain what precisely he has contributed to our understanding.

Let me say at once, to dispel a natural apprehension, that I am not going to represent him as a great economist. Although we owe to him both the term 'division of labour' and a clearer view of the nature of this phenomenon, and although no less an authority than

---

'Lecture on a master mind' delivered to the British Academy on 23 March 1966 and reprinted from the *Proceedings of the British Academy*, vol. LII, London, 1967.

Lord Keynes has given him high praise for other parts of his economic work, it will not be on this ground that I shall claim eminence for him. With the exception I have mentioned — which is a big one — what Mandeville has to say on technical economics seems to me to be rather mediocre, or at least unoriginal — ideas widely current in his time which he uses merely to illustrate conceptions of a much wider bearing.

Even less do I intend to stress Mandeville's contributions to the theory of ethics, in the history of which he has his well-established place. But though a contribution to our understanding of the genesis of moral rules is part of his achievement, it appears to me that the fact that he is regarded as primarily a moralist has been the chief obstacle to an appreciation of his main achievement.

I should be much more inclined to praise him as a really great psychologist,[2] if this is not too weak a term for a great student of human nature; but even this is not my main aim, though it brings me nearer to my contention. The Dutch doctor, who about 1696, in his late twenties, started to practise in London as a specialist in the diseases of the nerves and the stomach, that is, as a psychiatrist,[3] and continued to do so for the following 37 years, clearly acquired in the course of time an insight into the working of the human mind which is very remarkable and sometimes strikingly modern. He clearly prided himself on this understanding of human nature more than on anything else. That we do not know why we do what we do, and that the consequences of our decisions are often very different from what we imagine them to be, are the two foundations of that satire on the conceits of a rationalist age which was his initial aim.

What I do mean to claim for Mandeville is that the speculations to which that *jeu d'esprit* led him mark the definite breakthrough in modern thought of the twin ideas of evolution and of the spontaneous formation of an order, conceptions which had long been in coming, which had often been closely approached, but which just then needed emphatic statement because seventeenth-century rationalism had largely submerged earlier progress in this direction. Though Mandeville may have contributed little to the answers of particular questions of social and economic theory, he did, by asking the right questions, show that there was an object for a theory in this field. Perhaps in no case did he precisely show *how* an order formed itself without design, but he made it abundantly clear that it *did*, and thereby raised the questions to which theoretical analysis, first in the social sciences and later in biology, could address itself.[4]

II

Mandeville is perhaps himself a good illustration of one of his main contentions in that he probably never fully understood what was his main discovery. He had begun by laughing about the foibles and pretences of his contemporaries, and that poem in Hudibrastic verse which he published in 1705 as *The Grumbling Hive, or Knaves Turned Honest* was probably little more than an exercise in the new language he had come to love and of which in so short a time he had acquired a remarkable mastery. Yet though this poem is all that most people today know about him, it gives yet little indication of his important ideas. It also seems at first to have attracted no attention among serious people. The idea that

> The worst of all the multitude
> Did something for the common good

was but the seed from which his later thought sprang. It was not until nine years later, when he republished the original poem with an elaborate and wholly serious prose commentary, that the trend of his thought became more clearly visible; and only a further nine years later, with a second edition of the *Fable of the Bees, or Private Vices Public Benefits*, a book about twenty times as long as the original poem, that his ideas suddenly attracted wide attention and caused a public scandal. Finally, it was really only after yet another six years, when in 1728, at the age of 58, he added a second volume to it, that the bearing of his thought became quite clear. By that time, however, he had become a bogey man, a name with which to frighten the godly and respectable, an author whom one might read in secret to enjoy a paradox, but whom everybody knew to be a moral monster by whose ideas one must not be infected.

Yet almost everybody read him[5] and few escaped infection. Though the very title of the book, as the modern editor observes,[6] was apt 'to throw many good people into a kind of philosophical hysterics which left them no wit to grasp what he was driving at', the more the outraged thundered, the more the young read the book. If Dr. Hutchinson could give no lecture without attacking *The Fable of the Bees*, we may be sure that his student Adam Smith very soon turned to it. Even half a century later Dr. Samuel Johnson is said to have described it as a book that every young man had on his shelves in the mistaken belief that it was a wicked book.[7] Yet by then it had done its work and its chief contributions had become the basis of the approach to social philosophy of David Hume and his successors.

III

But does even the modern reader quite see what Mandeville was driving at? And how far did Mandeville himself? His main general thesis emerges only gradually and indirectly, as it were as a by-product of defending his initial paradox that what are private vices are often public benefits. By treating as vicious everything done for selfish purposes, and admitting as virtuous only what was done in order to obey moral commands, he had little difficulty in showing that we owed most benefits of society to what on such a rigoristic standard must be called vicious. This was no new discovery but as old almost as any reflection on these problems. Had not even Thomas Aquinas had to admit that *multae utilitates impedirentur si omnia peccata districte prohiberentur* — that much that is useful would be prevented if all sins were strictly prohibited?[8] The whole idea was so familiar to the literature of the preceding century, particularly through the work of La Rochefoucauld and Bayle, that it was not difficult for a witty and somewhat cynical mind, steeped from early youth in the ideas of Erasmus and Montaigne, to develop it into a grotesque of society. Yet by making his starting-point the particular moral contrast between the selfishness of the motives and the benefits which the resulting actions conferred on others, Mandeville saddled himself with an incubus of which neither he nor his successors to the present day could ever quite free themselves.

But as in his successive prose works Mandeville defends and develops the initial paradox, it becomes increasingly evident that it was but a special case of a much more general principle for which the particular contrast which had provoked all the moral indignation was almost irrelevant. His main contention became simply that in the complex order of society the results of men's actions were very different from what they had intended, and that the individuals, in pursuing their own ends, whether selfish or altruistic, produced useful results for others which they did not anticipate or perhaps even know; and, finally, that the whole order of society, and even all that we call culture, was the result of individual strivings which had no such end in view, but which were channelled to serve such ends by institutions, practices, and rules which also had never been deliberately invented but had grown up by the survival of what proved successful.

It was in the elaboration of this wider thesis that Mandeville for the first time developed all the classical paradigmata of the spontaneous growth of orderly social structures: of law and morals, of language, the market, and of money, and also of the growth of technological knowledge. To understand the significance of this it is necessary to be aware of the conceptual scheme into which these phenomena had somewhat uneasily been fitted during the preceding 2,000 years.

IV

The ancient Greeks, of course, had not been unaware of the problem which the existence of such phenomena raised; but they had tried to cope with it with a dichotomy which by its ambiguity produced endless confusion, yet became so firm a tradition that it acted like a prison from which Mandeville at last showed the way of escape.

The Greek dichotomy which had governed thinking so long, and which still has not lost all its power, is that between what is natural (*physei*) and that which is artificial or conventional (*thesei* or *nomō*).[9] It was obvious that the order of nature, the *kosmos*, was given independently of the will and actions of men, but that there existed also other kinds of order (for which they had a distinct word, *taxis*, for which we may envy them) which were the result of the deliberate arrangements of men. But if everything that was clearly independent of men's will and their actions was in this sense obviously 'natural', and everything that was the intended result of men's action 'artificial', this left no distinct place for any order which was the result of human actions but not of human design. That there existed among the phenomena of society such spontaneous orders was often perceived. But as men were not aware of the ambiguity of the established natural/artificial terminology, they endeavoured to express what they perceived in terms of it, and inevitably produced confusion: one would describe a social institution as 'natural' because it had never been deliberately designed, while another would describe the same institution as 'artificial' because it resulted from human actions.

It is remarkable how close, nevertheless, some of the ancient thinkers came to an understanding of the evolutionary processes that produced social institutions. There appears to have existed in all free countries a belief that a special providence watched over their affairs which turned their unsystematic efforts to their benefit. Aristophanes refers to this when he mentions that[10]

> There is a legend of the olden times
> That all our foolish plans and vain conceits
> Are overruled to work the public good.

—a sentiment not wholly unfamiliar in this country. And at least the Roman lawyers of classical times were very much aware that the Roman legal order was superior to others because, as Cato is reported to have said, it

> was based upon the genius, not of one man, but of many: it was founded, not in one generation, but in a long period of several centuries and many ages of men. For, said he, there never has lived a man possessed of so great a genius that nothing could escape him, nor could the combined powers of all men living at one time possibly make all the provisions for the future without the aid of actual experience and the test of time.[11]

This tradition was handed on, chiefly through the theories of the law of nature; and it is startling how far the older theorists of the law of nature, before they were displaced by the altogether different rationalist natural law school of the seventeenth century, penetrated into the secrets of the spontaneous development of social orders in spite of the handicap of the term 'natural'. Gradually even this unfortunate word became almost a technical term for referring to human institutions which had never been invented or designed by men, but had been shaped by the force of circumstances. Especially in the works of the last of the Schoolmen, the Spanish Jesuits of the sixteenth century, it led to a systematic questioning of how things would have ordered themselves if they had not otherwise been arranged by the deliberate efforts of government; they thus produced what I should call the first modern theories of society if their teaching had not been submerged by the rationalist tide of the following century.[12]

V

Because, however great an advance the work of a Descartes, a Hobbes, and a Leibniz may have meant in other fields, for the understanding of social growth processes it was simply disastrous. That to Descartes Sparta seemed eminent among Greek nations because its laws were the product of design and, 'originated by a single individual, they all tended to a single end'[13] is characteristic of that constructivistic rationalism which came to rule. It came to be thought that not only all cultural institutions were the product of deliberate construction, but that all that was so designed was necessarily superior to all mere growth. Under this influence the traditional conception of the law of nature was transformed from the idea of something which had formed itself by gradual adaptation to the 'nature of things', into the idea of something which a natural reason with which man had been originally endowed would enable him to design.

I do not know how much of the older tradition was preserved through this intellectual turmoil, and particularly how much of it may still have reached Mandeville. This would require an intimate knowledge of the seventeenth-century Dutch discussion of legal and social problems which is still largely inaccessible to one who does not read Dutch. There are many other reasons why a thorough study of this period of Dutch thought, which probably had great influence on English intellectual development at the end of that and the beginning of the next century, has long seemed to me one of the great desiderata of intellectual history. But until that gap is filled I can, so far as my particular problem is concerned, only surmise that a closer study would probably show that there are some threads connecting Mandeville with that group of late Schoolmen and particularly its Flemish member, Leonard Lessius of Louvain.[14]

Apart from this likely connexion with the older continental theorists of the law of nature, another probable source of inspiration for Mandeville was the English theorists of the common law, particularly Sir Matthew Hale. Their work had in some respects preserved, and in other respects made unnecessary in England, a conception of what the natural law theorists had been aiming at; and in the work of Hale Mandeville could have found much that would have helped him in the speculations about the growth of cultural institutions which increasingly became his central problem.[15]

Yet all these were merely survivals of an older tradition which had been swamped by the constructivistic rationalism of the time, the most powerful expositor of which in the social field was the chief target of Hale's argument, Thomas Hobbes. How ready men still were, under the influence of a powerful philosophy flattering to the human mind, to return to the naive design theories of human institutions, much more in accord with the ingrained propensity of our thinking to interpret everything anthropomorphically, we will understand better when we remember that distinguished renaissance scholars could still as a matter of course search for personal inventors of all the institutions of culture.[16] The renewed efforts to trace the political order to some deliberate act, an original agreement or contract, was much more congenial to this view than the more sophisticated accounts of their evolution which had been attempted earlier.

VI

To his contemporaries 'Mandeville's reduction of all action to open or disguised selfishness'[17] may indeed have seemed little more than another version of Hobbes, and to have disguised the fact that it led to wholly different conclusions. His initial stress on selfishness still carried a suggestion that man's actions were guided by wholly rational considerations, while the tenor of his argument becomes increasingly that it is not insight but restraints imposed upon men by the institutions and traditions of society which make their actions appear rational. While he still seems most concerned to show that it is merely pride (or 'self-liking')[18] which determines men's actions, he becomes in fact much more interested in the origin of the rules of conduct which pride makes men obey but whose origin and rationale they do not understand. After he has convinced himself that the reasons for which men observe rules are very different from the reasons which made these rules prevail, he gets increasingly intrigued about the origin of these rules whose significance for the orderly process of society is quite unconnected with the motives which make individual men obey them.

This begins to show itself already in the prose commentary on the poem and the other pieces which make up part I of the *Fable*, but blossoms forth in full only in part II. In part I Mandeville draws his illustrations largely from economic affairs because, as he thinks, 'the sociableness of man arises from those two things, *viz.*, the multiplicity of his desires, and the continuous opposition he meets with in his endeavours to satisfy them'.[19] But this leads him merely to those mercantilist considerations about the beneficial effects of luxury which caused the enthusiasm of Lord Keynes. We find here also that magnificent description of all the activities spread over the whole earth that go to the making of a piece of crimson cloth[20] which so clearly inspired Adam Smith and provided the basis for the explicit introduction of the division of labour in part II.[21] Already underlying this discussion there is clearly an awareness of the spontaneous order which the market produces.

VII

I would not wish to dwell on this at any length, however, if it were not for the fact that Mandeville's long recognized position as an anticipator of Adam Smith's argument for economic liberty has recently been challenged by Professor Jacob Viner,[22] than whom there is no greater authority on such matters. With all due respect, however, it seems to me that Professor Viner has been misled by a phrase which Mandeville repeatedly uses, namely his allusions to the 'dextrous management by which the skillful politician might turn private vices into public benefits'.[23] Professor Viner interprets this to mean that Mandeville favours what we now call government interference or intervention, that is, a specific direction of men's economic activities by government.

This, however, is certainly not what Mandeville meant. His aim comes out fairly unmistakably already in the little noticed subtitle to the second 1714 printing of the *Fable*, which describes it as containing 'Several Discourses, to demonstrate, that Human Frailties, . . . may be turned to the Advantage of the Civil Society, and made to supply the Place of *Moral Virtues*'.[24] What I believe he wants to say by this is precisely what Josiah Tucker expressed more clearly 40 years later when he wrote that 'that *universal* mover in human nature, SELF-LOVE, may receive such a direction in this case (as in all others) as to promote the public interest by those efforts it shall make towards pursuing its own'.[25] The means through which in the opinion of Mandeville and Tucker individual efforts are given such a direction, however, are by no means any particular commands of government but institutions and particularly general rules of just conduct. It seems to me that Mr. Nathan Rosenberg is wholly right when, in his reply to Professor Viner, he argues that in Mandeville's view, just as in Adam Smith's, the proper function of government is 'to establish the rules of the game by the creation of a framework of wise laws', and that Mandeville is searching for a system where 'arbitrary exertions of government power would be minimized'.[26] Clearly an author who could argue, as Mandeville had already in part I of the *Fable*, that 'this proportion as to numbers in every trade finds itself, and is never better kept than when nobody meddles or interferes with it',[27] and who in conclusion of part II speaks about 'how the short-sighted wisdom, of perhaps well-meaning people, may rob us of a felicity, that would flow spontaneously from the nature of every large society, if none were to divert or interrupt this stream',[28] was quite as much (or as little)[29] an advocate of laissez faire as Adam Smith.

I do not attach much importance to this question and would have relegated it to a footnote if in connexion with it the baneful effect of the old dichotomy of the 'natural' and the 'artificial' had not once again made an appearance. It was Elie Halévy who had first suggested that Mandeville and Adam Smith had based their argument on a 'natural identity of interests', while Helvetius (who undoubtedly was greatly indebted to Mandeville and Hume), and, following Helvetius, Jeremy Bentham, were thinking of an 'artificial identification of interests';[30] and Professor Viner suggests that Helvetius had derived this conception of an artificial identification of interests from Mandeville.[31] I am afraid this seems to me the kind of muddle to which the natural/artificial dichotomy inevitably leads. What Mandeville was concerned with was that institutions which man had not deliberately made — though it is the task of the legislator to improve them — bring it about that the divergent interests of the individuals are reconciled. The identity of interests was thus neither 'natural' in the sense that it was independent of institutions which had been formed by men's actions, nor 'artificial' in the sense that it was brought about by deliberate arrangement, but the result of spontaneously grown institutions which had developed because they made those societies prosper which tumbled upon them.

VIII

It is not surprising that from this angle Mandeville's interest became increasingly directed to the question of how those institutions grew up which bring it about that men's divergent interests are reconciled. Indeed this theory of the growth of law, not through the design of some wise legislator but through a long process of trial and error, is probably the most remarkable of those sketches of the evolution of institutions which make his investigation into the origin of society which constitutes part II of the *Fable* so remarkable a work. His central thesis becomes

> that we often ascribe to the excellency of man's genius, and the depth of his penetration, what is in reality owing to the length of time, and the experience of many generations, all of them very little differing from one another in natural parts and sagacity.[32]

He develops it with reference to laws by saying that

> there are very few, that are the work of one man, or of one generation; the greatest part of them are the product, the joint labour of several ages. . . . The wisdom I speak of, is not the offspring of a fine understanding, or intense thinking, but of sound and deliberate judgment, acquired from a long experience in business, and a multiplicity of observations. By this sort of wisdom, and length of time, it may be brought about, that there may be no greater difficulty in governing a large city, than (pardon the lowness of the simile) there is in weaving of stockings.[33]

When by this process the laws 'are brought to as much perfection, as art and human wisdom can carry them, the whole machinery can be made to play of itself, with as little skill, as is required to wind up a clock'.[34]

Of course Mandeville is not fully aware of how long would be the time required for the development of the various institutions — or of the length of time actually at his disposal for accounting for it. He is often tempted to telescope this process of adaptation to circumstances,[35] and does not pull himself up to say explicitly, as Hume later did in a similar context, that 'I here only suppose those reflections to be formed at once, which in fact arise insensibly and by degrees'.[36] He still vacillates between the then predominant pragmatic-rationalist and his new genetic or evolutionary view.[37] But what makes the latter so much more significant in his work than it was in the application to particular topics by Matthew Hale or John Law,[38] who probably did it better in their particular fields, is that he applies it to society at large and extends it to new topics. He still struggles to free himself from the constructivistic preconceptions. The burden of his argument is throughout that most of the institutions of society are not the result of design, but how 'a most beautiful superstructure may be raised upon a rotten and despicable foundation,'[39] namely men's pursuit of their selfish interests, and how, as 'the order, economy, and the very existence of civil society . . . is entirely built upon the variety of our wants . . . so the whole superstructure is made up of the reciprocal services which men do to each other'.[40]

IX

It is never wise to overload a lecture with quotations which, taken out of their context, rarely convey to the listener what they suggest to the reader of the consecutive exposition. So I will merely briefly mention the further chief applications to which Mandeville puts these ideas. Starting from the observation of how the skills of sport involve movements the purpose of which the acting person does not know,[41] and how similarly the skills of the arts and trades have been raised to 'prodigious height . . . by the uninterrupted labour and joint experience of many generations, though none but men of ordinary capacity should ever be employed in them',[42] he maintains that manners in speaking, writing, and ordering actions are generally followed by what we regard as 'rational creatures . . . without thinking and knowing what they are about'.[43] The most remarkable application of this, in which Mandeville appears to have been wholly a pioneer, is to the evolution of language which, he maintains, has also come into the world 'by slow degrees, as all other arts and sciences'.[44] When we remember that not long before even John Locke had regarded words as arbitrarily 'invented',[45] it would seem that Mandeville is the chief source of that rich speculation on the growth of language which we find in the second half of the eighteenth century.

All this is part of an increasing preoccupation with the process which we would now call cultural transmission, especially through education. He explicitly distinguishes what is 'adventitious and acquired by culture'[46] from what is innate, and makes his spokesman in the dialogue of part II stress that 'what you call natural, is evidently artificial and acquired by education'.[47] All this leads him in the end to argue that 'it was with our thought as it is with speech'[48] and that

> human wisdom is the child of time. It was not the contrivance of one man, nor could it have been the business of a few years, to es-

> tablish a notion, by which a rational creature is kept in awe for fear of itself, and an idol is set up, that shall be its own worshipper.[49]

Here the anti-rationalism, to use for once the misleading term which has been widely used for Mandeville and Hume, and which we had now better drop in favour of Sir Karl Popper's 'critical rationalism', comes out most clearly. With it Mandeville seems to me to have provided the foundations on which David Hume was able to build. Already in part II of the *Fable* we meet more and more frequently terms which are familiar to us through Hume, as when Mandeville speaks of the 'narrow bounds of human knowledge'[50] and says that

> we are convinced, that human understanding is limited; and by the help of very little reflection, we may be as certain, that the narrowness of its bounds, its being so limited, is the very thing, the sole cause, which palpably hinders us from driving into our origins by dint of penetration.[51]

And in *The Origin of Honour*, which came out when Hume was 21 and according to his own testimony was 'planning' the *Treatise on Human Nature*, but had not yet started 'composing' it,[52] we find the wholly Humean passage that

> all human creatures are swayed and wholly governed by their passions, whatever fine notions we may flatter ourselves with; even those who act suitably to their knowledge, and strictly follow the dictates of their reason, are not less compelled to do so by some passion or other, that sets them to work, than others, who bid defiance and act contrary to both, and whom we call slaves to their passions.[53]

X

I do not intend to pitch my claim on behalf of Mandeville higher than to say that he made Hume possible.[54] It is indeed my estimate of Hume as perhaps the greatest of all modern students of mind and society which makes Mandeville appear to me so important. It is only in Hume's work that the significance of Mandeville's efforts becomes wholly clear, and it was through Hume that he exercised his most lasting influence. Yet to have given Hume[55] some of his leading conceptions seems to me sufficient title for Mandeville to qualify as a master mind.

How much Mandeville's contribution meant we recognize when we look at the further development of those conceptions which Hume was the first and greatest to take up and elaborate. This development includes, of course, the great Scottish moral philosophers of the second half of the century, above all Adam Smith and Adam Ferguson, the latter of whom, with his phrase about the 'results of human action but not of human design',[56] has provided not only the best brief statement of Mandeville's central problem but also the best definition of the task of all social theory. I will not claim in favour of Mandeville that his work also led via Helvetius to Bentham's particularistic utilitarianism which, though the claim is true enough, meant a relapse into that constructivistic rationalism which it was Mandeville's main achievement to have overcome. But the tradition which Mandeville started includes also Edmund Burke, and, largely through Burke, all those 'historical schools' which, chiefly on the Continent, and through men like Herder[57] and Savigny,[58] made the idea of evolution a commonplace in the social sciences of the nineteenth century long before Darwin. And it was in this atmosphere of evolutionary thought in the study of society, where 'Darwinians before Darwin' had long thought in terms of the prevailing of more effective habits and practices, that Charles Darwin at last applied the idea systematically to biological organisms.[59] I do not, of course, mean to suggest that Mandeville had any direct influence on Darwin (though David Hume probably had). But it seems to me that in many respects Darwin is the culmination of a development which Mandeville more than any other single man had started.

Yet Mandeville and Darwin still have one thing in common: the scandal they caused had ultimately the same source, and Darwin in this respect finished what Mandeville had begun. It is difficult to remember now, perhaps most difficult for those who hold religious views in their now prevailing form, how closely religion was not long ago still associated with the 'argument from design'. The discovery of an astounding order which no man had designed was for most men the chief evidence for the existence of a personal creator. In the moral and political sphere Mandeville and Hume did show that the sense of justice and probity on which the order in this sphere rested, was not originally implanted in man's mind but had, like that mind itself, grown in a process of gradual evolution which at least in principle we might learn to understand. The revulsion against this suggestion was quite as great as that caused more than a century later when it was shown that the marvels of the organism could no longer be adduced as proof of special design. Perhaps I should have said that the process began with Kepler and Newton. But if it began and ended with a growing insight into what determined the *kosmos* of nature, it seems that the shock caused by the discovery that the moral and political *kosmos* was also the result of a process of evolution and not of design, contributed no less to produce what we call the modern mind.

Notes

1. Any serious work done today on Mandeville must be deeply indebted to the splendid edition of *The Fable of the Bees* which the late Professor F. B. Kaye published in 1924 through the Oxford University Press. All information about Mandeville and his work used in this lecture is taken from this edition and references to its two volumes will be simply 'i' and 'ii'. Though my opinion of Mandeville's importance is based on earlier acquaintance with most of his works, when I came to write this lecture I had access only to this edition of the *Fable* and two modern reprints of the *Letter to Dion*; all quotations from other works are taken from Kaye's Introduction and Notes to his edition. At least Mandeville's *Origin of Honour* (1732) and his *Free Thoughts on Religion etc.* (1720), and probably also some of his other works, would, however, deserve to be made more accessible; it would be a great boon if the Oxford University Press could be persuaded to expand its magnificent production of the *Fable* into an edition of Mandeville's collected works.

2. Professor Kaye has duly drawn attention to the more remarkable of Mandeville's psychological insights, especially to his modern conception of an *ex post* rationalization of actions directed by emotions (see i, p. lxxvii, and cf. pp. lxiii – lxiv), to which I would like to add references to his observations of the manner in which a man born blind would, after gaining sight, learn to judge distances (i, p. 227), and to his interesting conception of the structure and function of the brain (ii, p. 165).

3. Mandeville's work on psychiatry seems to have had a considerable reputation. *A Treatise on Hypochondriac and Hysteric Passions* which he published in 1711 had to be reprinted in the same year and was republished in an enlarged version in 1730 with the word 'Diseases' substituted for 'Passions' in the title.

4. Cf. Leslie Stephen, *History of English Thought in the 18th Century*, 2nd ed., London, 1881, i, p. 40: 'Mandeville anticipates, in many respects, the views of modern philosophers. He gives a kind of conjectural history de-

scribing the struggle for existence by which man gradually elevated himself above the wild beasts, and formed societies for mutual protection'.

5. There is perhaps no other comparable work of which one can be equally confident that all contemporary writers in the field knew it, whether they explicitly refer to it or not. Alfred Espinas ('La Troisième phase de la dissolution du mercantilisme', *Revue internationale de sociologie*, 1902, p. 162) calls it 'un livre dont nous nous sommes assurés que la plupart des hommes du XVIIIe siècle ont pris connaissance'.

6. F. B. Kaye in i, p. xxxix.

7. I borrow this quotation, which I have not been able to trace, from Joan Robinson, *Economic Philosophy*, London, 1962, p. 15.

8. *Summa Theologia*, II. ii, q. 78 i.

9. Cf. F. Heinimann, *Nomos und Physis*, Basel, 1945, and my essay 'The result of human action but not of human design' in my *Studies in Philosophy, Politics and Economics*, London and Chicago, 1967.

10. *Ecclesiazusae*, 473; the translation is that by B. B. Rogers in the Loeb edition, iii, p. 289.

11. M. Tullius Cicero, *De re publica* ii, 1, 2, Loeb ed. by C. W. Keyes, p. 113. Cf. also the Attic orator Antiphon, *On the Choreutes*, par. 2 (in *Minor Attic Orators*, Loeb ed. by K. J. Maidment, p. 247), where he speaks of laws having 'the distinction of being the oldest in this country, . . . and that is the surest token of good laws, as time and experience show mankind what is imperfect'.

12. On Luis Molina, from this angle the most important of these sixteenth-century Spanish Jesuits, and some of his predecessors see my essay cited in footnote 9, p. 254.

13. R. Descartes, *A Discourse on Method*, part II, Everyman ed. London, 1926, p. 11.

14. Leonard Lessius, *De justitia et jure*, 1606.

15. On Sir Matthew Hale see now particularly J. G. A. Pocock, *The Ancient Constitution and the Feudal Law*, Cambridge, 1957, esp. pp. 171 et seq. I would like to make amends here for inadvertently not referring to this excellent book in *The Constitution of Liberty*, 1960, for the final revision of which I had much profited from Mr. Pocock's work.

16. Cf. Pocock, op. cit., p. 19: 'This was the period in which Polydore Vergil wrote his *De inventoribus rerum* on the assumption that every invention could be traced to an individual discoverer; and in the field of legal history Macchiavelli would write with what seems singular naiveté of the man "chi ordinó" so complex a creation of history as the monarchy of France' — with footnote references to Denys Hay, *Polydore Vergil*, Oxford, 1953, chapter III, Niccoló Macchiavelli, *Discorsi* I, xvi, and Pierre Mesnard, *L'Essor de la philosophie politique au XVIe: siècle*, Paris, 1951, p. 83.

17. F. B. Kaye, i, p. lxiii.

18. See Chiaki Nishiyama, *The Theory of Self-Love: An Essay in the Methodology of the Social Sciences, and Especially of Economics, with Special Reference to Bernard Mandeville*, University of Chicago Ph.D. thesis (mimeographed), 1960.

19. i, p. 344.

20. i, p. 356. Already Dugald Stewart in his *Lectures on Political Economy* (*Collected Works*, vii, p. 323) suggests that this passage in Mandeville 'clearly suggested to Adam Smith one of the finest passages of *The Wealth of Nations*'.

21. ii, p. 284.

22. Introduction to Bernard Mandeville, *A Letter to Dion* (1732), edited for The Augustan Reprint Society, Los Angeles, University of California, 1953, and reprinted in Professor Viner's *The Long View and the Short*, Chicago, 1958, pp. 332 – 42. For the predominant and, I believe, truer opinion, cf. Albert Schatz, *L'Individualisme économique et social*, Paris, 1907, p. 62, who describes the *Fable* as 'l'ouvrage capital où se trouvent tous les germes essentiels de la philosophie économique et sociale de l'individualisme'.

23. i, pp. 51, 369, ii, p. 319; also *Letter to Dion*, p. 36.

24. Cf. the title page reproduced in ii, p. 393. It is not described as a second edition, which term was reserved to the edition of 1723.

25. Josiah Tucker, *The Elements of Commerce and Theory of Taxes* (1755), in R. L. Schuyler, *Josiah Tucker, A Selection from His Economic and Political Writings*, New York, 1931, p. 92.

26. Nathan Rosenberg, 'Mandeville and laissez faire', *Journal of the History of Ideas*, XXIV, 1963, pp. 190, 193. Cf. ii, p. 335, where Mandeville argues that, though it would be preferable to have all power in the hands of the good, 'the best of all then not being to be had, let us look out for the next best, and we shall find, that of all possible means to secure and perpetuate to nations their establishment, and whatever they value, there is no better method than with wise laws to guard and entrench their constitution and to contrive such forms of administration, that the commonweal can receive no great detriment from the want of knowledge or probity of ministers, if any of them should prove less able and honest than we would wish them'.

27. i, pp. 299 – 300.

28. ii, p. 353.

29. Cf. J. Viner, 'Adam Smith and laissez faire', *Journal of Political Economy*, xxxv, 1927 and reprinted in *The Long View and the Short*.

30. Elie Halévy, *The Growth of Philosophical Radicalism*, London, 1928, pp. 15 – 17.

31. *The Long View and the Short*, p. 342.

32. ii. p. 142.

33. ii, p. 322.

34. ii, p. 323.

35. N. Rosenberg, loc. cit., p. 194.

36. David Hume, *A Treatise on Human Nature*, ed. T. H. Green and T. H. Grose, ii, p. 274.

37. Cf. Paul Sakmann, *Bernard de Mandeville und die Bienenfabel-Controverse*, Freiburg i.B., 1897, p. 141. Although partly superseded by Kaye's edition, this is still the most comprehensive study of Mandeville.

38. In his *Money and Trade Considered with a Proposal for Supplying the Nation with Money*, Edinburgh, 1705, which thus appeared in the same year as Mandeville's original poem, John Law gave what Carl Menger rightly described as the first adequate account of the development of money. There is no ground for believing that Mandeville knew it, but the date is interesting as showing that the evolutionary idea was somehow 'in the air'.

39. ii, p. 64.

40. ii, p. 349.

41. ii, pp. 140 – 41.

42. ii, p. 141.

43. Ibid.

44. ii, p. 287.

45. John Locke, *Essay Concerning Human Understanding*, III. ii. 1.

46. ii, p. 89.

47. ii, p. 270.

48. ii, p. 269.

49. *The Origin of Honour* (1732), quoted, i, p. 47 n.

50. ii, p. 104. Cf. David Hume, 'Enquiry', in *Essays*, ed. T. H. Green and T. H. Grose, ii, p. 6: 'Man is a reasonable being; and as such, receives from science his proper food and nourishment: But so narrow are the bounds of human understanding, that little satisfaction can be hoped for in this particular, either from the extent or security of his acquisitions'.

51. ii, p. 315.

52. Cf. E. C. Mossner, *The Life of David Hume*, London, 1954, p. 74.

53. *The Origin of Honour*, p. 31, quoted, i, p. lxxix.

54. Cf. Simon N. Patten, *The Development of English Thought*, New York, 1910, pp. 212 – 13: 'Mandeville's immediate successor was Hume. . . . If my interpretation is correct, the starting-point of Hume's development lay in the writings of Mandeville'. Also O. Bobertag's observation in his German translation of *Mandeville's Bienenfabel*, Munich, 1914, p. xxv: 'Im 18. Jahrhundert gibt es nur einen Mann, der etwas gleich Grosses — und Grösseres — geleistet hat, David Hume'.

55. The same may also be true concerning Montesquieu. See on this Joseph Dedieu, *Montesquieu et la tradition politique anglaise*, Paris, 1909, pp. 260 – 61, and 307 n.

56. Adam Ferguson, *An Essay on the History of Civil Society*, Edinburgh, 1767, p. 187: 'Every step and every movement of the multitude, even in what are termed enlightened ages, are made with equal blindness to the future; and nations stumble upon establishments, which are indeed the result of human action, but not the execution of any human design. If Cromwell said, That a man never mounts higher than when he knows not wither he is going; it may with more reason be affirmed of communities, that they admit of the greatest revolutions where no change is intended, and that the most refined politicians do not always know wither they are leading the state by their projects'.

57. It may deserve notice that J. G. Herder seems to have been the earliest instance where the influence of Mandeville joined with that of the somewhat similar ideas of G. Vico.

58. It would seem as if it had been largely by way of Savigny that those ideas of Mandeville and Hume eventually reached Carl Menger and thus returned to economic theory. It was in the sociological parts of his *Untersuchungen über die Methode* (1883, translated as *Problems of Economics and Sociology*, ed. Louis Schneider, Urbana, Ill., 1963) that Carl Menger not only restated the general theory of the formation of law, morals, money, and the market in a manner which, I believe, had never again been attempted since Hume, but that he also expressed the fundamental insight that (p. 94 of the translation): 'This genetic insight is inseparable from the idea of theoretical science'. Perhaps it also deserves notice here, since this seems not to be generally known, that, through his pupil Richard Thurnwald, Menger exercised some influence on the rise of modern cultural anthropology, the discipline which more than any other has in our day concentrated on what were the central problems of the Mandeville-Hume-Smith-Ferguson tradition. Cf. also the long extracts from Mandeville now given in J. S. Slotkin (ed.), *Readings in Early Anthropology*, London, 1965.

59. On the influence on Charles Darwin of conceptions derived from social theory see E. Radl, *Geschichte der biologischen Theorie*, ii, Leipzig, 1909, especially p. 121.

THE PLACE OF MENGER'S *GRUNDSÄTZE* IN THE HISTORY OF ECONOMIC THOUGHT

·10·

When the *Grundsätze* appeared in 1871, it was only 95 years since the *Wealth of Nations,* only 54 since Ricardo's *Principles,* and a mere 23 since the great restatement of classical economics by John Stuart Mill. It is well to begin by recalling these intervals, lest we should look for a mark on contemporary economics (100 years later) which should be greater than it in fact appears to be. There has of course occurred, in the latter part of this 100 years, another revolution — which has shifted interest to aspects of economic analysis that were little cultivated in the earlier part of the century, the time when the impact of Menger's work was chiefly felt. Yet in a longer perspective the 'micro-economic' phase, which owed much of its character to Menger, had considerable duration. It lasted for more than a quarter of the nearly two centuries that have elapsed since Adam Smith.

It is also important, for proper appreciation of Menger, that we do not underestimate what had been achieved before. It is mislead-

---

Reprinted from J. R. Hicks and W. Weber (eds.), *Carl Menger and the Austrian School of Economics,* Oxford, 1973.

Editors' note: An extensive scholarly biography of Carl Menger is being prepared by his son, Karl Menger, and will be published as a volume of The International Carl Menger Library series (Munich: Philosophia-Verlag).

ing to think of the preceding period, 1820 – 70, as simply dominated by Ricardian orthodoxy. At least in the first generation after Ricardo there had been plenty of new ideas. Both within the body of classical economics as finally expounded by John Stuart Mill and even more outside it there had been accumulated an array of tools of analysis from which later generations were able to build an elaborate and coherent structure of theory after the concept of marginal utility provided the basis of the unification. If there ever was a time in which a quasi-Ricardian orthodoxy was dominant, it was after John Stuart Mill had so persuasively restated it. Yet even his *Principles* contain very important developments which go far beyond Ricardo. And even before the publication of that work there had been most important contributions which Mill did not integrate in his synthesis. There had been not only Cournot, Thünen, and Longfield with their crucial work on the theory of price and on marginal productivity, but also a number of other important contributions to the analysis of demand and supply — not to speak of those anticipations of the marginal-utility analysis that were overlooked at the time but later found to be contained in the works of Lloyd, Dupuit, and Gossen. Most of the material was thus available from which it was almost inevitable that somebody should sooner or later undertake a re-construction of the whole body of economic theory — as Alfred Marshall ultimately did, and probably would have done in a not very different fashion if the marginal revolution had not taken place before.

That the reaction against classical economics did take the particular form it did — that at almost the same time William Stanley Jevons in England, Carl Menger at Vienna, and Léon Walras at Lausanne made the subjective value of goods to individuals the starting-point for their reconstruction — was probably as much as anything due to the fact that in his theory of value Mill had explicitly returned to Ricardo. In the work of Menger and Walras their theories of value do not indeed so directly spring from a reaction against Mill as is true in the case of Jevons. But what stood out so clearly in Mill, namely that he lacked a general theory of value which explained the determination of all prices by a uniform principle, was scarcely less true of the systems and textbooks of economic theory that were generally used on the Continent. Though many of them contained much shrewd analysis of the factors that contributed to the determination of price in particular situations, they all lacked a general theory under which the particular instances could be subsumed. It is true that even the demand and supply curves apparatus was beginning to be used; it perhaps deserves mention that the edition of the German textbook by Karl Heinrich Rau, which Menger carefully studied before he wrote the *Grundsätze,* contains at the end a diagram using such curves. But in general it remains true that the prevailing theories offered altogether different explanations of the determination of prices of augmentable and of non-augmentable goods; and in the case of the former they traced the prices of the products to their cost of production, that is to the prices of the factors used, which in turn were not adequately explained. This kind of theory could hardly satisfy. It is indeed quite difficult to understand how a scholar of the penetration and transparent intellectual honesty of John Stuart Mill could have singled out what was so soon felt to be the weakest part of his system for the confident assertion that 'there is nothing in the laws of value which remains for the present or any future writer to clear up; the theory of the subject is complete'.[1] That this foundation of the whole edifice of economic theory was inadequate was only too painfully evident to a number of critical thinkers of the time.

Yet it would probably not be just to suggest that the widespread disillusionment about the prevailing body of economic theory, which becomes noticeable soon after the great success of Mill's work, was due entirely or even chiefly to this fault. There were other circumstances that shook the confidence in the economic theory that had so triumphantly conquered public opinion during the preceding generation, such as in the case of Mill his abandonment of the wage-fund theory which had played so important a part in his work and for which he had nothing to substitute. There was further the growing influence of the historical school which tended to question the value of all attempts at a general theory of economic phenomena. And the fact that the conclusions of the prevailing economic theory seemed to stand in the way of various new social aspirations produced a hostile attitude towards it which made the most of its undeniable defects.

But, though the contrary has been asserted, I can find no indication that Jevons, Menger, or Walras, in their efforts to rebuild economic theory, were moved by any desire to revindicate the practical conclusions that had been drawn from classical economics. Such indications as we have of their sympathies are on the side of the current movements for social reform. Their scientific work seems to me to have sprung entirely from their awareness of the inadequateness of the prevailing body of theory in explaining how the market order in fact operated. And the source of inspiration in all three cases seems to have been an intellectual tradition which, at least since Fernando Galiani in the eighteenth century, had run side by side with the labour and cost theories deriving from John Locke and Adam Smith. I cannot here spare the time to trace the now fairly well-explored history of this utility tradition in the theory of value. But while in the case of Jevons and Walras their indebtedness to particular earlier authors is fairly clear, it is less easy in the case of Menger to discover to whom he owed the decisive suggestions. It is true that on the whole the German literature, on which he mainly drew in his early studies, had devoted more attention to the relation between value and utility than the English writers had done. Yet none of the works that he knew came very close to the solution of the problem at which he ultimately arrived; for it seems certain that he did not know, before he wrote the *Grundsätze,* the one German work in which he had been largely anticipated, that of Herman Heinrich Gossen. Nor does it seem likely that the local environment in which he worked can have provided much stimulus to the pursuit of the problems with which he was concerned. He seems to have indeed worked in complete isolation, and in old age still regretfully told a young economist that in his youth he had had none of the opportunities for discussion that later generations enjoyed.[2] Indeed, Vienna could not have seemed at the time a likely place from which a major contribution to economic theory could be expected.

We know, however, very little about Menger's youth and education and I cannot help regretting that so little work has been done by Austrians to throw more light on it.[3] What little work has been done in modern times about the origin and history of his ideas has been done elsewhere and can scarcely replace what might be done from Austrian sources.[4] Even if the material for a proper biography of Menger does not exist, it should at least be possible to obtain a clearer picture than we have of the general intellectual background of his studies and early work. I must here confine myself to stating a few relevant facts, most of which I owe to the publications of Professor Emil Kauder.[5]

There had not been in Austria that great vogue of Smithian economics or that reception of English and French ideas in the field of economics that had swept most parts of Germany during the first half of the last century. Until as late as 1846 economics was in fact taught at the Austrian universities on the basis of the eighteenth-century cameralist textbook of Joseph von Sonnenfels. In that year it was at last replaced by the work that Menger apparently used as a student, J. Kudler's *Grundlehren der Volkswirthschaft.* In that work he would have found some discussion of the relation of value to utility and especially of the significance of the different urgency of the needs that the various commodities served. We have, however, no evidence that until some time after he left the university Menger began seriously to concern himself with these problems. He is reported to have himself said that his interest in them was aroused through having to write, as a young civil servant, reports on market conditions and through having become aware in doing this how little established theory did help to account for price changes. The earliest preserved notes in his copy of the textbook by Rau mentioned above suggest that by 1867, that is at the age of 27, he had started seriously to think about those questions and had already come fairly close to his ultimate solution. These extensive marginal annotations in his copy of the Rau volume, which with Menger's economic library is preserved at the Hitotsubashi University of Toyko, have been edited by the Japanese, with the assistance of Professor Kauder, under the title of a 'First Draft of the *Grundsätze*',[6] but they can hardly be called that. Though they show that he had already arrived at his conception of the value of a good to an individual as depending on the particular want, for the satisfaction of which it is a condition; though they manifest the characteristic impatience with vague hints in this direction that is bound to be felt by one who had already arrived at a clearer view; they still (perhaps inevitably from their nature) fall far short of the methodical approach which distinguishes the *Grundsätze*. I conclude that the book was really worked out between 1867 and 1871, largely with reference to the extensive German discussions to which the footnotes refer.

What makes the exposition of the *Grundsätze* so effective is its persistent slow approach to its main object. We find Menger elaborating the properties, first of a useful object, then of a good, then of a scarce or economic good, from which he proceeds to the factors determining its value; then he passes to define a marketable commodity (with various degrees of marketability) which takes him ultimately to money. And at every stage Menger stresses (in a manner that to the modern reader, to whom these things have become commonplace, may well seem tedious) how these properties depend (1) on the wants of the person who is acting, and (2) upon his knowledge of the facts and circumstances that make the satisfaction of his need depend on that particular object. He continually emphasizes that these attributes do not inhere in things (or services) as such; that they are not properties that can be discovered by studying the things in isolation. They are entirely a matter of relations between things and the persons who take action about them. It is the latter who, from their knowledge of their subjective wants, and of the objective conditions for satisfying those wants, are led to attribute to physical things a particular degree of importance.

The most obvious result of this analysis is of course the solution of the old paradox of value, through the distinction between the total and the marginal utility of a good. Menger does not yet use the term 'marginal utility' which (or more precisely its German equivalent, *Grenznutzen*) was introduced only 13 years later by Friedrich von Wieser. But he makes the distinction fully clear by showing for the simplest possible case of a given quantity of a particular kind of consumers' good that can be used to satisfy different wants (each of which declines in urgency as it is more fully satisfied), that the importance of any one unit of it will depend on that of the last need for the satisfaction of which the available total quantity is still sufficient. But if he had stopped at this point he would neither have gone beyond what several predecessors, unknown to him, had already seen, nor would he in all probability have made a greater impact than they had made. What later were called (also by Wieser) the two laws of Gossen, namely the decreasing utility of the successive satisfaction of any want, and the equalization of the utilities to which the satisfaction of the different wants that a given good served would be carried, were for Menger no more than the starting-point for the application of the same basic ideas to much more complex relations.

What makes Menger's analysis so much more impressive than that of any of his predecessors is that he applied the basic idea systematically to situations in which the satisfaction of a want is only indirectly (or partially) dependent on a particular good. His painstaking description of the causal connections between the goods and the satisfaction of the wants that they serve enables him to bring out such basic relations as those of complementarity, of consumers' goods as well as of factors of production, of the distinction between goods of a lower or higher order, of the variability of the proportions in which the factors of production can be used, and, finally and most importantly, of costs as determined by the utility that the goods used for a particular purpose might have had in alternative uses. It was this extension of the derivation of the value of a good from its utility, from the case of given quantities of consumers' goods to the general case of all goods, including the factors, of production, that was Menger's main achievement.

In thus providing, as a basis for his explanation of the value of goods, a sort of typology of the possible structures of the means-ends relationship Menger laid the foundation of what later has been called the pure logic of choice or the economic calculus. It contains at least the elements of the analysis of consumer-behaviour and of producer-behaviour; the two essential parts of modern micro-economic price theory. It is true that his immediate followers developed mainly the former, and in particular did not take up the bare hint we find in Menger of a marginal-productivity analysis which is essential for an adequate understanding of producer-behaviour. The development of this essential complement, the theory of the firm, was largely left to Alfred Marshall and his school. Yet enough of it is suggested by Menger for it to be possible for him to claim that he has provided all the essential elements for the achievement of his ultimate aim, an explanation of prices which should be derived from an analysis of the conduct of the individual participants in the market process.

The consistent use of the intelligible conduct of individuals as the building stones from which to construct models of complex market structures is of course the essence of the method that Menger himself described as 'atomistic' (or occasionally, in manuscript notes, as 'compositive') and that later came to be known as methodological individualism. Its character is best expressed by his emphatic statement in the Preface to the *Grundsätze* in which he says that his aim is 'to trace the complex phenomena of the social economy to their simplest elements which are still accessible to certain observation'. But while he stresses that in doing this he is employing the empirical procedure common to all sciences, he implies at the same time that, unlike the physical sciences which analyse the directly observed phenomena into hypothetical elements, in the social sciences we start from our acquaintance with the elements and use them to build models of possible configurations of the complex structures into which they can combine and which are not in the same manner accessible to direct observation as are the elements.

This raises a number of important issues, on the most difficult of which I can touch only briefly. Menger believes that in observing the actions of other persons we are assisted by a capacity of *understanding* the meaning of such actions in a manner in which we cannot understand physical events. This is closely connected with one of the senses in which at least Menger's followers spoke of the 'subjective' character of their theories, by which they meant, among other things, that they were based on our capacity to comprehend the intended meaning of the observed actions. 'Observation', as Menger uses the term, has thus a meaning that modern behaviourists would not accept; and it implies a *Verstehen* ('understanding') in the sense in which Max Weber later developed the concept. It seems to me that there is still much that could be said in defence of the original position of Menger (and of the Austrians generally) on this issue. But since the later development of the indifference-curve technique and particularly of the 'revealed preference' approach, which were designed to avoid the reliance on such introspective knowledge, have shown that at least in principle the hypothesis about individual behaviour that micro-economic theory requires can be stated independently of these 'psychological' assumptions, I will pass over this important point and will turn to another difficulty raised by the adherence to methodological individualism in all its forms.

The fact is, of course, that if we were to derive from our knowledge of individual behaviour specific predictions about changes of the complex structures into which the individual actions combine, we should need full information about the conduct of every single individual who takes part. Menger and his followers were certainly aware that we could never obtain all this information. But they evidently believed that common observation did supply us with a sufficiently complete catalogue of the various *types* of individual conduct that were likely to occur, and even with adequate knowledge of the probability that certain typical situations would occur. What they tried to show was that, starting from these known elements, it could be shown that they could be combined only into certain types of stable structures but not into others. In this sense such a theory would indeed lead to predictions of the kind of structures that would occur, that are capable of falsification. It is true, however, that these predictions would refer only to certain properties that those structures would possess, or indicate certain ranges within which these structures can vary, and rarely, if ever, to predictions of particular events or changes within these structures. To derive such predictions of specific events from this sort of micro-theory we should have to know, not only the types of individual elements of which the complex structures were made up, but the specific properties of every single element of which the particular structure was made up. Micro-economic theory, at least apart from such instances which it could operate with a fairly plausible *ceteris paribus* assumption, remains thus confined to what I have called elsewhere 'pattern predictions'—predictions of the kinds of structures that could be formed from the available kinds of elements. This limitation of the powers of specific prediction, which I believe is true of all theories of phenomena characterized by what Warren Weaver has called 'organized complexity' (to distinguish them from the phenomena of unorganized complexity where we can replace the information about the individual elements, by statistically ascertained probabilities about the occurrence of certain elements),[7] is certainly valid for large parts of micro-economic theory. The position that prevails here is well illustrated by an often quoted statement by Vilfredo Pareto concerning the limited applicability of the systems of equations by which the Walrasian School describes the equilibrium position of a whole economic system. He explicitly stated that these systems of equations 'had by no means the purpose to arrive at a numerical calculation of prices' and that it would be 'absurd' to assume that we could know all the particular facts on which these concrete magnitudes depended.[8]

It seems to me that Carl Menger was quite aware of this limitation of the predictive power of the theory he developed and was content with it because he felt that more could not be achieved in this field. There is to me even a certain refreshing realism about this modest aim which is content, for instance, to indicate only certain limits within which a price will settle down rather than a definite point. Even Menger's aversion against the use of mathematics seems to me directed against a pretence of greater precision than he thought could be achieved. Connected with this is also the absence in Menger's work of the conception of a general equilibrium. If he had continued his work it would probably have become even more apparent than it is in the introductory part (which is the *Grundsätze*) that what he was aiming at was rather to provide tools for what we now call process analysis than for a theory of static equilibrium. In this respect his work and that of the Austrians generally is, of course, very different from the grand view of a whole economic system that Walras gave us.

The limitation on the power of specific prediction to which I have referred seems to me to apply to the whole body of micro-theory which was gradually built up on the foundations of marginal-utility analysis. It was ultimately the desire of achieving more than this modest aim that led to an increasing dissatisfaction with this sort of micro-theory and to attempts to replace it with a theory of a different type.

Before I turn to this reaction against the type of theory of which Menger's work is the prototype, I should say a few words about the curious manner in which his influence operated during the time when it was greatest. There have probably been few books that had an effect as great as the *Grundsätze* in spite of the fact that this work was read by no more than a comparatively small number of people. The effect of the book was chiefly indirect; it became significant only after a considerable interval. Though we commonly date the marginal revolution from the year in which the works of Menger and Jevons were published, the fact is that for the next 10 years or so we shall seek in vain for signs in the literature that they had any effect. Of Menger's book we know that during that early period it had a few careful readers which included not only Eugen von Böhm-Bawerk and Friedrich von Wieser but also Alfred Marshall;[9] but it was only when the two former in the middle of the 1880s published works based on Menger's ideas that these began to be more widely discussed. It is only from this later date, so far as the general development of economic theory is concerned, that we can speak of an effective marginal revolution. And the works that were widely read at that time were those of Böhm-Bawerk and Wieser rather than that of Menger. While the former were soon translated into English, Menger's book had to wait 80 years till it was made available in an English version.

This delay in the effect of Menger's work was probably also the reason why Menger himself, rather than continuing his theoretical work, turned to a defence of the theoretical method of the social science in general. By the time he started on his second book, the *Studies in Method* (*Untersuchungen über die Methoden der Socialwissenschaften*), which appeared in 1883, he must indeed have been under the impression that his first book had had no effect whatever; not because it was thought wrong, but because the economists of the time, at least in the German-speaking world, regarded economic theory in general as irrelevant and uninteresting. It was natural, though perhaps regrettable, that in these circumstances it seemed more important to Menger to vindicate the importance of theoretical analysis than to complete the systematic exposition of his theory. But if in consequence the spreading and development of his theories were left almost wholly to the younger members of the Austrian School, there can be little doubt that during the 50 years from the mid 1880s to the mid 1930s they had, at least outside Britain where Alfred Marshall's ideas dominated, the greatest influence on the development of what, somewhat inappropriately, is now usually called neo-classical economics. For this we have the testimony of Knut Wicksell, who was probably the best-qualified judge because he was equally familiar with all the different strands of marginal theory, and who, in 1921 in an obituary of Carl Menger, could write that 'no book since Ricardo's *Principles* has had such a great influence on the development of economics as Menger's *Grundsätze*'.[10]

If 50 years later this statement could hardly be repeated, this is, of course, the consequence of the great shift of interest from micro- to macro-economics, due chiefly, though not entirely, to the work of Lord Keynes. Some tendency in this direction was already discernible before the appearance of the *General Theory* and was due to an increasing dissatisfaction with those limitations of the predictive powers of micro-theory to which I have already referred. It was largely a growing demand for greater deliberate control of the economic process (which required more knowledge of the specific effects to be expected from particular measures) that led to the endeavour to use the obtainable statistical information as the foundation for such predictions. This desire was strongly supported by certain methodological beliefs, such as that in order to be truly scientific a theory must lead to specific predictions, that it must refer to measurable magnitudes, and that it must be possible to ascertain constant relationships between the quantitative changes in the relations between those aggregates that are statistically measurable. I have already suggested that it seems to me that a theory with much more modest aims may still be testable in the sense of being refutable by observation; and I will now add that it seems by no means certain that the more ambitious aims can be realized. It cannot, however, be denied that if it were possible to establish that some such relationships are in fact constant over reasonably long periods of time, this would greatly increase the predictive power and therefore the usefulness of economic theory. I am not sure that, in spite of all the efforts devoted to this task during the last 25 years, this aim has yet been achieved. My impression is that it will be found that in general such constancies are confined to states which must be defined in micro-economic terms, and that in consequence we shall have to rely on a diagnosis of the situation in micro-economic terms in order to decide whether such quantitative relationships between aggregates as were observed in the past can still be expected to prevail. I rather expect, therefore, that it will be the needs of macro-economics that will in the future give a new stimulus to the further development of micro-economic theory.

Perhaps I should add that the marked lack of interest that so many of the younger economists have shown for micro-theory in the immediate past is a result of the particular form that macro-economic theory took during that period. It had been developed by Keynes chiefly as a theory of employment which, at least as a first approach, proceeded on the assumption that there existed unused reserves of all the different factors of production. The deliberate disregard of the fact of scarcity that this involved led to the treatment of relative prices as historically determined and not requiring theoretical explanation. This sort of theory may, perhaps, have been relevant for the kind of general unemployment that prevailed during the Great Depression. But it is not of much help for the kind of unemployment with which we are faced now or that we are likely to experience in the future. The appearance and growth of unemployment in an inflationary period shows only too clearly that employment is not simply a function of total demand but is determined by that structure of prices and production that only micro-theory can help us to understand.

It seems to me that signs can already be discerned of a revival of interest in the kind of theory that reached its first high point a generation ago — at the end of the period during which Menger's influence had been mainly felt. His ideas had by then, of course, ceased to be the property of a distinct Austrian School but had become merged in a common body of theory which was taught in most parts of the world. But though there is no longer a distinct Austrian School, I believe there is still a distinct Austrian tradition from which we may hope for many further contributions to the future development of economic theory. The fertility of its approach is by no means exhausted and there are still a number of tasks to which it can be profitably applied. But these tasks for the future will be the subject of later papers. What I have tried to do is merely to sketch the general role that Menger's ideas have played during the hundred years that have passed since the appearance of his first and most important work. How much his influence is still a live influence I expect the following papers will show.

NOTES

1. J. S. Mill, *Principles of Political Economy* (1848 and later), book III, chapter I, §1.

2. L. von Mises, *The Historical Setting of the Austrian School of Economics*, New Rochelle, N.Y., 1969, p. 10.

3. My own sketch of Menger's life which I wrote in 1934 in London as an Introduction to his *Collected Works* can in no way fill this gap. It could in the circumstances be no more than a compilation from the available printed

sources, supplemented only by information supplied by Menger's son and some of his pupils.

4. See particularly G. J. Stigler, 'The development of utility theory', *Journal of Political Economics,* 58, 1950, and reprinted in the author's *Essays in the History of Economics,* Chicago, 1965; R. S. Howey, *The Rise of the Marginal Utility School 1870 – 1889,* Lawrence, Kansas, 1960; R. Hansen, 'Der Methodenstreit in den Socialwissenschaften zwischen Gustav Schmoller und Karl Menger: seine wissenschaftshistorische und wissenschaftstheoretische Bedeutung' in A. Diemer (ed.), *Beiträge zur Entwicklung der Wissenschaftstheorie im 19. Jahrhundert,* Meisenheim am Glan, 1968; and the writings of Emil Kauder listed in note 5.

5. Emil Kauder, 'The retarded acceptance of marginal utility theory', *Quarterly Journal of Economics,* 67, 1953; 'Intellectual and political roots of the older Austrian school', *Zeitschrift für Nationalökonomie,* 17, 1958; 'Menger and his library', *Economic Review,* Hitotsubashi University, 10, 1959; 'Aus Mengers nachgelassenen Papieren', *Weltwirtschaftliches Archiv* 89, 1962; and *A History of Marginal Utility Theory,* Princeton, 1965.

6. *Carl Mengers erster Entwurf zu seinem Hauptwerk 'Grundsätze' geschrieben als Anmerkungen zu den 'Grundsätzen der Volkswirthschaftslehre' von Karl Heinrich Rau,* Library of Hitotsubashi University, Tokyo, 1963 (mimeographed), and cf. also *Carl Mengers Zusätze zu 'Grundsätze der Volkswirthschaftslehre',* published in 1961 by the same institution and in the same form.

7. Warren Weaver, 'Science and complexity', *The Rockefeller Foundation Annual Report,* 1958.

8. V. Pareto, *Manuel d'économie politique,* 2nd ed., Paris, 1926, p. 223.

9. Alfred Marshall's copy of the *Grundsätze,* preserved in the Marshall library at Cambridge, contains detailed marginal annotations summarizing the main steps in the argument but without comment. They seem to me to be written in Marshall's handwriting of an early date.

10. Knut Wicksell, *Ekonomisk Tidskrift,* 1921, p. 124, reprinted in his *Selected Papers,* London, 1952, p. 191.

THEORETICAL BASIS OF THE HAYEKIAN SYSTEM

♦ ♦ ♦ ♦

• *PART* • *FOUR* •

The Use of Knowledge in Society

·11·

I

What is the problem we wish to solve when we try to construct a rational economic order? On certain familiar assumptions the answer is simple enough. *If* we possess all the relevant information, *if* we can start out from a given system of preferences, and *if* we command complete knowledge of available means, the problem which remains is purely one of logic. That is, the answer to the question of what is the best use of the available means is implicit in our assumptions. The conditions which the solution of this optimum problem must satisfy have been fully worked out and can be stated best in mathematical form: put at their briefest, they are that the marginal rates of substitution between any two commodities or factors must be the same in all their different uses.

This, however, is emphatically *not* the economic problem which society faces. And the economic calculus which we have developed to solve this logical problem, though an important step toward the solution of the economic problem of society, does not yet provide

---

Reprinted from the *American Economic Review,* XXXV, No. 4 (September, 1945), 519–30.

an answer to it. The reason for this is that the "data" from which the economic calculus starts are never for the whole society "given" to a single mind which could work out the implications and can never be so given.

The peculiar character of the problem of a rational economic order is determined precisely by the fact that the knowledge of the circumstances of which we must make use never exists in concentrated or integrated form but solely as the dispersed bits of incomplete and frequently contradictory knowledge which all the separate individuals possess. The economic problem of society is thus not merely a problem of how to allocate "given" resources — if "given" is taken to mean given to a single mind which deliberately solves the problem set by these "data." It is rather a problem of how to secure the best use of resources known to any of the members of society, for ends whose relative importance only these individuals know. Or, to put it briefly, it is a problem of the utilization of knowledge which is not given to anyone in its totality.

This character of the fundamental problem has, I am afraid, been obscured rather than illuminated by many of the recent refinements of economic theory, particularly by many of the uses made of mathematics. Though the problem with which I want primarily to deal in this paper is the problem of a rational economic organization, I shall in its course be led again and again to point to its close connections with certain methodological questions. Many of the points I wish to make are indeed conclusions toward which diverse paths of reasoning have unexpectedly converged. But, as I now see these problems, this is no accident. It seems to me that many of the current disputes with regard to both economic theory and economic policy have their common origin in a misconception about the nature of the economic problem of society. This misconception in turn is due to an erroneous transfer to social phenomena of the habits of thought we have developed in dealing with the phenomena of nature.

II

In ordinary language we describe by the word "planning" the complex of interrelated decisions about the allocation of our available resources. All economic activity is in this sense planning; and in any society in which many people collaborate, this planning, whoever does it, will in some measure have to be based on knowledge which, in the first instance, is not given to the planner but to somebody else, which somehow will have to be conveyed to the planner. The various ways in which the knowledge on which people base their plans is communicated to them is the crucial problem for any theory explaining the economic process, and the problem of what is the best way of utilizing knowledge initially dispersed among all the people is at least one of the main problems of economic policy — or of designing an efficient economic system.

The answer to this question is closely connected with that other question which arises here, that of *who* is to do the planning. It is about this question that all the dispute about "economic planning" centers. This is not a dispute about whether planning is to be done or not. It is a dispute as to whether planning is to be done centrally, by one authority for the whole economic system, or is to be divided among many individuals. Planning in the specific sense in which the term is used in contemporary controversy necessarily means central planning — direction of the whole economic system according to one unified plan. Competition, on the other hand, means decentralized planning by many separate persons. The halfway house between the two, about which many people talk but which few like when they see it, is the delegation of planning to organized industries, or, in other words, monopolies.

Which of these systems is likely to be more efficient depends mainly on the question under which of them we can expect that fuller use will be made of the existing knowledge. This, in turn, depends on whether we are more likely to succeed in putting at the disposal of a single central authority all the knowledge which ought to be used but which is initially dispersed among many different individuals, or in conveying to the individuals such additional knowledge as they need in order to enable them to dovetail their plans with those of others.

III

It will at once be evident that on this point the position will be different with respect to different kinds of knowledge. The answer to our question will therefore largely turn on the relative importance of the different kinds of knowledge: those more likely to be at the disposal of particular individuals and those which we should with greater confidence expect to find in the possession of an authority made up of suitably chosen experts. If it is today so widely assumed that the latter will be in a better position, this is because one kind of knowledge, namely, scientific knowledge, occupies now so prominent a place in public imagination that we tend to forget that it is not the only kind that is relevant. It may be admitted that, as far as scientific knowledge is concerned, a body of suitably chosen experts may be in the best position to command all the best knowledge available — though this is of course merely shifting the difficulty to the problem of selecting the experts. What I wish to point out is that, even assuming that this problem can be readily solved, it is only a small part of the wider problem.

Today it is almost heresy to suggest that scientific knowledge is not the sum of all knowledge. But a little reflection will show that there is beyond question a body of very important but unorganized knowledge which cannot possibly be called scientific in the sense of knowledge of general rules: the knowledge of the particular circumstances of time and place. It is with respect to this that practically every individual has some advantage over all others because he possesses unique information of which beneficial use might be made, but of which use can be made only if the decisions depending on it are left to him or are made with his active co-operation. We need to remember only how much we have to learn in any occupation after we have completed our theoretical training, how big a part of our working life we spend learning particular jobs, and how valuable an asset in all walks of life is knowledge of people, of local conditions, and of special circumstances. To know of and put to use a machine not fully employed, or somebody's skill which could be better utilized, or to be aware of a surplus stock which can be drawn upon during an interruption of supplies, is socially quite as useful as the knowledge of better alternative techniques. The shipper who earns his living from using otherwise empty or half-filled journeys of tramp-steamers, or the estate agent whose whole knowledge is almost exclusively one of temporary opportunities, or the *arbitrageur* who gains from local differences of commodity prices — are all performing eminently useful functions based on special knowledge of circumstances of the fleeting moment not known to others.

It is a curious fact that this sort of knowledge should today be generally regarded with a kind of contempt and that anyone who by such knowledge gains an advantage over somebody better equipped with theoretical or technical knowledge is thought to have acted almost disreputably. To gain an advantage from better knowledge of facilities of communication or transport is sometimes regarded as almost dishonest, although it is quite as important that society make use of the best opportunities in this respect as in using the latest scientific discoveries. This prejudice has in a considerable measure affected the attitude toward commerce in general compared with that toward production. Even economists who regard themselves as definitely immune to the crude materialist fallacies of the past constantly commit the same mistake where activities directed toward the acquisition of such practical knowledge are concerned — apparently because in their scheme of things all such knowledge is supposed to be "given." The common idea now seems to be that all such knowledge should as a matter of course be readily at the command of everybody, and the reproach of irrationality leveled against the existing economic order is frequently based on the fact that it is not so available. This view disregards the fact that the method by which such knowledge can be made as widely available as possible is precisely the problem to which we have to find an answer.

IV

If it is fashionable today to minimize the importance of the knowledge of the particular circumstances of time and place, this is closely connected with the smaller importance which is now attached to change as such. Indeed, there are few points on which the assumptions made (usually only implicitly) by the "planners" differ from those of their opponents as much as with regard to the significance and frequency of changes which will make substantial alterations of production plans necessary. Of course, if detailed economic plans could be laid down for fairly long periods in advance and then closely adhered to, so that no further economic decisions of importance would be required, the task of drawing up a comprehensive plan governing all economic activity would be much less formidable.

It is, perhaps, worth stressing that economic problems arise always and only in consequence of change. As long as things continue as before, or at least as they were expected to, there arise no new problems requiring a decision, no need to form a new plan. The belief that changes, or at least day-to-day adjustments, have become less important in modern times implies the contention that economic problems also have become less important. This belief in the decreasing importance of change is, for that reason, usually held by the same people who argue that the importance of economic considerations has been driven into the background by the growing importance of technological knowledge.

Is it true that, with the elaborate apparatus of modern production, economic decisions are required only at long intervals, as when a new factory is to be erected or a new process to be introduced? Is it true that, once a plant has been built, the rest is all more or less mechanical, determined by the character of the plant, and leaving little to be changed in adapting to the ever changing circumstances of the moment?

The fairly widespread belief in the affirmative is not, as far as I can ascertain, borne out by the practical experience of the businessman. In a competitive industry at any rate — and such an industry alone can serve as a test — the task of keeping cost from rising requires constant struggle, absorbing a great part of the energy of the manager. How easy it is for an inefficient manager to dissipate the differentials on which profitability rests and that it is possible, with the same technical facilities, to produce with a great variety of costs are among the commonplaces of business experience which do not seem to be equally familiar in the study of the economist. The very strength of the desire, constantly voiced by producers and engineers, to be allowed to proceed untrammeled by considerations of money costs, is eloquent testimony to the extent to which these factors enter into their daily work.

One reason why economists are increasingly apt to forget about the constant small changes which make up the whole economic picture is probably their growing preoccupation with statistical aggregates, which show a very much greater stability than the movements of the detail. The comparative stability of the aggregates cannot, however, be accounted for — as the statisticians occasionally seem to be inclined to do — by the "law of large numbers" or the mutual compensation of random changes. The number of elements with which we have to deal is not large enough for such accidental forces to produce stability. The continuous flow of goods and services is maintained by constant deliberate adjustments, by new dispositions made every day in the light of circumstances not known the day before, by B stepping in at once when A fails to deliver. Even the large and highly mechanized plant keeps going largely because of an environment upon which it can draw for all sorts of unexpected needs: tiles for its roof, stationery or its forms, and all the thousand and one kinds of equipment in which it cannot be self-contained and which the plans for the operation of the plant require to be readily available in the market.

This is, perhaps, also the point where I should briefly mention the fact that the sort of knowledge with which I have been concerned is knowledge of the kind which by its nature cannot enter into statistics and therefore cannot be conveyed to any central authority in statistical form. The statistics which such a central authority would have to use would have to be arrived at precisely by abstracting from minor differences between the things, by lumping together, as resources of one kind, items which differ as regards location, quality, and other particulars, in a way which may be very significant for the specific decision. It follows from this that central planning based on statistical information by its nature cannot take direct account of these circumstances of time and place and that the central planner will have to find some way or other in which the decisions depending on them can be left to the "man on the spot."

V

If we can agree that the economic problem of society is mainly one of rapid adaptation to changes in the particular circumstances of time and place, it would seem to follow that the ultimate decisions must be left to the people who are familiar with these circumstances, who know directly of the relevant changes and of the resources immediately available to meet them. We cannot expect that this problem will be solved by first communicating all this knowledge to a central board which, after integrating all knowledge, issues its orders. We must solve it by some form of decentralization. But this answers only part of our problem. We need decentralization because only thus can we insure that the knowledge of the particular circumstances of time and place will be promptly used. But the "man on the spot" cannot decide solely on the basis of his limited but intimate knowledge of the facts of his immediate surroundings. There still remains the problem of communicating to him such further information as he needs to fit his decisions into the whole pattern of changes of the larger economic system.

How much knowledge does he need to do so successfully? Which of the events which happen beyond the horizon of his immediate knowledge are of relevance to his immediate decision, and how much of them need he know?

There is hardly anything that happens anywhere in the world that *might* not have an effect on the decision he ought to make. But he need not know of these events as such, nor of *all* their effects. It does not matter for him *why* at the particular moment more screws of one size than of another are wanted, *why* paper bags are more readily available than canvas bags, or *why* skilled labor, or particular machine tools, have for the moment become more difficult to obtain. All that is significant for him is *how much more or less* difficult to procure they have become compared with other things with which he is also concerned, or how much more or less urgently wanted are the alternative things he produces or uses. It is always a question of the relative importance of the particular things with which he is concerned, and the causes which alter their relative importance are of no interest to him beyond the effect on those concrete things of his own environment.

It is in this connection that what I have called the "economic calculus" (or the Pure Logic of Choice) helps us, at least by analogy, to see how this problem can be solved, and in fact is being solved, by the price system. Even the single controlling mind, in possession of all the data for some small, self-contained economic system, would not — every time some small adjustment in the allocation of resources had to be made — go explicitly through all the relations between ends and means which might possibly be affected. It is indeed the great contribution of the Pure Logic of Choice that it has demonstrated conclusively that even such a single mind could solve this kind of problem only by constructing and constantly using rates of equivalence (or "values," or "marginal rates of substitution"), that is, by attaching to each kind of scarce resource a numerical index which cannot be derived from any property possessed by that particular thing, but which reflects, or in which is condensed, its significance in view of the whole means-end structure. In any small change he will have to consider only these quantitative indices (or "values") in which all the relevant information is concentrated; and, by adjusting the quantities one by one, he can appropriately rearrange his dispositions without having to solve the whole puzzle *ab initio* or without needing at any stage to survey it at once in all its ramifications.

Fundamentally, in a system in which the knowledge of the relevant facts is dispersed among many people, prices can act to coordinate the separate actions of different people in the same way as subjective values help the individual to co-ordinate the parts of his plan. It is worth contemplating for a moment a very simple and commonplace instance of the action of the price system to see what precisely it accomplishes. Assume that somewhere in the world a new opportunity for the use of some raw material, say, tin, has arisen, or that one of the sources of supply of tin has been eliminated. It does not matter for our purpose — and it is significant that it does not matter — which of these two causes has made tin more scarce.

All that the users of tin need to know is that some of the tin they used to consume is now more profitably employed elsewhere and that, in consequence, they must economize tin. There is no need for the great majority of them even to know where the more urgent need has arisen, or in favor of what other needs they ought to husband the supply. If only some of them know directly of the new demand, and switch resources over to it, and if the people who are aware of the new gap thus created in turn fill it from still other sources, the effect will rapidly spread throughout the whole economic system and influence not only all the uses of tin but also those of its substitutes and the substitutes of these substitutes, the supply of all the things made of tin, and their substitutes, and so on; and all this without the great majority of those instrumental in bringing about these substitutions knowing anything at all about the original cause of these changes. The whole acts as one market, not because any of its members survey the whole field, but because their limited individual fields of vision sufficiently overlap so that through many intermediaries the relevant information is communicated to all. The mere fact that there is one price for any commodity — or rather that local prices are connected in a manner determined by the cost of transport, etc. — brings about the solution which (it is just conceptually possible) might have been arrived at by one single mind possessing all the information which is in fact dispersed among all the people involved in the process.

VI

We must look at the price system as such a mechanism for communicating information if we want to understand its real function — a function which, of course, it fulfils less perfectly as prices grow more rigid. (Even when quoted prices have become quite rigid, however, the forces which would operate through changes in price still operate to a considerable extent through changes in the other terms of the contract.) The most significant fact about this system is the economy of knowledge with which it operates, or how little the individual participants need to know in order to be able to take the right action. In abbreviated form, by a kind of symbol, only the most essential information is passed on and passed on only to those concerned. It is more than a metaphor to describe the price system as a kind of machinery for registering change, or a system of telecommunications which enables individual producers to watch merely the movement of a few pointers, as an engineer might watch the hands of a few dials, in order to adjust their activities to changes of which they may never know more than is reflected in the price movement.

Of course, these adjustments are probably never "perfect" in the sense in which the economist conceives of them in his equilibrium analysis. But I fear that our theoretical habits of approaching the problem with the assumption of more or less perfect knowledge on the part of almost everyone has made us somewhat blind to the true function of the price mechanism and led us to apply rather misleading standards in judging its efficiency. The marvel is that in a case like that of a scarcity of one raw material, without an order being issued, without more than perhaps a handful of people knowing the cause, tens of thousands of people whose identity could not be ascertained by months of investigation, are made to use the material or its products more sparingly; that is, they move in the right direction. This is enough of a marvel even if, in a constantly changing world, not all will hit it off so perfectly that their profit rates will always be maintained at the same even or "normal" level.

I have deliberately used the word "marvel" to shock the reader out of the complacency with which we often take the working of this mechanism for granted. I am convinced that if it were the result of deliberate human design, and if the people guided by the price changes understood that their decisions have significance far beyond their immediate aim, this mechanism would have been acclaimed as one of the greatest triumphs of the human mind. Its misfortune is the double one that it is not the product of human design and that the people guided by it usually do not know why they are made to do what they do. But those who clamor for "conscious direction" — and who cannot believe that anything which has evolved without design (and even without our understanding it) should solve problems which we should not be able to solve consciously — should remember this: The problem is precisely how to extend the span of our utilization of resources beyond the span of the control of any one mind; and, therefore, how to dispense with the need of conscious control and how to provide inducements which will make the individuals do the desirable things without anyone having to tell them what to do.

The problem which we meet here is by no means peculiar to economics but arises in connection with nearly all truly social phenomena, with language and with most of our cultural inheritance, and constitutes really the central theoretical problem of all social science. As Alfred Whitehead has said in another connection, "It is a profoundly erroneous truism, repeated by all copy-books and by eminent people when they are making speeches, that we should cultivate the habit of thinking what we are doing. The precise opposite is the case. Civilization advances by extending the number of important operations which we can perform without thinking about them." This is of profound significance in the social field. We make constant use of formulas, symbols, and rules whose meaning we do not understand and through the use of which we avail ourselves of the assistance of knowledge which individually we do not possess. We have developed these practices and institutions by building upon habits and institutions which have proved successful in their own sphere and which have in turn become the foundation of the civilization we have built up.

The price system is just one of those formations which man has learned to use (though he is still very far from having learned to make the best use of it) after he had stumbled upon it without understanding it. Through it not only a division of labor but also a coordinated utilization of resources based on an equally divided knowledge has become possible. The people who like to deride any suggestion that this may be so usually distort the argument by insinuating that it asserts that by some miracle just that sort of system has spontaneously grown up which is best suited to modern civilization. It is the other way around: man has been able to develop that division of labor on which our civilization is based because he happened to stumble upon a method which made it possible. Had he not done so, he might still have developed some other, altogether different, type of civilization, something like the "state" of the termite ants, or some other altogether unimaginable type. All that we can say is that nobody has yet succeeded in designing an alternative system in which certain features of the existing one can be preserved which are dear even to those who most violently assail it — such as particularly the extent to which the individual can choose his pursuits and consequently freely use his own knowledge and skill.

VII

It is in many ways fortunate that the dispute about the indispensability of the price system for any rational calculation in a complex society is now no longer conducted entirely between camps holding different political views. The thesis that without the price system we could not preserve a society based on such extensive division of labor as ours was greeted with a howl of derision when it was first advanced by von Mises twenty-five years ago. Today the difficulties which some still find in accepting it are no longer mainly political, and this makes for an atmosphere much more conducive to reasonable discussion. When we find Leon Trotsky arguing that "economic accounting is unthinkable without market relations"; when Professor Oscar Lange promises Professor von Mises a statue in the marble halls of the future Central Planning Board; and when Professor Abba P. Lerner rediscovers Adam Smith and emphasizes that the essential utility of the price system consists in inducing the individual, while seeking his own interest, to do what is in the general interest, the differences can indeed no longer be ascribed to political prejudice. The remaining dissent seems clearly to be due to purely intellectual, and more particularly methodological, differences.

A recent statement by Joseph Schumpeter in his *Capitalism, Socialism, and Democracy* provides a clear illustration of one of the methodological differences which I have in mind. Its author is preeminent among those economists who approach economic phenomena in the light of a certain branch of positivism. To him these phenomena accordingly appear as objectively given quantities of commodities impinging directly upon each other, almost, it would seem, without any intervention of human minds. Only against this background can I account for the following (to me startling) pronouncement. Professor Schumpeter argues that the possibility of a rational calculation in the absence of markets for the factors of production follows for the theorist "from the elementary proposition that consumers in evaluating ('demanding') consumers' goods *ipso facto* also evaluate the means of production which enter into the production of these goods."[1]

Taken literally, this statement is simply untrue. The consumers do nothing of the kind. What Professor Schumpeter's "*ipso facto*" presumably means is that the valuation of the factors of production is implied in, or follows necessarily from, the valuation of consumers' goods. But this, too, is not correct. Implication is a logical relationship which can be meaningfully asserted only of propositions simultaneously present to one and the same mind. It is evident, however, that the values of the factors of production do not depend solely on the valuation of the consumers' goods but also on the conditions of supply of the various factors of production. Only to a mind to which all these facts were simultaneously known would the answer necessarily follow from the facts given to it. The practical problem, however, arises precisely because these facts are never so given to a single mind, and because, in consequence, it is necessary that in the solution of the problem knowledge should be used that is dispersed among many people.

The problem is thus in no way solved if we can show that all the facts, *if* they were known to a single mind (as we hypothetically assume them to be given to the observing economist), would uniquely determine the solution; instead we must show how a solution is produced by the interactions of people each of whom possesses only partial knowledge. To assume all the knowledge to be given to a single mind in the same manner in which we assume it to be given to us as the explaining economists is to assume the problem away and to disregard everything that is important and significant in the real world.

That an economist of Professor Schumpeter's standing should thus have fallen into a trap which the ambiguity of the term "datum" sets to the unwary can hardly be explained as a simple error. It suggests rather that there is something fundamentally wrong with an approach which habitually disregards an essential part of the phenomena with which we have to deal: the unavoidable imperfection of man's knowledge and the consequent need for a process by which knowledge is constantly communicated and acquired. Any approach, such as that of much of mathematical economics with its simultaneous equations, which in effect starts from the assumption that people's *knowledge* corresponds with the objective *facts* of the situation, systematically leaves out what is our main task to explain. I am far from denying that in our system equilibrium analysis has a useful function to perform. But when it comes to the point where it misleads some of our leading thinkers into believing that the situation which it describes has direct relevance to the solution of practical problems, it is high time that we remember that it does not deal with the social process at all and that it is no more than a useful preliminary to the study of the main problem.

NOTES

1. *Capitalism, Socialism, and Democracy* (New York: Harper & Bros., 1942), p. 175. Professor Schumpeter is, I believe, also the original author of the myth that Pareto and Barone have "solved" the problem of socialist calculation. What they, and many others, did was merely to state the conditions which a rational allocation of resources would have to satisfy and to point out that these were essentially the same as the conditions of equilib-

rium of a competitive market. This is something altogether different from showing how the allocation of resources satisfying these conditions can be found in practice. Pareto himself (from whom Barone has taken practically everything he has to say), far from claiming to have solved the practical problem, in fact explicitly denies that it can be solved without the help of the market. See his *Manuel d'économie pure* (2d ed., 1927), pp. 233–34. The relevant passage is quoted in an English translation at the beginning of my article on "Socialist Calculation: The Competitive 'Solution,'" in *Economica,* VIII, No. 26 (new ser., 1940), 125; reprinted below as chapter viii [in *Individualism and Economic Order*].

PHILOSOPHICAL CONSEQUENCES

·12·

PRE-SENSORY EXPERIENCE AND PURE EMPIRICISM

If the account of the determination of mental qualities which we have given is correct, it would mean that the apparatus by means of which we learn about the external world is itself the product of a kind of experience. It is shaped by the conditions prevailing in the environment in which we live, and it represents a kind of generic reproduction of the relations between the elements of this environment which we have experienced in the past; and we interpret any new event in the environment in the light of that experience. If this conclusion is true, it raises necessarily certain important philosophical questions on which in this last chapter we shall attempt some tentative observations.

These consequences arise mainly from the role which we have assigned to the action of the pre-sensory experience or 'linkages' in determining the sensory qualities. Especially the elimination of the hypothetical 'pure' or 'primary' core of sensations, supposed not to be due to earlier experience, but either to involve some direct communication of properties of the external objects, or to constitute irreducible mental atoms or elements, disposes of various philosophical puzzles which arise from the lack of meaning of those hypotheses.

According to the traditional view, experience begins with the reception of sensory data possessing constant qualities which either reflect corresponding attributes belonging to the perceived external objects, or are uniquely correlated with such attributes of the elements of the physical world. These sensory data are supposed to form the raw material which the mind accumulates and learns to arrange in various manners. The theory developed here challenges the basic distinction implied in that conception: the distinction between sensory perception of given qualities and the operations which the intellect is supposed to perform on these data in order to arrive at an understanding of the given phenomenal world.

According to our theory, the characteristic attributes of the sensory qualities, or the classes into which different events are placed in the process of perception, are not attributes which are possessed by these events and which are in some manner 'communicated' to the mind; they are regarded as consisting entirely in the 'differentiating' responses of the organism by which the qualitative classification or order of these events is created; and it is contended that this classification is based on the connexions created in the nervous system by past linkages. Every sensation, even the 'purest', must therefore be regarded as an interpretation of an event in the light of the past experience of the individual or the species.

The process of experience thus does not begin with sensations or perceptions, but necessarily precedes them: it operates on physiological events and arranges them into a structure or order which becomes the basis of their 'mental' significance; and the distinction between the sensory qualities, in terms of which alone the conscious mind can learn about anything in the external world, is the result of such pre-sensory experience. We may express this also by stating that experience is not a function of mind or consciousness, but that mind and consciousness are rather products of experience.

Every sensory experience of an event in the external world is therefore likely to possess 'attributes' (or to be in a manner distinguished from other sensory events) to which no similar attributes of the external events correspond. These 'attributes' are the significance which the organism has learnt to assign to a class of events on the basis of the past associations of events of this class with certain other classes of events. It is only in so far as the nervous system has learnt thus to treat a particular stimulus as a member of a certain class of events, determined by the connexions which all the corresponding impulses possess with the same impulses representing other classes of events, that an event can be perceived at all, i.e., that it can obtain a distinct position in the system of sensory qualities.

If the distinctions between the different sensory qualities of which our conscious experience appears to be built up are thus themselves determined by pre-sensory experiences (linkages), the whole problem of the relation between experience and knowledge assumes a new complexion. So far as experience in the narrow sense, i.e., conscious sensory experience, is meant, it is then clearly not true that all that we know is due to such experience. Experience of this kind would rather become possible only after experience in the wider sense of linkages has created the order of sensory qualities — the order which determines the qualities of the constituents of conscious experience.

Sense experience therefore presupposes the existence of a sort of accumulated 'knowledge', of an acquired order of the sensory impulses based on their past co-occurrence; and this knowledge, although based on (pre-sensory) experience, can never be contradicted by sense experiences and will determine the forms of such experiences which are possible.

John Locke's famous fundamental maxim of empiricism that *nihil est in intellectu quod non antea fuerit in sensu* is therefore not correct if meant to refer to conscious sense experience. And it does not justify the conclusion that all we know (*quod est in intellectu*) must be subject to confirmation or contradiction by sense experience. From our explanation of the formation of the order of sensory qualities itself it would follow that there will exist certain general principles to which all sensory experiences must conform (such as that two distinct colours cannot be in the same place) — relations between the parts of such experiences which must always be true.

A certain part at least of what we know at any moment about the external world is therefore not learnt by sensory experience, but is rather implicit in the means through which we can obtain such experience; it is determined by the order of the apparatus of classification which has been built up by pre-sensory linkages. What we experience consciously as qualitative attributes of the external events is determined by relations of which we are not consciously aware but which are implicit in these qualitative distinctions, in the sense that they affect all that we do in response to these experiences.

All that we can perceive is thus determined by the order of sensory qualities which provides the 'categories' in terms of which sense experience can alone take place. Conscious experience, in particular, always refers to events defined in terms of relations to other events which do not occur in that particular experience.[1]

We thus possess 'knowledge' about the phenomenal world which, because it is in this manner implicit in all sensory experience, must be true of all that we can experience through our senses. This does not mean, however, that this knowledge must also be true of the physical world, that is, of the order of the stimuli which cause our sensations. While the conditions which make sense perception possible — the apparatus of classification which treats them as similar or different — must affect all sense perception, it does not for this reason also govern the order of the events in the physical world.

It requires a deliberate effort to divest oneself of the habitual assumption that all we have learned from experience must be true of the external (physical) world.[2] But since all we can ever learn from experience are generalizations about certain kinds of events, and since no number of particular instances can ever prove such a generalization, knowledge based entirely on experience may yet be entirely false. If the significance which a certain group of stimuli has acquired for us is based entirely on the fact that in the past they have regularly occurred in combination with certain other stimuli, this may or may not be an adequate basis for a classification which will enable us to make true predictions. We have earlier [*The Sensory Order*, chapter 5] given a number of reasons why we must expect that the classifications of events in the external world which our senses perform will not strictly correspond to a classification of these events based solely on the similarity or the differences of their behaviour towards each other.

While there can thus be nothing in our mind which is not the result of past linkages (even though, perhaps, acquired not by the individual but by the species), the experience that the classification based on the past linkages does not always work, i.e., does not always lead to valid predictions, forces us to revise that classification. In the course of this process of reclassification we not only establish new relations between the data given within a fixed framework of reference, i.e., between the elements of given classes: but since the framework consists of the relations determining the classes, we are led to adjust that framework itself.

The reclassification, or breaking up of the classes formed by the implicit relations which manifest themselves in our discrimination of sensory qualities, and the replacement of these classes by new classes defined by explicit relations, will occur whenever the expectations resulting from the existing classification are disappointed, or when beliefs so far held are disproved by new experiences. The immediate effects of such conflicting experiences will be to introduce inconsistent elements into the model of the external world; and such inconsistencies can be eliminated only if what formerly were treated as elements of the same class are now treated as elements of different classes.

The reclassification which is thus performed by the mind is a process similar to that through which we pass in learning to read aloud a language which is not spelled phonetically. We learn to give identical symbols different values according as they appear in combination with different other symbols, and to recognize different groups of symbols as being equivalent without even noticing the individual symbols.

While the process of reclassification involves a change of the frame of reference, or of what is a priori true of all statements which can be made about the objects defined with respect to that frame of reference, it alters merely the particular presuppositions of all statements, but does not change the fact that such presuppositions must be implied in all statements that can be made. In fact, far from being diminished, the a priori element will tend to increase as in the course of this process the various objects are increasingly defined by explicit relations existing between them.

The new experiences which are the occasion of, and which enter into, the new classifications or definitions of objects, is necessarily presupposed by anything which we can learn about these objects and cannot be contradicted by anything which we can say about the objects thus defined. There is, therefore, on every level, or in every universe of discourse, a part of our knowledge which, although it is the result of experience, cannot be controlled by experience, because it constitutes the ordering principle of that universe by which we distinguish the different kinds of objects of which it consists and to which our statements refer.

The more this process leads us away from the immediately given sensory qualities, and the more the elements described in terms of these qualities are replaced by new elements defined in terms of consciously experienced relations, the greater becomes the part of our knowledge which is embodied in the definitions of the elements, and which therefore is necessarily true. At the same time the part of our knowledge which is subject to control by experiences becomes correspondingly smaller.

This progressive growth of the tautological character of our knowledge is a necessary consequence of our endeavour so to readjust our classification of the elements as to make statements about them true. We have no choice but either to accept the classification effected by our senses, and in consequence to be unable correctly to predict the behaviour of the objects thus defined; or to redefine the objects on the basis of the observed differences in their behaviour with respect to each other, with the result that not only the differences which are the basis of our classification become necessarily true of the objects thus classified, but also that it becomes less and less possible to say of any particular sensory object with any degree of certainty to which of our theoretical classes it belongs.

This difficulty does not become too serious so long as we merely redefine a particular object in relational terms. But as we continue this process of reclassification, those other objects must in turn also be redefined in a similar manner. In the course of this process we are soon forced to take into account not only relations existing between a given object and other objects which are actually observed in conjunction with the former, but also relations which have existed in the past between that and other objects, and even relations which can be described only in hypothetical terms: relations which might have been observed between this and other objects in circumstances which did not in fact exist and which, if they had existed, would not have left the identity of the object unchanged.

Several chemical substances may, e.g., be completely indistinguishable to the senses so long as they remain in their given state. The reason why chemistry classifies them as different substances is that in certain circumstances and in combination with certain other substances they will 'react' differently. But most of these chemical reactions involve a change in the character of the substance, so that the identical quantity of a given substance, which has been tested for the reaction which is the basis of its classification, cannot be available after it has been established to which class it belongs. Only by such unverifiable assumptions as that the quantity of the substance from which we have drawn the sample is completely homogeneous, so that what we have found out about various samples applies also to the rest, can we arrive at the conclusion that the particular sensory object belongs to a definite theoretical class.

The sense data, or the sensory qualities of the objects about which we make statements, thus are pushed steadily further back; and when we complete the process of defining all objects by explicit relations instead of by the implicit relations inherent in our sensory distinctions, those sense data disappear completely from the system. In the end the system of explicit definitions becomes both all-comprehensive and self-contained or circular; all the elements in the universe are defined by their relations to each other, and all we know about that universe becomes contained in those definitions. We should obtain a self-contained model capable of reproducing all the combinations of events which we can observe in the external world, but should have no way of ascertaining whether any particular event in the external world corresponded to a particular part of our model.

Science thus tends necessarily towards an ultimate state in which all knowledge is embodied in the definitions of the objects with which it is concerned; and in which all true statements about these objects therefore are analytical or tautological and could not be disproved by any experience. The observation that any object did not behave as it should could then only mean that it was not an object of the kind it was thought to be. With the disappearance of all sensory data from the system, laws (or theories) would no longer exist in it apart from the definitions of the objects to which they applied, and for that reason could never be disproved.

Such a completely tautological or self-contained system of knowledge about the world would not be useless. It would constitute a model of the world from which we could read off what kind of events are possible in that world and what are not. It would often allow us, on the basis of a fairly complete history of a particular sensory object, to state with a high degree of probability that it fits into one and only one possible place in our model, and that in consequence it is likely to behave in a certain manner in circumstances which would have to be similarly described. But it would never enable us to identify with certainty a particular sensory object with a particular part of our model, or with certainty to predict how the former will behave in given circumstances.

A strict identification of any point of our theoretical model of the world with a particular occurrence in the sensory world would be possible only if we were in a position to complete our model of the physical world by including in it a complete model of the working of our brain — that is, if we were able to explain in detail the manner in which our senses classify the stimuli. This, however, as will be shown in section 6 of this chapter [The Limits of Explanation, p. 243], is a task which that same brain can never accomplish.

In conclusion of this section it should, perhaps, be emphasized that, in so far as we have been led into opposition to some of the theses traditionally associated with empiricism, we have been led to their rejection not from an opposite point of view, but on the contrary, by a more consistent and radical application of its basic idea. Precisely because all our knowledge, including the initial order of our different sensory experiences of the world, is due to experience, it must contain elements which cannot be contradicted by experience. It must always refer to classes of elements which are defined by certain relations to other elements, and it is valid only on the assumption that these relations actually exist. Generalization based on experience must refer to classes of objects or events and can have relevance to the world only in so far as these classes are regarded as given irrespective of the statement itself. Sensory experience presupposes, therefore, an order of experienced objects which precedes that experience and which cannot be contradicted by it, though it is itself due to other, earlier experience.

Phenomenalism and the Inconstancy of Sensory Qualities

If the classification of events in the external world effected by our senses proves not to be a 'true' classification, i.e. not one which enables us adequately to describe the regularities in this world, and if the properties which our senses attribute to these events are not objective properties of these individual events, but merely attributes defining the classes to which our senses assign them, this means that we cannot regard the phenomenal world in any sense as more 'real' than the constructions of science: we must assume the existence of an objective world (or better, of an objective order of the events which we experience in their phenomenal order) towards the recognition of which the phenomenal order is merely a first approximation. The task of science is thus to try and approach ever more closely towards a reproduction of this objective order — a task which it can perform only by replacing the sensory order of events by a new and different classification.[3]

By saying that there 'exists' an 'objective' world different from the phenomenal world we are merely stating that it is possible to construct an order or classification of events which is different from that which our senses show us and which enables us to give a more consistent account of the behaviour of the different events in that world. Or, in other words, it means that our knowledge of the phenomenal world raises problems which can be answered only by altering the picture which our senses give us of that world, i.e. by altering our classification of the elements of which it consists. That this is possible and necessary is, in fact, a postulate which underlies all our efforts to arrive at a scientific explanation of the world.

Any purely phenomenalistic interpretation of the task of science, or any attempt to reduce this task to merely a complete description of the phenomenal world, thus must break down because our senses do not effect such a classification of the different events that what appears to us as alike will also always behave in the same manner. The basic thesis of phenomenalism (and positivism) that 'all *phenomena* are subject to invariable laws' is simply not true if the term phenomenon is taken in its strict meaning of things as they appear to us.

The ideal of science as merely a complete description of phenomena, which is the positivist conclusion derived from the phenomenalistic approach, therefore proves to be impossible. Science consists rather in a constant search for new classes, for 'constructs' which are so defined that general propositions about the behaviour of their elements are universally and necessarily true. For this purpose these classes cannot be defined in terms of sensory properties of the particular individual events perceived by the individual person; they must be defined in terms of their relations to other individual events.

Such a definition of any class of events, in terms of their relations to other classes of events instead of in terms of any sensory properties which they individually possess, cannot be confined to the former, or even to all the events which together constitute the complete situation existing at a particular moment. The events referred to in the definition of those with which we have actually to deal have to be defined in a similar purely 'relational' manner. The ultimate aim of this procedure must be to define all classes of events exclusively in terms of their relations to each other and without any reference to their sensory properties. It has been well said that 'for science an object expresses itself in the totality of relations possible between it and other objects'.[4] We have already seen that such a complete system of explanation would necessarily be tautological, because all that could be predicted by it would necessarily follow from the definitions of the objects to which it referred.

If the theory outlined here is correct, there exists an even more fundamental objection to any consistently phenomenalist interpretation of science. It would appear that not only are the events of the world, if defined in terms of their sensory attributes, not subject to invariable laws, so that situations presenting the same appearance to our senses may produce different results; but also that the phenomenal world (or the order of the sensory qualities from which it is built up) is itself not constant but variable, and that it will in some measure change its appearance as a result of that very process of reclassification which we must perform in order to explain it.

If it is true, as we have argued, that the 'higher' mental activities are merely a repetition at successive levels of processes of classification of essentially the same character as those by which the different sensory qualities have come to be distinguished in the first instance, it would seem almost inevitable that this process of reclassification will in some measure also affect the distinctions between the different sensory qualities from which it starts. The nature of the process by which the difference between sensory qualities are determined makes it probable that they will remain variable and that the distinctions between them will be modified by new experiences. This would mean that the phenomenal world itself would not be constant but would be incessantly changing in a direction to a closer reproduction of the relations existing in the physical world. If in the course of this process the sensory data themselves alter their character, the ideal of a purely descriptive science becomes altogether impossible.

That the sensory qualities which attach to particular physical events are thus in principle themselves variable[5] is no less important even though we must probably regard them as *relatively* stable compared with the continuous changes of the scheme of classification in terms of which abstract thought proceeds, almost certainly in so far as the course of the life of the individual is concerned. But we should still have to consider more seriously than we are wont to do, what is amply confirmed by ordinary experience, namely that as a result of the advance of our explanation of the world we also come to 'see' this world differently, i.e. that we not merely recognize new laws which connect the given phenomena, but that these events are themselves likely to change their appearance to us.

Such variations of the sensory qualities attributed to given events could, of course, never be ascertained by direct comparisons of past and present sensations, since the memory images of past sensations would be subject to the same changes as the current sensations. The only possibility of testing this conclusion would be provided by experiments with discrimination such as have been suggested in the preceding chapter [*The Sensory Order*, chapter 7].

It deserves, perhaps, to be mentioned that, although the theory developed here was suggested in the first instance by the psychological views which Ernst Mach has outlined in his *Analysis of Sensations* and elsewhere, its systematic development leads to a refutation of his and similar phenomenalist philosophies: by destroying the conception of elementary and constant sensations as ultimate constituents of the world, it restores the necessity of a belief in an objective physical world which is different from that presented to us by our senses.[6]

Similar considerations apply to the views expounded on these matters by William James, John Dewey and the American realists and developed by Bertrand Russell. The latter's view according to which 'the stuff of the world' consists of 'innumerable transient particulars' such as a patch of colour which is 'both physical and psychical' in fact is explicitly based on the assumption that 'sensations are what is common to the mental and the physical world', and that their essence is 'their independence from past experience'. The whole of this 'neutral monism' seems to be based on entirely untenable psychological conceptions.[7]

Another interesting consequence following from our theory is that a stimulus whose occurrence in conjunction with other stimuli showed no regularities whatever could never be perceived by our senses. This would seem to mean that we can know only such kinds of events as show a certain degree of regularity in their occurrence in relations with others, and that we could not know anything about events which occurred in a completely irregular manner. The fact that the world which we know seems wholly an orderly world may thus be merely a result of the method by which we perceive it. Everything which we can perceive we perceive necessarily as an element of a class of events which obey certain regularities. There could be in this sense no class of events showing no regularities, because there would be nothing which could constitute them for us into a distinct class.

Dualism and Materialism

Because the account of the determination of mental qualities which has been given here explains them by the operation of processes of the same kind as those which we observe in the material world, it is likely to be described as a 'materialistic' theory. Such a description in itself would matter very little if it were not for certain erroneous ideas associated with the term materialism which not only would prejudice some people against a theory thus described but, what is more important, would also suggest that it implies certain conclusions which are almost the opposite of those which in fact follow from it. In the true sense of the word 'materialistic' it might even be argued that our theory is less materialistic than the dualistic theories which postulate a distinct mind 'substance'.

The dualistic theories are a product of the habit, which man has acquired in his early study of nature, of assuming that in every instance where he observed a peculiar and distinct process it must be due to the presence of a corresponding peculiar and distinct substance. The recognition of such a peculiar material substance came to be regarded as an adequate explanation of the process produced.

It is a curious fact that, although in the realm of nature in general we no longer accept as an adequate explanation the postulate of a peculiar substance possessing the capacity of producing the phenomena we wish to explain, we still resort to this old habit where mental events are concerned. The mind 'stuff' or 'substance' is a conception formed in analogy to the different kinds of matter supposedly responsible for the different kinds of material phenomena. It is, to use an old term in its literal sense, the result of a 'hylomorphic' manner of thinking. Yet in whatever manner we define substance, to think of mind as a substance is to ascribe to mental events some attributes for whose existence we have no evidence and which we postulate solely on the analogy of what we know of material phenomena.[8]

In the strict sense of the terms employed an account of mental phenomena which avoids the conception of a distinct mental substance is therefore the opposite of materialistic, because it does not attribute to mind any property which we derive from our acquaintance with matter. In being content to regard mind as a peculiar order of events, different from the order of events which we encounter in the physical world, but determined by the same kind of forces as those that rule in that world, it is indeed the only theory which is not materialistic.[9]

Superficially there may seem to exist a closer connexion between the theory presented here and the so-called 'double aspect theories' of the relations between mind and body. To scribe our theory as such, however, would be misleading. What could be regarded as the 'physical aspect' of this double-faced entity would not be the individual neural processes but only the complete order of all these processes; but this order, if we knew it in full, would then not be another aspect of what we know as mind but would be mind itself. We cannot directly observe how this order is formed by its physical elements, but can only infer it. But if we could complete the theoretical reconstruction of this order from its elements and then disregard all the properties of the elements which are not relevant to the existence of this order as a whole, we should have a complete description of the order we call mind — just as in describing a machine we can disregard many properties of its parts, such as their colour, and consider only those which are essential to the functioning of the machine as a whole.

This order which we call mind is thus the order prevailing in a particular part of the physical universe — that part of it which is ourselves. It is an order which we 'know' in a way which is different from the manner in which we know the order of the physical universe around us. What we have tried to do here is to show that the same kind of regularities which we have learnt to discover in the world around us are in principle also capable of building up an order like that constituting our mind. That such a kind of sub-order can be formed within that order which we have discovered in the external universe does not yet mean, however, that we must be able to explain how the particular order which constitutes our mind is placed in that more comprehensive order. In order to achieve this it would be necessary to construct, with special reference to the human mind, a detailed reproduction of the model-object relation which it involves such as we have sketched schematically before in order to illustrate the general principle [*The Sensory Order*, chapter 5]. While our theory leads us to deny any ultimate dualism of the forces governing the realms of mind and that of the physical world respectively, it forces us at the same time to recognize that for practical purposes we shall always have to adopt a dualistic view. It does this by showing that any explanation of mental phenomena which we can hope ever to attain cannot be sufficient to 'unify' all our knowledge, in the sense that we should become able to substitute statements about particular physical events (or classes of physical events) for statements about mental events without thereby changing the meaning of the statement.

In this specific sense we shall never be able to bridge the gap between physical and mental phenomena; and for practical purposes, including in this the procedure appropriate to the different sciences, we shall permanently have to be content with a dualistic view of the world. This, however, raises a further problem which must be more systematically considered in the remaining sections of this chapter.

The Nature of Explanation

What remains now is to restate briefly what the theory outlined in the preceding pages is meant to explain, and how far it can be expected to account for particular mental processes. This makes it necessary to make more precise than we have yet done what we mean by 'explanation'. This is a peculiarly relevant question since 'explanation' is itself one of the mental processes which the theory intends to explain.

It has been suggested before [*The Sensory Order*, chapter 5] that explanation consists in the formation in the brain of a model of the complex of events to be explained, a model the parts of which are defined by their position in a more comprehensive structure of relationships which constitutes the semi-permanent framework from which the representations of individual events receive their meaning.

This notion of the 'model', which the brain is assumed to be capable of building, has, of course, been often used in this connexion,[10] and by itself it does not get us very far. Indeed, if it is conceived, as is usually the case, as a separate model of the particular phenomenon to be explained, it is not at all clear what is meant by it. The analogy with a mechanical model is not directly applicable. A mechanical model derives its significance from the fact that the properties of its individual parts are assumed to be known and in some respects to correspond to the properties of the parts of the phenomenon which it reproduces. It is from this knowledge of the different properties of the parts that we derive our knowledge of how the particular combination of these parts will function.

In general, the possibility of forming a model which explains anything presupposes that we have at our disposal distinct elements whose action in different circumstances is known irrespective of the particular model in which we use them. In the case of a mechanical model it is the physical properties of the individual parts which are supposed to be known. In a mathematical 'model' the 'properties' of the parts are defined by functions which show the values they will assume in different circumstances, and which are capable of being combined into various systems of equations which constitute the models.

The weakness of the ordinary use of the concept of the model as an account of the process of explanation consists in the fact that this conception presupposes, but does not explain, the existence of the different mental entities from which such a model could be built. It does not explain in what sense or in which manner the parts of the model correspond to the parts of the original, or what are the properties of the elements from which the model is built.

The concept of a model that is being formed in the brain is helpful only after we have succeeded in accounting for the different properties of the parts from which it is built. Such an account is provided by the explanation of the determination of sensory (and other mental) qualities by their position in the more comprehensive semi-permanent structure of relationships, the 'map' of the world which past experience has created in the brain, which has been described in the preceding pages. It is the position of the impulse in the connected network of fibres which brings it about that its occurrence together with other impulses will produce certain further impulses. The formation of the model appears thus merely a particular case of that process of joint or simultaneous classification of a group of impulses of which each has its determined significance apart from the particular combination or model in which it now occurs.

We can schematically represent this process of joint classification which produces a model in the following manner: the different elements, the mental qualities from which the model is built, are classes of impulses which we may call *A*, *B*, *C*, etc., and which are defined as an *a* (member of *A*) producing *x* (and perhaps some other impulses) when it occurs in company with *o*, *p*, . . ., but producing *v*, *z*, . . . when it occurs in company with *r*, *s*, . . . etc., etc., and similarly for all members of the classes *B*, *C*, etc. In this definition any given class of impulses may, of course, occur both in a 'primary' character, that is as an element of a class to be defined by the impulses which any element of this class will evoke, and in a 'secondary' character as an evoked impulse which determines the class to which some other impulses belong. Impulses of the class *A* will appear not only in statements like 'if (*a*, *o*, *p*) then *x*' and 'if (*a*, *r*, *s*) then (*y*, *z* . . .)', but also in statements like 'if (*b*, *c*, *q*) then (*a*, *t*)', etc.

Given such a determination of the different significance of impulses of the different classes, it follows that any given combination of such impulses will produce impulses standing for other classes, and these in turn others, and so on, somewhat as in the following schematic representation:

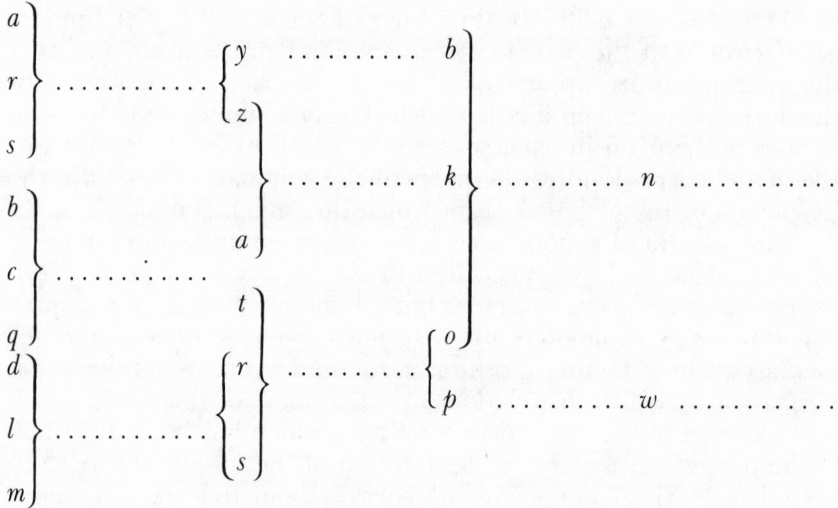

The particular result produced is thus recognized to be the effect of the simultaneous occurrence of certain elements in a particular constellation which, if we had known of their presence, would have enabled us to predict the result. Once we have formed such a model we are in a position to say on which of the various elements in the actual situation the observed result depends, and how it would be modified if any of these elements were changed; this is what an explanation enables us to do.

Explanation of the Principle

It follows from what has been said so far about explanation that it will always refer to classes of events, and that it will account only for those properties which are common to the elements of the class. Explanation is always generic in the sense that it always refers to features which are common to all phenomena of a certain kind, and it can never explain everything to be observed on a particular set of events.

But although all explanation must refer to the common features of a class of phenomena, there are evidently different degrees to which an explanation can be general, or to which it may approach to a full explanation of a particular set of events. The model may reproduce only the few common features of a great variety of phenomena, or it may reproduce a much larger number of features common to a smaller number of instances. In general, it will be true that the simpler the model, the wider will be the range of particular phenomena of which it reproduces one aspect, and the more complex the model, the more will its range of application be restricted.[11] In this respect the relation of the model to the object is similar to that between the connotation and the denotation (or the 'intension' and the 'extension') of a concept.

Most explanations (or theories) with which we are familiar are intended to show a common principle which operates in a large number of particular instances which in other respects may differ widely from each other. We have referred already earlier [*The Sensory Order*, chapter 2] to such explanations as 'explanations of the principle'.[12] The difference between such 'explanations of the principle' and more detailed explanations is, of course, merely one of the degree of their generality, and strictly speaking no explanation can be more than an explanation of the principle. It will be convenient, however, to reserve the name 'explanation of the principle' for explanations of a high degree of generality, and to contrast them with explanations of the detail.

The usual kind of explanation which we give, e.g., of the functioning of a clockwork, will in our sense be merely an explanation of the principle. It will merely show how the kind of phenomena which we call clockworks are produced: the manner in which a pair of hands can be made to revolve at constant speeds, etc. In the same 'general' way most of us are familiar with the principles on which a steam engine, an atomic bomb, or certain kinds of simple organisms function, without therefore necessarily being able to give a sufficiently detailed explanation of any one of these objects so that we should be able to construct it or precisely to predict its behaviour. Even where we are able to construct one of these objects, say a clockwork, the knowledge of the principle involved will not be sufficient to predict more than certain general aspects of its operation. We should never be able, for instance, before we have built it, to predict precisely how fast it will move or precisely where its hands will be at a particular moment of time.

If in general we are not more aware of this distinction between explanations merely of the principle and more detailed explanations, this is because usually there will be no great difficulty about elaborating any explanation of the principle so as to make it approximate to almost any desired degree to the circumstances of a particular situation. By increasing the complexity of the model we can usually obtain a close reproduction of any particular feature in which we are interested.

The distinction between the explanation of the principle on which a wide class of phenomena operate and the more detailed explanation of particular phenomena is reflected in the familiar distinction between the 'theoretical' and the more 'applied' parts of the different sciences. 'Theoretical physics', 'theoretical chemistry' or 'theoretical biology' are concerned with the explanation of the principles common to all phenomena which we call physical, chemical or biological.

Strictly speaking we should, of course, not be entitled to speak at all of phenomena of a certain kind unless we know some common principles which apply to the explanation of the phenomena of that kind. The various ways in which atoms are combined into molecules, e.g., constitute the common principles of all the phenomena which we call chemical. It is quite possible that an observed phenomenon, supposed to be, say, chemical, such as a change in the colour of a certain substance, may on investigation prove to be an event of a different kind, e.g., an optical event, such as a change in the light falling on the substance.

While it is true that a theoretical class of phenomena can be definitely established only after we have found a common principle of explanation applying to all its members, that is, a model of high degree of generality reproducing the features they all have in common, we will yet often know of a range of phenomena which seem to be similar in some respect and where we therefore expect to find a common principle of explanation without, however, as yet knowing such a principle. The difference between such prima facie or 'empirical' classes of phenomena, and the theoretical classes derived from a common principle of explanation, is that the empirical class is limited to phenomena actually observed, while the theoretical class enables us to define the range over which phenomena of the kind in question may vary.

The class of events which we call 'mental' has so far on the whole been an empirical class in this sense. What has been attempted here might be described as a sketch of a 'theoretical psychology' in the same sense in which we speak of theoretical physics or theoretical biology. We have attempted an explanation of the principle by which we may account for the peculiarities which are common to all processes which are commonly called mental. The question which arises now is how far in the sphere of mental processes we can hope to develop the explanation of the principle into more detailed explanations, especially into explanations that would enable us to predict the course of particular mental events.

The Limits of Explanation

It is by no means always and necessarily true that the achievement of an explanation of the principle on which the phenomena of a certain class operate enables us to proceed to explanations of the more concrete detail. There are several fields in which practical difficulties prevent us from thus elaborating known explanations of the principle to the point where they would enable us to predict particular events. This is often the case when the phenomena are very complex, as in meteorology or biology; in these instances, the number of variables which would have to be taken into account is greater than that which can be ascertained or effectively manipulated by the human mind. While we may, e.g., possess full theoretical knowledge of the mechanism by which waves are formed and propagated on the surface of water, we shall probably never be able to predict the shape and movements of the wave that will form on the ocean at a particular place and moment of time.

Apart from these practical limits to explanation, which we may hope continuously to push further back, there also exists, however, an absolute limit to what the human brain can ever accomplish by way of explanation — a limit which is determined by the nature of the instrument of explanation itself, and which is particularly relevant to any attempt to explain particular mental processes.

If our account of the process of explanation is correct, it would appear that any apparatus or organism which is to perform such operations must possess certain properties determined by the properties of the events which it is to explain. If explanation involves that kind of joint classification of many elements which we have described as 'model-building', the relation between the explaining agent and the explained object must satisfy such formal relations as must exist between any apparatus of classification and the individual objects which it classifies.

The proposition which we shall attempt to establish is that any apparatus of classification must possess a structure of a higher degree of complexity than is possessed by the objects which it classifies;

and that, therefore, the capacity of any explaining agent must be limited to objects with a structure possessing a degree of complexity lower than its own. If this is correct, it means that no explaining agent can ever explain objects of its own kind, or of its own degree of complexity, and, therefore, that the human brain can never fully explain its own operations. This statement possesses, probably, a high degree of prima facie plausibility. It is, however, of such importance and far-reaching consequences, that we must attempt a stricter proof.

We shall attempt such a demonstration at first for the simple processes of classification of individual elements, and later apply the same reasoning to those processes of joint classification which we have called model-building. Our first task must be to make clear what we mean when we speak of the 'degree of complexity' of the objects of classification and of the classifying apparatus. What we require is a measure of this degree of complexity which can be expressed in numerical terms.

So far as the objects of classification are concerned, it is necessary in the first instance to remember that for our purposes we are not interested in all the properties which a physical object may possess in an objective sense, but only in those 'properties' according to which these objects are to be classified. For our purposes the complete classification of the object is its complete definition, containing all that with which we are concerned in respect to it.

The degree of complexity of the objects of classification may then be measured by the number of different classes under which it is subsumed, or the number of different 'heads' under which it is classified. This number expresses the maximum number of points with regard to which the response of the classifying apparatus to this object may differ from its responses to any one other object which it is also capable of classifying. If the object in question is classified under n heads, it can evidently differ from any one other object that is classified by the same apparatus in n different ways.

In order that the classifying apparatus should be able to respond differently to any two objects which are classified differently under any one of these n heads, this apparatus will clearly have to be capable of distinguishing between a number of classes much larger than n. If any individual object may or may not belong to any one of the n classes $A, B, C, \ldots N$, and if all individual objects differing from each other in their membership of any one of these classes are to be treated as members of separate classes, then the number of different classes of objects to which the classifying apparatus will have to be able to respond differently will, according to a simple theorem of combinatorial analysis, have to be 2^{n+1}.

The number of different responses (or groups of responses), of which the classifying apparatus is capable, or the number of different classes it is able to form, will thus have to be of a definitely higher order of magnitude than the number of classes to which any individual object of classification can belong. This remains true when many of the individual classes to which a particular object belongs are mutually exclusive or disjunct, so that it can belong only to either A_1 or A_2 or A_3 . . . and to either B_1 or B_2 or B_3 . . ., etc. If in such a case the number of variable 'attributes' which distinguish elements of A_1 from elements of A_2 and of A_3, and elements of B_1 from those of B_2 and B_3, etc., is m and each of these m different variable attributes may assume n different 'values', although any one element will belong to at most m different classes, the number of distinct combinations of attributes to which the classifying apparatus will have to respond will still be equal to n^m.

In the same way in which we have used the number of different classes to which any one element can be assigned as the measure of the degree of its complexity, we can use the number of different classes to which the classifying apparatus will have to respond differently as the measure of complexity of that apparatus. It is evidently this number which indicates the variety of ways in which any one scheme of classification for a given set of elements may differ from any other scheme of classification for the different schemes of classification which can be applied to the given set of elements. Such a scheme for classifying the different possible schemes of classification would in turn have to possess a degree of complexity as much greater than that of any of the latter as their degree of complexity exceeds the complexity of any one of the elements.

What is true of the relationship between the degree of complexity of the different elements to be classified and that of the apparatus which can perform such classification, is, of course, equally true of that kind of joint or simultaneous classification which we have called 'model-building'. It differs from the classification of individual elements merely by the fact that the range of possible differences between different constellations of such elements is already of a higher order of magnitude than the range of possible differences between the individual elements, and that in consequence any apparatus capable of building models of all the different possible constellations of such elements must be of an even higher order of complexity.

An apparatus capable of building within itself models of different constellations of elements must be more complex, in our sense, than any particular constellation of such elements of which it can form a model, because, in addition to showing how any one of these elements will behave in a particular situation, it must be capable also of representing how any one of these elements would behave in any one of a large number of other situations. The 'new' result of the particular combination of elements which it is capable of predicting is derived from its capacity of predicting the behaviour of each element under varying conditions.

The significance of these abstract considerations will become clearer if we consider as illustrations some instances in which this or a similar principle applies. The simplest illustration of the kind is probably provided by a machine designed to sort out certain objects according to some variable property. Such a machine will clearly have to be capable of indicating (or of differentially responding to) a greater number of different properties than any one of the objects to be sorted will possess. If, e.g., it is designed to sort out objects according to their length, any one object can possess only one length, while the machine must be capable of a different response to many different lengths.

An analogous relationship, which makes it impossible to work out on any calculating machine the (finite) number of distinct operations which can be performed with it, exists between that number and the highest result which the machine can show. If that limit were, e.g., 999,999,999, there will already be 500,000,000 additions of two different figures giving 999,999,999 as a result, 499,999,999 pairs of different figures the addition of which gives 999,999,998 as a result, etc. etc., and therefore a very much larger number of different additions of pairs of figures only than the machine can show. To this would have to be added all additions of more than two figures and all the different instances of the other operations which the machine can perform. The number of distinct calculations it can perform therefore will be clearly of a higher order of magnitude than the highest figure it can enumerate.

Applying the same general principle to the human brain as an apparatus of classification it would appear to mean that, even though we may understand its modus operandi in general terms, or, in other words, possess an explanation of the principle on which it operates, we shall never, by means of the same brain, be able to arrive at a detailed explanation of its working in particular circumstances, or be able to predict what the results of its operations will be. To achieve this would require a brain of a higher order of complexity, though it might be built on the same general principles. Such a brain might be able to explain what happens in our brain, but it would in turn still be unable fully to explain its own operations, and so on.

The impossibility of explaining the functioning of the human brain in sufficient detail to enable us to substitute a description in physical terms for a description in terms of mental qualities, applies thus only in so far as the human brain is itself to be used as the instrument of classification. It would not only not apply to a brain built on the same principle but possessing a higher order of complexity, but, paradoxical as this may sound, it also does not exclude the logical possibility that the knowledge of the principle on which the brain operates might enable us to build a machine fully reproducing the action of the brain and capable of predicting how the brain will act in different circumstances.

Such a machine, designed by the human mind yet capable of 'explaining' what the mind is incapable of explaining without its help, is not a self-contradictory conception in the sense in which the idea of the mind directly explaining its own operations involves a contradiction. The achievement of constructing such a machine would not differ in principle from that of constructing a calculating machine which enables us to solve problems which have not been solved before, and the results of whose operations we cannot, strictly speaking, predict beyond saying that they will be in accord with the principles built into the machine. In both instances our knowledge merely of the principle on which the machine operates will enable us to bring about results of which, before the machine produces them, we know only that they will satisfy certain conditions.

It might appear at first as if this impossibility of a full explanation of mental processes would apply only to the mind as a whole, and not to particular mental processes, a full explanation of which might still enable us to substitute for the description of a particular mental process a fully equivalent statement about a set of physical events. Such a complete explanation of any particular mental process would, if it were possible, of course be something different from, and something more far-reaching than, the kind of partial explanation which we have called 'explanation of the principle'.

In order to provide a full explanation of even one particular mental process, such an explanation would have to run entirely in physical terms, and would have to contain no references to any other mental events which were not also at the same time explained in physical terms. Such a possibility is ruled out, however, by the fact, that the mind as an order is a 'whole' in the strict sense of the term: the distinct character of mental entities and of their mode of operation is determined by their relations to (or their position in the system of) all other mental entities. No one of them can, therefore, be explained without at the same time explaining all the others, or the whole structure of relationships determining their character.

So long as we cannot explain the mind as a whole, any attempt to explain particular mental processes must therefore contain references to other mental processes and will thus not achieve a full reduction to a description in physical terms. A full translation of the description of any set of events from the mental to the physical language would thus presuppose knowledge of the complete set of 'rules of correspondence'[13] by which the two languages are related, or a complete account of the orders prevailing in the two worlds.

This conclusion may be expressed differently by saying that a mental process could be identified with (or 'reduced to') a particular physical process only if we were able to show that it occupies in the whole order of mental events a position which is identical with the position which the physical events occupy in the physical order of the organism. The former is a mental process because it occupies a certain position in the whole order of mental process (i.e., because of the manner in which it can affect, and be affected by, other mental processes), and this position in an order can be explained in physical terms only by showing how an equivalent order can be built up from physical elements. Only if we could achieve this could we substitute for our knowledge of mental events a statement of the order existing in a particular part of the physical world.

The Division of the Sciences and the 'Freedom of the Will'

The conclusion to which our theory leads is thus that to us not only mind as a whole but also all individual mental processes must forever remain phenomena of a special kind which, although produced by the same principles which we know to operate in the physical world, we shall never be able fully to explain in terms of physical laws. Those whom it pleases may express this by saying that in some ultimate sense mental phenomena are 'nothing but' physical processes; this, however, does not alter the fact that in discussing mental processes we will never be able to dispense with the use of mental terms, and that we shall have permanently to be content with a practical dualism, a dualism based not on any assertion of an objective difference between the two classes of events, but on the demonstrable limitations of the powers of our own mind fully to comprehend the unitary order to which they belong.

From the fact that we shall never be able to achieve more than an 'explanation of the principle' by which the order of mental events is determined, it also follows that we shall never achieve a complete 'unification' of all sciences in the sense that all phenomena of which it treats can be described in physical terms.[14] In the study of human action, in particular, our starting point will always have to be our direct knowledge of the different kinds of mental events, which to us must remain irreducible entities.

The permanent cleavage between our knowledge of the physical world and our knowledge of mental events goes right through what is commonly regarded as the one subject of psychology. Since the theoretical psychology which has been sketched here can never be developed to the point at which it would enable us to substitute for the description of particular mental events descriptions in terms of particular physical events, and since it has therefore nothing to say about particular kinds of mental events, but is confined to describing the *kind* of physical processes by which the various types of mental processes can be produced, any discussion of mental events which is to get beyond such a mere 'explanation of the principle' will have to start from the mental entities which we know from direct experience.

This does not mean that we may not be able in a different sense to 'explain' particular mental events: it merely means that the type of explanation at which we aim in the physical sciences is not applicable to mental events. We can still use our direct ('introspective') knowledge of mental events in order to 'understand', and in some measure even to predict, the results to which mental processes will lead in certain conditions. But this introspective psychology, the part of psychology which lies on the other side of the great cleavage which divides it from the physical sciences, will always have to take our direct knowledge of the human mind for its starting point. It will derive its statements about some mental processes from its knowledge about other mental processes, but it will never be able to bridge the gap between the realm of the mental and the realm of the physical.

Such a *verstehende* psychology, which starts from our given knowledge of mental processes, will, however, never be able to explain why we must think thus and not otherwise, why we arrive at particular conclusions. Such an explanation would presuppose a knowledge of the physical conditions under which we would arrive at different conclusions. The assertion that we can explain our own knowledge involves also the belief that we can at any one moment of time both act on some knowledge and possess some additional knowledge about how the former is conditioned and determined. The whole idea of the mind explaining itself is a logical contradiction — nonsense in the literal meaning of the word — and a result of the prejudice that we must be able to deal with mental events in the same manner as we deal with physical events.[15]

In particular, it would appear that the whole aim of the discipline known under the name of 'sociology of knowledge' which aims at explaining why people as a result of particular material circumstances hold particular views at particular moments, is fundamentally misconceived. It aims at precisely that kind of specific explanation of mental phenomena from physical facts which we have tried to show to be impossible. All we can hope to do in this field is to aim at an explanation of the principle such as is attempted by the general theory of knowledge or epistemology.

It may be noted in passing that these considerations also have some bearing on the age-old controversy about the 'freedom of the will'. Even though we may know the general principle by which all human action is causally determined by physical processes, this would not mean that to us a particular human action can ever be recognizable as the necessary result of a particular set of physical circumstances. To us human decisions must always appear as the result of the whole of a human personality — that means the whole of a person's mind — which, as we have seen, we cannot reduce to something else.[16]

The recognition of the fact that for our understanding of human action familiar mental entities must always remain the last determinants to which we can penetrate, and that we cannot hope to replace them by physical facts, is, of course, of the greatest importance for all the disciplines which aim at an understanding and interpretation of human action. It means, in particular, that the devices developed by the natural sciences for the special purpose of replacing a description of the world in sensory or phenomenal terms by one in physical terms lose their raison d'être in the study of intelligible human action. This applies particularly to the endeavour to replace all qualitative statements by quantitative expressions or by descriptions which run exclusively in terms of explicit relations.[17]

The impossibility of any complete 'unification' of all our scientific knowledge into an all-comprehensive physical science has hardly less significance, however, for our understanding of the physical world than it has for our study of the consequences of human action. We have seen how in the physical sciences the aim is to build models of the connexions of the events in the external world by breaking up the classes known to us as sensory qualities and by replacing them by classes explicitly defined by the relations of the events to each other; also how, as this model of the physical world becomes more and more perfect, its application to any particular phenomenon in the sensory world becomes more and more uncertain.

A definite co-ordination of the model of the physical world thus constructed with the picture of the phenomenal world which our senses give us would require that we should be able to complete the task of the physical sciences by an operation which is the converse of their characteristic procedure: we should have to be able to show in what manner the different parts of our model of the physical world will be classified by our mind. In other words, a complete explanation of even the external world as we know it would presuppose a complete explanation of the working of our senses and our mind. If the latter is impossible, we shall also be unable to provide a full explanation of the phenomenal world.

Such a completion of the task of science, which would place us in a position to explain in detail the manner in which our sensory picture of the external world represents relations existing between the parts of this world, would mean that this reproduction of the world would have to include a reproduction of that reproduction (or a model of the model-object relation) which would have to include a reproduction of that reproduction of that reproduction, and so on ad infinitum. The impossibility of fully explaining any picture which our mind forms of the external world therefore also means that it is impossible ever fully to explain the 'phenomenal' external world. The very conception of such a completion of the task of science is a contradiction in terms. The quest of science is, therefore, by its nature a never-ending task in which every step ahead with necessity creates new problems.

Our conclusion, therefore, must be that *to us* mind must remain forever a realm of its own which we can know only through directly experiencing it, but which we shall never be able fully to explain or to 'reduce' to something else. Even though we may know that mental events of the kind which we experience can be produced by the same forces which operate in the rest of nature, we shall never be able to say which are the particular physical events which 'correspond' to a particular mental event.

Notes

1. K. Lorenz, 'Die angeborenen Formen möglicher Erfahrung' (*Z.f. Tierpsychol*, 5, 1943), p. 352.

2. H. von Helmholtz, *Die Tatsachen der Wahrnehmung* (Berlin, 1879). *Helmholtz's Treatise on Physiological Optics*, translated from the third German ed. by James P. C. Southall, Vol. III, *The Perception of Vision* (The Optical Society of America, 1925), p. 14: 'Here we still have to explain how experience counteracts experience, and how illusions can be produced by factors derived from experiences, when it might seem *as if experience could not teach anything except what was true*. In this matter we must remember, as we intimated above, that the sensations are interpreted just as they arise when they are stimulated in the normal way, and when the organ of sense is used normally'. (Italics ours.)

3. Cf., M. Planck, 'The meanings and limits of exact science' [*Scientific Autobiography*, N. Y., 1942 (1949)] p. 108.

4. College Mathematics Staff of the University of Chicago, *Fundamental Mathematics* (University of Chicago, 3rd. edition, I, 1948), p. 92.

5. This changeability of the sensory qualities apparently was already recognized by Protagoras, who according to Sextus Empiricus taught that the sensations 'are transformed and altered according to the times of life and to all the other conditions of the body'. R. G. Bury trans., *Outlines of Pyrrhonianism* (Loeb Classical Library, I, Book I), p. 218.

6. Cf., K. Koffka, *Principles of Gestalt Psychology* (London, Kegan Paul, 1935), p. 63: 'Mach was an excellent psychologist, who saw many of the most fundamental problems of psychology which, a whole generation later, many psychologists failed even to understand; at the same time he had a philosophy which made it impossible to give fruitful solutions to these problems'.

7. B. Russell, *Analysis of Mind* (London, Allen and Unwin, 1921), p. 144.

8. This seems to me to be true despite the efforts of C. D. Broad, *The Mind and its Place in Nature* (London, Kegan Paul, 1925), to give substance a meaning independent of its material connotations. On the mind substance theory see now G. Ryle, *The Concept of Mind* (London, Hutchinson, 1949).

9. Cf., W. Metzger, *Psychologie: Die Entwicklung ihrer Grundannahmen seit der Einführung des Experiments*, Wissenschaftliche Forschungsberichte, Naturwissenschaftliche Reihe, Band 52, (Dresden und Leipzig, Theodor Steinkopf, 1941), p. 23: 'Diese, im eigentlichen Sinn "materialistische" Auffas-

sung . . . lebt in der Psychologie bis an die Schwelle unserer Zeit fort: in der Alltagspsychologie in der kaum ausrottbaren Ansicht von der Seele als zweitem, stofflichen Etwas, das mit dem Körper während des Lebens "verbunden sei", in ihm wohne . . .'

10. See particularly K. J. W. Craik, *The Nature of Explanation* (Cambridge University Press, 1943) and K. Lorenz, 'Die angeborenen Formen möglicher Erfahrung' (*Z. f. Tierpsychol*, 5, 1943), pp. 343 and 351.

11. Cf., M. Petrovitch, *Mechanisms communs aux phenomenes disparates* (Paris, Félix Alcan, 1921), passim.

12. See also F. A. Hayek, 'Scientism and the Study of Society' (*Economica*, N. S., 1942), p. 290.

13. H. Margenau, *The Nature of Physical Reality* (New York, McGraw-Hill, 1950), pp. 60, 69, 450.

14. The term 'physical' must here be understood in the strict sense in which it has been defined in the first chapter [in *The Sensory Order*] and not be confused with the sense in which it is used, e.g., by O. Neurath or R. Carnap when they speak of their 'physical language'. In our sense their 'physical language', since it refers to the phenomenal or sensory qualities of the objects, is not 'physical' at all. Their use of this term rather implies a metaphysical belief in the ultimate 'reality' and constancy of the phenomenal world for which there is little justification. Cf., O. Neurath, *Einheitswissenschaft und Psychologie* (Vienna, Gerold, 1933), and R. Carnap, 'Logical Foundations of the Unity of Science' (*Encyclopaedia of Unified Science*, Vol. I, No. I, University of Chicago Press, 1934).

15. On this and the subject of the next paragraph cf., F. A. Hayek, 'Scientism and the Study of Society' (*Economica*, N. S., 1944), pp. 31 et seq.

16. It may also be mentioned, although this has little immediate connexion with our main subject, that since the word 'free' has been formed to describe a certain subjective experience and can scarcely be defined except by reference to that experience, it could at most be asserted that the term is meaningless. But this would make any denial of the existence of free will as meaningless as its assertion.

17. For a fuller discussion of this point see F. A. Hayek, 'Scientism and the Study of Society' (*Economica*, N. S., 1942), p. 290 ff.

Competition as a Discovery Procedure

·13·

I

It is difficult to defend economists against the charge that for some 40 to 50 years they have been discussing competition on assumptions that, *if* they were true of the real world, would make it wholly uninteresting and useless. If anyone really knew all about what economic theory calls the *data,* competition would indeed be a very wasteful method of securing adjustment to these facts. It is thus not surprising that some people have been led to the conclusion that we can either wholly dispense with the market, or that its results should be used only as a first step towards securing an output of goods and services which we can then manipulate, correct, or redistribute in any manner we wish. Others, who seem to derive their conception of competition solely from modern textbooks, have not unnaturally concluded that competition does not exist.

This lecture was originally delivered, without the present section II, to a meeting of the Philadelphia Society at Chicago on 29 March 1968 and later, on 5 July 1968, in German, without the present final section, to the Institut für Weltwirtschaft of the University of Kiel. Only the German version has been published before, first in the series of 'Kieler Vorträge', N.S. 56, Kiel, 1968, and then reprinted in my collected essays entitled *Freiburger Studien,* Tübingen, 1969.

Against this, it is salutary to remember that, *wherever* the use of competition can be rationally justified, it is on the ground that we do *not* know in advance the facts that determine the actions of competitors. In sports or in examinations, no less than in the award of government contracts or of prizes for poetry, it would clearly be pointless to arrange for competition, if we were certain beforehand who would do best. As indicated in the title of this lecture, I propose to consider competition as a procedure for the discovery of such facts as, without resort to it, would not be known to anyone, or at least would not be utilised.[1]

This may at first appear so obvious and incontestable as hardly to deserve attention. Yet, some interesting consequences that are not so obvious immediately follow from the explicit formulation of the above apparent truism. One is that competition is valuable *only* because, and so far as, its results are unpredictable and on the whole different from those which anyone has, or could have, deliberately aimed at. Further, that the generally beneficial effects of competition must include disappointing or defeating some particular expectations or intentions.

Closely connected with this is an interesting methodological consequence. It goes far to account for the discredit into which the micro-economic approach to theory has fallen. Although this theory seems to me to be the only one capable of explaining the role of competition, it is no longer understood, even by some professed economists. It is therefore worthwhile to say at the outset a few words about the methodological peculiarity of any theory of competition, because it has made its conclusions suspect to many of those who habitually apply an over-simplified test to decide what they are willing to accept as scientific. The necessary consequence of the reason why we use competition is that, *in those cases in which it is interesting*, the validity of the theory can never be tested empirically. We can test it on conceptual models, and we might conceivably test it in artificially created real situations, where the facts which competition is intended to discover are already known to the observer. But in such cases it is of no practical value, so that to carry out the experiment would hardly be worth the expense. If we do not know the facts we hope to discover by means of competition, we can never ascertain how effective it has been in discovering those facts that might be discovered. All we can hope to find out is that, on the whole, societies which rely for this purpose on competition have achieved their aims more successfully than others. This is a conclusion which the history of civilisation seems eminently to have confirmed.

The peculiarity of competition—which it has in common with scientific method—is that its performance cannot be tested in particular instances where it is significant, but is shown only by the fact that the market will prevail in comparison with any alternative arrangements. The advantages of accepted scientific procedures can never be proved scientifically, but only demonstrated by the common experience that, on the whole, they are better adapted to delivering the goods than alternative approaches.[2]

The difference between economic competition and the successful procedures of science consists in the fact that the former is a method of discovering particular facts relevant to the achievement of specific, temporary purposes, while science aims at the discovery of what are sometimes called 'general facts', which are regularities of events. Science concerns itself with unique, particular facts only to the extent that they help to confirm or refute theories. Because these refer to general, permanent features of the world, the discoveries of science have ample time to prove their value. In contrast, the benefits of particular facts, whose usefulness competition in the market discovers, are in a great measure transitory. So far as the theory of scientific method is concerned, it would be as easy to discredit it on the ground that it does not lead to testable predictions about what science will discover, as it is to discredit the theory of the market on the ground that it fails to predict particular results the market will achieve. This, in the nature of the case, the theory of competition cannot do in any situation in which it is sensible to employ it. As we shall see, its capacity to predict is necessarily limited to predicting the kind of pattern, or the abstract character of the order that will form itself, but does not extend to the prediction of particular facts.[3]

II

Having relieved myself of this pet concern, I shall return to the central subject of this lecture, by pointing out that economic theory sometimes appears at the outset to bar its way to a true appreciation of the character of the process of competition, because it starts from the assumption of a 'given' supply of scarce goods. But which goods are scarce goods, or which things are goods, and how scarce or valuable they are—these are precisely the things which competition has to discover. Provisional results from the market process at each stage alone tell individuals what to look for. Utilisation of knowledge widely dispersed in a society with extensive division of labour cannot rest on individuals knowing all the particular uses to which well-known things in their individual environment might be put. Prices direct their attention to what is worth finding out about market offers for various things and services. This means that the, in some respects always unique, combinations of individual knowledge and skills, which the market enables them to use, will not merely, or even in the first instance, be such knowledge of facts as they could list and communicate if some authority asked them to do so. The knowledge of which I speak consists rather of a capacity to find out particular circumstances, which becomes effective only if possessors of this knowledge are informed by the market which kinds of things or services are wanted, and how urgently they are wanted.[4]

This must suffice to indicate what kind of knowledge I am referring to when I call competition a discovery procedure. Much would have to be added to clothe the bare bones of this abstract statement with concrete flesh, so as to show its full practical importance. But I must be content with thus briefly indicating the absurdity of the usual procedure of starting the analysis with a situation in which all the facts are supposed to be known. This is a *state* of affairs which economic theory curiously calls 'perfect competition'. It leaves no room whatever for the *activity* called competition, which is presumed to have already done its task. However, I must hurry on to examine a question, on which there exists even more confusion — namely, the meaning of the contention that the market adjusts activities spontaneously to the facts it discovers — or the question of the purpose for which it uses this information.

The prevailing confusion here is largely due to mistakenly treating the order which the market produces as an 'economy' in the strict sense of the word, and judging results of the market process by criteria which are appropriate only to such a single organised community serving a given hierarchy of ends. But such a hierarchy of ends is not relevant to the complex structure composed of countless individual economic arrangements. The latter, unfortunately, we also describe by the same word 'economy', although it is something fundamentally different, and must be judged by different standards. An economy, in the strict sense of the word, is an organisation or arrangement in which someone deliberately allocates resources to a unitary order of ends. Spontaneous order produced by the market is nothing of the kind; and in important respects it does not behave like an economy proper. In particular, such spontaneous order differs because it does *not* ensure that what general opinion regards as more important needs are always satisfied before the less important ones. This is the chief reason why people object to it. Indeed, the whole of socialism is nothing but a demand that the market order (or catallaxy, as I like to call it, to prevent confusion with an economy proper)[5] should be turned into an economy in the strict sense, in which a common scale of importance determines which of the various needs are to be satisfied, and which are not to be satisfied.

The trouble with this socialist aim is a double one. As is true of every deliberate organisation, only the knowledge of the organiser can enter into the design of the economy proper, and all the members of such an economy, conceived as a deliberate organisation, must be guided in their actions by the unitary hierarchy of ends which it serves. On the other hand, advantages of the spontaneous order of the market, or the catallaxy, are correspondingly two. Knowledge that is used in it is that of all its members. Ends that it serves are the separate ends of those individuals, in all their variety and contrariness.

Out of this fact arise certain intellectual difficulties which worry not only socialists, but all economists who want to assess the accomplishments of the market order; because, if the market order does not serve a definite order of ends, indeed if, like any spontaneously formed order, it cannot legitimately be said to *have* particular ends, it is also not possible to express the value of the results as a sum of its particular individual products. What, then, do we mean when we claim that the market order produces in some sense a maximum or optimum?

The fact is, that, though the existence of a spontaneous order not made for a particular purpose cannot be properly said to have a purpose, it may yet be highly conducive to the achievement of many different individual purposes not known as a whole to any single person, or relatively small group of persons. Indeed, rational action is possible only in a fairly orderly world. Therefore it clearly makes sense to try to produce conditions under which the chances for any individual taken at random to achieve his ends as effectively as possible will be very high — even if it cannot be predicted which particular aims will be favoured, and which not.

As we have seen, the results of a discovery procedure are in their nature unpredictable; and all we can expect from the adoption of an effective discovery procedure is to improve the chances for unknown people. The only common aim which we can pursue by the choice of this technique of ordering social affairs is the general kind of pattern, or the abstract character, of the order that will form itself.

III

Economists usually ascribe the order which competition produces as an equilibrium — a somewhat unfortunate term, because such an equilibrium presupposes that the facts have already all been discovered and competition therefore has ceased. The concept of an 'order' which, at least for the discussion of problems of economic policy, I prefer to that of equilibrium, has the advantage that we can meaningfully speak about an order being approached to various degrees, and that order can be preserved throughout a process of change. While an economic equilibrium never really exists, there is some justification for asserting that the kind of order of which our theory describes an ideal type, is approached in a high degree.

This order manifests itself in the first instance in the circumstance that the expectations of transactions to be effected with other members of society, on which the plans of all the several economic subjects are based, can be mostly realised. This mutual adjustment of individual plans is brought about by what, since the physical sciences have also begun to concern themselves with spontaneous orders, or 'self-organising systems', we have learnt to call 'negative feedback'. Indeed, as intelligent biologists acknowledge, 'long before Claude Bernard, Clerk Maxwell, Walter B. Cannon, or Norbert Wiener developed cybernetics, Adam Smith has just as clearly used the idea in *The Wealth of Nations.* The 'invisible hand' that regulated prices to a nicety is clearly this idea. In a free market, says Smith in effect, prices are regulated by negative feedback'.[6]

We shall see that the fact that a high degree of coincidence of expectations is brought about by the systematic disappointment of some kind of expectations is of crucial importance for an understanding of the functioning of the market order. But to bring about a mutual adjustment of individual plans is not all that the market achieves. It also secures that whatever is being produced will be produced by people who can do so more cheaply than (or at least as cheaply as) anybody who does not produce it (and cannot devote his energies to produce something else comparatively even more cheaply), and that each product is sold at a price lower than that at which anybody who in fact does not produce it could supply it. This, of course, does not exclude that some may make considerable profits over their costs if these costs are much lower than those of the next efficient potential producer. But it does mean that of the combination of commodities that is in fact produced, as much will be produced as we know to bring about by any known method. It will of course not be as much as we might produce if all the knowledge anybody possessed or can acquire were commanded by some one agency, and fed into a computer (the cost of finding out would, however, be considerable). Yet we do injustice to the achievement of the market if we judge it, as it were, from above, by comparing it with an ideal standard which we have no known way of achieving. If we judge it, as we ought to, from below, that is, if the comparison in this case is made against what we could achieve by any other method — especially against what would be produced if competition were prevented, so that only those to whom some authority had conferred the right to produce or sell particular things were allowed to do so. All we need to consider is how difficult it is in a competitive system to discover ways of supplying to consumers better or cheaper goods than they already get. Where such unused opportunities seem to exist we usually find that they remain undeveloped because their use is either prevented by the power of authority (including the enforcement of patent privileges), or by some private misuse of power which the law ought to prohibit.

It must not be forgotten that in this respect the market only brings about an approach towards some point on that n-dimensional surface, by which pure economic theory represents the horizon of all possibilities to which the production of any one proportional combination of commodities and services could conceivably be carried. The market leaves the particular combination of goods, and its distribution among individuals, largely to unforeseeable circumstances — and, in this sense, to accident. It is, as Adam Smith already understood,[7] as if we had agreed to play a game, partly of skill and partly of chance. This competitive game, at the price of leaving the share of each individual in some measure to accident, ensures that the real equivalent of whatever his share turns out to be, is as large as we know how to make it. The game is, to use up-to-date language, not a zero-sum game, but one through which, by playing it according to the rules, the pool to be shared is enlarged, leaving individual shares in the pool in a great measure to chance. A mind knowing all the facts could select any point he liked on the surface and distribute this product in the manner he thought right.

But the only point on, or tolerably near, the horizon of possibilities which we know how to reach is the one at which we shall arrive if we leave its determination to the market. The so-called 'maximum' which we thus reach naturally cannot be defined as a sum of particular things, but only in terms of the chances it offers to unknown people to get as large a real equivalent as possible for their relative shares, which will be determined partly by accident. Simply because its results cannot be assessed in terms of a single scale of values, as is the case in an economy proper, it is very misleading to assess the results of a catallaxy as if it were an economy.

IV

Misinterpretation of the market order as an economy that can and ought to satisfy different needs in a certain order of priority, shows itself particularly in the efforts of policy to correct prices and incomes in the interest of what is called 'social justice'. Whatever meaning social philosophers have attached to this concept, in the practice of economic policy it has almost always meant one thing, and one thing only: the protection of certain groups against the necessity to descend from the absolute or relative material position which they have for some time enjoyed. Yet this is not a principle on which it is possible to act generally without destroying the foundations of the market order. Not only continuous increase, but in certain circumstances even mere maintenance of the existing level of incomes, depends on adaptation to unforeseen changes. This necessarily involves the relative, and perhaps even the absolute, share of some having to be reduced, although they are in no way responsible for the reduction.

The point to keep constantly in mind is that *all* economic adjustment is made necessary by unforeseen changes; and the whole reason for employing the price mechanism is to tell individuals that what they are doing, or can do, has for some reason for which they are not responsible become less or more demanded. Adaptation of the whole order of activities to changed circumstances rests on the remuneration derived from different activities being changed, without regard to the merits or faults of those affected.

The term 'incentives' is often used in this connection with somewhat misleading connotations, as if the main problem were to induce people to exert themselves sufficiently. However, the chief guidance which prices offer is not so much how to act, but *what to do.* In a continuously changing world even mere maintenance of a given level of wealth requires incessant changes in the direction of the efforts of some, which will be brought about only if the remuneration of some activities is increased and that of others decreased. With these adjustments, which under relatively stable conditions are needed merely to maintain the income stream, no 'surplus' is available which can be used to compensate those against whom prices turn. Only in a rapidly growing system can we hope to avoid absolute declines in the position of some groups.

Modern economists seem in this connection often to overlook that even the relative stability shown by many of those aggregates which macro-economics treats as data, is itself the result of a micro-economic process, of which changes in relative prices are an essential part. It is only thanks to the market mechanism that someone else is induced to step in and fill the gap caused by the failure of anyone to fulfil the expectations of his partners. Indeed, all those aggregate demand and supply curves with which we like to operate are not really objectively given facts, but results of the process of competition going on all the time. Nor can we hope to learn from statistical information what changes in prices or incomes are necessary in order to bring about adjustments to the inevitable changes.

The chief point, however, is that in a democratic society it would be wholly impossible by commands to bring about changes which are not felt to be just, and the necessity of which could never be clearly demonstrated. Deliberate regulation in such a political system must always aim at securing prices which appear to be just. This means in practice preservation of the traditional structure of incomes and prices. An economic system in which each gets what others think he deserves would necessarily be a highly inefficient system — quite apart from its being also an intolerably oppressive system. Every 'incomes policy' is therefore more likely to prevent than to facilitate those changes in the price and income structures that are required to adapt the system to new circumstances.

It is one of the paradoxes of the present world that the communist countries are probably freer from the incubus of 'social justice', and more willing to let those bear the burden against whom developments turn, than are the 'capitalist' countries. For some Western countries at least the position seems hopeless, precisely because the ideology dominating their politics makes changes impossible that are necessary for the position of the working class to rise sufficiently fast to lead to the disappearance of this ideology.

V

If even in highly developed economic systems competition is important as a process of exploration in which prospectors search for unused opportunities that, when discovered, can also be used by others, this is to an even greater extent true of underdeveloped societies. My first attention has been deliberately given to problems of preserving an efficient order for conditions in which most resources and techniques are generally known, and constant adaptations of activities are made necessary only by inevitably minor changes, in order to maintain a given level of incomes. I will not consider here the undoubted role competition plays in the advance of technological knowledge. But I do want to point out how much more important it must be in countries where the chief task is to discover yet unknown opportunities of a society in which in the past competition has not been active. It may not be altogether absurd, although largely erroneous, to believe that we can foresee and control the structure of society which further technological advance will produce in already highly developed countries. But it is simply fantastic to believe that we can determine in advance the social structure in a country where the chief problem still is to discover what material and human resources are available, or that for such a country we can predict the particular consequences of any measures we may take.

Apart from the fact that there is in such countries so much more to be discovered, there is still another reason why the greatest freedom of competition seems to be even more important there than in more advanced countries. This is that required changes in habits and customs will be brought about only if the few willing and able to experiment with new methods can make it necessary for the many to follow them, and at the same time to show them the way. The required discovery process will be impeded or prevented, if the many are able to keep the few to the traditional ways. Of course, it is one of the chief reasons for the dislike of competition that it not only shows how things can be done more effectively, but also confronts those who depend for their incomes on the market with the alternative of imitating the more successful or losing some or all of their income. Competition produces in this way a kind of impersonal compulsion which makes it necessary for numerous individuals to adjust their way of life in a manner that no deliberate instructions or commands could bring about. Central direction in the service of so-called 'social justice' may be a luxury rich nations can afford, perhaps for a long time, without too great an impairment of their incomes. But it is certainly not a method by which poor countries can accelerate their adaptation to rapidly changing circumstances, on which their growth depends.

Perhaps it deserves mention in this connection that possibilities of growth are likely to be greater the more extensive are a country's yet unused opportunities. Strange though this may seem at first sight, a high rate of growth is more often than not evidence that opportunities have been neglected in the past. Thus, a high rate of growth can sometimes testify to bad policies of the past rather than good policies of the present. Consequently it is unreasonable to expect in already highly developed countries as high a rate of growth as can for some time be achieved in countries where effective utilisation of resources was previously long prevented by legal and institutional obstacles.

From all I have seen of the world the proportion of private persons who are prepared to try new possibilities, if they appear to them to promise better conditions, and if they are not prevented by the pressure of their fellows, is much the same everywhere. The much lamented absence of a spirit of enterprise in many of the new countries is not an unalterable characteristic of the individual inhabitants, but the consequence of restraints which existing customs and institutions place upon them. This is why it would be fatal in such societies for the collective will to be allowed to direct the efforts of individuals, instead of governmental power being confined to protecting individuals against the pressures of society. Such protection for private initiatives and enterprise can only ever be achieved through the institution of private property and the whole aggregate of libertarian institutions of law.

Notes

1. Since I wrote this my attention has been drawn to a paper by Leopold von Wiese on 'Die Konkurrenz, vorwiegend in soziologisch-systematischer Betrachtung', *Verhandlungen des 6. Deutschen Soziologentages,* 1929, where, on p. 27, he discusses the 'experimental' nature of competition.

2. Cf. the interesting studies of the late Michael Polanyi in *The Logic of Liberty,* London, 1951, which show how he has been led from the study of scientific method to the study of competition in economic affairs; and see also K. R. Popper, *The Logic of Scientific Discovery,* London, 1959.

3. On the nature of 'pattern prediction' see my essay on 'The theory of complex phenomena' in *Studies in Philosophy, Politics and Economics,* London and Chicago, 1967.

4. Cf. Samuel Johnson in J. Boswell, *Life of Samuel Johnson,* L. F. Powell's revision of G. B. Hill's edition, Oxford, 1934, vol. II, p. 365 (18 April 1775): 'Knowledge is of two kinds. We know a subject ourselves, or we know where we can find information about it'.

5. For a fuller discussion see now my *Law, Legislation and Liberty,* vol. II, *The Mirage of Social Justice,* London and Chicago, 1976, pp. 107 – 20.

6. G. Hardin, *Nature and Man's Fate* (1951), Mentor ed. 1961, p. 54.

7. Adam Smith, *The Theory of Moral Sentiments,* London, 1759, part VI, chapter 2, penultimate paragraph, and part VII, section II, chapter 1.

The Pretence of Knowledge

· 14 ·

The particular occasion of this lecture, combined with the chief practical problem which economists have to face today, have made the choice of its topic almost inevitable. On the one hand the still recent establishment of the Nobel Memorial Prize in Economic Science marks a significant step in the process by which, in the opinion of the general public, economics has been conceded some of the dignity and prestige of the physical sciences. On the other hand, the economists are at this moment called upon to say how to extricate the free world from the serious threat of accelerating inflation which, it must be admitted, has been brought about by policies which the majority of economists recommended and even urged governments to pursue. We have indeed at the moment little cause for pride: as a profession we have made a mess of things.

It seems to me that this failure of the economists to guide policy more successfully is closely connected with their propensity to imitate as closely as possible the procedures of the brilliantly successful physical sciences — an attempt which in our field may lead to outright error. It is an approach which has come to be described as the

---

Nobel Memorial Lecture, delivered at Stockholm, 11 December 1974, and reprinted from *Les Prix Nobel en 1974,* Stockholm, 1975.

'scientistic' attitude — an attitude which, as I defined it some thirty years ago, 'is decidedly unscientific in the true sense of the word, since it involves a mechanical and uncritical application of habits of thought to fields different from those in which they have been formed'.[1] I want today to begin by explaining how some of the gravest errors of recent economic policy are a direct consequence of this scientistic error.

The theory which has been guiding monetary and financial policy during the last thirty years, and which I contend is largely the product of such a mistaken conception of the proper scientific procedure, consists in the assertion that there exists a simple positive correlation between total employment and the size of the aggregate demand for goods and services; it leads to the belief that we can permanently assure full employment by maintaining total money expenditure at an appropriate level. Among the various theories advanced to account for extensive unemployment, this is probably the only one in support of which strong quantitative evidence can be adduced. I nevertheless regard it as fundamentally false, and to act upon it, as we now experience, as very harmful.

This brings me to the crucial issue. Unlike the position that exists in the physical sciences, in economics and other disciplines that deal with essentially complex phenomena, the aspects of the events to be accounted for about which we can get quantitative data are necessarily limited and may not include the important ones. While in the physical sciences it is generally assumed, probably with good reason, that any important factor which determines the observed events will itself be directly observable and measurable, in the study of such complex phenomena as the market, which depend on the actions of many individuals, all the circumstances which will determine the outcome of a process, for reasons which I shall explain later, will hardly ever be fully known or measurable. And while in the physical sciences the investigator will be able to measure what, on the basis of a prima facie theory, he thinks important, in the social sciences often that is treated as important which happens to be accessible to measurement. This is sometimes carried to the point where it is demanded that our theories must be formulated in such terms that they refer only to measurable magnitudes.

It can hardly be denied that such a demand quite arbitrarily limits the facts which are to be admitted as possible causes of the events which occur in the real world. This view, which is often quite naively accepted as required by scientific procedure, has some rather paradoxical consequences. We know, of course, with regard to the market and similar social structures, a great many facts which we cannot measure and on which indeed we have only some very imprecise and general information. And because the effects of these facts in any particular instance cannot be confirmed by quantitative evidence, they are simply disregarded by those sworn to admit only what they regard as scientific evidence: they thereupon happily proceed on the fiction that the factors which they can measure are the only ones that are relevant.

The correlation between aggregate demand and total employment, for instance, may only be approximate, but as it is the *only* one on which we have quantitative data, it is accepted as the only causal connection that counts. On this standard there may thus well exist better 'scientific' evidence for a false theory, which will be accepted because it is more 'scientific', than for a valid explanation, which is rejected because there is no sufficient quantitative evidence for it.

Let me illustrate this by a brief sketch of what I regard as the chief actual cause of extensive unemployment — an account which will also explain why such unemployment cannot be lastingly cured by the inflationary policies recommended by the now fashionable theory. This correct explanation appears to me to be the existence of discrepancies between the distribution of demand among the different goods and services and the allocation of labour and other resources among the production of those outputs. We possess a fairly good 'qualitative' knowledge of the forces by which a correspondence between demand and supply in the different sectors of the economic system is brought about, of the conditions under which it will be achieved, and of the factors likely to prevent such an adjustment. The separate steps in the account of this process rely on facts of everyday experience, and few who take the trouble to follow the argument will question the validity of the factual assumptions, or the logical correctness of the conclusions drawn from them. We have indeed good reason to believe that unemployment indicates that the structure of relative prices and wages has been distorted (usually by monopolistic or governmental price fixing), and that in order to restore equality between the demand and the supply of labour in all sectors changes of relative prices and some transfers of labour will be necessary.

But when we are asked for quantitative evidence for the particular structure of prices and wages that would be required in order to assure a smooth continuous sale of the products and services offered, we must admit that we have no such information. We know, in other words, the general conditions in which what we call, somewhat misleadingly, an equilibrium will establish itself: but we never know what the particular prices or wages are which would exist if the market were to bring about such an equilibrium. We can merely say what the conditions are in which we can expect the market to establish prices and wages at which demand will equal supply. But we can never produce statistical information which would show how much the prevailing prices and wages *deviate* from those which would secure a continuous sale of the current supply of labour. Though this account of the causes of unemployment is an empirical theory, in the sense that it might be proved false, for example if, with a constant money supply, a general increase of wages did not lead to unemployment, it is certainly not the kind of theory which we could use to obtain specific numerical predictions concerning the rates of wages, or the distribution of labour, to be expected.

Why should we, however, in economics, have to plead ignorance of the sort of facts on which, in the case of a physical theory, a scientist would certainly be expected to give precise information? It is probably not surprising that those impressed by the example of the physical sciences should find this position very unsatisfactory and should insist on the standards of proof which they find there. The reason for this state of affairs is the fact, to which I have already briefly referred, that the social sciences, like much of biology but unlike most fields of the physical sciences, have to deal with structures of *essential* complexity, i.e. with structures whose characteristic properties can be exhibited only by models made up of relatively large numbers of variables. Competition, for instance, is a process which will produce certain results only if it proceeds among a fairly large number of acting persons.

In some fields, particularly where problems of a similar kind arise in the physical sciences, the difficulties can be overcome by using, instead of specific information about the individual elements, data about the relative frequency, or the probability, of the occurrence of the various distinctive properties of the elements. But this is true only where we have to deal with what has been called by Dr. Warren Weaver (formerly of the Rockefeller Foundation), with a distinction which ought to be much more widely understood, 'phenomena of unorganized complexity', in contrast to those 'phenomena of organized complexity' with which we have to deal in the social sciences.[2] Organized complexity here means that the character of the structures showing it depends not only on the properties of the individual elements of which they are composed, and the relative frequency with which they occur, but also on the manner in which the individual elements are connected with each other. In the explanation of the working of such structures we can for this reason not replace the information about the individual elements by statistical information, but require full information about each element if from our theory we are to derive specific predictions about individual events. Without such specific information about the individual elements we shall be confined to what on another occasion I have called mere pattern predictions — predictions of some of the general attributes of the structures that will form themselves, but not containing specific statements about the individual elements of which the structures will be made up.[3]

This is particularly true of our theories accounting for the determination of the systems of relative prices and wages that will form themselves on a well-functioning market. Into the determination of these prices and wages there will enter the effects of particular information possessed by every one of the participants in the market process — a sum of facts which in their totality cannot be known to the scientific observer, or to any other single brain. It is indeed the source of the superiority of the market order, and the reason why, when it is not suppressed by the powers of government, it regularly displaces other types of order, that in the resulting allocation of resources more of the knowledge of particular facts will be utilized which exists only dispersed among uncounted persons, than any one person can possess. But because we, the observing scientists, can thus never know all the determinants of such an order, and in consequence also cannot know at which particular structure of prices and wages demand would everywhere equal supply, we also cannot measure the deviations from that order; nor can we statistically test our theory that it is the deviations from that 'equilibrium' system of prices and wages which make it impossible to sell some of the products and services at the prices at which they are offered.

Before I continue with my immediate concern, the effects of all this on the employment policies currently pursued, allow me to define more specifically the inherent limitations of our numerical knowledge which are so often overlooked. I want to do this to avoid giving the impression that I generally reject the mathematical method in economics. I regard it in fact as the great advantage of the mathematical technique that it allows us to describe, by means of algebraic equations, the general character of a pattern even where we are ignorant of the numerical values which will determine its particular manifestation. We could scarcely have achieved that comprehensive picture of the mutual interdependencies of the different events in a market without this algebraic technique. It has led to the illusion, however, that we can use this technique for the determination and prediction of the numerical values of those magnitudes; and this has led to a vain search for quantitative or numerical constants. This happened in spite of the fact that the modern founders of mathematical economics had no such illusions. It is true that their systems of equations describing the pattern of a market equilibrium are so framed that *if* we were able to fill in all the blanks of the abstract formulae, i.e. *if* we knew all the parameters of these equations, we could calculate the prices and quantities of all commodities and services sold. But, as Vilfredo Pareto, one of the founders of this theory, clearly stated, its purpose cannot be 'to arrive at a numerical calculation of prices', because, as he said, it would be 'absurd' to assume that we could ascertain all the data.[4] Indeed, the chief point was already seen by those remarkable anticipators of modern economics, the Spanish schoolmen of the sixteenth century, who emphasized that what they call *pretium mathematicum,* the mathematical price, depended on so many particular circumstances that it could never be known to man but was known only to God.[5] I sometimes wish that our mathematical economists would take this to heart. I must confess that I still doubt whether their search for measurable magnitudes has made significant contributions to our *theoretical* understanding of economic phenomena — as distinct from their value as a description of particular situations. Nor am I prepared to accept the excuse that this branch of research is still very young: Sir William Petty, the founder of econometrics, was after all a somewhat senior colleague of Sir Isaac Newton in the Royal Society!

There may be few instances in which the superstition that only measurable magnitudes can be important has done positive harm in the economic field: but the present inflation and employment problems are a very serious one. Its effect has been that what is probably the true cause of extensive unemployment has been disregarded by the scientistically minded majority of economists, because its operation could not be confirmed by directly observable relations between measurable magnitudes, and that an almost exclusive concentration on quantitatively measurable surface phenomena has produced a policy which has made matters worse.

It has, of course, to be readily admitted that the kind of theory which I regard as the true explanation of unemployment is a theory of somewhat limited content because it allows us to make only very general predictions of the *kind* of events which we must expect in a given situation. But the effects on policy of the more ambitious constructions have not been very fortunate and I confess that I prefer true but imperfect knowledge, even if it leaves much indetermined and unpredictable, to a pretence of exact knowledge that is likely to be false. The credit which the apparent conformity with recognized scientific standards can gain for seemingly simple but false theories may, as the present instance shows, have grave consequences.

In fact, in the case discussed, the very measures which the dominant 'macro-economic' theory has recommended as a remedy for unemployment, namely the increase of aggregate demand, have become a cause of a very extensive misallocation of resources which is likely to make later large-scale unemployment inevitable. The continuous injection of additional amounts of money at points of the economic system where it creates a temporary demand which must cease when the increase of the quantity of money stops or slows down, together with the expectation of a continuing rise of prices, draws labour and other resources into employments which can last only so long as the increase of the quantity of money continues at the same rate — or perhaps even only so long as it continues to accelerate at a given rate. What this policy has produced is not so much a level of employment that could not have been brought about in other ways, as a distribution of employment which cannot be indefinitely maintained and which after some time can be maintained only by a rate of inflation which would rapidly lead to a disorganization of all economic activity. The fact is that by a mistaken theoretical view we have been led into a precarious position in which we cannot prevent substantial unemployment from reappearing; not because, as this view is sometimes misrepresented, this unemployment is deliberately brought about as a means to combat inflation, but because it is now bound to occur as a deeply regrettable but inescapable consequence of the mistaken policies of the past as soon as inflation ceases to accelerate.

I must, however, now leave these problems of immediate practical importance which I have introduced chiefly as an illustration of the momentous consequences that may follow from errors concerning abstract problems of the philosophy of science. There is as much reason to be apprehensive about the long run dangers created in a much wider field by the uncritical acceptance of assertions which have the *appearance* of being scientific as there is with regard to the problems I have just discussed. What I mainly wanted to bring out by the topical illustration is that certainly in my field, but I believe also generally in the sciences of man, what looks superficially like the most scientific procedure is often the most unscientific, and, beyond this, that in these fields there are definite limits to what we can expect science to achieve. This means that to entrust to science — or to deliberate control according to scientific principles — more than scientific methods can achieve may have deplorable effects. The progress of the natural sciences in modern times has of course so much exceeded all expectations that any suggestion that there may be some limits to it is bound to arouse suspicion. Especially all those will resist such an insight who have hoped that our increasing power of prediction and control, generally regarded as the characteristic result of scientific advance, applied to the processes of society, would soon enable us to mould society entirely to our liking. It is indeed true that, in contrast to the exhilaration which the discoveries of the physical sciences tend to produce, the insights which we gain from the study of society more often have a dampening effect on our aspirations; and it is perhaps not surprising that the more impetuous younger members of our profession are not always prepared to accept this. Yet the confidence in the unlimited power of science is only too often based on a false belief that the scientific method consists in the application of a ready-made technique, or in imitating the form rather than the substance of scientific procedure, as if one needed only to follow some cooking recipes to solve all social problems. It sometimes almost seems as if the technique of science were more easily learnt than the thinking that shows us what the problems are and how to approach them.

The conflict between what in its present mood the public expects science to achieve in satisfaction of popular hopes and what is really in its power is a serious matter because, even if the true scientists should all recognize the limitations of what they can do in the field of human affairs, so long as the public expects more there will always be some who will pretend, and perhaps honestly believe, that they can do more to meet popular demands than is really in their power. It is often difficult enough for the expert, and certainly in many instances impossible for the layman, to distinguish between legitimate and illegitimate claims advanced in the name of science. The enormous publicity recently given by the media to a report pronouncing in the name of science on *The Limits to Growth,* and the silence of the same media about the devastating criticism this report has received from the competent experts,[6] must make one feel somewhat apprehensive about the use to which the prestige of science can be put. But it is by no means only in the field of economics that far-reaching claims are made on behalf of a more scientific direction of all human activities and the desirability of replacing spontaneous processes by 'conscious human control'. If I am not mistaken, psychology, psychiatry and some branches of sociology, not to speak about the so-called philosophy of history, are even more affected by what I have called the scientistic prejudice, and by specious claims of what science can achieve.[7]

If we are to safeguard the reputation of science, and to prevent the arrogation of knowledge based on a superficial similarity of procedure with that of the physical sciences, much effort will have to be directed toward debunking such arrogations, some of which have by now become the vested interests of established university departments. We cannot be grateful enough to such modern philosophers of science as Sir Karl Popper for giving us a test by which we can distinguish between what we may accept as scientific and what not — a test which I am sure some doctrines now widely accepted as scientific would not pass. There are some special problems, however, in connection with those essentially complex phenomena of which social structures are so important an instance, which make me wish to restate in conclusion in more general terms the reasons why in these fields not only are there absolute obstacles to the prediction of specific events, but why to act as if we possessed scientific knowledge enabling us to transcend them may itself become a serious obstacle to the advance of the human intellect.

The chief point we must remember is that the great and rapid advance of the physical sciences took place in fields where it proved that explanation and prediction could be based on laws which accounted for the observed phenomena as functions of comparatively few variables — either particular facts or relative frequencies of events. This may even be the ultimate reason why we single out these realms as 'physical' in contrast to those more highly organized structures which I have here called essentially complex phenomena. There is no reason why the position must be the same in the latter as in the former fields. The difficulties which we encounter in the latter are not, as one might at first suspect, difficulties about formulating theories for the explanation of the observed events — although they cause also special difficulties about testing proposed explanations and therefore about eliminating bad theories. They are due to the chief problem which arises when we apply our theories to any particular situation in the real world. A theory of essentially complex phenomena must refer to a large number of particular facts; and to derive a prediction from it, or to test it, we have to ascertain all these particular facts. Once we succeeded in this there should be no particular difficulty about deriving testable predictions — with the help of modern computers it should be easy enough to insert these data into the appropriate blanks of the theoretical formulae and to derive a prediction. The real difficulty, to the solution of which science has little to contribute, and which is sometimes indeed insoluble, consists in the ascertainment of the particular facts.

A simple example will show the nature of this difficulty. Consider some ball game played by a few people of approximately equal skill. If we knew a few particular facts in addition to our general knowledge of the ability of the individual players, such as their state of attention, their perceptions and the state of their hearts, lungs, muscles, etc., at each moment of the game, we could probably predict the outcome. Indeed, if we were familiar both with the game and the teams we should probably have a fairly shrewd idea on what the outcome will depend. But we shall of course not be able to ascertain those facts and in consequence the result of the game will be outside the range of the scientifically predictable, however well we may know what effects particular events would have on the result of the game. This does not mean that we can make no predictions at all about the course of such a game. If we know the rules of the different games we shall, in watching one, very soon know which game is being played and what kinds of actions we can expect and what kind not. But our capacity to predict will be confined to such general characteristics of the events to be expected and not include the capacity of predicting particular individual events.

This corresponds to what I have called earlier the mere pattern predictions to which we are increasingly confined as we penetrate from the realm in which relatively simple laws prevail into the range of phenomena where organized complexity rules. As we advance we find more and more frequently that we can in fact ascertain only some but not all the particular circumstances which determine the outcome of a given process; and in consequence we are able to predict only some but not all the properties of the result we have to expect. Often all that we shall be able to predict will be some abstract characteristic of the pattern that will appear — relations between kinds of elements about which individually we know very little. Yet, as I am anxious to repeat, we will still achieve predictions which can be falsified and which therefore are of empirical significance.

Of course, compared with the precise predictions we have learnt to expect in the physical sciences, this sort of mere pattern predictions is a second best with which one does not like to have to be content. Yet the danger of which I want to warn is precisely the belief that in order to have a claim to be accepted as scientific it is necessary to achieve more. This way lies charlatanism and worse. To act on the belief that we possess the knowledge and the power which enable us to shape the processes of society entirely to our liking, knowledge which in fact we do *not* possess, is likely to make us do much harm. In the physical sciences there may be little objection to trying to do the impossible; one might even feel that one ought not to discourage the over-confident because their experiments may after all produce some new insights. But in the social field the erroneous belief that the exercise of some power would have beneficial consequences is likely to lead to a new power to coerce other men being conferred on some authority. Even if such power is not in itself bad, its exercise is likely to impede the functioning of those spontaneous ordering forces by which, without understanding them, man is in fact so largely assisted in the pursuit of his aims. We are only beginning to understand on how subtle a communication system the functioning of an advanced industrial society is based — a communications system which we call the market and which turns out to be a more efficient mechanism for digesting dispersed information than any that man has deliberately designed.

If man is not to do more harm than good in his efforts to improve the social order, he will have to learn that in this, as in all other fields where essential complexity of an organized kind prevails, he cannot acquire the full knowledge which would make mastery of the events possible. He will therefore have to use what knowledge he can achieve, not to shape the results as the craftsman shapes his handiwork, but rather to cultivate a growth by providing the appropriate environment, in the manner in which the gardener does this for his plants. There is danger in the exuberant feeling of ever growing power which the advance of the physical sciences has engendered and which tempts man to try, 'dizzy with success', to use a characteristic phrase of early communism, to subject not only our natural but also our human environment to the control of a human will. The recognition of the insuperable limits to his knowledge ought indeed to teach the student of society a lesson in humility which should guard him against becoming an accomplice in men's fatal striving to control society — a striving which makes him not only a tyrant over his fellows, but which may well make him the destroyer of a civilization which no brain has designed but which has grown from the free efforts of millions of individuals.

NOTES

1. 'Scientism and the study of society', *Economica,* vol. IX, no. 35, August 1942, reprinted in *The Counter-Revolution of Science,* Chicago, 1952.

2. Warren Weaver, 'A quarter century in the natural sciences', *The Rockefeller Foundation Annual Report 1958,* chapter I, 'Science and complexity'.

3. See my essay 'The theory of complex phenomena' in *The Critical Approach to Science and Philosophy. Essays in Honor of K. R. Popper,* ed. M. Bunge, New York, 1964, and reprinted (with additions) in my *Studies in Philosophy, Politics and Economics,* London and Chicago, 1967.

4. V. Pareto, *Manuel d'économie politique,* 2nd ed., Paris, 1927, pp. 223–24.

5. See, for example, Luis Molina, *De iustitia et iure,* Cologne, 1596–1600, tom. II, disp. 347, no. 3, and particularly Johannes de Lugo, *Disputationum de iustitia et iure tomus secundus,* Lyon, 1642, disp. 26, sect. 4, no. 40.

6. See *The Limits to Growth: A Report of the Club of Rome's Project on the Predicament of Mankind,* New York, 1972; for a systematic examination of this by a competent economist, cf. Wilfred Beckerman, *In Defence of Economic Growth,* London, 1974, and, for a list of earlier criticisms by experts, Gottfried Haberler, *Economic Growth and Stability,* Los Angeles, 1974, who rightly calls their effect 'devastating'.

7. I have given some illustrations of these tendencies in other fields in my inaugural lecture as Visiting Professor at the University of Salzburg, *Die Irrtümer des Konstruktivismus und die Grundlagen legitimer Kritik gesellschaftlicher Gebilde,* Munich, 1970, now reissued for the Walter Eucken Institute, at Freiburg i.B., by J. C. B. Mohr, Tübingen, 1975.

HAYEK'S POLITICAL ECONOMY: A PHILOSOPHICAL-REALISTIC CONCEPT

♦ ♦ ♦ ♦ ♦

• *PART • FIVE* •

Why I Am Not a Conservative

·15·

I

At a time when most movements that are thought to be progressive advocate further encroachments on individual liberty,[1] those who cherish freedom are likely to expend their energies in opposition. In this they find themselves much of the time on the same side as those who habitually resist change. In matters of current politics today they generally have little choice but to support the conservative parties. But, though the position I have tried to define is also often described as "conservative," it is very different from that to which this name has been traditionally attached. There is danger in the confused condition which brings the defenders of liberty and the true conservatives together in common opposition to developments which threaten their different ideals equally. It is therefore important to distinguish clearly the position taken here from that which has long been known — perhaps more appropriately — as conservatism.

Conservatism proper is a legitimate, probably necessary, and certainly widespread attitude of opposition to drastic change. It has, since the French Revolution, for a century and a half played an important role in European politics. Until the rise of socialism its opposite was liberalism. There is nothing corresponding to this conflict in the history of the United States, because what in Europe was called "liberalism" was here the common tradition on which the American polity had been built: thus the defender of the American tradition was a liberal in the European sense.[2] This already existing confusion was made worse by the recent attempt to transplant to America the European type of conservatism, which, being alien to the American tradition, has acquired a somewhat odd character. And some time before this, American radicals and socialists began calling themselves "liberals." I will nevertheless continue for the moment to describe as liberal the position which I hold and which I believe differs as much from true conservatism as from socialism. Let me say at once, however, that I do so with increasing misgivings, and I shall later have to consider what would be the appropriate name for the party of liberty. The reason for this is not only that the term "liberal" in the United States is the cause of constant misunderstandings today, but also that in Europe the predominant type of rationalistic liberalism has long been one of the pacemakers of socialism.

Let me now state what seems to me the decisive objection to any conservatism which deserves to be called such. It is that by its very nature it cannot offer an alternative to the direction in which we are moving. It may succeed by its resistance to current tendencies in slowing down undesirable developments, but, since it does not indicate another direction, it cannot prevent their continuance. It has, for this reason, invariably been the fate of conservatism to be dragged along a path not of its own choosing. The tug of war between conservatives and progressives can only affect the speed, not the direction, of contemporary developments. But, though there is need for a "brake on the vehicle of progress,"[3] I personally cannot be content with simply helping to apply the brake. What the liberal must ask, first of all, is not how fast or how far we should move, but where we should move. In fact, he differs much more from the collectivist radical of today than does the conservative. While the last generally holds merely a mild and moderate version of the prejudices of his time, the liberal today must more positively oppose some of the basic conceptions which most conservatives share with the socialists.

II

The picture generally given of the relative position of the three parties does more to obscure than to elucidate their true relations. They are usually represented as different positions on a line, with the socialists on the left, the conservatives on the right, and the liberals somewhere in the middle. Nothing could be more misleading. If we want a diagram, it would be more appropriate to arrange them in a triangle with the conservatives occupying one corner, with the socialists pulling toward the second and the liberals toward the third. But, as the socialists have for a long time been able to pull harder, the conservatives have tended to follow the socialist rather than the liberal direction and have adopted at appropriate intervals of time those ideas made respectable by radical propaganda. It has been regularly the conservatives who have compromised with socialism and stolen its thunder. Advocates of the Middle Way[4] with no goal of their own, conservatives have been guided by the belief that the truth must lie somewhere between the extremes — with the result that they have shifted their position every time a more extreme movement appeared on either wing.

The position which can be rightly described as conservative at any time depends, therefore, on the direction of existing tendencies. Since the development during the last decades has been generally in a socialist direction, it may seem that both conservatives and liberals have been mainly intent on retarding that movement. But the main point about liberalism is that it wants to go elsewhere, not to stand still. Though today the contrary impression may sometimes be caused by the fact that there was a time when liberalism was more widely accepted and some of its objectives closer to being achieved, it has never been a backward-looking doctrine. There has never been a time when liberal ideals were fully realized and when liberalism did not look forward to further improvement of institutions. Liberalism is not averse to evolution and change; and where spontaneous change has been smothered by government control, it wants a great deal of change of policy. So far as much of current governmental action is concerned, there is in the present world very little reason for the liberal to wish to preserve things as they are. It would seem to the liberal, indeed, that what is most urgently needed in most parts of the world is a thorough sweeping-away of the obstacles to free growth.

This difference between liberalism and conservatism must not be obscured by the fact that in the United States it is still possible to defend individual liberty by defending long-established institutions. To the liberal they are valuable not mainly because they are long established or because they are American but because they correspond to the ideals which he cherishes.

III

Before I consider the main points on which the liberal attitude is sharply opposed to the conservative one, I ought to stress that there is much that the liberal might with advantage have learned from the work of some conservative thinkers. To their loving and reverential study of the value of grown institutions we owe (at least outside the field of economics) some profound insights which are real contributions to our understanding of a free society. However reactionary in politics such figures as Coleridge, Bonald, De Maistre, Justus Möser, or Donoso Cortès may have been, they did show an understanding of the meaning of spontaneously grown institutions such as language, law, morals, and conventions that anticipated modern scientific approaches and from which the liberals might have profited. But the admiration of the conservatives for free growth generally applies only to the past. They typically lack the courage to welcome the same undesigned change from which new tools of human endeavors will emerge.

This brings me to the first point on which the conservative and the liberal dispositions differ radically. As has often been acknowledged by conservative writers, one of the fundamental traits of the conservative attitude is a fear of change, a timid distrust of the new as such,[5] while the liberal position is based on courage and confidence, on a preparedness to let change run its course even if we cannot predict where it will lead. There would not be much to object to if the conservatives merely disliked too rapid change in institutions and public policy; here the case for caution and slow process is indeed strong. But the conservatives are inclined to use the powers of government to prevent change or to limit its rate to whatever appeals to the more timid mind. In looking forward, they lack the faith in the spontaneous forces of adjustment which makes the liberal accept changes without apprehension, even though he does not know how the necessary adaptations will be brought about. It is, indeed, part of the liberal attitude to assume that, especially in the economic field, the self-regulating forces of the market will somehow bring about the required adjustments to new conditions, although no one can foretell how they will do this in a particular instance. There is perhaps no single factor contributing so much to people's frequent reluctance to let the market work as their inability to conceive how some necessary balance, between demand and supply, between exports and imports, or the like, will be brought about without deliberate control. The conservative feels safe and content only if he is assured that some higher wisdom watches and supervises change, only if he knows that some authority is charged with keeping the change "orderly."

This fear of trusting uncontrolled social forces is closely related to two other characteristics of conservatism: its fondness for authority and its lack of understanding of economic forces. Since it distrusts both abstract theories and general principles,[6] it neither understands those spontaneous forces on which a policy of freedom relies nor possesses a basis for formulating principles of policy. Order appears to the conservatives as the result of the continuous attention of authority, which, for this purpose, must be allowed to do what is required by the particular circumstances and not be tied to rigid rule. A commitment to principles presupposes an understanding of the general forces by which the efforts of society are co-ordinated, but it is such a theory of society and especially of the economic mechanism that conservatism conspicuously lacks. So unproductive has conservatism been in producing a general conception of how a social order is maintained that its modern votaries, in trying to construct a theoretical foundation, invariably find themselves appealing almost exclusively to authors who regarded themselves as liberal. Macaulay, Tocqueville, Lord Acton, and Lecky certainly considered themselves liberals, and with justice; and even Edmund Burke remained an Old Whig to the end and would have shuddered at the thought of being regarded as a Tory.

Let me return, however, to the main point, which is the characteristic complacency of the conservative toward the action of established authority and his prime concern that this authority be not weakened rather than that its power be kept within bounds. This is difficult to reconcile with the preservation of liberty. In general, it can probably be said that the conservative does not object to coercion or arbitrary power so long as it is used for what he regards as the right purposes. He believes that if government is in the hands of decent men, it ought not be too much restricted by rigid rules. Since he is essentially opportunist and lacks principles, his main hope must be that the wise and the good will rule — not merely by example, as we all must wish, but by authority given to them and enforced by them.[7] Like the socialist, he is less concerned with the problem of how the powers of government should be limited than with that of who wields them; and, like the socialist, he regards himself as entitled to force the value he holds on other people.

When I say that the conservative lacks principles, I do not mean to suggest that he lacks moral conviction. The typical conservative is indeed usually a man of very strong moral convictions. What I mean is that he has no political principles which enable him to work with people whose moral values differ from his own for a political order in which both can obey their convictions. It is the recognition of such principles that permits the co-existence of different sets of values that makes it possible to build a peaceful society with a minimum of force. The acceptance of such principles means that we agree to tolerate much that we dislike. There are many values of the conservative which appeal to me more than those of the socialists; yet for a liberal the importance he personally attaches to specific goals is no sufficient justification for forcing others to serve them. I have little doubt that some of my conservative friends will be shocked by what they will regard as "concessions" to modern views that I have made in Part III of this book [*The Constitution of Liberty*]. But, though I may dislike some of the measures concerned as much as they do and might vote against them, I know of no general principles to which I could appeal to persuade those of a different view that those measures are not permissible in the general kind of society which we both desire. To live and work successfully with others requires more than faithfulness to one's concrete aims. It requires an intellectual commitment to a type of order in which, even on issues which to one are fundamental, others are allowed to pursue different ends.

It is for this reason that to the liberal neither moral nor religious ideals are proper objects of coercion, while both conservatives and socialists recognize no such limits. I sometimes feel that the most conspicuous attribute of liberalism that distinguishes it as much from conservatism as from socialism is the view that moral beliefs concerning matters of conduct which do not directly interfere with the protected sphere of other persons do not justify coercion. This may also explain why it seems to be so much easier for the repentant socialist to find a new spiritual home in the conservative fold than in the liberal.

In the last resort, the conservative position rests on the belief that in any society there are recognizably superior persons whose inherited standards and values and position ought to be protected and who should have a greater influence on public affairs than others. The liberal, of course, does not deny that there are some superior people — he is not an egalitarian — but he denies that anyone has authority to decide who these superior people are. While the conservative inclines to defend a particular established hierarchy and wishes authority to protect the status of those whom he values, the liberal feels that no respect for established values can justify the resort to privilege or monopoly or any other coercive power of the state in order to shelter such people against the forces of economic change. Though he is fully aware of the important role that cultural and intellectual elites have played in the evolution of civilization, he also believes that these elites have to prove themselves by their capacity to maintain their position under the same rules that apply to all others.

Closely connected with this is the usual attitude of the conservative to democracy. I have made it clear earlier that I do not regard majority rule as an end but merely as a means, or perhaps even as the least evil of those forms of government from which we have to choose. But I believe that the conservatives deceive themselves when they blame the evils of our time on democracy. The chief evil is unlimited government, and nobody is qualified to wield unlimited power.[8] The powers which modern democracy possesses would be even more intolerable in the hands of some small elite.

Admittedly, it was only when power came into the hands of the majority that further limitation of the power of government was thought unnecessary. In this sense democracy and unlimited government are connected. But it is not democracy but unlimited government that is objectionable, and I do not see why the people should not learn to limit the scope of majority rule as well as that of any other form of government. At any rate, the advantages of democracy as a method of peaceful change and of political education seem to be so great compared with those of any other system that I can have no sympathy with the anti-democratic strain of conservatism. It is not who governs but what government is entitled to do that seems to me the essential problem.

That the conservative opposition to too much government control is not a matter of principle but is concerned with the particular aims of government is clearly shown in the economic sphere. Conservatives usually oppose collectivist and directivist measures in the industrial field, and here the liberal will often find allies in them. But at the same time conservatives are usually protectionists and have frequently supported socialist measures in agriculture. Indeed, though the restrictions which exist today in industry and commerce are mainly the result of socialist views, the equally important restrictions in agriculture were usually introduced by conservatives at an even earlier date. And in their efforts to discredit free enterprise many conservative leaders have vied with the socialists.[9]

IV

I have already referred to the differences between conservatism and liberalism in the purely intellectual field, but I must return to them because the characteristic conservative attitude here not only is a serious weakness of conservatism but tends to harm any cause which allies itself with it. Conservatives feel instinctively that it is new ideas more than anything else that cause change. But, from its point of view rightly, conservatism fears new ideas because it has no distinctive principles of its own to oppose to them; and, by its distrust of theory and its lack of imagination concerning anything except that which experience has already proved, it deprives itself of the weapons needed in the struggle of ideas. Unlike liberalism with its fundamental belief in the long-range power of ideas, conservatism is bound by the stock of ideas inherited at a given time. And since it does not really believe in the power of argument, its last resort is generally a claim to superior wisdom, based on some self-arrogated superior quality.

This difference shows itself most clearly in the different attitudes of the two traditions to the advance of knowledge. Though the liberal certainly does not regard all change as progress, he does regard the advance of knowledge as one of the chief aims of human effort and expects from it the gradual solution of such problems and difficulties as we can hope to solve. Without preferring the new merely because it is new, the liberal is aware that it is of the essence of human achievement that it produces something new; and he is prepared to come to terms with new knowledge, whether he likes its immediate effects or not.

Personally, I find that the most objectionable feature of the conservative attitude is its propensity to reject well-substantiated new knowledge because it dislikes some of the consequences which seem to follow from it — or, to put it bluntly, its obscurantism. I will not deny that scientists as much as others are given to fads and fashions and that we have much reason to be cautious in accepting the conclusions that they draw from their latest theories. But the reasons for our reluctance must themselves be rational and must be kept separate from our regret that the new theories upset our cherished beliefs. I can have little patience with those who oppose, for instance, the theory of evolution or what are called "mechanistic" explanations of the phenomena of life simply because of certain moral consequences which at first seem to follow from these theories, and still less with those who regard it as irreverent or impious to ask certain questions at all. By refusing to face the facts, the conservative only weakens his own position. Frequently the conclusions which rationalist presumption draws from new scientific insights do not at all follow from them. But only by actively taking part in the elaboration of the consequences of new discoveries do we learn whether or not they fit into our world picture and, if so, how. Should our moral beliefs really prove to be dependent on factual assumptions shown to be incorrect, it would be hardly moral to defend them by refusing to acknowledge facts.

Connected with the conservative distrust of the new and the strange is its hostility to internationalism and its proneness to a strident nationalism. Here is another source of its weakness in the struggle of ideas. It cannot alter the fact that the ideas which are changing our civilization respect no boundaries. But refusal to acquaint one's self with new ideas merely deprives one of the power of effectively countering them when necessary. The growth of ideas is an international process, and only those who fully take part in the discussion will be able to exercise a significant influence. It is no real argument to say that an idea is un-American, un-British, or un-German, nor is a mistaken or vicious ideal better for having been conceived by one of our compatriots.

A great deal more might be said about the close connection between conservatism and nationalism, but I shall not dwell on this point because it may be felt that my personal position makes me unable to sympathize with any form of nationalism. I will merely add that it is this nationalistic bias which frequently provides the bridge from conservatism to collectivism: to think in terms of "our" industry or resource is only a short step away from demanding that these national assets be directed in the national interest. But in this respect the Continental liberalism which derives from the French Revolution is little better than conservatism. I need hardly say that nationalism of this sort is something very different from patriotism and that an aversion to nationalism is fully compatible with a deep attachment to national traditions. But the fact that I prefer and feel reverence for some of the traditions of my society need not be the cause of hostility to what is strange and different.

Only at first does it seem paradoxical that the anti-internationalism of the conservative is so frequently associated with imperialism. But the more a person dislikes the strange and thinks his own ways superior, the more he tends to regard it as his mission to "civilize" others[10] — not by the voluntary and unhampered intercourse which the liberal favors, but by bringing them the blessings of efficient government. It is significant that here again we frequently find the conservatives joining hands with the socialists against the liberals — not only in England, where the Webbs and their Fabians were outspoken imperialists, or in Germany, where state socialism and colonial expansionism went together and found the support of the same group of "socialists of the chair," but also in the United States, where even at the time of the first Roosevelt it could be observed: "the Jingoes and the Social Reformers have gotten together; and have formed a political party, which threatened to capture the Government and use it for their program of Caesaristic paternalism, a danger which now seems to have been averted only by the other parties having adopted their program in a somewhat milder degree and form."[11]

V

There is one respect, however, in which there is justification for saying that the liberal occupies a position midway between the socialist and the conservative: he is as far from the crude rationalism of the socialist, who wants to reconstruct all social institutions according to a pattern prescribed by his individual reason, as from the mysticism to which the conservative so frequently has to resort. What I have described as the liberal position shares with conservatism a distrust of reason to the extent that the liberal is very much aware that we do not know all the answers and that he is not sure that the answers he has are certainly the right ones or even that we can find all the answers. He also does not disdain to seek assistance from whatever non-rational institutions or habits have proved their worth. The liberal differs from the conservative in his willingness to face this ignorance and to admit how little we know, without claiming the authority of supernatural sources of knowledge where his reason fails him. It has to be admitted that in some respects the liberal is fundamentally a skeptic[12] — but it seems to require a certain degree of diffidence to let others seek their happiness in their own fashion and to adhere consistently to that tolerance which is an essential characteristic of liberalism.

There is no reason why this need mean an absence of religious belief on the part of the liberal. Unlike the rationalism of the French Revolution, true liberalism has no quarrel with religion, and I can only deplore the militant and essentially illiberal antireligionism which animated so much of nineteenth-century Continental liberalism. That this is not essential to liberalism is clearly shown by its English ancestors, the Old Whigs, who, if anything, were much too closely allied with a particular religious belief. What distinguishes the liberal from the conservative here is that, however profound his own spiritual beliefs, he will never regard himself as entitled to impose them on others and that for him the spiritual and the temporal are different spheres which ought not to be confused.

VI

What I have said should suffice to explain why I do not regard myself as a conservative. Many people will feel, however, that the position which emerges is hardly what they used to call "liberal." I must, therefore, now face the question of whether this name is today the appropriate name for the party of liberty. I have already indicated that, though I have all my life described myself as a liberal, I have done so more recently with increasing misgivings — not only because in the United States this term constantly gives rise to misunderstanding, but also because I have become more and more aware of the great gulf that exists between my position and the rationalistic Continental liberalism or even the English liberalism of the utilitarians.

If liberalism still meant what it meant to an English historian who in 1827 could speak of the revolution of 1688 as "the triumph of those principles which in the language of the present day are denominated liberal or constitutional"[13] or if one could still, with Lord Acton, speak of Burke, Macaulay, and Gladstone as the three greatest liberals, or if one could still, with Harold Laski, regard Tocqueville and Lord Acton as "the essential liberals of the nineteenth century,"[14] I should indeed be only too proud to describe myself by that name. But, much as I am tempted to call their liberalism true liberalism, I must recognize that the majority of Continental liberals stood for ideas to which these men were strongly opposed, and that they were led more by a desire to impose upon the world a preconceived rational pattern than to provide opportunity for free growth. The same is largely true of what has called itself Liberalism in England at least since the time of Lloyd George.

It is thus necessary to recognize that what I have called "liberalism" has little to do with any political movement that goes under that name today. It is also questionable whether the historical associations which that name carries today are conducive to the success of any movement. Whether in these circumstances one ought to make an effort to rescue the term from what one feels is its misuse is a question on which opinions may well differ. I myself feel more and more that to use it without long explanations causes too much confusion and that as a label it has become more of a ballast than a source of strength.

In the United States, where it has become almost impossible to use "liberal" in the sense in which I have used it, the term "libertarian" has been used instead. It may be the answer; but for my part I find it singularly unattractive. For my taste it carries too much the flavor of a manufactured term and of a substitute. What I should want is a word which describes the party of life, the party that favors free growth and spontaneous evolution. But I have racked my brain unsuccessfully to find a descriptive term which commends itself.

VII

We should remember, however, that when the ideals which I have been trying to restate first began to spread through the Western world, the party which represented them had a generally recognized name. It was the ideals of the English Whigs that inspired what later came to be known as the liberal movement in the whole of Europe[15] and that provided the conceptions that the American colonists carried with them and which guided them in their struggle for independence and in the establishment of their constitution.[16] Indeed, until the character of this tradition was altered by the accretions due to the French Revolution, with its totalitarian democracy and socialist leanings, "Whig" was the name by which the party of liberty was generally known.

The name died in the country of its birth partly because for a time the principles for which it stood were no longer distinctive of a particular party, and partly because the men who bore the name did not remain true to those principles. The Whig parties of the nineteenth century, in both Britain and the United States, finally brought discredit to the name among the radicals. But it is true that, since liberalism took the place of Whiggism only after the movement for liberty had absorbed the crude and militant rationalism of the French Revolution, and since our task must largely be to free that tradition from the overrationalistic, nationalistic, and socialistic influences which have intruded into it, Whiggism is historically the correct name for the ideas in which I believe. The more I learn about the evolution of ideas, the more I have become aware that I am simply an unrepentant Old Whig — with the stress on the "old."

To confess one's self an Old Whig does not mean, of course, that one wants to go back to where we were at the end of the seventeenth century. It has been one of the purposes of this book to show that the doctrines then first stated continued to grow and develop until about seventy or eighty years ago, even though they were no longer the chief aim of a distinct party. We have since learned much that should enable us to restate them in a more satisfactory and effective form. But, though they require restatement in the light of our present knowledge, the basic principles are still those of the Old Whigs. True, the later history of the party that bore that name has made some historians doubt where there was a distinct body of Whig principles; but I can but agree with Lord Acton that, though some of "the patriarchs of the doctrine were the most infamous of men, the notion of a higher law above municipal codes, with which Whiggism began, is the supreme achievement of Englishmen and their bequest to the nation"[17] — and, we may add, to the world. It is the doctrine which is at the basis of the common tradition of the Anglo-Saxon countries. It is the doctrine from which Continental liberalism took what is valuable in it. It is the doctrine on which the American system of government is based. In its pure form it is represented in the United States, not by the radicalism of Jefferson, nor by the conservatism of Hamilton or even of John Adams, but by the ideas of James Madison, the "father of the Constitution."[18]

I do not know whether to revive that old name is practical politics. That to the mass of people, both in the Anglo-Saxon world and elsewhere, it is today probably a term without definite associations is perhaps more an advantage than a drawback. To those familiar with the history of ideas it is probably the only name that quite expresses what the tradition means. That, both for the genuine conservative and still more for the many socialists turned conservative, Whiggism is the name for their pet aversion shows a sound instinct on their part. It has been the name for the only set of ideals that has consistently opposed all arbitrary power.

VIII

It may well be asked whether the name really matters so much. In a country like the United States, which on the whole still has free institutions and where, therefore, the defense of the existing is often a defense of freedom, it might not make so much difference if the defenders of freedom call themselves conservatives, although even here the association with the conservatives by disposition will often be embarrassing. Even when men approve of the same arrangements, it must be asked whether they approve of them because they exist or because they are desirable in themselves. The common resistance to the collectivist tide should not be allowed to obscure the fact that the belief in integral freedom is based on an essentially forward-looking attitude and not on any nostalgic longing for the past or a romantic admiration for what has been.

The need for a clear distinction is absolutely imperative, however, where, as is true in many parts of Europe, the conservatives have already accepted a large part of the collectivist creed — a creed that has governed policy for so long that many of its institutions have come to be accepted as a matter of course and have become a source of pride to "conservative" parties who created them.[19] Here the believer in freedom cannot but conflict with the conservative and take an essentially radical position, directed against popular prejudices, entrenched positions, and firmly established privileges. Follies and abuses are no better for having long been established principles of policy.

Though *quieta non movere* may at times be a wise maxim for the statesman, it cannot satisfy the political philosopher. He may wish policy to proceed gingerly and not before public opinion is prepared to support it, but he cannot accept arrangements merely because current opinion sanctions them. In a world where the chief need is once more, as it was at the beginning of the nineteenth century, to free the process of spontaneous growth from the obstacles and encumbrances that human folly has erected, his hopes must rest on persuading and gaining the support of those who by disposition are "progressives," those who, though they may now be seeking change in the wrong direction, are at least willing to examine critically the existing and to change it wherever necessary.

I hope I have not misled the reader by occasionally speaking of "party" when I was thinking of groups of men defending a set of intellectual and moral principles. Party politics of any one country has not been the concern of this book. The question of how the principles I have tried to reconstruct by piecing together the broken fragments of a tradition can be translated into a program with mass appeal, the political philosopher must leave to "that insidious and crafty animal, vulgarly called a statesman or politician, whose councils are directed by the momentary fluctuations of affairs."[20] The task of the political philosopher can only be to influence public opinion, not to organize people for action. He will do so effectively only if he is not concerned with what is now politically possible but consistently defends the "general principles which are always the same."[21] In this sense I doubt whether there can be such a thing as a conservative political philosophy. Conservatism may often be a useful practical maxim, but it does not give us any guiding principles which can influence long-range developments.

NOTES

1. This has now been true for over a century, and as early as 1855 J. S. Mill could say (see my *John Stuart Mill and Harriet Taylor* [London and Chicago, 1951], p. 216) that "almost all the projects of social reformers of these days are really *liberticide*."

2. B. Crick, "The Strange Quest for an American Conservatism," *Review of Politics*, XVII (1955), 365, says rightly that "the normal American who calls himself 'A Conservative' is, in fact, a liberal." It would appear that the reluctance of these conservatives to call themselves by the more appropriate name dates only from its abuse during the New Deal era.

3. The expression is that of R. G. Collingwood, *The New Leviathan* (Oxford: Oxford University Press, 1942), p. 209.

4. Cf. the characteristic choice of this title for the programmatic book by the present British Prime Minister Harold Macmillan, *The Middle Way* (London, 1938).

5. Cf. Lord Hugh Cecil, *Conservatism* ("Home University Library" [London, 1912]), p. 9: "Natural Conservatism . . . is a disposition averse from change; and it springs partly from a distrust of the unknown."

6. Cf. the revealing self-description of a conservative in K. Feiling, *Sketches in Nineteenth Century Biography* (London, 1930), p. 174: "Taken in bulk, the Right have a horror of ideas, for is not the practical man, in Disraeli's words, 'one who practises the blunders of his predecessors'? For long tracts of their history they have indiscriminately resisted improvement, and in claiming to reverence their ancestors often reduce opinion to aged individual prejudice. Their position becomes safer, but more complex, when we add that this Right wing is incessantly overtaking the Left; that it lives by repeated inoculation of liberal ideas, and thus suffers from a never-perfected state of compromise."

7. I trust I shall be forgiven for repeating here the words in which on an earlier occasion I stated an important point: "The main merit of the

individualism which [Adam Smith] and his contemporaries advocated is that it is a system under which bad men can do least harm. It is a social system which does not depend for its functioning on our finding good men for running it, or on all men becoming better than they now are, but which makes use of men in all their given variety and complexity, sometimes good and sometimes bad, sometimes intelligent and more often stupid" (*Individualism and Economic Order* [London and Chicago 1948]), p. 11).

8. Cf. Lord Acton in *Letters of Lord Acton to Mary Gladstone*, ed. H. Paul (London, 1913), p. 73: "The danger is not that a particular class is unfit to govern Every class is unfit to govern. The law of liberty tends to abolish the reign of race over race, of faith over faith, of class over class."

9. J. R. Hicks has rightly spoken in this connection of the "caricature drawn alike by the young Disraeli, by Marx and by Goebbels" ("The Pursuit of Economic Freedom," *What We Defend*, ed. E. F. Jacob [Oxford: Oxford University Press, 1942], p. 96). On the role of the conservatives in this connection see also my Introduction to *Capitalism and the Historians* (Chicago: University of Chicago Press, 1954), pp. 19 ff.

10. Cf. J. S. Mill, *On Liberty*, ed. R. B. McCallum (Oxford, 1946), p. 83: "I am not aware that any community has a right to force another to be civilised."

11. J. W. Burgess, *The Reconciliation of Government with Liberty* (New York, 1915), p. 380.

12. Cf. Learned Hand, *The Spirit of Liberty*, ed. I. Dilliard (New York, 1952), p. 190: "The Spirit of liberty is the spirit which is not too sure that it is right." See also Oliver Cromwell's often quoted statement in his *Letter to the General Assembly of the Church of Scotland*, August 3, 1650: "I beseech you, in the bowels of Christ, think it possible you may be mistaken." It is significant that this should be the probably best-remembered saying of the only "dictator" in British history!

13. H. Hallam, *Constitutional History* (1827) ("Everyman" ed.), III, 90. It is often suggested that the term "liberal" derives from the early nineteenth-century Spanish party of the *liberales*. I am more inclined to believe that it derives from the use of the term by Adam Smith in such passages as *W.o.N.*, II, 41: "the liberal system of free exportation and free importation" and p. 216: "allowing every man to pursue his own interest in his own way, upon the liberal plan of equality, liberty, and justice."

14. Lord Acton in *Letters to Mary Gladstone*, p. 44. Cf. also his judgment of Tocqueville in *Lectures on the French Revolution* (London, 1910), p. 357: "Tocqueville was a Liberal of the purest breed — a Liberal and nothing else, deeply suspicious of democracy and its kindred, equality, centralisation, and utilitarianism." Similarly in the *Nineteenth Century*, XXXIII (1893), 885. The statement by H. J. Laski occurs in "Alexis de Tocqueville and Democracy," in *The Social and Political Ideas of Some Representative Thinkers of the Victorian Age*, ed. F. J. C. Hearnshaw (London, 1933), p. 100, where

he says that "a case of unanswerable power could, I think, be made out for the view that he [Tocqueville] and Lord Acton were the essential liberals of the nineteenth century."

15. As early as the beginning of the eighteenth century, an English observer could remark that he "scarce ever knew a foreigner settled in England, whether of Dutch, German, French, Italian, or Turkish growth, but became a Whig in a little time after his mixing with us" (quoted by G. H. Guttridge, *English Whiggism and the American Revolution* [Berkeley: University of California Press, 1942], p. 3).

16. In the United States the nineteenth-century use of the term "Whig" has unfortunately obliterated the memory of the fact that in the eighteenth it stood for the principles which guided the revolution, gained independence, and shaped the Constitution. It was in Whig societies that the young James Madison and John Adams developed their political ideals (cf. E. M. Burns, *James Madison* [New Brunswick, N.J.: Rutgers University Press, 1938], p. 4); it was Whig principles which, as Jefferson tells us, guided all the lawyers who constituted such a strong majority among the signers of the Declaration of Independence and among the members of the Constitutional Convention (see *Writings of Thomas Jefferson* ["Memorial ed". (Washington, 1905)], XVI, 156). The profession of Whig principles was carried to such a point that even Washington's soldiers were clad in the traditional "blue and buff" colors of the Whigs, which they shared with the Foxites in the British Parliament and which was preserved down to our own days on the covers of the *Edinburgh Review*. If a socialist generation has made Whiggism its favorite target, this is all the more reason for the opponents of socialism to vindicate the name. It is today the only name which correctly describes the beliefs of the Gladstonian liberals, of the men of the generation of Maitland, Acton, and Bryce, the last generation for whom liberty rather than equality or democracy was the main goal.

17. Lord Acton, *Lectures on Modern History* (London, 1906), p. 218 (I have slightly rearranged Acton's clauses to reproduce briefly the sense of his statement).

18. Cf. S. K. Padover in his Introduction to *The Complete Madison* (New York, 1953), p. 10: "In modern terminology, Madison would be labeled a middle-of-the-road liberal and Jefferson a radical." This is true and important, though we must remember what E. S. Corwin ("James Madison: Layman, Publicist, and Exegete," *New York University Law Review*, XXVII [1952], 285) has called Madison's later "surrender to the overweening influence of Jefferson."

19. Cf. the British Conservative party's statement of policy, *The Right Road for Britain* (London, 1950), pp. 41 – 42, which claims, with considerable justification, that "this new conception [of the social services] was developed [by] the Coalition Government with a majority of Conservative Ministers and the full approval of the Conservative majority in the House

of Commons. . . . [We] set out the principle for the schemes of pensions, sickness and unemployment benefit, industrial injuries benefit and a national health scheme."

20. A. Smith, *W.o.N.*, I, 432.

21. Ibid.

PRINCIPLES AND EXPEDIENCY

·16·

*The frequent recurrence to fundamental principles is absolutely necessary to preserve the blessings of liberty.**

INDIVIDUAL AIMS AND COLLECTIVE BENEFITS

The thesis of this book [*Law, Legislation and Liberty*, vol. I] is that a condition of liberty in which all are allowed to use their knowledge for their purposes, restrained only by rules of just conduct of universal application, is likely to produce for them the best conditions for achieving their aims; and that such a system is likely to be achieved and maintained only if all authority, including that of the majority of the people, is limited in the exercise of coercive power by general principles to which the community has committed itself. Individual freedom, wherever it has existed, has been largely the product of a

*The Constitution of the State of North Carolina. The idea is probably derived from David Humes's, *Essays*, in *Works* III, p. 482: 'A government, says Machiavelli, must often be brought back to its original principles.' An earlier version of this chapter appeared in *Towards Liberty, Essays in Honor of Ludwig von Mises* (Menlo Park, Calif., 1971), vol. I.

prevailing respect for such principles which, however, have never been fully articulated in constitutional documents. Freedom has been preserved for prolonged periods because such principles, vaguely and dimly perceived, have governed public opinion. The institutions by which the countries of the Western world have attempted to protect individual freedom against progressive encroachment by government have always proved inadequate when transferred to countries where such traditions did not prevail. And they have not provided sufficient protection against the effects of new desires which even among the peoples of the West now often loom larger than the older conceptions — conceptions that made possible the periods of freedom when these peoples gained their present position.

I will not undertake here a fuller definition of the term "freedom" or enlarge upon why we regard individual freedom as so important. That I have attempted in another book.[1] But a few words should be said about why I prefer the short formula by which I have repeatedly described the condition of freedom, namely a state in which each can use his knowledge for his purposes, to the classic phrase of Adam Smith, 'every man, so long as he does not violate the laws of justice [being] left perfectly free to pursue his own interests in his own way.'[2] The reason for my preference is that the latter formula unnecessarily and unfortunately suggests, without intending to, a connection of the argument for individual freedom with egotism or selfishness. The freedom to pursue his own aims is, however, at least as important for the complete altruist as for the most selfish. Altruism, to be a virtue, certainly does not presuppose that one has to follow another person's will. But it is true that much pretended altruism manifests itself in a desire to make others serve the ends which the 'altruist' regards as important.

We need not return here to the undeniable fact that the beneficial effects on others of one's efforts will often become visible to one only if one acts as part of a concerted effort of many in accordance with a coherent plan, and that it may often be difficult for the isolated individual to do much about the evils that deeply concern him. But it is, of course, part of his freedom that for such purposes he can join (or create) organizations which will enable him to take part in concerted action. And though some of the ends of the altruist will be achievable only by collective action, purely selfish ends too will as often be achieved through it. There is no necessary connection between altruism and collective action, or between egotism and individual action.

Freedom Can Be Preserved Only by Following Principles and Is Destroyed by Following Expediency

From the insight that the benefits of civilization rest on the use of more knowledge than can be used in any deliberately concerted effort, it follows that it is not in our power to build a desirable society by simply putting together the particular elements that by themselves appear desirable. Although probably all beneficial improvement must be piecemeal, if the separate steps are not guided by a body of coherent principles, the outcome is likely to be a suppression of individual freedom.

The reason for this is very simple, although not generally understood. Since the value of freedom rests on the opportunities it provides for unforeseen and unpredictable actions, we will rarely know what we lose through a particular restriction of freedom. Any such restriction, any coercion other than the enforcement of general rules, will aim at the achievement of some foreseeable particular result, but what is prevented by it will usually not be known. The direct effects of any interference with the market order will be near and clearly visible in most cases, while the more indirect and remote effects will mostly be unknown and will therefore be disregarded.[3] We shall never be aware of all the costs of achieving particular results by such interference.

And so, when we decide each issue solely on what appear to be its individual merits, we always over-estimate the advantages of central direction. Our choice will regularly appear to be one between a certain known and tangible gain and the mere probability of the prevention of some unknown beneficial action by unknown persons. If the choice between freedom and coercion is thus treated as a matter of expediency,[4] freedom is bound to be sacrificed in almost every instance. As in the particular instance we shall hardly ever know what would be the consequence of allowing people to make their own choice, to make the decision in each instance depend only on the foreseeable particular results must lead to the progressive destruction of freedom. There are probably few restrictions on freedom which could not be justified on the grounds that we do not know the particular loss they will cause.

That freedom can be preserved only if it is treated as a supreme principle which must not be sacrificed for particular advantages was fully understood by the leading liberal thinkers of the nineteenth century, one of whom even described liberalism as 'the system of principles.'[5] Such is the chief burden of their warnings concerning 'What is seen and what is not seen in political economy'[6] and about the 'pragmatism that contrary to the intentions of its representatives inexorably leads to socialism.'[7]

All these warnings were, however, thrown to the wind, and the progressive discarding of principles and the increasing determination during the last hundred years to proceed pragmatically[8] is one of the most important innovations in social and economic policy. That we should foreswear all principles or 'isms' in order to achieve greater mastery over our fate is even now proclaimed as the new wisdom of our age. Applying to each task the 'social techniques' most appropriate to its solution, unfettered by any dogmatic belief, seems to some the only manner of proceeding worthy of a rational and scientific age.[9] 'Ideologies', that is sets of principles, have become generally as unpopular as they have always been with aspiring dictators such as Napoleon I or Karl Marx, the two men who gave the word its modern derogatory meaning.

If I am not mistaken, this fashionable contempt for 'ideology', or for all general principles or 'isms', is a characteristic attitude of disillusioned socialists who, because they have been forced by the inherent contradictions of their own ideology to discard it, have concluded that all ideologies must be erroneous and that in order to be rational one must do without one. But to be guided only, as they imagine it to be possible, by explicit particular purposes which one consciously accepts, and to reject all general values whose conduciveness to particular desirable results cannot be demonstrated (or to be guided only by what Max Weber calls 'purposive rationality') is an impossibility. Although, admittedly, an ideology is something which cannot be 'proved' (or demonstrated to be true), it may well be something whose widespread acceptance is the indispensable condition for most of the particular things we strive for.

Those self-styled modern 'realists' have only contempt for the old-fashioned reminder that if one starts unsystematically to interfere with the spontaneous order there is no practicable halting point and that it is therefore necessary to choose between alternative systems. They are pleased to think that by proceeding experimentally and therefore 'scientifically' they will succeed in fitting together in piecemeal fashion a desirable order by choosing for each particular desired result what science shows them to be the most appropriate means of achieving it.

Since warnings against this sort of procedure have often been misunderstood, as one of my earlier books has, a few more words about their intentions may be appropriate. What I meant to argue in *The Road to Serfdom*[10] was certainly not that whenever we depart, however slightly, from what I regard as the principles of a free society, we shall ineluctably be driven to go the whole way to a totalitarian system. It was rather what in more homely language is expressed when we say: 'If you do not mend your principles you will go to the devil.' That this has often been understood to describe a necessary process over which we have no power once we have embarked on it, is merely an indication of how little the importance of principles for the determination of policy is understood, and particularly how completely overlooked is the fundamental fact that by our political actions we unintentionally produce the acceptance of principles which will make further action necessary.

What is overlooked by those unrealistic modern 'realists' who pride themselves on the modernity of their view is that they are advocating something which most of the Western world has indeed been doing for the past two or three generations, and which is responsible for the conditions of present politics. The end of the liberal era of principles might well be dated at the time when, more than eighty years ago, W. S. Jevons pronounced that in economic and social policy 'we can lay down no hard and fast rules, but must treat every case in detail upon its merits.'[11] Ten years later Herbert Spencer could already speak of 'the reigning school of politics' by whom 'nothing less than scorn is shown for every doctrine which implies restraints on the doings of immediate expediency' or which relies on 'abstract principles.'[12]

This 'realistic' view which has not dominated politics for so long has hardly produced the results which its advocates desired. Instead of having achieved greater mastery over our fate we find ourselves in fact more frequently committed to a path which we have not deliberately chosen, and faced with 'inevitable necessities' of further action which, though never intended, are the result of what we have done.

The 'Necessities' of Policy are Generally the Consequences of Earlier Measures

The contention often advanced that certain political measures were inevitable has a curious double aspect. With regard to developments that are approved by those who employ this argument, it is readily accepted and used in justification of the actions. But when developments take an undesirable turn, the suggestion that this is not the effect of circumstances beyond our control, but the necessary consequence of our earlier decisions, is rejected with scorn. The idea that we are not fully free to pick and choose whatever combination of features we wish our society to possess, or to fit them together into a viable whole, that is, that we cannot build a desirable social order like a mosaic by selecting whatever particular parts we like best, and that many well-intentioned measures may have a long train of unforeseeable and undesirable consequences, seems to be intolerable to modern man. He has been taught that what he has made he can also alter at will to suit his wishes, and conversely, that what he can alter he must also have made in the first instance. He has not yet learnt that this naive belief derives from that ambiguity of the word 'made' which we discussed earlier.

In fact, of course, the chief circumstance which will make certain measures seem unavoidable is usually the result of our past actions and of the opinions which are now held. Most of the 'necessities' of policy are of our own creation. I am myself now old enough to have been told more than once by my elders that certain consequences of their policy which I foresaw would never occur, and later, when they did appear, to have been told by younger men that these had been inevitable and quite independent of what in fact was done.

The reason why we cannot achieve a coherent whole by just fitting together any elements we like is that the appropriateness of any particular arrangement within a spontaneous order will depend on all the rest of it, and that any particular change we make in it will tell us little about how it would operate in a different setting. An experiment can tell us only whether any innovation does or does not fit into a given framework. But to hope that we can build a coherent order by random experimentation with particular solutions of individual problems and without following guiding principles is an illusion. Experience tells us much about the effectiveness of different social and economic systems as a whole. But an order of the complexity of modern society can be designed neither as a whole, nor by shaping each part separately without regard to the rest, but only by consistently adhering to certain principles throughout a process of evolution.

This is not to say that these 'principles' must necessarily take the form of articulated rules. Principles are often more effective guides for action when they appear as no more than an unreasoned prejudice, a general feeling that certain things simply 'are not done'; while as soon as they are explicitly stated speculation begins about their correctness and their validity. It is probably true that in the eighteenth century the English, little given to speculation about general principles, were for this reason much more firmly guided by strong opinions about what kinds of political actions were permissible, than the French who tried so hard to discover and adopt such principles. Once the instinctive certainty is lost, perhaps as a result of unsuccessful attempts to put into words principles that had been observed 'intuitively', there is no way of regaining such guidance other than to search for a correct statement of what before was known implicitly.

The impression that the English in the seventeen and eighteenth centuries, through their gift of 'muddling through' and their 'genius for compromise', succeeded in building up a viable system without talking much about principles, while the French, with all their concern about explicit assumptions and clear formulations, never did so, may thus be misleading. The truth seems to be that while they talked little about principles, the English were much more surely guided by principles, while in France the very speculation about basic principles prevented any one set of principles from taking a firm hold.

The Danger of Attaching Greater Importance to the Predictable Rather Than to the Merely Possible Consequences of Our Actions

The preservation of a free system is so difficult precisely because it requires a constant rejection of measures which appear to be required to secure particular results, on no stronger grounds than that they conflict with a general rule, and frequently without our knowing what will be the costs of not observing the rule in the particular instance. A successful defence of freedom must therefore be dogmatic and make no concessions to expediency, even where it is not possible to show that, besides the known beneficial effects, some particular harmful result would also follow from its infringement. Freedom will prevail only if it is accepted as a general principle whose application to particular instances requires no justification. It is thus a misunderstanding to blame classical liberalism for having been too doctrinaire. Its defect was not that it adhered too stubbornly to principles, but rather that it lacked principles sufficiently definite to provide clear guidance, and that it often appeared simply to accept the traditional functions of government and to oppose all new ones. Consistency is possible only if definite principles are accepted. But the concept of liberty with which the liberals of the nineteenth century operated was in many respects so vague that it did not provide clear guidance.

People will not refrain from those restrictions on individual liberty that appear to them the simplest and most direct remedy of a recognized evil, if there does not prevail a strong belief in definite principles. The loss of such belief and the preference for expediency is in part a result of the fact that we no longer have any principles which can be rationally defended. The rules of thumb which at one time were accepted were not adequate to decide what is and what is not permissible in a free system. We have no longer even a generally understood name for what the term 'free system' only vaguely describes. Certainly neither 'capitalism' nor *laissez-faire* properly describe it; and both terms are understandably more popular with the enemies than with the defenders of a free system. 'Capitalism' is an appropriate name at most for the partial realization of such a system in a certain historical phase, but always misleading because it suggests a system which mainly benefits the capitalists, while in fact it is a system which imposes upon enterprise a discipline under which the managers chafe and which each endeavours to escape. *Laissez-faire* was never more than a rule of thumb. It indeed expressed protest against abuses of governmental power, but never provided a criterion by which one could decide what were the proper functions of government. Much the same applies to the terms 'free enterprise' or 'market economy' which, without a definition of the free sphere of the individual, say little. The expression 'liberty under the law', which at one time perhaps conveyed the essential point better than any other, has become almost meaningless because both 'liberty' and 'law' no longer have a clear meaning. And the only term that in the past was widely and correctly understood, namely 'liberalism', has 'as a supreme but unintended compliment been appropriated by the opponents of this ideal.'[13]

The lay reader may not be fully aware how much we have already moved away from the ideal expressed by those terms. While the lawyer or political scientist will at once see that what I shall be espousing is an ideal that has largely vanished and has never been fully realized, it is probably true that the majority of people believe that something like it still governs public affairs. It is because we have departed from the ideal so much further than most people realize, and because, unless this development is soon checked, it will by its own momentum transform society from a free into a totalitarian one, that we must reconsider the general principles guiding our political actions. We are still as free as we are because certain traditional but rapidly vanishing prejudices have impeded the process by which the inherent logic of the changes we have already made tends to assert itself in an ever widening field. In the present state of opinion the ultimate victory of totalitarianism would indeed be no more than the final victory of the ideas already dominant in the intellectual sphere over a merely traditionalist resistance.

Spurious Realism and the Required Courage to Consider Utopia

With respect to policy, the methodological insight that in the case of complex spontaneous orders we will never be able to determine more than the general principles on which they operate or to predict the particular changes that any event in the environment will bring about, has far-reaching consequences. It means that where we rely on spontaneous ordering forces we shall often not be able to foresee the particular changes by which the necessary adaptation to altered external circumstances will be brought about, and sometimes perhaps not even be able to conceive in what manner the restoration of a disturbed 'equilibrium' or 'balance' can be accomplished. This ignorance of how the mechanism of the spontaneous order will solve such a 'problem' which we know must be solved somehow if the overall order is not to disintegrate, often produces a panic-like alarm and the demand for government action for the restoration of the disturbed balance.

Often it is even the acquisition of a partial insight into the character of the spontaneous overall order that becomes the cause of the demands for deliberate control. So long as the balance of trade, or the correspondence of supply and demand of any particular commodity, adjusted itself spontaneously after any disturbance, men rarely asked themselves how this happened. But, once they became aware of the necessity of such constant readjustments, they felt that somebody must be made responsible for deliberately bringing them about. The economist, from the very nature of his schematic picture of the spontaneous order, could counter such apprehension only by the confident assertion that the required new balance would establish itself somehow if we did not interfere with the spontaneous forces; but, as he is usually unable to predict precisely how this would happen, his assertions were not very convincing.

Yet when it is possible to foresee how the spontaneous forces are likely to restore the disturbed balance, the situation becomes even worse. The necessity of adaptation to unforeseen events will always mean that someone is going to be hurt, that someone's expectations will be disappointed or his efforts frustrated. This leads to the demand that the required adjustment be brought about by deliberate guidance, which in practice must mean that authority is to decide who is to be hurt. The effect of this is often that necessary adjustments will be prevented whenever they can be foreseen.

What helpful insight science can provide for the guidance of policy consists in an understanding of the general nature of the spontaneous order, and not in any knowledge of the particulars of a concrete situation, which it does not and cannot possess. The true appreciation of what science has to contribute to the solution of our political tasks, which in the nineteenth century was fairly general, has been obscured by the new tendency derived from a now fashionable misconception of the nature of scientific method: the belief that science consists of a collection of particular observed facts, which is erroneous so far as science in general is concerned, but doubly misleading where we have to deal with the parts of a complex spontaneous order. Since all the events in any part of such an order are interdependent, and an abstract order of this sort has no recurrent concrete parts which can be identified by individual attributes, it is necessarily vain to try to discover by observation regularities in any of its parts. The only theory which in this field can lay claim to scientific status is the theory of the order as a whole; and such a theory (although it has, of course, to be tested on the facts) can never be achieved inductively by observation but only through constructing mental models made up from the observable elements.

The myopic view of science that concentrates on the study of particular facts because they alone are empirically observable, and whose advocates even pride themselves on not being guided by such a conception of the overall order as can be obtained only by what they call 'abstract speculation', by no means increases our power of shaping a desirable order, but in fact deprives us of all effective guidance for successful action. The spurious 'realism' which deceives itself in believing that it can dispense with any guiding conception of the nature of the overall order, and confines itself to an examination of particular 'techniques' for achieving particular results, is in reality highly unrealistic. Especially when this attitude leads, as it frequently does, to a judgment of the advisability of particular measures by consideration of the 'practicability' in the given political climate of opinion, it often tends merely to drive us further into an impasse. Such must be the ultimate results of successive measures which all tend to destroy the overall order that their advocates at the same time tacitly assume to exist.

It is not to be denied that to some extent the guiding model of the overall order will always be an utopia, something to which the existing situation will be only a distant approximation and which many people will regard as wholly impractical. Yet it is only by constantly holding up the guiding conception of an internally consistent model which could be realized by the consistent application of the same principles, that anything like an effective framework for a functioning spontaneous order will be achieved. Adam Smith thought that 'to expect, indeed, that freedom of trade should ever be entirely restored in Great Britain is as absurd as to expect an Oceana or Utopia should ever be established in it.'[14] Yet seventy years later, largely as a result of his work, it was achieved.

Utopia, like ideology, is a bad word today; and it is true that most utopias aim at radically redesigning society and suffer from internal contradictions which make their realization impossible. But an ideal picture of a society which may not be wholly achievable, or a guiding conception of the overall order to be aimed at, is nevertheless not only the indispensable precondition of any rational policy, but also the chief contribution that science can make to the solution of the problems of practical policy.

The Role of the Lawyer in Political Evolution

The chief instrument of deliberate change in modern society is legislation. But however carefully we may think out beforehand every single act of law-making, we are never free to redesign completely the legal system as a whole, or to remake it out of the whole cloth according to a coherent design. Law-making is necessarily a continuous process in which every step produces hitherto unforeseen consequences for what we can or must do next. The parts of a legal system are not so much adjusted to each other according to a comprehensive overall view, as gradually adapted to each other by the successive application of general principles to particular problems — principles, that is, which are often not even explicitly known but merely implicit in the particular measures that are taken. For those who imagine it possible to arrange deliberately all the particular activities of a Great Society according to a coherent plan, it should indeed be a sobering reflection that this has not proved possible even for such a part of the whole as the system of law. Few facts show more clearly how prevailing conceptions will bring about a continuous change, producing measures that in the beginning nobody had desired or foreseen but which appear inevitable in due course, than the process of the change of law. Every single step in this process is determined by problems that arise when the principles laid down by (or implicit in) earlier decisions are applied to circumstances which were then not foreseen. There is nothing specially mysterious about these 'inner dynamics of the law' which produce change not willed as a whole by anybody.

In this process the individual lawyer is necessarily more an unwitting tool, a link in a chain of events that he does not see as a whole, than a conscious initiator. Whether he acts as a judge or as the drafter of a statute, the framework of general conceptions into which we must fit his decision is given to him, and his task is to apply these general principles of the law, not to question them. However much he may be concerned about the future implications of his decisions, he can judge them only in the context of all the other recognized principles of the law that are given to him. This is, of course, as it ought to be; it is of the essence of legal thinking and of just decisions that the lawyer strives to make the whole system consistent.

It is often said that the professional bias of the lawyer is conservative.[15] In certain conditions, namely when some basic principles of the law have been accepted for a long time, they will indeed govern the whole system of law, its general spirit as well as every single rule and application within it. At such times it will possess great inherent stability. Every lawyer will, when he has to interpret or apply a rule which is not in accord with the rest of the system, endeavour so to bend it as to make it conform with the others. The legal profession as a whole may thus occasionally in effect even nullify the intention of the legislator, not out of disrespect for the law, but, on the contrary, because their technique leads them to give preference to what is still the predominant part of the law and to fit an alien element into it by so transforming it as to make it harmonize with the whole.

The situation is entirely different, however, when a general philosophy of the law which is not in accord with the greater part of the existing law has recently gained ascendancy. The same lawyers will, through the same habits and techniques, and generally as unwittingly, become a revolutionary force, as effective in transforming the law down to every detail as they were before in preserving it. The same forces which in the first condition make for lack of movement, will in the second tend to accelerate change until it has transformed the whole body of law much beyond the point that anyone foresaw or desired. Whether this process will lead to a new equilibrium or to a disintegration of the whole body of law in the sense in which we still chiefly understand the word, will depend on the character of the new philosophy.

We live in such a period of transformation of the law by inner forces and it is submitted that, if the principles which at present guide that process are allowed to work themselves out to their logical consequences, law as we know it as the chief protection of the freedom of the individual is bound to disappear. Already the lawyers in many fields have, as the instrument of a general conception which they have not made, become the tools, not of principles of justice, but of an apparatus in which the individual is made to serve the ends of his rulers. Legal thinking appears already to be governed to such an extent by new conceptions of the functions of law that, if these conceptions were consistently applied, the whole system of rules of individual conduct would be transformed into a system of rules of organization.

These developments have indeed been noticed with apprehension by many professional lawyers whose chief concern is still with what is sometimes described as 'lawyer's law', that is, those rules of just conduct which at one time were regarded as *the* law. But the leadership in jurisprudence, in the course of the process we have described, has shifted from the practitioners of private law to the public lawyer, with the result that today the philosophical preconceptions which govern the development of all law, including the private law, are almost entirely fashioned by men whose main concern is the public law or the rules of organization of government.

The Modern Development of Law Has Been Guided Largely by False Economics

It would, however, be unjust to blame the lawyers for this state of affairs more than the economists. The practising lawyer will indeed in general best perform his task if he just applies the general principles of the law which he has learned and which it is his duty consistently to apply. It is only in the theory of law, in the formulation and elaboration of those general principles, that the basic problem of their relation to a viable order of actions arises. For such a formulation and elaboration, an understanding of this order is absolutely essential if any intelligent choice between alternative principles is to be made. During the last two or three generations, however, a misunderstanding rather than an understanding of the character of this order has guided legal philosophy.

The economists in their turn, at least after the time of David Hume and Adam Smith, who were also philosophers of law, certainly showed no more appreciation of the significance of the system of legal rules, the existence of which was tacitly presupposed by their argument. They rarely put their account of the determination of a spontaneous order in a form which could be of much use to the legal theorist. But they have probably contributed unknowingly as much to the transformation of the whole social order as the lawyers have done.

This becomes evident when we examine the reason regularly given by the lawyers for the great changes that the character of law has undergone during the last hundred years. Everywhere, whether it be in English or American, French or German legal literature, we find alleged economic necessities given as the reasons for these changes. To the economist, reading the account by which the lawyers explain the transformation of the law, is a somewhat melancholy experience: he finds all the sins of his predecessors visited upon him. Accounts of the modern development of law are full of references to 'irreversible compelling forces' and 'inevitable tendencies' which are alleged to have imperatively called for the particular changes. The fact that 'all modern democracies' did this or that is adduced as proof of the wisdom or necessity of such changes.

These accounts invariably speak of a past *laissez-faire* period, as if there had been a time when no efforts were made to improve the legal framework so as to make the market operate more beneficially or to supplement its results. Almost without exception they base their argument on the *fable convenue* that free enterprise has operated to the disadvantage of the manual workers, and allege that 'early capitalism' or 'liberalism' had brought about a decline in the material standard of the working class. The legend, although wholly untrue,[16] has become part of the folklore of our time. The fact is, of course, that as the result of the growth of free markets, the reward of manual labour has during the past hundred and fifty years experienced an increase unknown in any earlier period of history. Most contemporary works on legal philosophy are full also of outdated clichés about the alleged self-destructive tendency of competition, or the need for 'planning' created by the increased complexity of the modern world, clichés deriving from the high tide of enthusiasm for 'planning' of thirty or forty years ago, when it was widely accepted and its totalitarian implications not yet clearly understood.

It is indeed doubtful whether as much false economics has been spread during the last hundred years by any other means as by the teaching of the young lawyers by their elders that 'it was necessary' this or that should have been done, or that such and such circumstances 'made it inevitable' that certain measures should be taken. It seems almost to be a habit of thought of the lawyer to regard the fact that the legislature has decided on something as evidence of the wisdom of that decision. This means, however, that his efforts will be beneficial or pernicious according to the wisdom or foolishness of the precedents by which he is guided, and that he is as likely to become the perpetuator of the errors as of the wisdom of the past. If he accepts as mandatory for him the observable trend of development, he is as likely to become simply the instrument through which changes he does not understand work themselves out as the conscious creator of a new order. In such a condition it will be necessary to seek for criteria of the desirability of developments elsewhere than within the science of law.

This is not to say that economics alone provides the principles that ought to guide legislation — although considering the influence that economic conceptions inevitably exercise, one must wish that such influence would come from good economics and not from that collection of myths and fables about economic development which seem today to govern legal thinking. Our contention is rather that the principles and preconceptions which guide the development of law inevitably come in part from outside the law and can be beneficial only if they are based on a true conception about how the activities in a Great Society can be effectively ordered.

The role of the lawyer in social evolution and the manner in which his actions are determined are indeed the best illustration of a truth of fundamental importance: namely that, whether we want it or not, the decisive factors which will determine that evolution will always be highly abstract and often unconsciously held ideas about what is right and proper, and not particular purposes or concrete desires. It is not so much what men consciously aim at, as their opinions about permissible methods, which determine not only what will be done but also whether anyone will have the power of doing it. This is the message reiterated by the greatest students of social affairs and always disregarded, namely that 'though men be much more governed by interest yet even interest itself, and all human affairs, are entirely governed by *opinion*.'[17]

Few contentions meet with such disbelief from most practical men, and are so much disregarded by the dominant school of political thought, as that, what is contemptuously dubbed as an ideology, has dominant power over those who believe themselves to be free from it even more than over those who consciously embrace it. Yet there are few things which must impress themselves more strongly on the student of the evolution of social institutions than the fact that what decisively determines them are not good or bad intentions concerning their immediate consequences, but the general preconceptions in terms of which particular issues are decided.

The power of abstract ideas rests largely on the very fact that they are not consciously held as theories but are treated by most people as self-evident truths which act as tacit presuppositions. That this dominant power of ideas is so rarely admitted is largely due to the oversimplified manner in which it is often asserted, suggesting that some great mind had the power of impressing on succeeding generations their particular conceptions. But which ideas will dominate, mostly without people ever being aware of them, is, of course, determined by a slow and immensely intricate process which we can rarely reconstruct in outline even in retrospect. It is certainly humbling to have to admit that our present decisions are determined by what happened long ago in a remote specialty without the general public ever knowing about it, and without those who first formulated the new conception being aware of what would be its consequences, particularly when it was not a discovery of new facts but a general philosophical conception which later affected particular decisions. These opinions not only the 'men in the street', but also the experts in the particular fields, accept unreflectingly and in general simply because they happen to be 'modern.'

It is necessary to realize that the sources of many of the most harmful agents in this world are often not evil men but highminded idealists, and that in particular the foundations of totalitarian barbarism have been laid by honourable and well-meaning scholars who never recognized the offspring they produced.[18] The fact is that, especially in the legal field, certain guiding philosophical preconceptions have brought about a situation where well-meaning theorists, highly admired to the present day even in free countries, have already worked out all the basic conceptions of a totalitarian order. Indeed, the communists, no less than the fascists or national socialists, had merely to use conceptions provided by generations of legal theorists in order to arrive at their doctrines.

What concerns us here is, however, not so much the past as the present. In spite of the collapse of the totalitarian regimes in the western world, their basic ideas have in the theoretical sphere continued to gain ground, so much so that to transform completely the legal system into a totalitarian one all that is needed now is to allow the ideas already reigning in the abstract sphere to be translated into practice.

Nowhere can this situation be more clearly seen than in Germany, which not only has largely provided the rest of the world with the philosophical conceptions that have produced the totalitarian regimes, but which also has been one of the first to succumb to this product of conceptions nurtured in the abstract sphere. Although the average German has by his experience probably been thoroughly purged of any conscious leaning towards the recognizable manifestations of totalitarianism, the basic philosophical conceptions have merely retreated into the abstract sphere, and now lurk in the hearts of grave and highly respected scholars, ready, unless discredited in time, again to take control of developments.

There is indeed no better illustration or more explicit statement of the manner in which philosophical conceptions about the nature of the social order affect the development of law than the theories of Carl Schmitt who, long before Hitler came to power, directed all his formidable intellectual energies to a fight against liberalism in all its forms;[19] who then became one of Hitler's chief legal apologists and still enjoys great influence among German legal philosophers and public lawyers; and whose characteristic terminology is as readily employed by German socialists as by conservative philosophers. His central belief, as he finally formulated it, is that from the 'normative' thinking of the liberal tradition law has gradually advanced through a 'decisionist' phase in which the will of the legislative authorities decided on particular matters, to the conception of a 'concrete order formation', a development which involves 'a reinterpretation of an ideal of the *nomos* as a total conception of law importing a concrete order and community.'[20] In other words, law is not to consist of abstract rules which make possible the formation of a spontaneous order by the free action of individuals through limiting the range of their actions, but is to be the instrument of arrangement or organization by which the individual is made to serve concrete purposes. This is the inevitable outcome of an intellectual development in which the self-ordering forces of society and the role of law in an ordering mechanism are no longer understood.

NOTES

1. See F. A. Hayek, *The Constitution of Liberty* (London and Chicago, 1960).

2. Adam Smith, *Wealth of Nations*, edited by E. Cannan (London, 1930), vol. 2, p. 184; see also John Locke, *Second Treatise on Government*, edited by P. Laslett (Cambridge, 1960), section 22: 'a liberty to follow my own will in all things, where the rules prescribe not.'

3. See A. V. Dicey, *Lectures on the Relation between Law and Public Opinion during the Nineteenth Century* (London, 1914), p. 257:

> The beneficial effect of State intervention, especially in the form of legislation, is direct, immediate, and so to speak visible, whilst its evil effects are gradual and indirect, and lie outside our sight. . . . Hence the majority of mankind must almost of necessity look with undue favour upon government intervention. This natural bias can be counteracted only by the existence, in a given society, . . . of a presumption or prejudice in favour of individual liberty, that is of *laissez-faire*.

Similarly, E. Küng, *Der Interventionismus* (Bern, 1941), p. 360: 'Die günstigen und gewollten Nachwirkungen der meisten wirtschaftspolitischen Massnahmen treten kurz nach ihrer Inkraftsetzung auf, die manchmal schwerer wirkenden Fernwirkungen erst später.'

4. As has been preached with such far-reaching effect on the American intellectuals by John Dewey: see for example, his essay 'Force and coercion,' *International Journal of Ethics*, xvi, 1916, especially p. 362. 'Whether the use of force is justified or not . . . is, in substance, a question of efficiency (including economy) of means in the accomplishment of ends.'

5. Benjamin Constant, 'De l'arbitraire', in *Oeuvres politiques*, edited by C. Louandre (Paris, 1874), pp. 71 – 72.

6. Frederic Bastiat, *Ce qu'on voit et ce qu'on ne voit pas en economie politique* (Paris, 1850), English translation in his *Selected Essays in Political Economy*, edited by G. B. de Huszar (Princeton, 1964), his last and most brilliant essay.

7. Carl Menger, *Problems of Economics and Sociology*, edited by L. Schneider (Urbana, Ill., 1963).

8. See W. Y. Elliott, *The Pragmatic Revolt in Politics* (New York, 1928).

9. On these lines particularly R. A. Dahl and Charles Lindblom, *Politics, Economics, and Welfare* (New York, 1953), pp. 3 – 18, e.g. p. 16:

'Techniques and not "isms" are the kernel of rational action in the Western world. Both socialism and capitalism are dead.' This is precisely the cause of our drift.

10. London and Chicago, 1944.

11. See Preface to W. S. Jevons, *The State in Relation to Labour* (London, 1882).

12. Herbert Spencer, *Justice: Being Part IV of the Principles of Ethics* (London, 1891), p. 44.

13. J. A. Schumpeter, *History of Economic Analysis* (New York, 1954), p. 394.

14. Adam Smith, op. cit. vol. I, p. 435.

15. See for example, Max Weber, *On Law in Economy and Society*, edited by Max Rheinstein (Cambridge, Mass., 1954), p. 298.

16. See the essays on *Capitalism and the Historians*, by various authors, edited by the present writer (London and Chicago, 1953).

17. David Hume, *Essays*, in *Works* III, p. 125, and compare the passages by J. S. Mill and Lord Keynes quoted on p. 113 and in note 14 to ch. 6 of my book, *The Constitution of Liberty*, to which may now be added a similar statement by G. Mazzini which I have seen quoted without source: 'Ideas rule the world and its events. A revolution is the passage of an idea from theory to practice. Whatever men say, material interests never have caused, and never will cause a revolution.'

18. It was therefore also not, as J. A. Schumpeter kindly suggested in a review of *The Road to Serfdom* in *Journal of Political Economy*, xiv, 1946, 'politeness to a fault' but profound conviction about what are the decisive factors if that book 'hardly ever attributes to opponents anything beyond intellectual error.'

19. As one of Carl Schmitt's followers, George Dahm, reviewing Schmitt's *Drei Arten des rechtswissenschaftlichen Denkens* (Hamburg, 1934), in *Zeitschrift für die gesamte Staatswissenschaft*, xcv, 1935, p. 181, wrote, all Schmitt's works 'sind von Anfang an auf ein bestimmtes Ziel gerichtet gewesen: die Entlarvung und Zerstörung des liberalen Rechtsstaates und die Überwindung des Gesetzgebungsstaates.' The most appropriate comment on Schmitt came from Johannes Huizinga, *Homo Ludens* (1944), English translation (London, 1947), p. 209:

> I know of no sadder and deeper fall from human reason than Schmitt's barbarous and pathetic delusion about the friend-foe principle. His inhuman cerebrations do not even hold water as a piece of formal logic. For it is not war that is serious but peace. . . . Only by transcending this pitiable friend-foe relationship will mankind enter into the dignity of man's estate. Schmitt's brand of 'seriousness' merely takes us back to the savage level.

20. See Carl Schmitt, op. cit., p. 11 et seq.

The Origins and Effects of Our Morals: A Problem for Science

·17·

What I propose to do in this lecture is to try condensing into manageable size the discussion of the topic indicated by the title, which as a draft chapter of the book I am working on exploded into unmanageable dimensions, by approaching it from a different angle. I will start out from one of my contentions of the preceding chapter in which I discuss the differences between the mechanics of organic, or Darwinian, and of cultural evolution. Next to the fact that the latter rests of course on the inheritance of acquired characteristics, the most important one seems to me now that cultural evolution is founded wholly on group selection, which in biological evolution seems to play only a minor role, if that. My chief contention will be that we owe to this fact that in some respects our morals endow us with capacities greater than our reason could do, namely the ability to adapt to conditions of which the individual mind could never be aware. It seems to me that what is sometimes called the "collective mind" of the group is nothing but the common moral tradition of its members, something different from and autonomous of the individual reasons, though of course constantly interacting with them.

The fact that cultural evolution operates chiefly through group selection has very important consequences. It is the reason why, as

---

From a speech delivered at the Hoover Institution, November 1, 1983.

David Hume so clearly understood, "the rules of morality are not the conclusions of our reason." The human groups have been selected for the effects of their habitual practices, effects of which the individuals were not and could not be aware. Customs are mostly group properties, beneficial only if they are common properties of its individual members but referring to reciprocal action. Morals have not only been designed by man, but man also usually does not understand their reason. In some fields, such as language and law, the fact that these institutions could develop only through group selection is obvious: language could clearly be of no use to its sole possessor, and the benefits derived from it will normally accrue to all those who can communicate through it. All the paradigms of culturally evolved institutions, morals, exchange, and money refer to such practices whose benefits transcend the individuals who practice them in the particular instances. The result is that whole groups may be helped by them to expand into what I shall call extended orders, through the effects of practices of which the individuals are not aware. Such practices can lead to the formation of orderly structures far exceeding the perception of those whose actions produce them. They make possible the adaptation of such actions to unknown circumstances and lead to the formation of an indefinitely expansible order which can develop only through group selection, that is, a selection of groups for common attributes possessed by them. They make possible the adaptation of such actions to unknown circumstances and lead to the formation of an indefinitely expansible order which can develop only through group selection, that is, a selection of groups for common attributes possessed by their members.

We may retrospectively discover at least the general character of the process that has produced the existing order of the division of labour, and this is, as we shall see, what political economy (or, as I prefer to call it, catallactics) has done. Its Scottish founders, David Hume, Adam Ferguson, and Adam Smith, also developed in this process those twin concepts of spontaneous order and evolution that have become the universal key to the explanation of all highly complex phenomena for which man formerly had to resort to the anthropomorphic explanation of design or creation by one manlike maker. Adam Smith's famous "invisible hand," still the butt of the mockery of silly rationalists, was in fact a very good name for the process of adaptation to effects mostly invisible to any human actor. That Charles Darwin was the first to produce convincing evidence for the operation of a process of selective evolution in the formation of biological species, for which he deserves the greatest possible admiration, but for which he and his successors elaborated a mechanism not directly applicable to cultural evolution, ought not to have deterred students of human interaction from continuing to develop for their purposes the original conception of the evolution of human institutions which, though operating through a different mechanism, still relies on the same principles of selection, namely the multiplication of individual lives. "Social Darwinism" was no doubt a mistake.

Since I have long argued that the conception of evolution originated in the humanities, I might perhaps mention that it has given me great satisfaction to discover recently that even the term "genetic" was first used (in German) by Herder, Wieland, and Schiller in the eighteenth century and by Wilhelm von Humboldt in the nineteenth in connection with the formation of language before it was introduced into English by Thomas Carlyle, and was still employed in its original sense by the economist Carl Menger, and that it was only seventy years ago that William Bateson made it an exclusive technical term for biological evolution through the title of a famous book.

But, to return to my central argument: the fact that the tradition of moral rules contains adaptions to circumstances in our environment which are not accessible by individual observation or not perceptible by reason, and that our morals are therefore a human equipment that is not only a creation of reason, but even in some respects superior to it because it contains guides to human action which reason alone could never have discovered or justified, explains why the value of traditional morals as an autonomous equipment is unintelligible to those intellectuals who are committed to a strict rationalism or positivism. A rationalist who "denies the acceptability of beliefs founded on anything but experience and reasoning," or a positivist believing that all "true knowledge is scientific in the sense of describing the coexistence and succession of observable phenomena" or even a believer in any "hedonistic ethics, utilitarianism [which] takes the pleasure and pain of everyone affected by it to be the criteria of an action's rightness" (these are all the very representative definitions of these concepts by Antony Quinton in the convenient *Fontana Dictionary of Modern Thought*) must reject traditional ethics as irrational. When one of the most influential thinkers of the last generation, John Maynard Keynes, could declare "I remain, and always will remain, an immoralist" (1938), and "conventional wisdom" became the pitying phrase with which the typical intellectual disposed of all conservative beliefs, it had profound political consequences. It is no exaggeration to say that the central aim of socialism is to discredit those traditional morals which keep us alive.

The two crucial groups of rules of conduct which the arrogance of the human intellect began to question because they were not the conclusions of our reason but wholly the product of cultural selections were those of several property (or, as David Hume described them, the rules of the stability of possessions, its transference by consent, and the keeping of promises) and those concerning the family. They are the chief rules of morals which are not intellectually founded and for this reason have, for the past two thousand years, been the object of recurrent attacks from rationalist reformers who, however, have themselves never succeeded in building a lasting community based on their anti-property and anti-family doctrines. Today I shall have to confine myself to the sources of the constant revolts of the intellectuals against the institution of several property, especially in the means of production, which became the foundation of socialism. It was Adam Smith who had recognized that it was the distinctly human product of cultural evolution, namely several property, that has become the foundation of human civilization. As he put it, "Nobody ever saw one animal by its gestures and natural cries signify to another this is mine, that is yours" (*Wealth of Nations*, p. 26). It is this product of cultural selection of which socialism now wants to deprive us, and it is this characteristic of socialism which makes me argue that socialism is not even half right but all wrong.

The full bearing of the profound insight with respect to the value of traditional morals at which David Hume arrived two hundred and fifty years ago is still far from being generally comprehended, and the failure to do so is the reason why the widespread opposition to the moral tradition by rationalist intellectuals is still far from being conclusively refuted. The insight shows that man owes some of his most important endowments, which enabled him to keep milliards of his kind alive through the operation of an extended order transcending anyone's perception, to an attitude which he acquired because group selection favoured in the process of cultural evolution those groups whose traditional rules of conduct enabled them through the market to adapt their actions to effects of which they were not aware. This undesigned moral tradition became an autonomous endowment of man, interacting with, yet different from, reason; and it is as indispensable for the formation of the extended order as reason itself.

This restatement was necessary to prepare for my next point: the conclusion that socialism is the logical consequence of rationalism does not mean that socialism is right, but rather that rationalist judgment of morals is mistaken. Man was neither clever enough to design the order from which billions of his kind now draw their sustenance nor even to recognize what he would have to know in order to direct these efforts successfully. What enabled him to achieve this was obedience to traditional customs which were selected by group evolution without his understanding them. We do not owe our ability to keep two hundred times as many human beings alive than we could five thousand years ago solely, or even chiefly, to our growing intellectual insight into scientific and technological problems, but at least as much, if not more, to a moral tradition of which both our innate instincts and our attempts at rational comprehension largely disapprove — a tradition which was kept alive essentially by a faith in supernatural forces which science now teaches us is factually wrong. As Adam Smith understood, it was "religion [which] in its crudest form gave a sanction to the rules of morality, long before the age of artificial reasoning and philosophy" (*Theory of Moral Sentiments*, p. 273). In fact, even agnostics ought to be grateful to the religious traditions which, for reasons they cannot accept, have preserved long enough those nonrational beliefs that made available the building elements of the extended order which we call civilization.

This order, as we can now recognize, is the product of the institution of several property which developed, not because some liked or understood its effects, but because it made possible the growth of the groups practising it to grow faster than others. Adam Smith of course also understood that "the most decisive mark of the prosperity of any country is the increase of the number of its inhabitants" (*Wealth of Nations*, p. 87). That the adoption of the convention of respecting individual property and the determination of prices on a competitive market were the only ways in which man could become able to exploit discoverable resources so intensely as to raise his increasing numbers seems to me incontestable; this *is* still contested by some who have missed the central teaching of economics.

I have to admit that even after sixty years as a professional economist, I can still see how difficult it must be for the layman to understand that with an equal, or even with a "just," distribution of the product, nearly all would have much less than they have now—for the existing world population probably not even enough to maintain its numbers. The present magnitude of the total product is a result of the inequality of its distribution—or more exactly, the result of the expectation of very difficult renumeration for the alternative uses of various skills and knowledge, expectations which alone can tell the individuals from moment to moment what to do to add to the aggregate.

The wishfully invented morals according to which each ought to have what he deserves in the light of his perceived merits or needs (already two conflicting criteria) are irreconcilable not only with personal freedom, but also with the guide mechanism that alone can tell the individual how to contribute as much as he can to the common product. Several property in the means of production is irreconcilable with a just distribution of the product, but it is an indispensable condition for the existence of this product in anything like its present size. Socialists offer us as a superior moral what is, in fact, a very inferior morality, yet alluring because they promise greater pleasure or enjoyment to people they would be unable to feed.

We do not have to deal, as some imagine, with a given product whose size is determined by generally known physical or technological facts. We must face the truth that it is not the magnitude of a given aggregate product which allows us to decide what to do with it, but rather the other way around: that a process which tells us how to reward the several contributions to this product is also the indispensable source of information for the individuals, telling them where they can make the aggregate product as large as possible. It is the relative renumeration of all the different factors of production by the market which alone can show us how we must arrange them to make the product as large as we can. This means not merely that only a very unequal distribution of incomes, but even only one whose particular order we cannot intellectually account for, will enable us to achieve an overall product sufficient to feed existing mankind.

The silliest sentence ever penned by a famous economist—and the one with the gravest consequences (the conversion of all the master's pupils, I believe, to Fabian socialism)—John Stuart Mill's "once the product is there, mankind, individually or collectively, can do with it whatever it pleases" is really an incredible stupidity, showing a complete unawareness of the crucial guide function of prices that informs us of the significant effects of remote events of which we know nothing. There is probably no better instance showing how this understanding was completely blocked by the classical labour theory of value — or any other belief in a causal determination of value by any particular antecedent event.

To return to the problem of evolution: the first requirement if such practices are to spread whose beneficial effects are not perceived by the individuals is that they are maintained long enough, or sufficiently stabilized, to become part of the generally expected conduct, and produce a sort of order whose advantages could operate during a prolonged period of competition with other orders. Since the effects which give a group this selective advantage are not known to the acting individuals, some other common beliefs must secure the stability of a tradition of group practices. The selection among alternative traditions will be affected by their different support to the proliferation of the group. Both the traditional rules of conduct and the beliefs which supported them had essentially the character of faiths, not recognized means for particular ends, but rather like conditions for membership of a group — or signs that made them recognizable as such to each other. The inducements to the kinds of actions which served the group better than other usages, and which were therefore regarded as "right," usually took the form of a threat of punishment which served as an effective restraint confining action to whichever was generally beneficial to the group as a whole. It was these "symbolic truths" of the religions, as we might call them, that alone were able to guide men in such a way that they had better prospects to "grow and multiply and conquer the world" than other beliefs.

Group selection thus does not primarily choose what the individuals recognize as serving their own ends, or what they desire. It will elect customs whose beneficial assistance to the survival of men are not perceived by the individuals. The group thereby becomes dependent for the very survival of its increased numbers on the observance by its members of practices which they cannot rationally justify, and which may conflict with both their innate instincts on the one hand, and their intellectual insight on the other. No doubt a society may be more successful because of its distinct moral tradition — as I believe the English were for a long time and the Swiss still are.

However, all this applies only to the grown morals of tradition and not to morals which have been invented to serve the satisfaction of human desires. But it seems to me to show that the whole conception of morals serving human pleasures is wrong and that in their very nature morals are traditional restraints placed on the pursuit of human pleasures, not by reason but by what has sometimes misleading been called "group experience." Hedonistic, utilitarian, or egalitarian morals, or conceptions like distributive justice, are all intellectual inventions which have never been tested and have never been shown that they improve, or even could secure, the preservation of the group. It is neither the striving for beauty, nor for justice, nor any other foreseen or intended aim of human evolution, which can perform the necessary function that alone selectively evoked morals can perform, namely to enhance the production of, or to maintain, more lives. The best illustration of the contemporary striving to manipulate morals to serve an invented ideal of human relations I have yet come across is probably the comment of a modern British philosopher on David Hume's interpretation of human morals: he argues that "although Hume uses the expression 'rules of conduct' to cover such things as property rules, 'justice' is now analytically tied to 'desert' and 'need,' so that one could quite properly say that some of what Hume calls 'rules of justice' were unjust" (B. M. Barry, *Analysis*, 1961:80). By "redefining" moral concepts one can of course try to turn them into tools for the satisfaction of our wishes, but at the same time they lose the power to guide us beyond the range of our conscious aims.

To demonstrate that rationalism may be wrong and that traditional morals may in some respects provide a surer guide to human action than rational knowledge is the main contention of this lecture.

The recognition of the limits of the powers of human reason has of course been the ultimate conclusion of many of our great thinkers of the past. Only since the seventeenth century has the hubris of modern man tended to forget this. Sir Karl Popper's new conception of "world 3" tends to correct this, though it will have to be a *very* critical rationalism to undo the harm which Cartesianism has done with its thesis that we ought not to believe anything which we cannot rationally prove, and to repair all the damage that the constructivistic conception of "social engineering" is constantly doing.

It seems to me that the limitations of the possible powers of reason and even the acceptance of some purely nonrational traditions can be justified by reason at least as well as, let us say, by relying on probabilities based on observed frequencies. I believe that I obey reason if I submit to traditional rules which I cannot rationally justify as long as I have, in the particular case, no strong rational grounds to the contrary, especially if there is no conflict with other similar rules which I am also inclined to accept. And I believe that one of the greatest achievements so far in discovering the unseen functions of traditional practices is the legitimation of several property by catallactics which now gives us a real chance of gradually improving its operation by eliminating all results of socialist misconceptions.

The exclusive reliance on rational insight as sufficient ground for human action is a grave intellectual error to which those secondhand dealers in ideas who regard themselves as intellectuals seem to be particularly prone. One might almost define them as those who are not intelligent enough to recognize the limits of reason and who in consequence deprive us of the only guide that has enabled us to produce order by structures based on more information than any human agency can use. Logically a strict rationalist or positivist is indeed bound to believe in central planning and socialism, and it is indeed quite difficult to find a positivist who is not a socialist.

I believe that the science of catallactics can demonstrate that the dispersed and market-determined distribution of property in the means of production is the only condition under which men can employ their, of necessity equally dispersed, abilities to make use of the greatest amount of information possible, and that this process can function only if those who dispose of this property are rewarded not according to some recognizable merit (or "justice"), but according to actual success.

It must be admitted, however, that some economists have blinded themselves to this insight by habitually referring to the relevant facts by the somewhat comic term "given data," which of course means no more than that the theorist must for his purposes *assume* particular facts to exist if he is to account for their effects without his or any other known person's having actual knowledge of them. His retrospective interpretation of how the market system operates does, however, not mean that we are now able to replace it by some deliberate arrangement. On the contrary, it proves that this is impossible, and that all we can do is to try by deliberate competitive experimentation gradually to improve the grown institutions which have enabled us to use so much more information than anyone possesses.

It may at first seem as if there exists a contradiction between the claim that we can explain how the rules of moral conduct were formed and to describe the effect they had on the general character of the resulting order on the one hand, and the assertion on the other that it is beyond our power to construct a wholly new and more beneficial system of morals. But this conclusion is indeed a necessary implication of the explanation I have given. If it is true that the selection of traditional rules of conduct produces an adaptation of men's actions to circumstances of which the individual minds cannot be aware, it also means that the explanation which we can give must be confined to a mere "explanation of the principle," as I have called it, enabling us not to decide what particular results will be produced by this process. Knowledge of our ignorance may be very important, especially if we recognize that we possess ways of adapting our actions to unknown facts. To somebody whose conception of science was shaped by mechanics, catallactics may well not look like science, but as the theories of natural phenomena advanced into more complex fields (even organic chemistry, or biology in particular), they came to look more and more like catallactics: the theory of biological evolution is as incapable of predictions of specific events as catallactics and was not confirmed by falsification since it could not make any specific predictions, or ever ascertain all the relevant marginal conditions, but was confined to asserting the probability of the formation of certain kinds of patterns or structures.

Catallactics is in fact an attempt to discover in retrospect why man succeeded to do better than he ever foresaw or understood. It is a sort of rational reconstruction of what he did not and could not have done deliberately on the fictitious assumption that the explainer knows the particular facts to the discovery of which the market prices guide the individuals. I am inclined to claim that only an economist, i.e. someone who understands the process of the formation of the extended order of cooperation, can explain the selective evolution of the morals of property and honesty — how they arose as well as what effects they had on the development of mankind. They are matters which are problems of science and not value problems. Socialism is of course an endeavour to persuade us to accept other and, as its advocates believe, better morals than those which have guided the development of Western civilization. Socialists try to immunize their proposals against scientific refutation by appealing to the principle of value freedom of science. But whether they can fulfill their promises and what would be the effects of the application of their proposals are questions of fact which only science is competent to answer. The question of desirability of the socialist programme arises only after the possibility of the achievement of its ends is made at least probable, but becomes wholly irrelevant if it is shown to be altogether impossible.

Socialism owes much of its support to the rationalists' animosity towards the traditional restraints on the pursuit of man's innate instincts. It hopes to guide cultural evolution in a direction where it will more fully gratify our pleasure, especially the enjoyment of beauty and the just reward of merits. But this conflicts with the fundamental function of morals: to keep alive that part of mankind which we feed only through the constant adaptation to incessant unforeseeable changes which enabled us to raise them in the first instance. Morals are not a matter of taste. They are very necessary but most unwelcome restraints telling us which of the things we would instinctively like to do we must not do if we are to preserve an order on which most of us depend for our survival but which we have neither made nor learnt to understand. The idea that morals are a device to get us what we want is wholly erroneous. On the contrary, they are a learned restraint which tells us which wishes we must forgo, initially to secure the survival of more men than we otherwise could, but soon in order merely to maintain the numbers of men which the extended order of human interaction has enabled us to raise. Karl Marx was perfectly right when he said that capitalism had created the proletariat. But it did so not by expropriating anybody of possessions they had, but by enabling many people to survive without owning any property of their own and who at least could not have raised offspring if others had not supplied them with tools.

We must resign ourselves to the fact that our morals do not lead us where we wish to go, that in particular they do not produce beauty, pleasure, or generally guide us to what we want, but rather warn us not to pursue some short ways to what we desire because to do so would cause damage to the order on which we all count to achieve what is possible. To put it crudely, our morals are materialistic and not idealistic, and must be so because their first function is to keep us alive, which they do in a manner that we still understand only imperfectly.

I can sympathize with the desire that man ought to direct his own evolution, but if this means that he ought to direct it to satisfy his pleasure, or towards what appears to him now noble and beautiful, I fear that he is wholly mistaken. Man has become as intelligent as he is because he did *not* go where he wished. If he had been allowed to follow his innate emotions, or to do what he liked, he would certainly never have achieved the powers which his intellect now confers on him. *The Fatal Conceit*, which is the subject of the book on which I am working, is devoted precisely to refute the erroneous belief that *Man Has Made Himself* (V. Gordon Childe, 1936). All of evolution that has increased our power was an adaptation to the as yet unknown. Planned evolution would be the end of evolution itself. Moral evolution in particular does not and cannot move in the direction that man wishes — and, if it did not follow human direction, would soon cease to help preserve what it has created. It would mean the pupil teaching the teacher.

It was my aim today to show how the strict rationalist who denies the acceptability of all beliefs founded on anything but experience and reasoning tends to become a barbarian unless he makes concessions to expediency. This is true even if, as he usually does, he puts aesthetic or other kinds of pleasures as the deliberate goals of his efforts. I sometimes have the impression that in a world that depends on traditions which the individual cannot rationally justify, some of the most intelligent men can become the most dangerous fools, aliens to and disturbers of the civilization in which they live.

We must learn to recognize that what the rationalists have habitually ridiculed as "the dead hand of tradition" may contain conditions for the existence of modern mankind. This appears to me a conclusion to which a sensible use of reason leads, and which at the same time exposes the falsity of the most important conclusions represented as the result of a consistent use of reason. The moral tradition remains a treasure which reason cannot replace, but can only endeavour to improve by immanent criticism, that is, by endeavouring to make a system which we cannot create as a whole, serve more consistently the same set of effects. Systems of morals are self-contained in the sense that all judgments of particular moral values must in turn also be in moral terms. We can judge a particular rule of moral conduct only in terms of a system of such rules which for that purpose we must treat as undoubted. To most people this will be simply part of the environment into which they were born. But to many in the modern world, the adoption of such a system is necessarily a gradual process in which each starts from the beliefs of his family and locality, and gradually moves to another system that he learns to regard as being in some sense superior. In this process the temptation to let oneself be guided by nonmoral considerations would clearly be very strong. In particular, desirable effects which deviant conduct might appear to have for the individuals or for the group might seem very alluring. But to claim moral superiority for such innovations implies a claim that not merely the particular modification but the whole moral system into which it fits is superior to possible alternatives. Such claims that any moral system is superior to others are today very unpopular, but seem to me implied in all strong moral beliefs. They demand a choice of a moral system as a whole as superior to all others — even if its adherents may be quite unable to see the system in which they believe as a whole.

Man will have to recognize that it is neither his inborn instincts nor his intelligence on which his future chiefly depends. It is his faith in traditional morals, which I fear have been progressively crumbling for the last few generations, a process which is gaining alarming speed. The order of interaction which maintains mankind still depends on it. But its authority has already been gravely weakened, and this has been done chiefly by the supercilious conceit of the so-called intellectuals, those "dupes of their own sophistry," as Adam Smith called them, who conceived that they could invent a better moral which they thought would more fully gratify their desires. Their reformist zeal has been directed in the first instance against that part of our moral tradition on which, as I have tried to show, our very survival mainly depends. They imagine that their invented but untried morals will produce more pleasant results. But that is a wrong standard for judging a system of morals. Morals are not something we can choose at pleasure. At least the general outline of those we have inherited are an irreplaceable means for keeping alive the number of humans they have called into being.

The present trend of opinion makes it seem quite possible that men, because they do not like it, will destroy the moral order that keeps them alive. Once we get into the downward slide with which such a decline will begin, it will be increasingly difficult to stop it. The more emergency measures governments will impose in order to cure particular sufferings, and the more additional powers we will have to give governments for that purpose, the faster the momentum of the descent will become. It seems to me now that at present the establishment of a single world government will merely increase the risk of ultimate complete catastrophe.

It is the humble recognition of the limitations of human reason which forces us to concede superiority to a moral order to which we owe our existence and which has its source *neither* in our innate instincts, which are still those of the savage, nor in our intelligence, which is not great enough to build what is better than it knows, but to a tradition which we must revere and care for even if we continuously experiment with improving its parts — not designing but humbly tinkering on a system which we must accept as given. Human reason's greatest achievement is to recognize not only its own unsurmountable limitations, but also the existence of a gradually evolved set of abstract rules of which it can avail itself to build better than it knows.

EQUALITY, VALUE, AND MERIT

·18·

I have no respect for the passion for equality, which seems to me merely idealizing envy.

Oliver Wendell Holmes, Jr.*

I

The great aim of the struggle for liberty has been equality before the law. This equality under the rules which the state enforces may be supplemented by a similar equality of the rules that men voluntarily obey in their relations with one another. This extension of the principle of equality to the rules of moral and social conduct is the chief expression of what is commonly called the democratic spirit — and probably that aspect of it that does most to make inoffensive the inequalities that liberty necessarily produces.

Equality of the general rules of law and conduct, however, is the only kind of equality conducive to liberty and the only equality which

*From *The Holmes-Laski Letters: The Correspondence of Mr. Justice Holmes and Harold J. Laski, 1916–1935* (Cambridge: Harvard University Press, 1953), II, 942. A German translation of an earlier version of this chapter has appeared in *Ordo*, Vol. X (1958).

we can secure without destroying liberty. Not only has liberty nothing to do with any other sort of equality, but it is even bound to produce inequality in many respects. This is the necessary result and part of the justification of individual liberty: if the result of individual liberty did not demonstrate that some manners of living are more successful than others, much of the case for it would vanish.

It is neither because it assumes that people are in fact equal nor because it attempts to make them equal that the argument for liberty demands that government treat them equally. This argument not only recognizes that individuals are very different but in a great measure rests on that assumption. It insists that these individual differences provide no justification for government to treat them differently. And it objects to the differences in treatment by the state that would be necessary if persons who are in fact very different were to be assured equal positions in life.

Modern advocates of a more far-reaching material equality usually deny that their demands are based on any assumption of the factual equality of all men.[1] It is nevertheless still widely believed that this is the main justification for such demands. Nothing, however, is more damaging to the demand for equal treatment than to base it on so obviously untrue an assumption as that of the factual equality of all men. To rest the case for equal treatment of national or racial minorities on the assertion that they do not differ from other men is implicitly to admit that factual inequality would justify unequal treatment; and the proof that some differences do, in fact, exist would not be long in forthcoming. It is of the essence of the demand for equality before the law that people should be treated alike in spite of the fact that they are different.

II

The boundless variety of human nature — the wide range of differences in individual capacities and potentialities — is one of the most distinctive facts about the human species. Its evolution has made it probably the most variable among all kinds of creatures. It has been well said that "biology, with variability as its cornerstone, confers on every human individual a unique set of attributes which give him a dignity he could not otherwise possess. Every newborn baby is an unknown quantity so far as potentialities are concerned because there are many thousands of unknown interrelated genes and gene-patterns which contribute to his make-up. As a result of nature and nurture the newborn infant may become one of the greatest of men or women ever to have lived. In every case he or she has the making of a distinctive individual. . . . If the differences are not very important, then freedom is not very important and the idea of individual worth is not very important."[2] The writer justly adds that the widely held uniformity theory of human nature, "which on the surface appears to accord with democracy . . . would in time undermine the very basic ideals of freedom and individual worth and render life as we know it meaningless."[3]

It has been the fashion in modern times to minimize the importance of congenital differences between men and to ascribe all the important differences to the influence of environment.[4] However important the latter may be, we must not overlook the fact that individuals are very different from the outset. The importance of individual differences would hardly be less if all people were brought up in very similar environments. As a statement of fact, it just is not true that "all men are born equal." We may continue to use this hallowed phrase to express the ideal that legally and morally all men ought to be treated alike. But if we want to understand what this ideal of equality can or should mean, the first requirement is that we free ourselves from the belief in factual equality.

From the fact that people are very different it follows that, if we treat them equally, the result must be inequality in their actual position,[5] and that the only way to place them in an equal position would be to treat them differently. Equality before the law and material equality are therefore not only different but are in conflict with each other; and we can achieve either the one or the other, but not both at the same time. The equality before the law which freedom requires leads to material inequality. Our argument will be that, though where the state must use coercion for other reasons, it should treat all people alike, the desire of making people more alike in their condition cannot be accepted in a free society as a justification for further and discriminatory coercion.

We do not object to equality as such. It merely happens to be the case that a demand for equality is the professed motive of most of those who desire to impose upon society a preconceived pattern of distribution. Our objection is against all attempts to impress upon society a deliberately chosen pattern of distribution, whether it be an order of equality or of inequality. We shall indeed see that many of those who demand an extension of equality do not really demand equality but a distribution that conforms more closely to human conceptions of individual merit and that their desires are as irreconcilable with freedom as the more strictly egalitarian demands.

If one objects to the use of coercion in order to bring about a more even or a more just distribution, this does not mean that one does not regard these as desirable. But if we wish to preserve a free society, it is essential that we recognize that the desirability of a particular object is not sufficient justification for the use of coercion. One may well feel attracted to a community in which there are no extreme contrasts between rich and poor and may welcome the fact that the general increase in wealth seems gradually to reduce those differences. I fully share these feelings and certainly regard the degree of social equality that the United States has achieved as wholly admirable.

There also seems no reason why these widely felt preferences should not guide policy in some respects. Wherever there is a legitimate need for government action and we have to choose between different methods of satisfying such a need, those that incidentally also reduce inequality may well be preferable. If, for example, in the law of intestate succession one kind of provision will be more conducive to equality than another, this may be a strong argument in its favor. It is a different matter, however, if it is demanded that, in order to produce substantive equality, we should abandon the basic postulate of a free society, namely, the limitation of all coercion by equal law. Against this we shall hold that economic inequality is not one of the evils which justify our resorting to discriminatory coercion or privilege as a remedy.

III

Our contention rests on two basic propositions which probably need only be stated to win fairly general assent. The first of them is an expression of the belief in a certain similarity of all human beings: it is the proposition that no man or group of men possesses the capacity to determine conclusively the potentialities of other human beings and that we should certainly never trust anyone invariably to exercise such a capacity. However great the differences between men may be, we have no ground for believing that they will ever be so great as to enable one man's mind in a particular instance to comprehend fully all that another responsible man's mind is capable of.

The second basic proposition is that the acquisition by any member of the community of additional capacities to do things which may be valuable must always be regarded as a gain for that community. It is true that particular people may be worse off because of the superior ability of some new competitor in their field; but any such additional ability in the community is likely to benefit the majority. This implies that the desirability of increasing the abilities and opportunities of any individual does not depend on whether the same can also be done for the others — provided, of course, that others are not thereby deprived of the opportunity of acquiring the same or other abilities which might have been accessible to them had they not been secured by that individual.

Egalitarians generally regard differently those differences in individual capacities which are inborn and those which are due to the influences of environment, or those which are the result of "nature" and those which are the result of "nurture." Neither, be it said at once, has anything to do with moral merit.[6] Though either may greatly affect the value which an individual has for his fellows, no more credit belongs to him for having been born with desirable qualities than for having grown up under favorable circumstances. The distinction between the two is important only because the former advantages are due to circumstances clearly beyond human control, while the latter are due to factors which we might be able to alter. The important question is whether there is a case for so changing our institutions as to eliminate as much as possible those advantages due to environment. Are we to agree that "all inequalities that rest on birth and inherited property ought to be abolished and none remain unless it is an effect of superior talent and industry"?[7]

The fact that certain advantages rest on human arrangements does not necessarily mean that we could provide the same advantages for all or that, if they are given to some, somebody else is thereby deprived of them. The most important factors to be considered in this connection are the family, inheritance, and education, and it is against the inequality which they produce that criticism is mainly directed. They are, however, not the only important factors of environment. Geographic conditions such as climate and landscape, not to speak of local and sectional differences in cultural and moral traditions, are scarcely less important. We can, however, consider here only the three factors whose effects are most commonly impugned.

So far as the family is concerned, there exists a curious contrast between the esteem most people profess for the institution and their dislike of the fact that being born into a particular family should confer on a person special advantages. It seems to be widely believed that, while useful qualities which a person acquires because of his native gifts under conditions which are the same for all are socially beneficial, the same qualities become somehow undesirable if they are the result of environmental advantages not available to others. Yet it is difficult to see why the same useful quality which is welcomed when it is the result of a person's natural endowment should be less valuable when it is the product of such circumstances as intelligent parents or a good home.

The value which most people attach to the institution of the family rests on the belief that, as a rule, parents can do more to prepare their children for a satisfactory life than anyone else. This means not only that the benefits which particular people derive from their family environment will be different but also that these benefits may operate cumulatively through several generations. What reason can there be for believing that a desirable quality in a person is less valuable to society if it has been the result of family background than if it has not? There is, indeed, good reason to think that there are some socially valuable qualities which will be rarely acquired in a single generation but which will generally be formed only by the continuous efforts of two or three. This means simply that there are parts of the cultural heritage of a society that are more effectively transmitted through the family. Granted this, it would be unreasonable to deny that a society is likely to get a better elite if ascent is not limited to one generation, if individuals are not deliberately made to start from the same level, and if children are not deprived of the chance to benefit from the better education and material environment which their parents may be able to provide. To admit this is merely to recognize that belonging to a particular family is part of the individual personality, that society is made up as much of families as of individuals, and that the transmission of the heritage of civilization within the family is as important a tool in man's striving toward better things as is the heredity of beneficial physical attributes.

IV

Many people who agree that the family is desirable as an instrument for the transmission of morals, tastes, and knowledge still question the desirability of the transmission of material property. Yet there can be little doubt that, in order that the former may be possible, some continuity of standards, of the external forms of life, is essential, and that this will be achieved only if it is possible to transmit not only immaterial but also material advantages. There is, of course, neither greater merit nor any greater injustice involved in some people being born to wealthy parents than there is in others being born to kind or intelligent parents. The fact is that it is no less of an advantage to the community if at least some children can start with the advantages which at any given time only wealthy homes can offer than if some children inherit great intelligence or are taught better morals at home.

We are not concerned here with the chief argument for private inheritance, namely, that it seems essential as a means to preserve the dispersal in the control of capital and as an inducement for its accumulation. Rather, our concern here is whether the fact that it confers unmerited benefits on some is a valid argument against the institution. It is unquestionably one of the institutional causes of inequality. In the present context we need not inquire whether liberty demands unlimited freedom of bequest. Our problem here is merely whether people ought to be free to pass on to children or others such material possessions as will cause substantial inequality.

Once we agree that it is desirable to harness the natural instincts of parents to equip the new generation as well as they can, there seems no sensible ground for limiting this to non-material benefits. The family's function of passing on standards and traditions is closely tied up with the possibility of transmitting material goods. And it is difficult to see how it would serve the true interest of society to limit the gain in material conditions to one generation.

There is also another consideration which, though it may appear somewhat cynical, strongly suggests that if we wish to make the best use of the natural partiality of parents for their children, we ought not to preclude the transmission of property. It seems certain that among the many ways in which those who have gained power and influence might provide for their children, the bequest of a fortune is socially by far the cheapest. Without this outlet, these men would look for other ways of providing for their children, such as placing them in positions which might bring them the income and the prestige that a fortune would have done; and this would cause a waste of resources and an injustice much greater than is caused by the inheritance of property. Such is the case with all societies in which inheritance of property does not exist, including the Communist. Those who dislike the inequalities caused by inheritance should therefore recognize that, men being what they are, it is the least of evils, even from their point of view.

V

Though inheritance used to be the most widely criticized source of inequality, it is today probably no longer so. Egalitarian agitation now tends to concentrate on the unequal advantages due to differences in education. There is a growing tendency to express the desire to secure equality of conditions in the claim that the best education we have learned to provide for some should be made gratuitously available for all and that, if this is not possible, one should not be allowed to get a better education than the rest merely because one's parents are able to pay for it, but only those and all those who can pass a uniform test of ability should be admitted to the benefits of the limited resources of higher education.

The problem of educational policy raises too many issues to allow of their being discussed incidentally under the general heading of equality. We shall have to devote a separate chapter to them at the end of this book [*The Constitution of Liberty*]. For the present we shall only point out that enforced equality in this field can hardly avoid preventing some from getting the education they otherwise might. Whatever we might do, there is no way of preventing those advantages which only some can have, and which it is desirable that some should have, from going to people who neither individually merit them nor will make as good a use of them as some other person might have done. Such a problem cannot be satisfactorily solved by the exclusive and coercive powers of the state.

It is instructive at this point to glance briefly at the change that the ideal of equality has undergone in this field in modern times. A hundred years ago, at the height of the classical liberal movement, the demand was generally expressed by the phrase *la carrière ouverte aux talents*. It was a demand that all man-made obstacles to the rise of some should be removed, that all privileges of individuals should be abolished, and that what the state contributed to the chance of improving one's conditions should be the same for all. That so long as people were different and grew up in different families this could not assure an equal start was fairly generally accepted. It was understood that the duty of government was not to ensure that everybody had the same prospect of reaching a given position but merely to make available to all on equal terms those facilities which in their nature depended on government action. That the results were bound to be different, not only because the individuals were different, but also because only a small part of the relevant circumstances depended on government action, was taken for granted.

This conception that all should be allowed to try has been largely replaced by the altogether different conception that all must be assured an equal start and the same prospects. This means little less than that the government, instead of providing the same circumstances for all, should aim at controlling all conditions relevant to a particular individual's prospects and so adjust them to his capacities as to assure him of the same prospects as everybody else. Such deliberate adaptation of opportunities to individual aims and capacities would, of course, be the opposite of freedom. Nor could it be justified as a means of making the best use of all available knowledge except on the assumption that government knows best how individual capacities can be used.

When we inquire into the justification of these demands, we find that they rest on the discontent that the success of some people often produces in those that are less successful, or, to put it bluntly, on envy. The modern tendency to gratify this passion and to disguise it in the respectable garment of social justice is developing into a serious threat to freedom. Recently an attempt was made to base these demands on the argument that it ought to be the aim of politics to remove all sources of discontent.[8] This would, of course, necessarily mean that it is the responsibility of government to see that nobody is healthier or possesses a happier temperament, a better-suited spouse or more prospering children, than anybody else. If really all unfulfilled desires have a claim on the community, individual responsibility is at an end. However human, envy is certainly not one of the sources of discontent that a free society can eliminate. It is probably one of the essential conditions for the preservation of such a society that we do not countenance envy, not sanction its demands by camouflaging it as social justice, but treat it, in the words of John Stuart Mill, as "the most anti-social and evil of all passions."[9]

VI

While most of the strictly egalitarian demands are based on nothing better than envy, we must recognize that much that on the surface appears as a demand for greater equality is in fact a demand for a juster distribution of the good things of this world and springs therefore from much more creditable motives. Most people will object not to the bare fact of inequality but to the fact that the differences in reward do not correspond to any recognizable differences in the merits of those who receive them. The answer commonly given to this is that a free society on the whole achieves this kind of justice.[10] This, however, is an indefensible contention if by justice is meant proportionality of reward to moral merit. Any attempt to found the case for freedom on this argument is very damaging to it, since it concedes that material rewards ought to be made to correspond to recognizable merit and then opposes the conclusion that most people will draw from this by an assertion which is untrue. The proper answer is that in a free system it is neither desirable nor practicable that material rewards should be made generally to correspond to what men recognize as merit and that it is an essential characteristic of a free society that an individual's position should not necessarily depend on the views that his fellows hold about the merit he has acquired.

This contention may appear at first so strange and even shocking that I will ask the reader to suspend judgment until I have further explained the distinction between value and merit.[11] The difficulty in making the point clear is due to the fact that the term "merit," which is the only one available to describe what I mean, is also used in a wider and vaguer sense. It will be used here exclusively to describe the attributes of conduct that make it deserving of praise, that is, the moral character of the action and not the value of the achievement.[12]

As we have seen throughout our discussion, the value that the performance or capacity of a person has to his fellows has no necessary connection with its ascertainable merit in this sense. The inborn as well as the acquired gifts of a person clearly have a value to his fellows which does not depend on any credit due to him for possessing them. There is little a man can do to alter the fact that his special talents are very common or exceedingly rare. A good mind or a fine voice, a beautiful face or a skilful hand, and a ready wit or an attractive personality are in a large measure as independent of a person's efforts as the opportunities or the experiences he has had. In all these instances the value which a person's capacities or services have for us and for which he is recompensed has little relation to anything that we can call moral merit or deserts. Our problem is whether it is desirable that people should enjoy advantages in proportion to the benefits which their fellows derive from their activities or whether the distribution of these advantages should be based on other men's views of their merits.

Reward according to merit must in practice mean reward according to assessable merit, merit that other people can recognize and agree upon and not merit merely in the sight of some higher power. Assessable merit in this sense presupposes that we can ascertain that a man has done what some accepted rule of conduct demanded of him and that this has cost him some pain and effort. Whether this has been the case cannot be judged by the result: merit is not a matter of the objective outcome but of subjective effort. The attempt to achieve a valuable result may be highly meritorious but a complete failure, and full success may be entirely the result of accident and thus without merit. If we know that a man has done his best, we will often wish to see him rewarded irrespective of the result; and if we know that a most valuable achievement is almost entirely due to luck or favorable circumstances, we will give little credit to the author.

We may wish that we were able to draw this distinction in every instance. In fact, we can do so only rarely with any degree of assurance. It is possible only where we possess all the knowledge which was at the disposal of the acting person, including a knowlege of his skill and confidence, his state of mind and his feelings, his capacity for attention, his energy and persistence, etc. The possibility of a true judgment of merit thus depends on the presence of precisely those conditions whose general absence is the main argument for liberty. It is because we want people to use knowledge which we do not possess that we let them decide for themselves. But insofar as we want them to be free to use capacities and knowledge of facts which we do not have, we are not in a position to judge the merit of their achievements. To decide on merit presupposes that we can judge whether people have made such use of their opportunities as they ought to have made and how much effort of will or self-denial this has cost them; it presupposes also that we can distinguish between that part of their achievement which is due to circumstances within their control and that part which is not.

VII

The incompatibility of reward according to merit with freedom to choose one's pursuit is most evident in those areas where the uncertainty of the outcome is particularly great and our individual estimates of the chances of various kinds of effort very different.[13] In those speculative efforts which we call "research" or "exploration," or in economic activities which we commonly describe as "speculation," we cannot expect to attract those best qualified for them unless we give the successful ones all the credit or gain, though many others may have striven as meritoriously. For the same reason that nobody can know beforehand who will be the successful ones, nobody can say who has earned greater merit. It would clearly not serve our purpose if we let all who have honestly striven share in the prize. Moreover, to do so would make it necessary that somebody have the right to decide who is to be allowed to strive for it. If in their pursuit of uncertain goals people are to use their own knowledge and capacities, they must be guided, not by what other people think they ought to do, but by the value others attach to the result at which they aim.

What is so obviously true about those undertakings which we commonly regard as risky is scarcely less true of any chosen object we decide to pursue. Any such decision is beset with uncertainty, and if the choice is to be as wise as it is humanly possible to make it, the alternative results anticipated must be labeled according to their value. If the remuneration did not correspond to the value that the product of a man's efforts has for his fellows, he would have no basis for deciding whether the pursuit of a given object is worth the effort and risk. He would necessarily have to be told what to do, and some other person's estimate of what was the best use of his capacities would have to determine both his duties and his remuneration.[14]

The fact is, of course, that we do not wish people to earn a maximum of merit but to achieve a maximum of usefulness at a minimum of pain and sacrifice and therefore a minimum of merit. Not only would it be impossible for us to reward all merit justly, but it would not even be desirable that people should aim chiefly at earning a maximum of merit. Any attempt to induce them to do this would necessarily result in people being rewarded differently for the same service. And it is only the value of the result that we can judge with any degree of confidence, not the different degrees of effort and care that it has cost different people to achieve it.

The prizes that a free society offers for the result serve to tell those who strive for them how much effort they are worth. However, the same prizes will go to all those who produce the same result, regardless of effort. What is true here of the remuneration for the same services rendered by different people is even more true of the relative remuneration for different services requiring different gifts and capacities: they will have little relation to merit. The market will generally offer for services of any kind the value they will have for those who benefit from them; but it will rarely be known whether it was necessary to offer so much in order to obtain these services, and often, no doubt, the community could have had them for much less. The pianist who was reported not long ago to have said that he would perform even if he had to pay for the privilege probably described the position of many who earn large incomes from activities which are also their chief pleasure.

VIII

Though most people regard as very natural the claim that nobody should be rewarded more than he deserves for his pain and effort, it is nevertheless based on a colossal presumption. It presumes that we are able to judge in every individual instance how well people use the different opportunities and talents given to them and how meritorious their achievements are in the light of all the circumstances which have made them possible. It presumes that some human beings are in a position to determine conclusively what a person is worth and are entitled to determine what he may achieve. It presumes, then, what the argument for liberty specifically rejects: that we can and do know all that guides a person's action.

A society in which the position of the individuals was made to correspond to human ideas of moral merit would therefore be the exact opposite of a free society. It would be a society in which people were rewarded for duty performed instead of for success, in which every move of every individual was guided by what other people thought he ought to do, and in which the individual was thus relieved of the responsibility and the risk of decision. But if nobody's knowledge is sufficient to guide all human action, there is also no human being who is competent to reward all efforts according to merit.

In our individual conduct we generally act on the assumption that it is the value of a person's performance and not his merit that determines our obligation to him. Whatever may be true in more intimate relations, in the ordinary business of life we do not feel that, because a man has rendered us a service at a great sacrifice, our debt to him is determined by this, so long as we could have had the same service provided with ease by somebody else. In our dealings with other men we feel that we are doing justice if we recompense value rendered with equal value, without inquiring what it might have cost the particular individual to supply us with these services. What determines our responsibility is the advantage we derive from what others offer us, not their merit in providing it. We also expect in our dealings with others to be remunerated not according to our subjective merit but according to what our services are worth to them. Indeed, so long as we think in terms of our relations to particular people, we are generally quite aware that the mark of the free man is to be dependent for his livelihood not on other people's views of his merit but solely on what he has to offer them. It is only when we think of our position or our income as determined by "society" as a whole that we demand reward according to merit.

Though moral value or merit is a species of value, not all value is moral value, and most of our judgments of value are not moral judgments. That this must be so in a free society is a point of cardinal importance; and the failure to distinguish between value and merit has been the source of serious confusion. We do not necessarily admire all activities whose product we value; and in most instances where we value what we get, we are in no position to assess the merit of those who have provided it for us. If a man's ability in a given field is more valuable after thirty years' work than it was earlier, this is independent of whether these thirty years were most profitable and enjoyable or whether they were a time of unceasing sacrifice and worry. If the pursuit of a hobby produces a special skill or an accidental invention turns out to be extremely useful to others, the fact that there is little merit in it does not make it any less valuable than if the result had been produced by painful effort.

This difference between value and merit is not peculiar to any one type of society — it would exist anywhere. We might, of course, attempt to make rewards correspond to merit instead of value, but we are not likely to succeed in this. In attempting it, we would destroy the incentives which enable people to decide for themselves what they should do. Moreover, it is more than doubtful whether even a fairly successful attempt to make rewards correspond to merit would produce a more attractive or even a tolerable social order. A society in which it was generally presumed that a high income was proof of merit and a low income of the lack of it, in which it was universally believed that position and remuneration corresponded to merit, in which there was no other road to success than the approval of one's conduct by the majority of one's fellows, would probably be much more unbearable to the unsuccessful ones than one in which it was frankly recognized that there was no necessary connection between merit and success.[15]

It would probably contribute more to human happiness if, instead of trying to make remuneration correspond to merit, we made clearer how uncertain is the connection between value and merit. We are probably all much too ready to ascribe personal merit where there is, in fact, only superior value. The possession by an individual or a group of a superior civilization or education certainly represents an important value and constitutes an asset for the community to which they belong; but it usually constitutes little merit. Popularity and esteem do not depend more on merit than does financial success. It is, in fact, largely because we are so used to assuming an often non-existent merit wherever we find value that we balk when, in particular instances, the discrepancy is too large to be ignored.

There is every reason why we ought to endeavor to honor special merit where it has gone without adequate reward. But the problem of rewarding action of outstanding merit which we wish to be widely known as an example is different from that of the incentives on which the ordinary functioning of society rests. A free society produces institutions in which, for those who prefer it, a man's advancement depends on the judgment of some superior or of the majority of his fellows. Indeed, as organizations grow larger and more complex, the task of ascertaining the individual's contribution will become more difficult; and it will become increasingly necessary that, for many, merit in the eyes of the managers rather than the ascertainable value of the contribution should determine the rewards. So long as this does not produce a situation in which a single comprehensive scale of merit is imposed upon the whole society, so long as a multiplicity of organizations compete with one another in offering different prospects, this is not merely compatible with freedom but extends the range of choice open to the individual.

IX

Justice, like liberty and coercion, is a concept which, for the sake of clarity, ought to be confined to the deliberate treatment of men by other men. It is an aspect of the intentional determination of those conditions of people's lives that are subject to such control. Insofar as we want the efforts of individuals to be guided by their own views about prospects and chances, the results of the individual's efforts are necessarily unpredictable, and the question as to whether the resulting distribution of incomes is just has no meaning.[16] Justice does require that those conditions of people's lives that are determined by government be provided equally for all. But equality of those conditions must lead to inequality of results. Neither the equal provision of particular public facilities nor the equal treatment of different partners in our voluntary dealings with one another will secure reward that is proportional to merit. Reward for merit is reward for obeying the wishes of others in what we do, not compensation for the benefits we have conferred upon them by doing what we thought best.

It is, in fact, one of the objections against attempts by government to fix income scales that the state must attempt to be just in all it does. Once the principle of reward according to merit is accepted as the just foundation for the distribution of incomes, justice would require that all who desire it should be rewarded according to that principle. Soon it would also be demanded that the same principle be applied to all and that incomes not in proportion to recognizable merit not be tolerated. Even an attempt merely to distinguish between those incomes or gains which are "earned" and those which are not will set up a principle which the state will have to try to apply but cannot in fact apply generally.[17] And every such attempt at deliberate control of some remunerations is bound to create further demands for new controls. The principle of distributive justice, once introduced, would not be fulfilled until the whole of society was organized in accordance with it. This would produce a kind of society which in all essential respects would be the opposite of a free society—a society in which authority decided what the individual was to do and how he was to do it.

X

In conclusion we must briefly look at another argument on which the demands for a more equal distribution are frequently based, though it is rarely explicitly stated. This is the contention that membership in a particular community or nation entitles the individual to a particular material standard that is determined by the general wealth of the group to which he belongs. This demand is in curious conflict with the desire to base distribution on personal merit. There is clearly no merit in being born into a particular community, and no argument of justice can be based on the accident of a particular individual's being born in one place rather than another. A relatively wealthy community in fact regularly confers advantages on its poorest members unknown to those born in poor communities. In a wealthy community the only justification its members can have for insisting on further advantages is that there is much private wealth that the government can confiscate and redistribute and that men who constantly see such wealth being enjoyed by others will have a stronger desire for it than those who know of it only abstractly, if at all.

There is no obvious reason why the joint efforts of the members of any group to ensure the maintenance of law and order and to organize the provision of certain services should give the members a claim to a particular share in the wealth of this group. Such claims would be especially difficult to defend where those who advanced them were unwilling to concede the same rights to those who did not belong to the same nation or community. The recognition of such claims on a national scale would in fact only create a new kind of collective (but not less exclusive) property right in the resources of the nation that could not be justified on the same grounds as individual property. Few people would be prepared to recognize the justice of these demands on a world scale. And the bare fact that within a given nation the majority had the actual power to enforce such demands, while in the world as a whole it did not yet have it, would hardly make them more just.

There are good reasons why we should endeavor to use whatever political organization we have at our disposal to make provision for the weak or infirm or for the victims of unforeseeable disaster. It may well be true that the most effective method of providing against certain risks common to all citizens of a state is to give every citizen protection against those risks. The level on which such provisions against common risks can be made will necessarily depend on the general wealth of the community.

It is an entirely different matter, however, to suggest that those who are poor, merely in the sense that there are those in the same community who are richer, are entitled to a share in the wealth of the latter or that being born into a group that has reached a particular level of civilization and comfort confers a title to a share in all its benefits. The fact that all citizens have an interest in the common provision of some services is no justification for anyone's claiming as a right a share in all the benefits. It may set a standard for what some ought to be willing to give, but not for what anyone can demand.

National groups will become more and more exclusive as the acceptance of this view that we have been contending against spreads. Rather than admit people to the advantages that living in their country offers, a nation will prefer to keep them out altogether; for, once admitted, they will soon claim as a right a particular share in its wealth. The conception that citizenship or even residence in a country confers a claim to a particular standard of living is becoming a serious source of international friction. And since the only justification for applying the principle within a given country is that its government has the power to enforce it, we must not be surprised if we find the same principle being applied by force on an international scale. Once the right of the majority to the benefits that minorities enjoy is recognized on a national scale, there is no reason why this should stop at the boundaries of the existing states.

Notes

1. See, e.g., R. H. Tawney, *Equality* (London, 1931), p. 47.

2. Roger J. Williams, *Free and Unequal: The Biological Basis of Individual Liberty* (Austin: University of Texas Press, 1953), pp. 23 and 70; cf. also J. B. S. Haldane, *The Inequality of Man* (London, 1932), and P. B. Medawar, *The Uniqueness of the Individual* (London, 1957).

3. Williams, op. cit., p. 152.

4. See the description of this fashionable view in H. M. Kallen's article "Behaviorism," *E.S.S.*, II, 498: "At birth human infants, regardless of their heredity, are as equal as Fords."

5. Cf. Plato, *Laws* vi. 757A: "To unequals equals become unequal."

6. Cf. F. H. Knight, *Freedom and Reform* (New York, 1947), p. 151: "There is no visible reason why anyone is more or less entitled to the earnings of inherited personal capacities than to those of inherited property in any other form"; and the discussion in W. Roepke, *Mass und Mitte* (Erlenbach and Zurich, 1950), pp. 65 – 75.

7. This is the position of R. H. Tawney as summarized by J. P. Plamenatz, "Equality of Opportunity," in *Aspects of Human Equality*, ed. L. Bryson and others (New York, 1956), p. 100.

8. C. A. R. Crosland, *The Future of Socialism* (London, 1956), p. 205.

9. J. S. Mill, *On Liberty*, ed. R. B. McCallum (Oxford, 1946), p. 70.

10. Cf. W. B. Gallie, "Liberal Morality and Socialist Morality," in *Phi-*

losophy, Politics, and Society, ed. P. Laslett (Oxford, 1956), pp. 123 – 25. The author represents it as the essence of "liberal morality" that it claims that rewards are equal to merit in a free society. This was the position of some nineteenth-century liberals which often weakened their argument. A characteristic example is W. G. Sumner, who argued (*What Social Classes Owe to Each Other*, reprinted in *Freeman*, VI [Los Angeles, n.d.], 141) that if all "have equal chances so far as chances are provided or limited by society," this will "produce inequal results — that is results which shall be proportioned to the merits of individuals." This is true only if "merit" is used in the sense in which we have used "value," without any moral connotations, but certainly not if it is meant to suggest proportionality to any endeavor to do the good or right thing, or to any subjective effort to conform to an ideal standard.

But, as we shall presently see, Mr. Gallie is right that, in the Aristotelian terms he uses, liberalism aims at commutative justice and socialism at distributive justice. But, like most socialists, he does not see that distributive justice is irreconcilable with freedom in the choice of one's activities: it is the justice of a hierarchic organization, not of a free society.

11. Although I believe that this distinction between merit and value is the same as that which Aristotle and Thomas Aquinas had in mind when they distinguished "distributive justice" from "commutative justice," I prefer not to tie up the discussion with all the difficulties and confusions which in the course of time have become associated with these traditional concepts. That what we call here "reward according to merit" corresponds to the Aristotelian distributive justice seems clear. The difficult concept is that of "commutative justice," and to speak of justice in this sense seems always to cause a little confusion. Cf. M. Solomon, *Der Begriff der Gerechtigkeit bei Aristoteles* (Leiden, 1937); and for a survey of the extensive literature G. del Vecchio, *Die Gerechtigkeit* (2nd ed.; Basel, 1950).

12. The terminological difficulties arise from the fact that we use the word merit also in an objective sense and will speak of the "merit" of an idea, a book, or a picture, irrespective of the merit acquired by the person who has created them. Sometimes the word is also used to describe what we regard as the "true" value of some achievement as distinguished from its market value. Yet even a human achievement which has the greatest value or merit in this sense is not necessarily proof of moral merit on the part of him to whom it is due. It seems that our use has the sanction of philosophical tradition. Cf., for instance, D. Hume, *Treatise*, II, 252: "The external performance has no merit. We must look within to find the moral quality. . . . The ultimate object of our praise and approbation is the motive, that produc'd them."

13. Cf. the important essay by A. A. Alchian, "Uncertainty, Evolution, and Economic Theory," *J.P.E.*, LVIII (1950), esp. 213 – 14, Sec. II, headed "Success Is Based on Results, Not Motivation." It probably is also no accident that the American economist who has done most to advance our un-

derstanding of a free society, F. H. Knight, began his professional career with a study of *Risk, Uncertainty, and Profit.* Cf. also B. de Jouvenel, *Power* (London, 1948), p. 298.

14. It is often maintained that justice requires that remuneration be proportional to the unpleasantness of the job and that for this reason the street cleaner or the sewage worker ought to be paid more than the doctor or office worker. This, indeed, would seem to be the consequence of the principle of remuneration according to merit (or "distributive justice"). In a market such a result would come about only if all people were equally skilful in all jobs so that those who could earn as much as others in the more pleasant occupations would have to be paid more to undertake the distasteful ones. In the actual world those unpleasant jobs provide those whose usefulness in the more attractive jobs is small an opportunity to earn more than they could elsewhere. That persons who have little to offer their fellows should be able to earn an income similar to that of the rest only at a much greater sacrifice is inevitable in any arrangement under which the individual is allowed to choose his own sphere of usefulness.

15. Cf. Crosland, op. cit., p. 235: "Even if all the failures could be convinced that they had an equal chance, their discontent would still not be assuaged; indeed it might actually be intensified. When opportunities are known to be unequal, and the selection clearly biased towards wealth or lineage, people can comfort themselves for failure by saying that they never had a proper chance — the system was unfair, the scales too heavily weighted against them. But if the selection is obviously by merit, this source of comfort disappears, and failure induces a total sense of inferiority, with no excuse or consolation; and this, by a natural quirk of human nature, actually increases the envy and resentment at the success of others." Cf. also chap. xxiv, at n. 8. I have not yet seen Michael Young, *The Rise of the Meritocracy* (London, 1958), which, judging from reviews, appears to bring out these problems very clearly.

16. See the interesting discussion in R. G. Collingwood, "Economics as a Philosophical Science," *Ethics*, Vol. XXXVI (1926), who concludes (p. 174): "A just price, a just wage, a just rate of interest, is a contradiction in terms. The question what a person ought to get in return for his goods and labor is a question absolutely devoid of meaning. The only valid questions are what he *can* get in return for his goods or labor, and whether he ought to sell them at all."

17. It is, of course, possible to give the distinction between "earned" and "unearned" incomes, gains, or increments a fairly precise legal meaning, but it then rapidly ceases to correspond to the moral distinction which provides its justification. Any serious attempt to apply the moral distinction in practice soon meets the same insuperable difficulties as any attempt to assess subjective merit. How little these difficulties are generally understood by philosophers (except in rare instances, as that quoted in the preceding note) is well illustrated by a discussion in L. S. Stebbing, *Thinking to Some Purpose*

("Pelican Books" [London, 1939]), p. 184, in which, as an illustration of a distinction which is clear but not sharp, she chooses that between "legitimate" and "excess" profits and asserts: "The distinction is clear between 'excess profits' (or 'profiteering') and 'legitimate profits,' although it is not a sharp distinction."

WHITHER DEMOCRACY?

·19·

I

The concept of democracy has one meaning — I believe the true and original meaning — for which I hold it a high value well worth fighting for. Democracy has not proved to be a certain protection against tyranny and oppression, as once it was hoped. Nevertheless, as a convention which enables any majority to rid itself of a government it does not like, democracy is of inestimable value.

For this reason I am more and more disquieted by the growing loss of faith in democracy among thinking people. This can no longer be overlooked. It is becoming serious just as — and perhaps partly because — the magic word democracy has become so all-powerful that all the inherited limitations on governmental power are breaking down before it. Sometimes it seems as if the sum of demands which are now everywhere advanced in the name of democracy have so alarmed even just and reasonable people that a serious reaction against democracy, as such, is a real danger. Yet it is not the basic conception of democracy, but additional connotations which have in the course of time been added to the original meaning of a partic-

---

A lecture delivered to the Institute of Public Affairs, New South Wales, at Sydney, 8 October 1976.

ular kind of decision-making procedure, which now endanger the belief in a democracy so enlarged in content. What is happening is indeed precisely that which some had apprehended concerning democracy in the nineteenth century. A wholesome method of arriving at widely acceptable political decisions has become the pretext for enforcing substantially egalitarian aims.

The advent of democracy in the last century brought a decisive change in the range of governmental powers. For centuries efforts had been directed towards limiting the powers of government; and the gradual development of constitutions served no other purpose than this. Suddenly it was believed that the control of government by elected representatives of the majority made any other checks on the powers of government unnecessary, so that all the various constitutional safeguards which had been developed in the course of time could be dispensed with.

Thus arose unlimited democracy — and it is unlimited democracy, not just democracy, which is the problem of today. All democracy that we know today in the West is more or less unlimited democracy. It is important to remember that, if the peculiar institutions of the unlimited democracy we have today should ultimately prove a failure, this need not mean that democracy itself was a mistake, but only that we tried it in the wrong way. While personally I believe that democratic decision on all issues on which there is general agreement that some government action is necessary is an indispensable method of peaceful change, I also feel that a form of government in which any temporary majority can decide that any matter it likes should be regarded as 'common affairs' subject to its control is an abomination.

II

The greatest and most important limitation upon the powers of democracy, which was swept away by the rise of an omnipotent representative assembly, was the principle of the 'separation of powers'. We shall see that the root of the trouble is that so-called 'legislatures', which the early theorists of representative government (and particularly John Locke) conceived to be limited to making laws in a very specific narrow sense of that word, have become omnipotent governmental bodies. The old ideal of the 'Rule of Law', or of 'Government under the Law', has thereby been destroyed. The 'sovereign' Parliament can do whatever the representatives of the majority find expedient to do in order to retain majority support.

But to call 'law' everything that the elected representatives of the majority resolve, and to describe as 'Government under the Law' all the directives issued by them — however discriminating in favour of, or to the detriment of, some groups of individuals — is a very bad joke. It is in truth lawless government. It is a mere play on words to maintain that, so long as a majority approves of acts of government, the rule of law is preserved. The rule of law was regarded as a safeguard of individual freedom, because it meant that coercion was permissible only to enforce obedience to general rules of individual conduct equally applicable to all, in an unknown number of future instances. Arbitrary oppression — that is coercion undefined by any rule by the representatives of the majority — is no better than arbitrary action by any other ruler. Whether it requires that some hated person should be boiled and quartered, or that his property should be taken from him, comes in this respect to the same thing. Although there is good reason for preferring limited democratic government to a non-democratic one, I must confess to preferring non-democratic government under the law to unlimited (and therefore essentially lawless) democratic government. Government under the law seems to me to be the higher value, which it was once hoped that democratic watch-dogs would preserve.

I believe indeed that the suggestion of a reform, to which my critique of the present institutions of democracy will lead, would result in a truer realisation of the common *opinion* of the majority of citizens than the present arrangements for the gratification of the *will* of the separate interest groups which add up to a majority.

It is not suggested that the democratic claim of the elected representatives of the people to have a decisive word in the direction of government is any less strong than their claim to determine what the law shall be. The great tragedy of the historical development is that these two distinct powers were placed in the hands of one and the same assembly, and that government consequently ceased to be subject to law. The triumphant claim of the British Parliament to have become sovereign, and so able to govern subject to no law, may prove to have been the death-knell of both individual freedom and democracy.

III

This development may have been historically unavoidable. Certainly, it is not logically cogent. It is not difficult to imagine how development could have taken place along different lines. When in the eighteenth century the House of Commons successfully claimed exclusive power over the public purse, in effect it thereby gained exclusive control of government. If at this time the House of Lords had been in a position to concede this only on condition that the development of *the* law (that is, the private and criminal law which limits the powers of all government) should be exclusively *its* concern — a development not unnatural with the House of Lords being the highest court of law — such a division between a governmental and a legislative assembly might have been achieved and a restraint of government by law preserved. Politically, however, it was impossible to confer such legislative power on the representatives of a privileged class.

Prevailing forms of democracy, in which the sovereign representative assembly at one and the same time makes law and directs government, owe their authority to a delusion. This is the pious belief that such a democratic government will carry out the will of the people. It may be true of democratically elected legislatures in the strict sense of makers of law, in the original sense of the term. That is, it may be true of elected assemblies whose power is limited to laying down universal rules of just conduct, designed to delimit against each other the domains of control over individuals, and intended to apply to an unknown number of future instances. About such rules governing individual conduct, which prevent conflicts most people may find themselves in at either end, a community is likely to form a predominant *opinion,* and agreement is likely to exist among the representatives of a majority. An assembly with such a definite limited task is therefore likely to reflect the *opinion* of the majority — and, being concerned only with general rules, has little occasion to reflect the *will* of particular interests on specific matters.

But the giving of *laws* in this classic sense of the word is the least part of the tasks of the assemblies which we still call 'legislatures'. Their main concern is government. For 'lawyers' law', as an acute observer of the British Parliament wrote more than seventy years ago, 'parliament has neither time nor taste'. So much indeed are activities, character and procedures of representative assemblies everywhere determined by their governmental tasks that their name 'legislature' no longer derives from their making laws. The relation has rather been reversed. We now call practically every resolution of these assemblies laws, solely because they derive from a legislature — however little they may have that character of a commitment to a general rule of just conduct, to the enforcement of which the coercive powers of government were supposed to be limited in a free society.

IV

But as every resolution of this sovereign governmental authority has 'the force of law', its governmental actions are also not limited by law. Nor can they, and this is even more serious, still claim to be authorised by the opinion of a majority of the people. In fact, grounds for supporting members of an omnipotent majority are wholly different from those for supporting a majority on which the actions of a true legislature rest. Voting for a limited legislator is choosing between alternative ways of securing an overall order resulting from the decisions of free individuals. Voting for a member of a body with power to confer special benefits, without being itself bound by general rules, is something entirely different. In such a democratically elected assembly with unlimited power to confer special benefits and impose special burdens on particular groups, a majority can be formed only by buying the support of numerous special interests, through granting them such benefits at the expense of a minority.

It is easy to threaten to withhold support even of general laws one approves of unless one's votes are paid for by special concessions to one's group. In an omnipotent assembly, decisions therefore rest on a sanctioned process of blackmail and corruption. This has long been a recognised part of the system, from which even the best cannot escape.

Such decisions on favours for particular groups have little to do with any agreement by the majority about the substance of governmental action, since in most respects the members of the majority will know little more than that they have conferred on some agency ill-defined powers to achieve some ill-defined objective. With regard to most measures, the majority of voters will have no reason to be for or against them, except that they know that in return for supporting those who advocate them, they are promised the satisfaction of some wishes of their own. It is the result of this bargaining process which is dignified as the 'will of the majority'.

What we call 'legislatures' are in fact bodies continually deciding on particular measures, and are authorising coercion for their execution, on which no genuine agreement among a majority exists, but for which the support of a majority has been obtained by *deals*.

In an omnipotent assembly which is concerned mainly with particulars and not with principles, majorities are therefore not based on agreement of opinions, but are formed by aggregations of special interests mutually assisting each other.

The apparently paradoxical fact is that a nominally all-powerful assembly — whose authority is not limited to, or rests on its committing itself to, general rules — is necessarily exceedingly weak and wholly depèndent on the support of those splinter groups which are bound to hold out for gifts which are at the government's command. The picture of the majority of such an assembly united by common moral convictions evaluating the merits of the claims of particular groups is of course a fantasy. It is a majority only because it has pledged itself not to a principle but to satisfying particular claims. The sovereign assembly is anything but sovereign in the use of its unlimited powers. It is rather quaint that the fact that 'all modern democracies' have found this or that necessary is sometimes quoted as proof of the desirability or equity of some measure. Most members of the majority often knew that a measure was stupid and unfair, but they had to consent to it, in order to remain members of a majority.

V

An unlimited legislature which is not prevented by convention or constitutional provisions from decreeing aimed and discriminatory measures of coercion, such as tariffs or taxes or subsidies, cannot avoid acting in such an unprincipled manner. Although attempts are inevitably made to disguise this purchase of support as beneficial assistance to the deserving, the moral pretence can hardly be taken seriously. Agreement of a majority on how to distribute the spoils it can extort from a dissenting minority can hardly claim any moral sanction for its proceedings — even if it invokes the figment of 'social justice' to defend it. What happens is that *political necessity created by the existing institutional set-up produces non-viable or even destructive moral beliefs.*

Agreement by the majority on sharing the booty gained by overwhelming a minority of fellow citizens, or deciding how much is to be taken from them, is not democracy. At least it is not that ideal of democracy which has any moral justification. Democracy itself is not egalitarianism. But unlimited democracy is bound to become egalitarian.

With regard to the fundamental immorality of all egalitarianism I will here point only to the fact that all our morals rest on the different esteem in which we hold people according to the manner in which they conduct themselves. While equality before the law — the treatment of all by government according to the same rules — appears to me to be an essential condition of individual freedom, that different treatment which is necessary in order to place people who are individually very different into the same material position seems to me not only incompatible with personal freedom, but highly immoral. But this is the kind of immorality towards which unlimited democracy is moving.

To repeat, it is not democracy but unlimited democracy which I regard as no better than any other unlimited government. The fatal error which gave the elected representative assembly unlimited powers is the superstition that a supreme authority must in its very nature be unlimited, because any limitation would presuppose another will above it, in which case it would not be a supreme power. But this is a misunderstanding deriving from the totalitarian-positivist conceptions of Francis Bacon and Thomas Hobbes, or the constructivism of Cartesian Rationalism, which fortunately in the Anglo-Saxon world was at least for a long time held back by the deeper understanding of Sir Edward Coke, Matthew Hale, John Locke and the Old Whigs.

In this respect the ancients were indeed often wiser than modern constructivistic thinking. A highest power need not be an unlimited power but may owe its authority to its commitment to general rules approved by public opinion. The judge-king of early times was not selected in order that whatever he said was to be right, but because, and so long as, what he pronounced was generally felt to be right. He was not the source but merely the interpreter of a law which rested on a diffused opinion, but which could lead to action only if articulated by the approved authority. And if the supreme authority alone could order action, it extended only so far as it had the support of the general assent to the principles on which it acted. The only and highest authority entitled to take decisions on common action might well be a limited authority — limited to decisions by which it committed itself to a general rule of which public opinion approved.

The secret of decent government is precisely that the supreme power must be limited power — a power that can lay down rules limiting all other power — and which thus can restrain but not command the private citizen. All other authority rests thus on its commitment to rules which its subjects recognise: what makes a community is the common recognition of the same rules.

Thus the elected supreme body need not have any other power than that of making laws in the classical sense of general rules guiding individual conduct. Nor need there be any power of coercing private citizens other than that of enforcing obedience to the rules of conduct thus laid down. Other branches of government, including an elected governmental assembly, should be bound and limited by the laws of the assembly confined to true legislation. These are the requirements that would secure genuine government under the law.

VI

Solution of the problem, as I have already suggested, seems to be to divide the truly legislative from the governmental tasks between distinct legislative and governmental assemblies. Naturally, little would be gained by merely having two such assemblies of essentially the present character, and merely charged with different tasks. Not only would two assemblies of essentially the same composition inevitably act in collusion, and thereby produce much the same sort of results as the existing assemblies. The character, procedures and composition of these have also been determined so completely by their predominant governmental tasks as to make them little suited for legislation proper.

Nothing is more illuminating in this respect than that the eighteenth-century theorists of representative government almost unanimously condemned an organisation of what they conceived as the legislature on party lines. They usually spoke of 'factions'. But their predominant concern with governmental matters made their organisation on party lines universally necessary. A government, to perform its tasks successfully, needs the support of an organised majority committed to a programme of action. And to give the people an option, there must be a similarly organised opposition capable of forming an alternative government.

For their strictly governmental functions, existing 'legislatures' appear to have become fairly well adapted and might well be allowed to continue in their present form, if their power over the private citizen were limited by a law laid down by another democratic assembly, which the former could not alter. It would, in effect, administer the material and personal resources placed at the disposal of government to enable it to render various services to the citizens at large. It might also determine the aggregate amount of revenue to be raised from the citizens each year to finance those services. But the determination of the share each citizen would be compelled to contribute to this total would have to be made by a true law; that is, the sort of obligatory and uniform rule of individual conduct which only the legislative assembly could lay down. It is difficult to conceive of a more salutary control of expenditure than such a system in which every member of the governmental assembly would know that to every expenditure he supported he and his constituents would have to contribute at a rate he could not alter!

The critical issue then becomes the composition of the legislative assembly. How can we at the same time make it truly representative of general opinion about what is right, and yet make it immune from any pressure of special interests? The legislative assembly constitutionally would be limited to passing general laws, so that any specific or discriminating order it issued would be invalid. It would owe its authority to its commitment to general rules. The constitution would define the properties such a rule must possess to be valid law, such as applicability to an unknown number of future instances, uniformity, generality, and so on. A constitutional court would gradually have to elaborate that definition as well as decide any conflict of competence between the two assemblies.

But this limitation to passing genuine laws would hardly suffice to prevent collusion of the legislative with a similarly composed governmental assembly, for which it would be likely to provide the laws which that assembly needed for its particular purposes, with results little different from those of the present system. What we want in the legislative assembly is clearly a body representing general opinion, and not particular interests; and it should therefore be composed of individuals who, once entrusted with this task, are independent from the support of any particular group. It should also consist of men and women who could take a long-term view, and would not be swayed by the temporary passions and fashions of a fickle multitude which they had to please.

VII

This would seem to require, in the first instance, independence of parties, and this could be secured by the second, independently necessary condition — namely, not being influenced by the desire for re-election. I imagine for this reason a body of men and women who, after having gained reputation and trust in the ordinary pursuits of life, were elected for a single long period of something like 15 years. To assure that they had gained sufficient experience and respect, and that they did not have to be concerned about securing a livelihood for the period after the end of their tenure, I would fix the age of election comparatively high, say at 45 years, and assure them for another 10 years after expiry of their mandate at 60 of some dignified posts as lay-judges or the like. The average age of the member of such an assembly would, at less than 53 years, still be lower than that of most comparable assemblies today.

The assembly would of course not be elected as a whole at one date, but every year those who had served their 15 years' period would be replaced by 45-year-olds. I would favour these annual elections of one-fifteenth of the membership to be made by their contemporaries, so that every citizen would vote only once in his life, in his forty-fifth year, for one of his contemporaries to become a legislator. This seems to me desirable not only because of old experience in military and similar organisations that contemporaries are usually the best judges of a man's character and abilities, but also because it would probably become the occasion of the growth of such institutions as local age clubs which would make elections on the basis of personal knowledge possible.

Since there would be no parties, there would of course be no nonsense about proportional representation. Contemporaries of a region would confer the distinction as a sort of prize for the most admired member of the class. There are many other fascinating questions which an arrangement of this sort raises, such as whether for this purpose some sort of indirect election might not be preferable (with the local clubs vying for the honour of one of their delegates being elected representative), but which it would not be appropriate to consider in an exposition of the general principle.

VIII

I do not think experienced politicians will find my description of the procedure in our present legislatures very wrong, though they will probably regard as inevitable and beneficial what to me seems avoidable and harmful. But they ought not to be offended by hearing it described as institutionalised blackmail and corruption, because it is we who maintain institutions which make it necessary for them thus to act if they are to be able to do any good.

To a certain extent the bargaining I have described is probably in fact inevitable in democratic *government*.

What I object to is that the prevailing institutions carry this into that supreme body which ought to make the rules of the game and restrain government. The misfortune is not that those kinds of things happen — in local administration they can probably not be avoided — but that they happen in that supreme body that has to make our laws, which are supposed to protect us against oppression and arbitrariness.

One further important and very desirable effect of separating the legislative from the governmental power would be that it would eliminate the chief cause of the accelerating centralisation and concentration of power. This is today the result of the fact that, as a consequence of the fusion of the legislative and the governmental power in the same assembly, it possesses powers which in a free society no authority should possess. Of course, more and more governmental tasks are pushed up to that body which can meet particular demands by making special laws for the purpose. If the powers of the central government were no greater than those of the regional or local governments, only those matters where a uniform national regulation would seem advantageous to all would be handled by the central government, and much that is now so handled would be devolved to lower units.

Once it is generally recognised that government under the law and unlimited powers of the representatives of the majority are irreconcilable, and all government is equally placed under the law, little more than external relations need to be entrusted to central *government* — as distinct from legislation — and the regional and local governments, limited by the same uniform laws with regard to the manner in which they could make their individual inhabitants contribute to their revenue, would develop into business-like corporations competing with each other for citizens who could vote with their feet for that corporation which offered them the highest benefits compared with the price charged.

In this manner we may still be able to preserve democracy and at the same time stop the drift towards what has been called 'totalitarian democracy', which to many people already appears irresistible.

The Principles of a Liberal Social Order

·20·

By 'liberalism' I shall understand here the conception of a desirable political order which in the first instance was developed in England from the time of the Old Whigs in the later part of the seventeenth century to that of Gladstone at the end of the nineteenth. David Hume, Adam Smith, Edmund Burke, T. B. Macaulay and Lord Acton may be regarded as its typical representatives in England. It was this conception of individual liberty under the law which in the first instance inspired the liberal movements on the Continent and which became the basis of the American political tradition. A few of the leading political thinkers in those countries like B. Constant and A. de Tocqueville in France, Immanuel Kant, Friedrich von Schiller and Wilhelm von Humboldt in Germany, and James Madison, John Marshall and Daniel Webster in the United States belong wholly to it.

This liberalism must be clearly distinguished from another, originally Continental European tradition, also called 'liberalism' of which what now claims this name in the United States is a direct descendant. This latter view, though beginning with an attempt to imitate

---

A paper submitted to the Tokyo Meeting of the Mont Pélèrin Society, September 1966, and published in *Il Politico,* December 1966.

the first tradition, interpreted it in the spirit of a constructivist rationalism prevalent in France and thereby made of it something very different, and in the end, instead of advocating limitations on the powers of government, ended up with the ideal of the unlimited powers of the majority. This is the tradition of Voltaire, Rousseau, Condorcet and the French Revolution which became the ancestor of modern socialism. English utilitarianism has taken over much of this Continental tradition and the late-nineteenth-century British liberal party, resulting from a fusion of the liberal Whigs and the utilitarian Radicals, was also a product of this mixture.

Liberalism and democracy, although compatible, are not the same. The first is concerned with the extent of governmental power, the second with who holds this power. The difference is best seen if we consider their opposites: the opposite of liberalism is totalitarianism, while the opposite of democracy is authoritarianism. In consequence, it is at least possible in principle that a democratic government may be totalitarian and that an authoritarian government may act on liberal principles. The second kind of 'liberalism' mentioned before has in effect become democratism rather than liberalism and, demanding *unlimited* power of the majority, has become essentially anti-liberal.

It should be specially emphasized that the two political philosophies which both describe themselves as 'liberalism' and lead in a few respects to similar conclusions, rest on altogether different philosophical foundations. The first is based on an evolutionary interpretation of all phenomena of culture and mind and on an insight into the limits of the powers of the human reason. The second rests on what I have called 'constructivist' rationalism, a conception which leads to the treatment of all cultural phenomena as the product of deliberate design, and on the belief that it is both possible and desirable to reconstruct all grown institutions in accordance with a preconceived plan. The first kind is consequently reverent of tradition and recognizes that all knowledge and all civilization rests on tradition, while the second type is contemptuous of tradition because it regards an independently existing reason as capable of designing civilization. (Cf. the statement by Voltaire: 'If you want good laws, burn those you have and make new ones.') The first is also an essentially modest creed, relying on abstraction as the only available means to extend the limited powers of reason, while the second refuses to recognize any such limits and believes that reason alone can prove the desirability of particular concrete arrangements.

(It is a result of this difference that the first kind of liberalism is at least not incompatible with religious beliefs and has often been held and even been developed by men holding strong religious beliefs, while the 'Continental' type of liberalism has always been antagonistic to all religion and politically in constant conflict with organized religions.)

The first kind of liberalism, which we shall henceforth alone consider, is itself not the result of a theoretical construction but arose from the desire to extend and generalize the beneficial effects which unexpectedly had followed on the limitations placed on the powers of government out of sheer distrust of the rulers. Only after it was found that the unquestioned greater personal liberty which the Englishman enjoyed in the eighteenth century had produced an unprecedented material prosperity were attempts made to develop a systematic theory of liberalism, attempts which in England never were carried very far while the Continental interpretations largely changed the meaning of the English tradition.

Liberalism thus derives from the discovery of a self-generating or spontaneous order in social affairs (the same discovery which led to the recognition that there existed an object for theoretical social sciences), an order which made it possible to utilize the knowledge and skill of all members of society to a much greater extent than would be possible in any order created by central direction, and the consequent desire to make as full use of these powerful spontaneous ordering forces as possible.

It was thus in their efforts to make explicit the principles of an order already existing but only in an imperfect form that Adam Smith and his followers developed the basic principles of liberalism in order to demonstrate the desirability of their general application. In doing this they were able to presuppose familiarity with the common law conception of justice and with the ideals of the rule of law and of government under the law which were little understood outside the Anglo-Saxon world; with the result that not only were their ideas not fully understood outside the English-speaking countries, but that they ceased to be fully understood even in England when Bentham and his followers replaced the English legal tradition by a constructivist utilitarianism derived more from Continental rationalism than from the evolutionary conception of the English tradition.

The central concept of liberalism is that under the enforcement of universal rules of just conduct, protecting a recognizable private domain of individuals, a spontaneous order of human activities of much greater complexity will form itself than could ever be produced by deliberate arrangement, and that in consequence the coercive activities of government should be limited to the enforcement of such rules, whatever other services government may at the same time render by administering those particular resources which have been placed at its disposal for those purposes.

The distinction between a *spontaneous order* based on abstract rules which leave individuals free to use their own knowledge for their own purposes, and an *organization or arrangement* based on commands, is of central importance for the understanding of the principles of a free society and must in the following paragraphs be explained in some detail, especially as the spontaneous order of a free society will contain many organizations (including the biggest organization, government), but the two principles of order cannot be mixed in any manner we may wish.

The first peculiarity of a spontaneous order is that by using its ordering forces (the regularity of the conduct of its members) we can achieve an order of a much more complex set of facts than we could ever achieve by deliberate arrangement, but that, while availing ourselves of this possibility of inducing an order of much greater extent than we otherwise could, we at the same time limit our power over the details of that order. We shall say that when using the former principle we shall have power only over the abstract character but not over the concrete detail of that order.

No less important is the fact that, in contrast to an organization, neither has a spontaneous order a purpose nor need there be agreement on the concrete results it will produce in order to agree on the desirability of such an order, because, being independent of any particular purpose, it can be used for, and will assist in the pursuit of, a great many different, divergent and even conflicting individual purposes. Thus the order of the market, in particular, rests not on common purposes but on reciprocity, that is on the reconciliation of different purposes for the mutual benefit of the participants.

The conception of the common welfare or of the public good of a free society can therefore never be defined as a sum of known particular results to be achieved, but only as an abstract order which as a whole is not oriented on any particular concrete ends but provides merely the best chance for any member selected at random successfully to use his knowledge for his purposes. Adopting a term of Professor Michael Oakeshott (London), we may call such a free society a *nomocratic* (law-governed) as distinguished from an unfree *telocratic* (purpose-governed) social order.

The great importance of the spontaneous order or nomocracy rests on the fact that it extends the possibility of peaceful co-existence of men for their mutual benefit beyond the small group whose members have concrete common purposes, or were subject to a common superior, and that it thus made the appearance of the *Great* or *Open Society* possible. This order which has progressively grown beyond the organizations of the family, the horde, the clan and the tribe, the principalities and even the empire or national state, and has produced at least the beginning of a world society, is based on the adoption — without and often against the desire of political authority — of rules which came to prevail because the groups who observed them were more successful; and it has existed and grown in extent long before men were aware of its existence or understood its operation.

The spontaneous order of the market, based on reciprocity or mutual benefits, is commonly described as an economic order; and in the vulgar sense of the term 'economic' the Great Society is indeed held together entirely by what are commonly called economic forces. But it is exceedingly misleading, and has become one of the chief sources of confusion and misunderstanding, to call this order an economy as we do when we speak of a national, social, or world economy. This is at least one of the chief sources of most socialist endeavour to turn the spontaneous order of the market into a deliberately run organization serving an agreed system of common ends.

An economy in the strict sense of the word in which we can call a household, a farm, an enterprise or even the financial administration of government an economy, is indeed an organization or a deliberate arrangement of a given stock of resources in the service of a unitary order of purposes. It rests on a system of coherent decisions in which a single view of the relative importance of the different competing purposes determines the uses to be made of the different resources.

The spontaneous order of the market resulting from the interaction of many such economies is something so fundamentally different from an economy proper that it must be regarded as a great misfortune that it has ever been called by the same name. I have become convinced that this practice so constantly misleads people that it is necessary to invent a new technical term for it. I propose that we call this spontaneous order of the market a *catallaxy* in analogy to the term 'catallactics', which has often been proposed as a substitute for the term 'economics'. (Both 'catallaxy' and 'catallactics' derive from the ancient Greek verb *katallattein* which, significantly, means not only 'to barter' and 'to exchange' but also 'to admit into the community' and 'to turn from enemy into friend'.)

The chief point about the catallaxy is that, as a spontaneous order, its orderliness does *not* rest on its orientation on a single hierarchy of ends, and that, therefore, it will *not* secure that for it as a whole the more important comes before the less important. This is the chief cause of its condemnation by its opponents, and it could be said that most of the socialist demands amount to nothing less than that the catallaxy should be turned into an economy proper (i.e., the purposeless spontaneous order into a purpose-oriented organization) in order to assure that the more important be never sacrificed to the less important. The defence of the free society must therefore show that it is due to the fact that we do not enforce a unitary scale of concrete ends, nor attempt to secure that some particular view about what is more and what is less important governs the whole of society, that the members of such a free society have as good a chance successfully to use their individual knowledge for the achievement of their individual purposes as they in fact have.

The extension of an order of peace beyond the small purpose-oriented organization became thus possible by the extension of purpose-independent ('formal') rules of just conduct to the relations with other men who did not pursue the same concrete ends or hold the same values except those abstract rules — rules which did not impose obligations for particular actions (which always presuppose a concrete end) but consisted solely in prohibitions from infringing the protected domain of each which these rules enable us to determine. Liberalism is therefore inseparable from the institution of private property which is the name we usually give to the material part of this protected individual domain.

But if liberalism presupposes the enforcement of rules of just conduct and expects a desirable spontaneous order to form itself only if appropriate rules of just conduct are in fact observed, it also wants to restrict the *coercive* powers of government to the enforcement of such rules of just conduct, including at least one prescribing a positive duty, namely, the rule requiring citizens to contribute according to uniform principles not only to the cost of enforcing those rules but also to the costs of the non-coercive service functions of government which we shall presently consider. Liberalism is therefore the same as the demand for the rule of law in the classical sense of the term according to which the coercive functions of government are strictly limited to the enforcement of uniform rules of law, meaning uniform rules of just conduct towards one's fellows. (The 'rule of law' corresponds here to what in German is called *materieller Rechtsstaat* as distinguished from the mere *formelle Rechtsstaat* which requires only that each act of government is authorized by legislation, whether such a law consists of a general rule of just conduct or not.)

Liberalism recognizes that there are certain other services which for various reasons the spontaneous forces of the market may not produce or may not produce adequately, and that for this reason it is desirable to put at the disposal of government a clearly circumscribed body of resources with which it can render such services to the citizens in general. This requires a sharp distinction between the coercive powers of government, in which its actions are strictly limited to the enforcement of rules of just conduct and in the exercise of which all discretion is excluded, and the provision of services by government, for which it can use only the resources put at its disposal for this purpose, has no coercive power or monopoly, but in the use of which resources it enjoys wide discretion.

It is significant that such a conception of a liberal order has arisen only in countries in which, in ancient Greece and Rome no less than in modern Britain, justice was conceived as something to be discovered by the efforts of judges or scholars and not as determined by the arbitrary will of any authority; that it always had difficulty in taking roots in countries in which law was conceived primarily as the product of deliberate legislation, and that it has everywhere declined under the joint influence of legal positivism and of democratic doctrine, both of which know no other criterion of justice than the will of the legislator.

Liberalism has indeed inherited from the theories of the common law and from the older (pre-rationalist) theories of the law of nature, and also presupposes, a conception of justice which allows us to distinguish between such rules of just individual conduct as are implied in the conception of the 'rule of law' and are required for the formation of a spontaneous order on the one hand, and all the particular commands issued by authority for the purpose of organization on the other. This essential distinction has been made explicit in the legal theories of two of the greatest philosophers of modern times, David Hume and Immanuel Kant, but has not been adequately restated since and is wholly uncongenial to the governing theories of our day.

The essential points of this conception of justice are (a) that justice can be meaningfully attributed only to human action and not to any state of affairs as such without reference to the question whether it has been, or could have been, deliberately brought about by somebody; (b) that the rules of justice have essentially the nature of prohibitions, or, in other words, that injustice is really the primary concept and the aim of rules of just conduct is to prevent unjust action; (c) that the injustice to be prevented is the infringement of the protected domain of one's fellow men, a domain which is to be ascertained by means of these rules of justice; and (d) that these rules of just conduct which are in themselves negative can be developed by consistently applying to whatever such rules a society has inherited the equally negative test of universal applicability — a test which, in the last resort, is nothing else than the self-consistency of the actions which these rules allow if applied to the circumstances of the real world. These four crucial points must be developed further in the following paragraphs.

Ad(*a*): Rules of just conduct can require the individual to take into account in his decisions only such consequences of his actions as he himself can foresee. The concrete results of the catallaxy for particular people are, however, essentially unpredictable; and since they are not the effect of anyone's design or intentions, it is meaningless to describe the manner in which the market distributed the good things of this world among particular people as just or unjust. This, however, is what the so-called 'social' or 'distributive' justice aims at in the name of which the liberal order of law is progressively destroyed. We shall later see that no test or criteria have been found or can be found by which such rules of 'social justice' can be assessed, and that, in consequence, and in contrast to the rules of just conduct, they would have to be determined by the arbitrary will of the holders of power.

Ad(*b*): No particular human action is fully determined without a concrete purpose it is meant to achieve. Free men who are to be allowed to use their own means and their own knowledge for their own purposes must therefore not be subject to rules which tell them what they must positively do, but only to rules which tell them what they must not do; except for the discharge of obligations an individual has voluntarily incurred, the rules of just conduct thus merely delimit the range of permissible actions but do not determine the particular actions a man must take at a particular moment. (There are certain rare exceptions to this, like actions to save or protect life, prevent catastrophes, and the like, where either rules of justice actually do require, or would at least generally be accepted as just rules if they required, some positive action. It would lead far to discuss here the position of such rules in the system.) The generally negative character of the rules of just conduct, and the corresponding primacy of the injustice which is prohibited, has often been noticed but scarcely ever been thought through to its logical consequences.

Ad(c): The injustice which is prohibited by rules of just conduct is any encroachment on the protected domain of other individuals, and they must therefore enable us to ascertain what is the protected sphere of others. Since the time of John Locke it is customary to describe this protected domain as property (which Locke himself had defined as 'the life, liberty, and possessions of a man'). This term suggests, however, a much too narrow and purely material conception of the protected domain which includes not only material goods but also various claims on others and certain expectations. If the concept of property is, however, (with Locke) interpreted in this wide sense, it is true that law, in the sense of rules of justice, and the institution of property are inseparable.

Ad(d): It is impossible to decide about the justice of any one particular rule of just conduct except within the framework of a whole system of such rules, most of which must for this purpose be regarded as unquestioned: values can always be tested only in terms of other values. The test of the justice of a rule is usually (since Kant) described as that of its 'universalizability', i.e., of the possibility of willing that the rules should be applied to all instances that correspond to the conditions stated in it (the 'categorical imperative'). What this amounts to is that in applying it to any concrete circumstances it will not conflict with any other accepted rules. The test is thus in the last resort one of the compatibility or non-contradictoriness of the whole system of rules, not merely in a logical sense but in the sense that the system of actions which the rules permit will not lead to conflict.

It will be noticed that only purpose-independent ('formal') rules pass this test because, as rules which have originally been developed in small, purpose-connected groups ('organizations') are progressively extended to larger and larger groups and finally universalized to apply to the relations between any members of an Open Society who have no concrete purposes in common and merely submit to the same abstract rules, they will in this process have to shed all references to particular purposes.

The growth from the tribal organization, all of whose members served common purposes, to the spontaneous order of the Open Society in which people are allowed to pursue their own purposes in peace, may thus be said to have commenced when for the first time a savage placed some goods at the boundary of his tribe in the hope that some member of another tribe would find them and leave in turn behind some other goods to secure the repetition of the offer. From the first establishment of such a practice which served reciprocal but not common purposes, a process has been going on for millennia which, by making rules of conduct independent of the particular purposes of those concerned, made it possible to extend these rules to ever wider circles of undetermined persons and eventually might make possible a universal peaceful order of the world.

The character of those universal rules of just individual conduct, which liberalism presupposes and wishes to improve as much as possible, has been obscured by confusion with that other part of law which determines the organization of government and guides it in the administration of the resources placed at its disposal. It is a characteristic of liberal society that the private individual can be coerced to obey only the rules of private and criminal law; and the progressive permeation of private law by public law in the course of the last eighty or hundred years, which means a progressive replacement of rules of conduct by rules of organization, is one of the main ways in which the destruction of the liberal order has been effected. A German scholar (Franz Böhm) has for this reason recently described the liberal order very justly as the *Privatrechtsgesellschaft* (private law society).

The difference between the order at which the rules of conduct of private and criminal law aim, and the order at which the rules of organization of public law aim, comes out most clearly if we consider that rules of conduct will determine an order of action only in combination with the particular knowledge and aims of the acting individuals, while the rules of organization of public law determine directly such concrete action in the light of particular purposes, or, rather, give some authority power to do so. The confusion between rules of conduct and rules of organization has been assisted by an erroneous identification of what is often called the 'order of law' with the order of actions, which in a free system is not fully determined by the system of laws but merely presupposes such system of laws as one of the conditions required for its formation. Not every system of rules of conduct which secures uniformity of action (which is how the 'order of law' is frequently interpreted) will, however, secure an order of action in the sense that the actions permitted by the rules will not conflict.

The progressive displacement of the rules of conduct of private and criminal law by a conception derived from public law is the process by which existing liberal societies are progressively transformed into totalitarian societies. This tendency has been most explicitly seen and supported by Adolf Hitler's 'crown jurist' Carl Schmitt who consistently advocated the replacement of the 'normative' thinking of liberal law by a conception of law which regards as its purpose the 'concrete order formation' (*konkretes Ordnungsdenken*).

Historically this development has become possible as a result of the fact that the same representative assemblies have been charged with the two different tasks of laying down rules of individual conduct and laying down rules and giving orders concerning the organization and conduct of government. The consequence of this has been that the term 'law' itself, which in the older conception of the 'rule of law' had meant only rules of conduct equally applicable to all, came to mean any rule of organization or even any particular command approved by the constitutionally appointed legislature. Such a conception of the rule of law which merely demands that a command be legitimately issued and not that it be a rule of justice equally applicable to all (what the Germans call the merely *formelle Rechtsstaat*), of course no longer provides any protection of individual freedom.

If it was the nature of the constitutional arrangements prevailing in all Western democracies which made this development possible, the driving force which guided it in the particular direction was the growing recognition that the application of uniform or equal rules to the conduct of individuals who were in fact very different in many respects, inevitably produced very different results for the different individuals; and that in order to bring about by government action a reduction in these unintended but inevitable differences in the material position of different people, it would be necessary to treat them not according to the same but according to different rules. This gave rise to a new and altogether different conception of justice, namely that usually described as 'social' or 'distributive' justice, a conception of justice which did not confine itself to rules of conduct for the individual but aimed at particular results for particular people, and which therefore could be achieved only in a purpose-governed organization but not in a purpose-independent spontaneous order.

The concepts of a 'just price', a 'just remuneration' or a 'just distribution of incomes' are of course very old; it deserves notice, however, that in the course of the efforts of two thousand years in which philosophers have speculated about the meaning of these concepts, not a single rule has been discovered which would allow us to determine what is in this sense just in a market order. Indeed the one group of scholars which have most persistently pursued the question, the schoolmen of the later middle ages and early modern times, were finally driven to define the just price or wage as that price or wage which would form itself on a market in the absence of fraud, violence or privilege — thus referring back to the rules of just conduct and accepting as a just result whatever was brought about by the just conduct of all individuals concerned. This negative conclusion of all the speculations about 'social' or 'distributive' justice was, as we shall see, inevitable, because a just remuneration or distribution has meaning only within an organization whose members act under command in the service of a common system of ends, but can have no meaning whatever in a catallaxy or spontaneous order which can have no such common system of ends.

A state of affairs as such, as we have seen, cannot be just or unjust as a mere fact. Only in so far as it has been brought about designedly or could be so brought about does it make sense to call just or unjust the actions of those who have created it or permitted it to arise. In the catallaxy, the spontaneous order of the market, nobody can foresee, however, what each participant will get, and the results for particular people are not determined by anyone's intentions; nor is anyone responsible for particular people getting particular things. We might therefore question whether a deliberate choice of the market order as the method for guiding economic activities, with the unpredictable and in a great measure chance incidence of its benefits, is a just decision, but certainly not whether, once we have decided to avail ourselves of the catallaxy for that purpose, the particular results it produces for particular people are just or unjust.

That the concept of justice is nevertheless so commonly and readily applied to the distribution of incomes is entirely the effect of an erroneous anthropomorphic interpretation of society as an organization rather than as a spontaneous order. The term 'distribution' is in this sense quite as misleading as the term 'economy', since it also suggests that something is the result of deliberate action which in fact is the result of spontaneous ordering forces. Nobody distributes income in a market order (as would have to be done in an organization) and to speak, with respect to the former, of a just or unjust distribution is therefore simple respect to the former, of a just or unjust distribution is therefore simple nonsense. It would be less misleading to speak in this respect of a 'dispersion' rather than a 'distribution' of incomes.

All endeavours to secure a 'just' distribution must thus be directed towards turning the spontaneous order of the market into an organization or, in other words, into a totalitarian order. It was this striving after a new conception of justice which produced the various steps by which rules of organization ('public law'), which were designed to make people aim at particular results, came to supersede the purpose-independent rules of just individual conduct, and which thereby gradually destroyed the foundations on which a spontaneous order must rest.

The ideal of using the coercive powers of government to achieve 'positive' (i.e., social or distributive) justice leads, however, not only necessarily to the destruction of individual freedom, which some might not think too high a price, but it also proves on examination a mirage or an illusion which cannot be achieved in any circumstances, because it presupposes an agreement on the relative importance of the different concrete ends which cannot exist in a great society whose members do not know each other or the same particular facts. It is sometimes believed that the fact that most people today desire social justice demonstrates that this ideal has a determinable content. But it is unfortunately only too possible to chase a mirage, and the consequence of this is always that the result of one's striving will be utterly different from what one had intended.

There can be no rules which determine how much everybody 'ought' to have unless we make some unitary conception of relative 'merits' or 'needs' of the different individuals, for which there exists no objective measure, the basis of a central allocation of all goods and services — which would make it necessary that each individual, instead of using *his* knowledge for *his* purposes, were made to fulfil a duty imposed upon him by somebody else, and were remunerated according to how well he has, in the opinion of others, performed this duty. This is the method of remuneration appropriate to a closed organization, such as an army, but irreconcilable with the forces which maintain a spontaneous order.

It ought to be freely admitted that the market order does not bring about any close correspondence between subjective merit or individual needs and rewards. It operates on the principle of a combined game of skill and chance in which the results for each individual may be as much determined by circumstances wholly beyond his control as by his skill or effort. Each is remunerated according to the value his particular services have to the particular people to whom he renders them, and this value of his services stands in no necessary relation to anything which we could appropriately call his merits and still less to his needs.

It deserves special emphasis that, strictly speaking, it is meaningless to speak of a value 'to society' when what is in question is the value of some services to certain people, services which may be of no interest to anybody else. A violin virtuoso presumably renders services to entirely different people from those whom a football star entertains, and the maker of pipes altogether different people from the maker of perfumes. The whole conception of a 'value to society' is in a free order as illegitimate an anthropomorphic term as its description as 'one economy' in the strict sense, as an entity which 'treats' people justly or unjustly, or 'distributes' among them. The results of the market process for particular individuals are neither the result of anybody's will that they should have so much, nor even foreseeable by those who have decided upon or support the maintenance of this kind of order.

Of all the complaints about the injustice of the results of the market order the one which appears to have had the greatest effect on actual policy, and to have produced a progressive destruction of the equal rules of just conduct and their replacement by a 'social' law aiming at 'social justice', however, was not the extent of the inequality of the rewards, nor their disproportion with recognizable merits, needs, efforts, pains incurred, or whatever else has been chiefly stressed by social philosophers, but the demands for protection against an undeserved descent from an already achieved position. More than by anything else the market order has been distorted by efforts to protect groups from a decline from their former position; and when government interference is demanded in the name of 'social justice' this now means, more often than not, the demand for the protection of the existing relative position of some group. 'Social justice' has thus become little more than a demand for the protection of vested interests and the creation of new privilege, such as when in the name of social justice the farmer is assured 'parity' with the industrial worker.

The important facts to be stressed here are that the positions thus protected were the result of the same sort of forces as those which now reduce the relative position of the same people, that their position for which they now demand protection was no more deserved or earned then the diminished position now in prospect for them, and that their former position could in the changed position be secured to them only by denying to others the same chances of ascent to which they owed their former position. In a market order the fact that a group of persons has achieved a certain relative position cannot give them a claim in justice to maintain it, because this cannot be defended by a rule which could be equally applied to all.

The aim of economic policy of a free society can therefore never be to assure particular results to particular people, and its success cannot be measured by any attempt at adding up the value of such particular results. In this respect the aim of what is called 'welfare economics' is fundamentally mistaken, not only because no meaningful sum can be formed of the satisfactions provided for different people, but because its basic idea of a maximum of need-fulfilment (or a maximum social product) is appropriate only to an economy proper which serves a single hierarchy of ends, but not to the spontaneous order of a catallaxy which has no common concrete ends.

Though it is widely believed that the conception of an optimal economic policy (or any judgment whether one economic policy is better than another) presupposes such a conception of maximizing aggregate real social income (which is possible only in value terms and therefore implies an illegitimate comparison of the utility to different persons), this is in fact not so. An optimal policy in a catallaxy may aim, and ought to aim, at increasing the chances of any member of society taken at random of having a high income, or, what amounts to the same thing, the chance that, whatever his share in total income may be, the real equivalent of this share will be as large as we know how to make it.

This condition will be approached as closely as we can manage, irrespective of the dispersion of incomes, if everything which is produced is being produced by persons or organizations who can produce it more cheaply than (or at least as cheaply as) anybody who does not produce it, and is sold at a price lower than that at which it would be possible to offer it for anybody who does not in fact so offer it. (This allows for persons or organizations to whom the costs of producing one commodity or service are lower than they are for those who actually produce it and who still produce something else instead, because their comparative advantage in that other production is still greater; in this case the total costs of their producing the first commodity would have to include the loss of the one which is not produced.)

It will be noticed that this optimum does not presuppose what economic theory calls 'perfect competition' but only that there are no obstacles to the entry into each trade and that the market functions adequately in spreading information about opportunities. It should also be specially observed that this modest and achievable goal has never yet been fully achieved because at all times and everywhere governments have both restricted access to some occupations and tolerated persons and organizations deterring others from entering occupations when this would have been to the advantage of the latter.

This optimum position means that as much will be produced of whatever combination of products and services is in fact produced as can be produced by any method that we know, because we can through such a use of the market mechanism bring more of the dispersed knowledge of the members of society into play than by any other. But it will be achieved only if we leave the share in the total, which each member will get, to be determined by the market mechanism and all its accidents, because it is only through the market determination of incomes that each is led to do what this result requires.

We owe, in other words, our chances that our unpredictable share in the total product of society represents as large an aggregate of goods and services as it does to the fact that thousands of others constantly submit to the adjustments which the market forces on them; and it is consequently also our duty to accept the same kind of changes in our income and position, even if it means a decline in our accustomed position and is due to circumstances we could not have foreseen and for which we are not responsible. The conception that we have 'earned' (in the sense of morally deserved) the income we had when we were more fortunate, and that we are therefore entitled to it so long as we strive as honestly as before and had no warning to turn elsewhere, is wholly mistaken. Everybody, rich or poor, owes his income to the outcome of a mixed game of skill and chance, the aggregate result of which and the shares in which are as high as they are only because we have agreed to play that game. And once we have agreed to play the game and profited from its results, it is a moral obligation on us to abide by the results even if they turn against us.

There can be little doubt that in modern society all but the most unfortunate and those who in a different kind of society might have enjoyed a legal privilege, owe to the adoption of that method an income much larger than they could otherwise enjoy. There is of course no reason why a society which, thanks to the market, is as rich as modern society should not provide *outside the market* a minimum security for all who in the market fall below a certain standard. Our point was merely that considerations of justice provide no justification for 'correcting' the results of the market and that justice, in the sense of treatment under the same rules, requires that each takes what a market provides in which every participant behaves fairly. There is only a justice of individual conduct but not a separate 'social justice'.

We cannot consider here the legitimate tasks of government in the administration of the resources placed at its disposal for the rendering of services to the citizens. With regard to these functions, for the discharge of which the government is given money, we will here only say that in exercising them government should be under the same rules as every private citizen, that it should possess no monopoly for a particular service of the kind, that it should discharge these functions in such a manner as not to disturb the much more comprehensive spontaneously ordered efforts of society, and that the means should be raised according to a rule which applies uniformly to all. (This, in my opinion, precludes an overall progression of the burden of taxation of the individuals, since such a use of taxation for purposes of redistribution could be justified only by such arguments as we have just excluded.) In the remaining paragraphs we shall be concerned only with some of the functions of government for the discharge of which it is given not merely money but power to enforce rules of private conduct.

The only part of these coercive functions of government which we can further consider in this outline are those which are concerned with the preservation of a functioning market order. They concern primarily the conditions which must be provided by law to secure the degree of competition required to steer the market efficiently. We shall briefly consider this question first with regard to enterprise and then with regard to labour.

With regard to enterprise the first point which needs underlining is that it is more important that government refrain from assisting monopolies than that it combat monopoly. If today the market order is confined only to a part of the economic activities of men, this is largely the result of deliberate government restrictions of competition. It is indeed doubtful whether, if government consistently refrained from creating monopolies and from assisting them through protective tariffs and the character of the law of patents for inventions and of the law of corporations, there would remain an element of monopoly significant enough to require special measures. What must be chiefly remembered in this connection is, firstly, that monopolistic positions are always undesirable but often unavoidable for objective reasons which we cannot or do not wish to alter; and, secondly, that all government-supervised monopolies tend to become government-protected monopolies which will persist when their justification has disappeared.

Current conceptions of anti-monopoly policy are largely misguided by the application of certain conceptions developed by the theory of perfect competition which are irrelevant to conditions where the factual presuppositions of the theory of perfect competition are absent. The theory of perfect competition shows that if on a market the number of buyers and sellers is sufficiently large to make it impossible for any one of them deliberately to influence prices, such quantities will be sold at prices which will equal marginal costs. This does not mean, however, that it is either possible or even necessarily desirable everywhere to bring about a state of affairs where large numbers buy and sell the same uniform commodity. The idea that in situations where we cannot, or do not wish to, bring about such a state, the producers should be held to conduct themselves as if perfect competition existed, or to sell at a price which would rule under perfect competition, is meaningless, because we do not know what would be the particular conduct required, or the price which would be formed, if perfect competition existed.

Where the conditions for perfect competition do not exist, what competition still can and ought to be made to achieve is nevertheless very remarkable and important, namely the conditions described above. It was pointed out then that this state will tend to be approached if nobody can be prevented by government or others to enter any trade or occupation he desired.

This condition would, I believe, be approached as closely as it is possible to secure this if, *firstly,* all agreements to restrain trade were without exception (not prohibited, but merely) made void and unenforceable, and, *secondly,* all discriminatory or other aimed actions towards an actual or potential competitor intended to make him observe certain rules of market conduct were to make liable for multiple damages. It seems to me that such a modest aim would produce a much more effective law than actual prohibitions under penalties, because no exceptions need to be made from such a declaration as invalid or unenforceable of all contracts in restraint of trade, while, as experience has shown, the more ambitious attempts are bound to be qualified by so many exceptions as to make them much less effective.

The application of this same principle that all agreements in restraint of trade should be invalid and unenforceable and that every individual should be protected against all attempts to enforce them by violence or aimed discrimination, is even more important with regard to labour. The monopolistic practices which threaten the functioning of the market are today much more serious on the side of labour than on the side of enterprise, and the preservation of the market order will depend, more than on anything else, on whether we succeed in curbing the latter.

The reason for this is that the developments in this field are bound to force government, and are already forcing many governments, into two kinds of measures which are wholly destructive of the market order: attempts authoritatively to determine the appropriate incomes of the various groups (by what is called an 'incomes policy') and efforts to overcome the wage 'rigidities' by an inflationary monetary policy. But since this evasion of the real issue by only temporarily effective monetary means must have the effect that those 'rigidities' will constantly increase, they are a mere palliative which can only postpone but not solve the central problem.

Monetary and financial policy is outside the scope of this paper. Its problems were mentioned only to point out that its fundamental and in the present situation insoluble dilemmas cannot be solved by any monetary means but only by a restoration of the market as an effective instrument for determining wages.

In conclusion, the basic principles of a liberal society may be summed up by saying that in such a society all coercive functions of government must be guided by the overruling importance of what I like to call THE THREE GREAT NEGATIVES: PEACE, JUSTICE AND LIBERTY. Their achievement requires that in its coercive functions government shall be confined to the enforcement of such prohibitions (stated as abstract rules) as can be equally applied to all, and to exacting under the same uniform rules from all a share of the costs of the other, noncoercive services it may decide to render to the citizens with the material and personal means thereby placed at its disposal.

A Model Constitution

· 21 ·

In all cases it must be advantageous to know what is the most perfect in the kind, that we may be able to bring any real constitution or form of government as near it as possible, by such gentle alterations and innovations as may not give too great a disturbance to society.

David Hume*

The Wrong Turn Taken by the Development of Representative Institutions

What can we do today, in the light of the experience gained, to accomplish the aims which, nearly two hundred years ago, the fathers of the Constitution of the United States of America for the first time attempted to secure by a deliberate construction? Though our aims may still be the same, there is much that we ought to have learnt from the great experiment and its numerous imitations. We know now why the hope of the authors of those documents, that through them they could effectively limit the powers of government, has been disappointed. They had hoped by a separation of the leg-

*David Hume, *Essays,* Part II, Essay XVI, 'The Idea of a Perfect Commonwealth'.

islative from executive as well as the judicial powers to subject government and the individuals to rules of just conduct. They could hardly have foreseen that, because the legislature was also entrusted with the direction of government, the task of stating rules of just conduct and the task of directing particular activities of government to specific ends would come to be hopelessly confounded, and that law would cease to mean only such universal and uniform rules of just conduct as would limit all arbitrary coercion. In consequence, they never really achieved that separation of powers at which they had aimed. Instead they produced in the USA a system under which, often to the detriment of the efficiency of government, the power of organizing and directing government was divided between the chief executive and a representative assembly elected at different times and on different principles and therefore frequently at loggerheads with each other.

We have already seen that the desire to have the laying down of rules of just conduct as well as the direction of current government in the hands of representative bodies need not mean that both these powers should be entrusted to the same body. The possibility of a different solution of the problem[1] is in fact suggested by an earlier phase of the development of representative institutions. The control of the conduct of government was, at least at first, brought about mainly through the control of revenue. By an evolution which started in Britain as early as the end of the fourteenth century the power of the purse had progressively devolved upon the House of Commons. When at last at the end of the seventeenth century the exclusive right of the Commons over 'money bills' was definitely conceded by the House of Lords, the latter, as the highest court in the country, still retained ultimate control of the development of the rules of common law. What would have been more natural than that, in conceding to the Commons sole control of the current conduct of government, the second chamber should have in return claimed the exclusive right to alter by statute the enforceable rules of just conduct?

Such a development was not really possible so long as the upper house represented a small privileged class. But in principle a division by functions instead of a division according to the different classes represented might have led to a situation in which the Commons would have obtained full power over the apparatus of government and all the material means put at its disposal, but would have been able to employ coercion only within the limits of the rules laid down by the House of Lords. In organizing and directing what was properly the task of government they would have been entirely free. To guide the actions of the officers of government concerning what was the property of the state they could have laid down any rules they agreed upon. But neither they nor their servants could have coerced private citizens except to make them obey the rules recognized or laid down by the Upper House. It would then have been entirely logical if the current affairs of government were conducted by a committee of the Lower House, or rather of its majority. Such a government would then in its powers over citizens have been entirely under a law which it would have had no power to alter in order to make it suit its particular purposes.

Such a separation of tasks would have required and gradually produced a sharp distinction between rules of just conduct and instructions to government. It would soon have shown the need for a superior judicial authority, capable of deciding conflicts between the two representative bodies, and by doing so, gradually building up an ever more precise distinction between the two kind of rules; the private (including criminal) and the public law, which are now confused because they are described by the same term, 'law'.

Instead of such a progressive clarification of the fundamental distinction the combination of wholly different tasks in the hands of one and the same body has led to an increasing vagueness of the concept of law. We have seen that the distinction is not an easy one to draw and that the task presents even modern legal thought with some hard problems. But it is not an impossible task. Though a wholly satisfactory solution may require further advance of our understanding. It is through such advance that all law has grown.

The Value of a Model of an Ideal Constitution

Assuming that a distinction between the two kinds of rules which we now call laws can be drawn clearly, its significance will be put into sharper focus if we sketch in some detail the sort of constitutional arrangements which would secure a real separation of powers between two distinct representative bodies whereby lawmaking in the narrow sense as well as government proper would be conducted democratically, but by different and mutually independent agencies. My purpose in presenting such a sketch is not to propose a constitutional scheme for present application. I certainly do not wish to suggest that any country with a firmly established constitutional tradition should replace its constitution by a new one drawn up on the lines suggested. But apart from the fact that the general principles discussed in the preceding pages will obtain more definite shape if I outline here a constitution embodying them, there are two further reasons which appear to make such a sketch worth while.

In the first instance, very few countries in the world are in the fortunate position of possessing a strong constitutional tradition. Indeed, outside the English-speaking world probably only the smaller countries of Northern Europe and Switzerland have such traditions. Most of the other countries have never preserved a constitution long enough to make it become a deeply entrenched tradition; and in many of them there is also lacking the background of traditions and beliefs which in the more fortunate countries have made constitutions work which did not explicitly state all that they presupposed, or which did not even exist in written form. This is even more true of those new countries which, without a tradition even remotely similar to the ideal of the Rule of Law which the nations of Europe have long held, have adopted from the latter the institutions of democracy without the foundations of beliefs and convictions presupposed by those institutions.

If such attempts to transplant democracy are not to fail, much of that background of unwritten traditions and beliefs, which in the successful democracies had for a long time restrained the abuse of the majority power, will have to be spelled out in such instruments of government for the new democracies. That most of such attempts have so far failed does not prove that the basic conceptions of democracy are inapplicable, but only that the particular institutions which for a time worked tolerably well in the West presuppose the tacit acceptance of certain other principles which were in some measure observed there but which, where they are not yet recognized, must be made as much a part of the written constitution as the rest. We have no right to assume that the particular forms of democracy which have worked with us must also work elsewhere. Experience seems to show that they do not. There is, therefore, every reason to ask how those conceptions which our kind of representative institutions tacitly presupposed can be explicitly put into such constitutions.

In the second instance, the principles embodied in the scheme to be outlined may be of relevance in connection with the contemporary endeavours to create new supra-national institutions. There seems to be a growing feeling that we may hope to achieve some sort of international law but that it is doubtful whether we can, or even whether we should, create a supra-national government beyond some pure service agencies. Yet if anything should be clear it is that, if these endeavours are not to fail, or even not to do more harm than good, these new supra-national institutions will for a long time have to be limited to restraining national governments from actions harmful to other countries, but possess no powers to order them to do particular things. Many of the objections which people understandably have to entrusting an international authority with the power of issuing orders to the several national governments might well be met if such a new authority were to be restricted to the establishment of general rules which merely prohibited certain kinds of actions of the member states or their citizens. But to achieve this we have yet to discover how the power of legislation, in the sense in which it was understood by those who believed in the separation ofpowers, can be effectively separated from the powers of government.

The Basic Principles

The basic clause of such a constitution would have to state that in normal times, and apart from certain clearly defined emergency situations, men could be restrained from doing what they wished, or coerced to do particular things, only in accordance with the recognized rules of just conduct designed to define and protect the individual domain of each; and that the accepted set of rules of this kind could be deliberately altered only by what we shall call the Legislative Assembly. This in general would have power only in so far as it proved its intention to be just by committing itself to universal rules intended to be applied in an unknown number of future instances and over the application of which to particular cases it had no further power. The basic clause would have to contain a definition of what can be law in this narrow sense of *nomos* which would enable a court to decide whether any particular resolution of the Legislative Assembly possessed the formal properties to make it law in this sense.

We have seen that such a definition could not rely only on purely logical criteria but would have to require that the rules should be intended to apply to an indefinite number of unknown future instances, to serve the formation and preservation of an abstract order whose concrete contents were unforeseeable, but not the achievement of particular concrete purposes, and finally to exclude all provisions intended or known to affect principally particular identifiable individuals or groups. It would also have to recognize that, though alterations of the recognized body of existing rules of just conduct were the exclusive right of the Legislative Assembly, the initial body of such rules would include not only the products of past legislation but also those not yet articulated conceptions implicit in past decisions by which the courts should be bound and which it would be their task to make explicit.

The basic clause would of course not be intended to define the functions of government but merely to define the limits of its coercive powers. Though it would restrict the means that government could employ in rendering services to the citizens, it would place no direct limit on the content of the services government might render. We shall have to return to this matter when we turn to the functions of the second representative body, the Governmental Assembly.

Such a clause would by itself achieve all and more than the traditional Bills of Rights were meant to secure; and it would therefore make any separate enumeration of a list of special protected fundamental rights unnecessary. This will be clear when it is remembered that none of the traditional Rights of Man, such as the freedom of speech, of the press, of religion, of assembly and association, or of the inviolability of the home or of letters, etc., can be, or ever have been, absolute rights that may not be limited by general rules of law. Freedom of speech does of course not mean that we are free to slander, libel, deceive, incite to crime or cause a panic by false alarm, etc., etc. All these rights are either tacitly or explicitly protected against restrictions only 'save in accordance with the law'. But this limitation, as has become only too clear in modern times, is meaningful and does not deprive the protection of those rights of all efficacy against the 'legislature', only if by 'law' is not meant every properly passed resolution of a representative assembly but only such rules as can be described as laws in the narrow sense here defined.

Nor are the fundamental rights, traditionally protected by Bills of Rights, the only ones that must be protected if arbitrary power is to be prevented, nor can all such essential rights which constitute individual liberty ever be exhaustively enumerated. Though, as has been shown before, the efforts to extend the concept to what are now called social and economic rights were misguided (see appendix to chapter 9 [*Law, Legislation and Liberty,* vol. 3]), there are many unforeseeable exercises of individual freedom which are no less deserving of protection other than those enumerated by various Bills of Rights. Those which are commonly explicitly named are those which at particular times were specially threatened, and particularly those which seemed to need safeguarding if democratic government was to work. But to single them out as being specially protected suggests that in other fields government may use coercion without being bound by general rules of law.

This, indeed, has been the reason why the original framers of the American Constitution did not at first wish to include in it a Bill of Rights, and why, when it was added, the ineffective and all but forgotten Ninth Amendment provided that 'the enumeration in the Constitution, of certain rights, shall not be construed to deny or disparage others retained by the people'. The enumeration of particular rights as being protected against infringements 'save in accordance with the law' indeed might seem to imply that in other respects the legislature is free to restrain or coerce people without committing itself to a general rule. And the extension of the term 'law' to almost any resolution of the legislature has lately made even this protection meaningless. The purpose of a constitution, however, is precisely to prevent even the legislature from all arbitrary restraints and coercion. And, as has been forcefully pointed out by a distinguished Swiss jurist,[2] the new possibilities which technological developments create may in the future make other liberties even more important than those protected by the traditional fundamental rights.

What the fundamental rights are intended to protect is simply individual liberty in the sense of the absence of arbitrary coercion. This requires that coercion be used only to enforce the universal rules of just conduct protecting the individual domains and to raise means to support the services rendered by government; and since what is implied here is that the individual can be restrained only in such conduct as may encroach upon the protected domain of others, he would under such a provision be wholly unrestricted in all actions which affected only his personal domain or that of other consenting responsible persons, and thus be assured all freedom that can be secured by political action. That this freedom may have to be temporarily suspended when those institutions are threatened which are intended to preserve it in the long run, and when it becomes necessary to join in common action for the supreme end of defending them, or to avert some other common danger to the whole society, is another matter which we shall take up later.

The Two Representative Bodies with Distinctive Functions

The idea of entrusting the task of stating the general rules of just conduct to a representative body distinct from the body which is entrusted with the task of government is not entirely new. Something like this was attempted by the ancient Athenians when they allowed only the *nomothetae,* a distinct body, to change the fundamental *nomos.*[3] As *nomos* is about the only term which has preserved at least approximately the meaning of general rules of just conduct, and as the term *nomothetae* was revived in a somewhat similar context in seventeenth century England[4] and again by J. S. Mill,[5] it will be convenient occasionally to use it as a name for that purely legislative body which the advocates of the separation of powers and the theorists of the Rule of Law had in mind, whenever it is necessary emphatically to distinguish it from the second representative body which we shall call the Governmental Assembly.

Such a distinctive legislative assembly would evidently provide an effective check on the decisions of an equally representative governmental body only if its membership were not composed in the same way; this would in practice appear to require that the two assemblies must not be chosen in the same manner, or for the same period. If the two assemblies were merely charged with different tasks but composed of approximately the same proportions of representatives of the same groups and especially parties, the legislature would probably simply provide those laws which the governmental body wanted for its purposes as much as if they were one body.

The different tasks also require that the different assemblies should represent the views of the electors in different respects. For the purpose of government proper it seems desirable that the concrete wishes of the citizens for particular results should find expression, or, in other words, that their particular interests should be represented; for the conduct of government a majority committed to a programme of action and 'capable of governing' is thus clearly needed. Legislation proper, on the other hand, should not be governed by interests but by opinion, i.e. by views about what *kind* of action is right or wrong — not as an instrument for the achievement of particular ends but as a permanent rule and irrespective of the effect on particular individuals or groups. In choosing somebody most likely to look effectively after their particular interests and in choosing persons whom they can trust to uphold justice impartially the people would probably elect very different persons: effectiveness in the first kind of task demands qualities very different from the probity, wisdom, and judgment which are of prime importance in the second.

The system of periodic election of the whole body of representatives is well designed not only to make them responsive to the fluctuating wishes of the electorate, but also to make them organize into parties and to render them dependent on the agreed aims of parties committed to support particular interests and particular programmes of actions. But it also in effect compels the individual member to submit to party discipline to get the support of the party for re-election.

To expect from an assembly of representatives charged with looking after particular interests the qualities which were expected by the classical theorists of democracy from a representative sample of the people at large is unreasonable. But this does not mean that if the people were asked to elect representatives who had no power to grant them particular favours they could not be induced to respond by designating those whose judgment they have learnt most to respect, especially if they had to choose among persons who already had made their reputation in the ordinary pursuits of life.

What would thus appear to be needed for the purposes of legislation proper is an assembly of men and women elected at a relatively mature age for fairly long periods, such as fifteen years, so that they would not have to be concerned about being re-elected, after which period, to make them wholly independent of party discipline, they should not be re-eligible nor forced to return to earning a living in the market but be assured of continued public employment in such honorific but neutral positions as lay judges, so that during their tenure as legislators they would be neither dependent on party support nor concerned about their personal future. To assure this only people who have already proved themselves in the ordinary business of life should be elected and the same time to prevent the assembly's containing too high a proportion of old persons, it would seem wise to rely on the old experience that a man's contemporaries are his fairest judges and to ask each group of people of the same age once in their lives, say in the calendar year in which they reached the age of 45, to select from their midst representatives to serve for fifteen years.

The result would be a legislative assembly of men and women between their 45th and 60th years, one-fifteenth of whom would be replaced every year. The whole would thus mirror that part of the population which had already gained experience and had had an opportunity to make their reputation, but who would still be in their best years. It should be specially noted that, although the under 45s would not be represented in such an assembly, the average age of the members — $52^1/_2$ years — would be less than that of most existing representative bodies, even if the strength of the older part were kept constant by replacement of those dropping out through death and disease, which in the normal course of events would seem unnecessary and would only increase the proportion of those with little experience in the business of legislating.

Various additional safeguards might be employed to secure the entire independence of these *nomothetae* from the pressure of particular interests or organized parties. Persons who had already served in the Governmental Assembly or in party organizations might be made ineligible for the Legislative Assembly. And even if many members might have closer attachment to certain parties, there would be little inducement for them to obey instructions of the party leadership or the government in power.

Members would be removable only for gross misconduct or neglect of duty by some group of their present or former peers on the principles which today apply to judges. The assurance after the end of their tenure and up to the age of retirement with a pension (that is for the time from their 60th to their 70th year) of a dignified position such as that of lay members of judicial courts would be an important factor contributing to their independence; indeed, their salary might be fixed by the Constitution at a certain percentage of the average of, say, the twenty most highly paid posts in the gift of government.

It could be expected that such a position would come to be regarded by each age class as a sort of prize to be awarded to the most highly respected of their contemporaries. As the Legislative Assembly should not be very numerous, comparatively few individuals would have to be elected every year. This might well make it advisable to employ an indirect method of election, with regionally appointed delegates electing the representative from their midst. Thus a further inducement would be provided for each district to appoint as delegates persons of such standing as would have the best chance of being chosen in the second poll.

It might at first seem as if such a purely legislative assembly would have very little work to do. If we think exclusively of those tasks which we have so far stressed, namely the revision of the body of private (including commercial and criminal) law, they would indeed appear to require action only at long intervals, and hardly provide adequate continuous occupation for a select group of highly competent persons. Yet this first impression is misleading. Though we have used private and criminal law as our chief illustrations, it must be remembered that all enforceable rules of conduct would have to have the sanction of this assembly. While, within the compass of this book, we have had little opportunity to go into detail on these matters we have repeatedly pointed out that those tasks include not only the principles of taxation but also all those regulations of safety and health, including regulations of production or construction, that have to be enforced in the general interest and should be stated in the form of general rules. These comprise not only what used to be called safety legislation but also all the difficult problems of creating an adequate framework for a functioning competitive market and the law of corporations which we have mentioned in the last chapter [in *Law, Legislation, and Liberty*].

Such matters have in the past had to be largely delegated by the legislature which had no time for careful consideration of the often highly technical issues involved, and have in consequence been placed in the hands of the bureaucracy or special agencies created for the purpose. Indeed, a 'legislature' chiefly concerned with the pressing matters of current government is bound to find it difficult to give such matters the attention they require. They are nevertheless matters not of administration but of legislation proper, and the danger that the bureaucracy, if the tasks are delegated to it, will assume discretionary and essentially arbitrary powers is considerable. There are no intrinsic reasons why the regulation of these matters should not take the form of general rules (as was still the rule in Britain before 1914), if it were seriously attempted by a legislature, instead of being considered from the point of view of the convenience of administrators ambitious of acquiring power. Probably most of the powers which bureaucracy has acquired, and which are in effect uncontrollable, are the result of delegation by legislatures.

Yet, though I am not really concerned about the members of the legislature lacking adequate occupation, I will add that I should regard it as by no means unfortunate but rather as desirable if a selected group of men and women, who had already made a reputation in the ordinary business of life, were then freed for part of their lives from the necessity or duty of devoting themselves to tasks imposed on them by circumstances so that they would be able to reflect on the principles of government or might take up whatever cause they thought important. A certain sprinkling of people who have leisure is essential if public spirit is to express itself in those voluntary activities where new ideals can manifest themselves. Such was the function of the man of independent means, and though I believe it to be a strong argument for his preservation, there is no reason why people who have acquired property should be the only ones given such an opportunity. If those who have been entrusted by their contemporaries with the highest confidence they can show were to be free to devote a substantial part of their time to tasks of their own choice, they may contribute much to the development of that 'voluntary sector' which is so necessary if government is not to assume overwhelming power. And if the position of a member of the legislature should not prove to be a very onerous one, it ought nevertheless to be made one of great honour and dignity so that in some respects the members of this democratically elected body would be able to play the role of what Max Weber has called the *honoratiores,* independent public figures who, apart from their functions as legislators, and without party ties, could take a leading part in various voluntary efforts.

So far as the chief task of these *nomothetae* is concerned, it may be felt that the main problem would probably not be whether they had enough work to do, but rather whether there would be a sufficient inducement for them to do it. It might be feared that the very degree of independence which they enjoyed might tempt them to become lazy. Though it seems to me not very likely that persons who had earlier made their mark in active life, and whose position would henceforth rest on public reputation should, once they were elected for fifteen years to a position in which they were practically irremovable, in such a manner neglect their duties, yet provisions might be made similar to those applying in the case of judges. Though they must be wholly independent of the governmental organization there might well be some supervision by some senate of former members of the body who in the case of neglect of duties might even be entitled to remove representatives. It would also be such a body which at the end of the tenure of membership of the Legislative Assembly would have to assign positions to each retiring member, ranging from that of a president of the Constitutional Court to that of a lay assessor of some minor judicial body.

The Constitution should, however, also guard against the eventuality of the Legislative Assembly becoming wholly inactive by providing that, while it should have exclusive powers to lay down general rules of just conduct, this power might devolve temporarily to the Governmental Assembly if the former did not respond within a reasonable period to a notice given by government that some rules should be laid down on a particular question. Such a constitutional provision would probably by its mere existence make it unnecessary that it should ever have to be invoked. The jealousy of the Legislative Assembly would probably operate strongly enough to assure that it would within a reasonable time answer any question of rules of just conduct which was raised.

Further Observations on Representation by Age Groups

Although only the general principle of the suggested model constitution is relevant to the main theme of this book, the method of representation by generations proposed for the Legislative Assembly offers so many interesting possibilities for the development of democratic institutions that it seems worthwhile to elaborate on it a little further. The fact that the members of each age class would know that some day they would have an important common task to perform might well lead to the early formation of local clubs of contemporaries, and since this would contribute towards the proper education of suitable candidates, such a tendency would seem to deserve public support, at least through the provision of regular meeting places and facilities for contacts between the groups of different localities. The existence in each locality of only one such publically assisted and recognised group for every age class might also help to prevent a splitting of groups on party lines.

Clubs of contemporaries might well be formed either at school-leaving age or at least when each class entered public life, say at the age of 18. They would possibly be more attractive if men of one age group were brought together with women two years or so younger. This might be achieved, without any objectionable legal discrimination, by allowing men and women at the age of eighteen to join either the then newly formed club or one of those formed in one of the preceding two or three years, in which case probably most men would prefer to join their own new club, while women would seem more likely to join one of those started in the preceding years. Such a choice would of course imply that those opting for the higher age class would permanently belong to it and vote for the delegate and be eligible as delegates and representatives earlier than would otherwise be the case.

The clubs would, by bringing together the contemporaries of all social classes, and preserving contacts between those who were together at school (and perhaps national service), but now go entirely different ways, provide a truly democratic link by serving to provide contacts cutting across all other stratifications and providing an education in, and an incentive for, interest in public institutions as well as training in parliamentry procedures. They would also provide a regular channel for the expression of dissent of those not yet represented in a Legislative Assembly. If they should occasionally also become platforms for party debates, their advantage would be that those leaning towards different parties would be induced to discuss the issues together, and would become conscious that they had the common task of representing the outlook of their generation and to qualify for possible later public service.

Though individual membership ought to be primarily in the local group, it should confer on a member the right to take part as visitors in the clubs of one's age class at places other than that of one's permanent residence; and if it were known that in each locality a particular age class met regularly at a particular time and place (as it is the case with Rotarians and similar organizations), this might become an important means of inter-local contacts. In many other respects such clubs would probably introduce an important element of social coherence, especially to the structure of urban society, and do much to reduce the existing occupational and class distinctions.

The rotating chairmanship of these clubs would provide the members with an opportunity to become acquainted with the suitability of potential candidates for election as delegates or representatives; in the case of indirect elections they might therefore be based on personal knowledge even in the second round and the delegates ultimately selected might thereafter act not only as chairmen but also as voluntary but officially recognized spokesmen of their respective age groups, a sort of special honorary 'ombudsmen', who would protect the interests of their age groups against authorities. The advantage of their performing such functions would be that in voting for them the members would be more likely to elect somebody whose integrity they trusted.

Though after the election of the representatives these clubs would have few further formal tasks they would probably continue as means of social contact which might in fact also be called upon in case of need to restore the number of representatives if by some unusual accidents it had been depleted much below normal strength — perhaps not to the full original number but at least so that the numerical strength of their age group was adequately represented.

The Governmental Assembly

We need say little here about the second or Governmental Assembly because for it the existing parliamentary bodies, which have developed mainly to serve governmental tasks, could serve as model. There is no reason why it should not be formed by periodic re-elections of the whole body on party lines,[6] and why its chief business should not be conducted by an executive committee of the majority. This would constitute the government proper and operate subject to the control and criticism of an organized opposition ready to offer an alternative government. Concerning the various possible arrangements with regard to methods of election, periods for which the representatives are elected, etc., the arguments to be considered would be more or less the same as those currently discussed and need not detain us here. Perhaps the case for securing an effective majority capable of conducting government would under this scheme even more strongly than it does now outweigh the case for an exact mirroring of the proportional distribution of the different interests in the population at large, and the case against proportional representation would therefore, in my opinion, become even stronger.

The one important difference between the position of such a representative Governmental Assembly and the existing parliamentary bodies would of course be that in all that it decided it would be bound by the rules of just conduct laid down by the Legislative Assembly, and that, in particular, it could not issue any orders to private citizens which did not follow directly and necessarily from the rules laid down by the latter. Within the limits of these rules the government would, however, be complete master in organizing the apparatus of government and deciding about the use of material and personal resources entrusted to the government.

A question which should be reconsidered is whether, with regard to the right to elect representatives to this Governmental Assembly, the old argument does not assume new strength that employees of government and all who received pensions or other support from government should have no vote. The argument was clearly not conclusive so long as it concerned the vote for a representative assembly whose primary task was conceived to be the laying down of universal rules of just conduct. Undoubtedly the civil servant or government pensioner is as competent to form an opinion on what is just as anybody else, and it would have appeared as invidious for such persons to be excluded from a right granted to many who are less informed and less educated. But it is an altogether different matter when what is at issue is not an opinion but frankly interest in seeing particular results achieved. Here neither the instruments of policy nor those who, without contributing to the means, merely share in the results, seem to have the same claim as the private citizen. That civil servants, old age pensioners, the unemployed, etc., should have a vote on how they should be paid out of the pocket of the rest, and their vote be solicited by a promise of a rise in their pay, is hardly a reasonable arrangement. Nor would it seem reasonable that, in addition to formulating projects for action, the government employees should also have a say on whether their projects should be adopted or not, or that those who are subject to orders by the Governmental Assembly should have a part in deciding what these orders ought to be.

The task of the governmental machinery, though it would have to operate within the framework of a law it could not alter, would still be very considerable. Though it would be under an obligation not to discriminate in the services it renders, the choice, organization, and aims of these services would still give it great power, limited only so far as coercion or other discriminatory treatment of the citizens was excluded. And though the manner in which it could raise funds would thus be restricted, the amount or the general purposes for which they are spent would not be, except indirectly.

The Constitutional Court

The whole arrangement rests on the possibility of drawing a sharp distinction between the enforceable rules of just conduct to be developed by the Legislative Assembly and binding the government and citizens alike, and all those rules of the organization and conduct of government proper which, within the limits of the law, it would be the task of the Governmental Assembly to determine. Though we have endeavoured to make the principle of the distinction clear, and the basic clause of the constitution would have to attempt to define what is to be considered law in the relevant sense of rules of just conduct, in practice the application of the distinction would undoubtedly raise many difficult problems, and all its implications could be worked out only through the continuous efforts of a special court. The problems would arise chiefly in the form of a conflict of competence between the two assemblies, generally through the questioning by one of the validity of the resolution passed by the other.

To give the court of last instance in these matters the required authority, and in view of the special qualification needed by its members, it would probably be desirable to establish it as a separate Constitutional Court. It would seem appropriate that in addition to professional judges its membership should include former members of the Legislative and perhaps also of the Governmental Assembly. In the course of gradually building up a body of doctrine it should probably be bound by its own former decisions, while whatever reversal of such decisions might seem necessary had best been left to an amending procedure provided by the constitution.

The only other point about this Constitutional Court that needs to be stressed here is that its decisions often would have to be, not that either of the two Assemblies were competent rather than the other to take certain kinds of action, but that nobody at all was entitled to take certain kinds of coercive measures. This would in particular apply, except in periods of emergency to be considered later, to all coercive measures not provided for by general rules of just conduct which were either traditionally recognized or explicitly laid down by the Legislative Assembly.

The scheme proposed also raises all kinds of problems concerning the organization of the administration of justice in general. To organize the judicial machinery would clearly seem an organizational and therefore governmental task, yet to place it into the hands of government might threaten the complete independence of the courts. So far as the appointment and promotion of judges is concerned, this might well be placed into the hands of that committee of former members of the Legislative Assembly which we suggested should decide about the employment of their fellows as lay judges and the like. And the independence of the individual judge might be secured by his salary being determined in the same manner as that which we have proposed for the determination of the salaries of the members of the Legislative Assembly, namely as a certain percentage of the average salary of a fixed number of the highest positions in the gift of government.

Quite a different problem is that of the technical organization of the courts, their non-judicial personnel and their material needs. To organize these might seem more clearly a matter of government proper, yet there are good reasons why in the Anglo-Saxon tradition the conception of a Ministry of Justice responsible for such matters has long been suspect. It might at least be considered whether such a task, which clearly should not be performed by the Legislative Assembly, might not be entrusted to that committee selected from its former members which we have already mentioned, and which thereby would become the permanent organizational body for the third, the judicial power, commanding for its purposes a block grant of financial means assigned to it by government.

All this is closely connected with another important and difficult issue which we have not yet considered and that even here we can barely touch upon. It is the whole question of competence for laying down the law of procedure as against substantive law. In general this, as all rules subsidiary to the enforcement of justice, should be a matter for the Legislative Assembly, though some points of a more organizational character that today are also regulated in the codes of procedure might well seem matters to be decided either by the special body suggested or by the Governmental Assembly. These are, however, technical questions which we cannot further consider here.

The General Structure of Authority

The function of the Legislative Assembly must not be confused with that of a body set up to enact or amend the Constitution. The functions of these two bodies would indeed be entirely different. Strictly speaking, a Constitution ought to consist wholly of organizational rules, and need touch on substantive law in the sense of universal rules of just conduct only by stating the general attributes such laws must possess in order to entitle government to use coercion for their enforcement.

But though the Constitution must define what can be substantive law in order to allocate and limit powers among the parts of the organization it sets up, it leaves the content of this law to be developed by the legislature and judiciary. It represents a protective superstructure designed to regulate the continuous process of developing an existing body of law and to prevent any confusion of the powers of government in enforcing the rules on which the spontaneous order of society rests, and those of using the material means entrusted to its administration for the rendering of services to the individuals and groups.

There is no need here to enter into a discussion of the appropriate procedure for establishing and amending the Constitution. But perhaps the relation between the body called upon for this task and those established *by* the Constitution can be further elucidated by our saying that the proposed scheme replaces the existing two-tiered arrangement with a three-tiered one: while the Constitution allocates and restricts powers, it should not prescribe positively how these powers are to be used. The substantive law in the sense of rules of just conduct would be developed by the Legislative Assembly which would be limited in its powers only by the provision of the Constitution defining the general attributes which enforceable rules of just conduct must possess. The Governmental Assembly and its government as its executive organ on the other hand would be restricted both by the rules of the Constitution and by the rules of just conduct laid down or recognized by the Legislative Assembly. This is what government under the law means. The government, the executive organ of the Governmental Assembly, would of course also be bound by the decision of that Assembly and might thus be regarded as the fourth tier of the whole structure, with the administrative bureaucratic apparatus as the fifth.

If it be asked where under such an arrangement 'sovereignty' rests, the answer is nowhere — unless it temporally resides in the hands of the constitution-making or constitution-amending body. Since constitutional government is limited government there can be no room in it for a sovereign body if sovereignty is defined as unlimited power. We have seen before that the belief that there must always be an unlimited ultimate power is a superstition deriving from the erroneous belief that all law derives from the deliberate decision of a legislative agency. But government never starts from a lawless state; it rests on and derives its support from the expectation that it will enforce the prevailing opinions concerning what is right.

It might be noticed that the hierarchy of tiers of authority is related to the periods for which the different agencies have to make provision. Ideally the Constitution ought to be intended for all time, though of course, as is true of any product of the human mind, defects will be discovered which will need correction by amendment. Substantive law, though also intended for an indefinite period, will need continual development and revision as new and unforeseen problems arise with which the judiciary cannot deal adequately. The administration of the resources entrusted to government for the purpose of rendering services to the citizens is in its nature concerned with short-term problems and has to provide satisfaction of particular needs as they arise, and commanding as means for this task not the private citizen but only the resources explicitly placed under its control.

Emergency Powers

The basic principle of a free society, that the coercive powers of government are restricted to the enforcement of universal rules of just conduct, and cannot be used for the achievement of particular purposes, though essential to the normal working of such a society, may yet have to be temporarily suspended when the long-run preservation of that order is itself threatened. Though normally the individuals need be concerned only with their own concrete aims, and in pursuing them will best serve the common welfare, there may temporarily arise circumstances when the preservation of the overall order becomes the overruling common purpose, and when in consequence the spontaneous order, on a local or national scale, must for a time be converted into an organization. When an external enemy threatens, when rebellion or lawless violence has broken out, or a natural catastrophe requires quick action by whatever means can be secured, powers of compulsory organization, which normally nobody possesses, must be granted to somebody. Like an animal in flight from mortal danger society may in such situations have to suspend temporarily even vital functions on which in the long run its existence depends if it is to escape destruction.

The conditions under which such emergency powers may be granted without creating the danger that they will be retained when the absolute necessity has passed are among the most difficult and important points a constitution must decide on. 'Emergencies' have always been the pretext on which the safeguards of individual liberty have been eroded — and once they are suspended it is not difficult for anyone who has assumed such emergency powers to see to it that the emergency will persist. Indeed if all needs felt by important groups that can be satisfied only by the exercise of dictatorial powers constitute an emergency, every situation is an emergency situation. It has been contended with some plausibility that whoever has the power to proclaim an emergency and on this ground to suspend any part of the constitution is the true sovereign.[7] This would seem to be true enough if any person or body were able to arrogate to itself such emergency powers by declaring a state of emergency.

It is by no means necessary, however, that one and the same agency should possess the power to declare an emergency and to assume emergency powers. The best precaution against the abuse of emergency powers would seem to be that the authority that can declare a state of emergency is made thereby to renounce the powers it normally possesses and to retain only the right of revoking at any time the emergency powers it has conferred on another body. In the scheme suggested it would evidently be the Legislative Assembly which would not only have to delegate some of its powers to the government, but also to confer upon this government powers which in normal circumstances nobody possesses. For this purpose an emergency committee of the Legislative Assembly would have to be in permanent existence and quickly accessible at all times. The committee would have to be entitled to grant limited emergency powers until the Assembly as a whole could be convened which itself then would have to determine both the extent and duration of the emergency powers granted to government. So long as it confirmed the existence of an emergency, any measures taken by government within the powers granted to it would have full force, including such specific commands to particular persons as in normal times nobody would have the power to issue. The Legislative Assembly, however, would at all times be free to revoke or restrict the powers granted, and after the end of the emergency to confirm or to revoke any measures proclaimed by the government, and to provide for compensation to those who in the general interest were made to submit to such extraordinary powers.

Another kind of emergency for which every constitution should provide is the possible discovery of a gap in its provisions, such as the appearance of questions of authority to which the constitutional rules do not give an answer. The possibility of a discovery of such lacunae in any scheme, however carefully thought out, can never be excluded: and there may well arise questions which require a prompt authoritative answer if the whole machinery of government is not to be paralysed. Yet though somebody should have the power to provide a temporary answer to such questions by *ad hoc* decisions, these decisions should remain in effect only until the Legislative Assembly, the Constitutional Court, or the normal apparatus for amending the Constitution has filled the gap by an appropriate regulation. Until then a normally purely ceremonial Head of State might well be given power to fill such gaps by provisional decisions.

The Division of Financial Powers

The field in which the constitutional arrangements here sketched would produce the most far-reaching changes would be that of finance. It is also the field in which the nature of these consequences can be best illustrated in such a condensed outline as is attempted here.

The central problem arises from the fact that the levying of contributions is necessarily an act of coercion and must therefore be done in accordance with general rules laid down by the Legislative Assembly, while the determination of both the volume and the direction of expenditure is clearly a governmental matter. Our scheme would therefore require that the uniform rules according to which the total means to be raised are apportioned among the citizens be laid down by the Legislative Assembly, while the total amount of expenditure and its direction would have to be decided by the Governmental Assembly.

Nothing would probably provide a more salutary discipline of expenditure than such a condition in which everybody voting for a particular outlay would know that the costs would have to be borne by him and his constituents in accordance with a predetermined rule which he could not alter. Except in those cases where the beneficiaries of a particular outlay could be clearly identified (although, once the service was provided for all it could not be withheld from those not voluntarily paying for it and the costs would therefore have to be raised by compulsion) as is the case with a motor tax for the provision of roads, or a wireless tax, or the various local and communal taxes for the finance of particular services, all expenditure decided upon would automatically lead to a corresponding increase of the general burden of taxes for all under the general scheme determined by the Legislative Assembly. There could then be no support for any expenditure based on the expectation that the burden could afterwards be shifted on to other shoulders: everyone would know that of all that would be spent he had to bear a fixed share.

Current methods of taxation have been shaped largely by the endeavour to raise funds in such a manner as to cause the least resistance or resentment on the part of the majority who had to approve the expenditure. They certainly were not designed to assure responsible decisions on expenditure, but on the contrary to produce the feeling that somebody else would pay for it. It is regarded as obvious that the methods of taxation should be adjusted to the amount to be raised, since in the past the need for additional revenue regularly led to a search for new sources of taxation. Additional expenditure thus always raised the question of who should pay for it. The theory and practice of public finance has been shaped almost entirely by the endeavour to disguise as far as possible the burden imposed, and to make those who will ultimately have to bear it as little aware of it as possible. It is probable that the whole complexity of the tax structure we have built up is largely the result of the efforts to persuade citizens to give the government more than they would knowingly consent to do.

To distinguish effectively the legislation on the general rules by which the tax burden is to be apportioned among the individuals from the determination of the total sums to be raised, would require such a complete re-thinking of all the principles of public finance that the first reaction of those familiar with the existing institutions will probably be to regard such a scheme as wholly impracticable. Yet nothing short of such a complete reconsideration of the institutional setting of financial legislation can probably stop that trend towards a continuing and progressive rise of that share of the income of society which is controlled by government. This trend, if allowed to continue, would before long swallow up the whole of society in the organization of government.

It is evident that taxation in accordance with a uniform rule can have no place for any overall progression of the total tax burden, although, as I have discussed elsewhere,[8] some progression of the direct taxes may not only be permissible but necessary to offset the tendency of indirect taxes to be regressive. I have in the same place also suggested some general principles by which we might so limit taxation as to prevent the shifting of the burden by a majority to the shoulders of a minority, but at the same time leave open the unobjectionable possibility of a majority conceding to a weak minority certain advantages.

Notes

1. The suggestion for the reconstruction of the representative assemblies has by now occupied me over a long period and I have sketched it in writing on numerous earlier occasions. The first, I believe, was a talk on 'New Nations and the Problem of Power' in the *Listener,* no. 64, London, 10 November 1960. See also 'Libertad bayo la Ley' in *Orientacion Economica,* Caracas, April 1962; 'Recht, Gesetz und Wirtschaftsfreiheit', *Hundert Jahre Industrie — und Handelskammer zu Dortmund* 1863 – 1963 (Dortmund, 1963; reprinted in the *Frankfurter Allgemeine Zeitung* 1/2 May 1963, and in my *Freiburger Studien* [Tübingen, 1969]); 'The Principles of a Liberal Social Order', *Il Politico,* December 1966, and reprinted in *Studies in Philosophy, Politics and Economics* (London and Chicago, 1967); 'Die Anschauungen der Mehrheit und die zeitgenössische Demokratie', *Ordo* 15/16 (Düsseldorf, 1963);

'The Constitution of a Liberal State', *Il Politico* 31, 1967; *The Confusion of Language in Political Thought* (Institute of Economic Affairs, London, 1968); and *Economic Freedom and Representative Government* (Institute of Economic Affairs, London, 1973). Most of the later ones are reprinted in my *New Studies in Philosophy, Politics, Economics and the History of Ideas* (London and Chicago, 1977). The latest statement is in *Three Lectures on Democracy, Justice and Socialism* (Sydney, 1977), also available in German, Spanish and Portuguese translations.

2. Z. Giacommetti, *Der Freiheitskatalog als Kodifikation der Freiheit* (Zürich, 1955).

3. Cf. A. R. W. Harris, 'Law Making at Athens at the End of the Fifth Century B.C.', *Journal of Hellenic Studies*, 1955, and further references given there.

4. E. G. Philip Hunton, *A Treatise on Monarchy* (London, 1643), p. 5.

5. J. S. Mill, *Considerations on Representative Government* (London, 1861), chapter 5.

6. While for the purposes of legislation a division of the assembly on party lines is altogether undesirable, for the purpose of government a two-party system is obviously desirable. There is, therefore, in neither instance a case for proportional representation, the general arguments against which have been powerfully marshalled in a work which, because of the date of its publication, has not received the attention it deserves: F. A. Hermens, *Democracy or Anarchy* (Notre Dame, Ind., 1941).

7. Carl Schmitt, 'Soziologie des Souverainitätsbegriffes und politische Theologie' in M Palyi (ed.), *Hauptprobleme der Soziologie, Erinnerungsgabe für Max Weber* (Munich, 1923), II, p. 5.

8. See my *The Constitution of Liberty* (London and Chicago, 1960), chapter 20.

INDEX